STUDIES IN JACOB BÖHME

Anne Judith Brown
circa 1857
(Mrs Edward Burton Penny)

STUDIES IN
JACOB BÖHME

BY
A. J. PENNY

WIPF & STOCK · Eugene, Oregon

"*All I venture to offer are germs of thought gathered on widely different planes, and on suitable mental ground they will not be altogether fruitless.*"—p. 86.

"*Tentative outlines of thought, if but firmly and clearly presented, may serve as skeleton maps serve in a school-room. They do not pretend to suffice; they only make ready a frame for larger knowledge to fill up.*"—p. 368.

"*Because there is a blessing upon all honest effort, I trust that clearer light may be thrown upon them by the unseen Helper who guides into all truth.*"—p. 366.

Wipf and Stock Publishers
199 W 8th Ave, Suite 3
Eugene, OR 97401

Studies in Jacob Böhme
By Penny, A. J.
ISBN 13: 978-1-4982-9366-2
Publication date 5/30/2016
Previously published by John M. Watkins, 1912

PREFACE

IN the Publisher's Note prefixed to the first volume of the proposed reprint of the complete works of Jacob Böhme (*Threefold Life*, 1909), it was stated that a reprint was contemplated of a small volume, privately printed, of Essays by Mrs A. J. Penny on Böhme. On searching the volumes of *Light*, and *Light and Life*, for the originals of these Essays, I was delighted to find that both magazines, but particularly *Light*, contain, in addition, many more articles by Mrs Penny that deal directly with Böhme's teachings. These articles are all reproduced here by kind permission of the respective Editors, to whom I tender my grateful acknowledgments and best thanks. The *New Church Independent*, Chicago, U.S.A., also contains many contributions from her pen, one only of which is here reprinted.

When the pages of *Light* were examined, notes were also made of the titles of other articles and letters by Mrs Penny, in addition to those dealing directly with Böhme. For the benefit of any student who would like to have at hand a ready reference to these, the list is printed as an Appendix to the present volume.

Mrs Penny was born on 9th April 1825. She was the thirteenth and youngest child of the Rev. Walter Brown, Rector of Stonesfield Oxon and Prebendary of Canterbury, and of Eliza his wife (née Cokayne Frith). From about her sixth year, when she lost both her parents,

Anne Judith Brown was brought up by her eldest sister. Whilst still a girl she became afflicted with spinal disease, from which she never completely recovered; and this entailed a severe discipline of suffering, which continued more or less during the whole of her life. Physical activity being thus largely denied her, she was left with more time for the cultivation of her literary tastes; for she had at an early age developed a pronounced love of reading, together with a marked tendency to independent thought and action. Thus about 1855 she began writing for young girls, her first publication being *Morning Clouds*. This was followed by *The Afternoon of Life*, *Problems of Human Nature*, *The Romance of a Dull Life*, *Wanted a Home*, and a few smaller volumes.

A year prior to the above date an old and revered friend, the Rev. Enoch Warriner, Rector of Foots Cray, Kent, who taught her much, and strongly influenced her by his life, introduced her to the works of Jacob Böhme. In these and all works bearing on them she from the first took an absorbing interest. One of her favourite authors (as an exponent of Böhme) was Louis-Claude de Saint-Martin ("le Philosophe Inconnu"), and it was in connection with her studies of this author that Miss A. J. Brown made the acquaintance of Mr Edward Burton Penny, to whom she was married on 3rd October 1865.

Mr and Mrs Penny were in complete accord in their high appreciation of Böhme; and it was by the express wish of her husband that Mrs Penny devoted herself exclusively to the study of Mysticism. Mr Penny died in March 1872.

It is deeply to be regretted that Mrs Penny was not enabled to write upon her favourite author in the more methodical and exhaustive manner of book form. Doubtless the hopelessness, in those days, of securing a publisher for such a work is quite sufficient to account for this. At the same time there is in print a fairly large output from her pen.

Possibly no writer in this country, except it be Dionysius Andreas Freher,[1] ever devoted more time to the study of Jacob Böhme than Mrs Penny. At the time of her death, which took place on 18th December 1893, Böhme had been her constant companion over a period of thirty-nine years; and not only was she familiar with the whole range of Böhme's writings, but she was also well versed in the writings of men who had themselves made a special study of Böhme.

That her interpretations will not on all points meet with unqualified acceptance, even by lovers of Böhme, goes without saying. The profundities with which he essayed to deal are of such a nature, that differences must inevitably arise in the minds of students as to the exact meaning and value to be attached to his expositions; nor will such differences be due solely to the matter of his work, but also to its manner, which was undoubtedly deeply influenced, both by the thought-forms of his age, and by the human element in the man, in contradistinction to the divine element, by virtue of which his knowledge came to him spontaneously and unsought.

However, Mrs Penny's marvellous gift for collating passages in illustration of her contentions will give the student ample opportunity for checking her statements; and the fruits of her industry in this direction, even as contained in the present volume, are by no means the least valuable service Mrs Penny has rendered her readers.[2]

[1] See Walton's *Memorial of William Law*, and *Threefold Life*, 1909, Appen. B.
[2] *N.B.*—All references are to the English translations of Böhme's works. In these the numbers of the paragraphs do not always correspond to the German originals.

In the *Threefold Life*, ch. v., par. 26, Böhme wrote: "We speak in two languages; and so we must be understood also by two languages, one whereof will despise this work, and the other will highly believe and love it; for every spirit taketh its own." Though we need not assume for one single moment that either loving or despising Böhme bespeaks anything more in the mind of the reader than an individual predilection—as devoid of merit in the one case, as of demerit in the other—we must admit that Böhme appeals to the few rather than to the many. It has ever been so in the past, and in all probability will continue so to be in the future. Of the few in the past who have loved Böhme, none has been more ardent than Mrs Penny; and for the few, in the present and in the future, this volume has been compiled from such of her published writings as are immediately available.

It will hardly be necessary to ask the reader to bear in mind that these pieces were contributed to periodical literature, and would therefore not receive the same careful revision that Mrs Penny might have given them, had she known that they would one day reappear in book form.

For a biographical note of Böhme, and a résumé of his teachings, the student would be well repaid for consulting the article "Böhme," by the Rev. G. W. Allen, in the recently published vol. ii. of Hastings' *Encyclopædia of Religion and Ethics*, and also the series of articles, entitled "An introduction to the Philosophy of Jacob Böhme," that Mr Allen is at the present time publishing in his quarterly magazine, *The Seeker*. Dr Alexander Whyte's monograph, *Jacob Behmen: An Appreciation*, is also exceedingly good.

In the case of a reader taking up Böhme for the first time, it cannot be too strongly borne in mind (1) that the author attained to the illumination in and by which the whole of his works were written, only after intense and prolonged spiritual struggles, and (2) that, in studying these writings, the mental attitude of the student is of more than ordinary importance; for Böhme contends, with unwearying iteration, that only and in so far as a man gives up his own self-will, and immerses himself unconditionally in the will of God, can man attain salvation, and *thereby* enlightenment in Divine Wisdom; for man, in his first-birth nature, is an alien to the "Principle" wherein alone divine wisdom resides, and unless he be born again, of water and of the Spirit, into another "Principle," an alien he will for ever remain. Not that Böhme contemns "reason" in its own proper sphere; for he has attempted to explain at considerable length the genesis, the nature, and the value of that Principle wherein reason is lord. But no power that man possesses will enable man, of and by his own will, to find or reach into God; not even man's highest endowment, as man.

"Self-reason, which, being void of God's spirit, is only taught and instructed from the bare letter . . . knoweth not the mind of the Lord, because the same is not in it. Its understanding is from the stars. . . . How can he judge of divine matters in whom the spirit of the Lord is not?"[1]

"Every spirit seeth no further than into its mother, out of which it hath its original, and wherein it standeth; for it is impossible for any spirit in its own natural power to look into another Principle and behold it, except it be regenerated therein."[2]

"Every spirit speaketh of its own mother, whose food it eateth and in whose property it liveth."[3]

[1] Epistles (1649), Ep. 2, pars. 22, 23.
[2] Three Principles, ch. vii., par. 1.
[3] Threefold Life, ch. v., par. 1.

"Christ said, 'Except ye turn and become as children, ye shall not see the kingdom of God.' Again, He said to Nicodemus, 'Except a man be born again, of water and of the spirit, he cannot enter into the kingdom of God; for that which is born of the flesh is flesh, and that which is born of the spirit is spirit.' Also the Scripture positively declareth that the fleshy natural man receiveth not the things of the spirit of God; for they are foolishness unto him, neither can he know or conceive them."[1]

"God bringeth not a new or strange spirit into us, but He openeth with His spirit our spirit, namely, the mystery of God's wisdom, which lieth in every man."[2]

"Through imagination, and an earnest serious desire, we become again impregnated of the Deity, and receive the new body in the old. The new doth not mix itself with the old; like as gold in the dross and rough stone is quite another thing, and hath another tincture and spirit than the rough matter in the stone; thus also is the new man in the old."[3]

"Pray God, the most High, that He would be pleased to open the door of knowledge, without which no man will understand my writings; for they surpass and transcend the astral reason; they apprehend and comprehend the divine birth; therefore there must also be the very like spirit to understand them aright; no speculation [or acute apprehension or notion of reason] reacheth them, unless the mind be illuminated from God—to the finding of which the way is faithfully shewn unto the seeking reader."[4]

[1] Of Regeneration, ch. i., pars. 1, 2.
[2] Epistles (1649), Ep. 2, par. 26.
[3] Ibid., Ep. 5, par. 10.
[4] Ibid., Ep. 16, pars. 8, 10.

That Böhme has himself faithfully shewn the reader the way to understand his writings is unconditionally endorsed by William Law, than whom no student of Böhme ever was, is, or probably ever will be,

"I will not conceal from you the simple childlike way which I walk in Christ Jesus; for I can write nothing of myself, but as of a child, which neither knoweth nor understandeth anything; neither hath ever been learned, but only that which the Lord vouchsafeth to know in me, according to the measure as He manifests Himself in me.

"For I never desired to know anything of the divine Mystery, much less understood I the way how to seek or find it. I knew nothing of it, as 'tis the condition of poor laymen in their simplicity. I sought only after the Heart of Jesus Christ, that I might hide myself therein from the wrathful anger of God, and the violent assaults of the devil. And I besought the Lord earnestly for his holy spirit, and his grace, that he would be pleased to bless and guide me in him, and take that away from me which did turn me away from him. And I resigned myself wholly to him, that I might not live to my own will, but to his; and that he only might lead and direct me; to the end that I might be his child in his Son Jesus Christ.

"In this my earnest Christian seeking and desire (wherein I suffered many a shrewd repulse, but at last being resolved rather to put my life to utmost hazard, than to give over and leave off) the Gate was opened unto me, that in one quarter of an hour I saw and knew more than if I had been many years together at

better qualified to give an opinion. In his *Way to Divine Knowledge* he wrote: "And now, Academicus, you may see how needless it is to ask me, or any one else, to help you to understand his [Böhme's] works: he himself has given you all the assistance that can be given. He has laid open before you, in the utmost plainness, both the nature of the Mystery, and the one only possible way that you can partake of it." *Way to Divine Knowledge*, 1752, p. 114; Reprint, 1893, p. 198. An absolutely priceless work, not merely to students of Böhme, but to every man who appreciates and seeks to understand the fundamental principles upon which is founded the divine wisdom as revealed to the world in and by our Lord Jesus Christ.

a university; at which I did exceedingly admire; and I knew not how it happened to me. And thereupon I turned my heart to praise God for it.

"I have written, not from the instruction or knowledge received from men; not from the learning or reading of books; but I have written out of my own book which was opened in me, being the noble similitude of God, the book of the noble and precious image (understand God's own similitude or likeness) was bestowed upon me to read. Therein I have studied, as a child in the house of its mother, which beholdeth what the Father doth, and in his childlike play doth imitate his father. I have no need of any other book.

"My book hath only three leaves: the same are the three Principles of eternity, wherein I can find all whatsoever Moses and the prophets, Christ and His apostles have taught and spoken. I can find therein the foundation of the world, and all Mysteries; yet not I, but the spirit of God doth it, according to the measure as he pleaseth.

"For I have besought and begged of him many hundred times, that if my knowledge did not make for his glory, and conduce to the bettering or benefit and instruction of my brethren, he would be pleased to take it from me, and preserve me only in his love. Yet I found that by my praying or earnest desiring I did only enkindle the fire more strongly in me. In such inflammation, knowledge and manifestation I made my writings.[1]

"Our whole writing and teaching aimeth at this, How we must seek, make, and lastly find ourselves; How we must generate or bring forth, that we may be one spirit with God, that God may be in us, and we in God; that God's love-spirit in us may be the willing and the doing. And that we withdraw from the

[1] Epistles (1649), Ep. 2, pars. 5-7, 14-16.

anguish source or quality, that we may introduce ourselves into the true similitude, in three worlds, that each of them may stand in their order, and that the light-world in us may be lord, that that may lead the dominion. That so the anguish-world may abide hidden in the light-world, as it doth also in God, and so be only a cause of the life of God's wonders."[1]

"God is an eternal seeker and finder of himself in the great wonders; and that which he findeth, he findeth in the power; he is the opener of the power: Nothing is like him, neither doth anything find him, but that which yieldeth itself to be his own, that entereth into him. That which denieth itself to be, in that thing the spirit of God is all things; for it is the only will in the eternal nothing; and yet it is all things, as God's spirit itself is. Therefore if you would fain find it, seek it not in me, but in yourself, though not in your reason either, which must be as dead, and your desire and will must be in God. And so God becometh the will and the deed in you: also the spirit of God bringeth your will into himself, and then you may well see what God is, and what spirit's child this hand is, and from what kind of spirit it writeth."[2]

"The will of the creature ought to sink wholly into itself with all its reason and desire, accounting itself an unworthy child that is no whit worthy of this so high a grace; nor should it arrogate any knowledge or understanding to itself, or desire of God to have any understanding in its creaturely self; but sincerely and simply sink down into the grace and love of God in Christ Jesus, and desire to be as it were dead to itself and its own reason, in the divine life, and wholly resign itself to the spirit of God in love, that he may do how and what he will with it, as with his own instrument.

[1] Incarnation, Part II., ch. x., pars. 24–26.
[2] Forty Questions, Ques. 1, pars. 57–58.

Its own reason ought not to enter upon any speculation in divine or in the ground of human matters; nor to will and desire anything but the grace of God in Christ. And as a child continually longeth after the breasts of the mother, so must its hunger be continually entering into the love of God, and not suffer itself to be broken off from that hunger by any means.[1]

"Let the will only, in all simplicity and unfeigned sincerity, directly cast itself into the mercy of God, and wholly lie down and shroud itself in the suffering and death of Christ, and surrender itself to God through Christ. As a child that betakes itself unto the lap of the mother, which willeth to do only that which is the will of the mother" ... "even so must our desire be only and wholly turned and directed to our first mother, from whom we, in Adam, departed and went into self-will. Therefore Christ said, 'Unless you be converted and become as children you cannot see the kingdom of God.'"[2]

"For the spirit born of God ... openeth to the mind the understanding and knowledge, so that man seeth himself in the bands of this world."[3]

"If God reveals himself in man, then he is in two kingdoms, and seeth with twofold eyes; and yet this way is not so hard and difficult as reason's seeking in outward things: it lieth all in the willing."[4]

"It is impossible for any man to have it, except it be given him out of grace in the love of God: and when that is given to a man, then that soul standeth in the knowledge in the wonders of God: which [soul] then speaketh not of things strange and afar off, but of the things wherein it standeth, and of itself; for it becometh seeing in the light of God, so that it can know itself."[5]

---

[1] True Resignation, ch. ii., pars. 5, 6.
[2] Epistles (1649), Ep. 2, par. 38, 39.
[3] Threefold Life, ch. v., par. 29.
[4] Ibid., ch. x., par. 10.
[5] Ibid., ch. i., par. 20.

"There is a gross deadness in the understanding, and though I write plain enough, yet I shall be still dumb to that deadened soul which is void of understanding, and yet I cannot help it; for it is said, You must be born anew, if you will see the kingdom of God."[1]

"There needeth not in our writings much toil, nor hard consideration or study. We write out of another Principle" [than the Principle in which outward reason takes its rise], "no reader understandeth us rightly in the ground, except his mind be born of God. There ought no historical skill and knowledge to be sought for in our writings; for as it is not possible to see God with earthly eyes, so also it is not possible that an unenlightened mind, in the earthliness, can comprehend the ground of our writings. Heavenly thoughts and meaning can comprehend it: like must be comprehended by like."[2]

"Leave off your laborious searching in reason, and enter into the will of God, into God's spirit, and cast outward reason away, and then your will is God's will, and God's spirit will seek you within you. And if he findeth your will in him, then he manifesteth himself in your will, as in his own propriety. For if you quit that will, then it is his, who is all things; and when he moveth, go you with him, for you have divine power; and then whatever you search, he is in it, and then nothing is hidden from the will. Thus you see in his light, and are his."[3]

"As we men with our [earthly] eyes which we have from this world cannot see God and the angels, which yet are every moment present to us, and the Deity itself is in us, and yet we are not able to comprehend it, except we put our imagination and earnest will into

---

[1] Three Principles, ch. viii., par. 35.
[2] Ibid., Appen., par. 23.
[3] Forty Questions, Ques. 1, pars. 60, 61.

God, and then God appeareth to us in the will, and filleth the mind; where we feel God and see him with our eyes [viz. the eyes of our mind]."[1]

Böhme was vividly aware that the knowledge that came to him was not the result of any intellectual effort on his part, and he repeatedly refers to this in his writings, at the same time explaining for the reader's benefit his Way or method. These interpolated passages of a personal nature crop up in the least expected places; usually they are passed over by the reader as of little value; this is unfortunate, as they really contain the most precious element in his teaching. And, if Böhme himself is to be accepted as a guide to lead others to the knowledge of that Divine Wisdom that he himself acquired, there is no mistaking the explicit qualification necessary in the reader for that attainment.

He avers that the knowledge that came to him, came purely and solely as the result of a change in the interior constitution of his own being, and not as the result of any effort on his part to acquire that knowledge directly. He was also thoroughly convinced that no man will enter fully into his meanings and understand his writings, unless he also undergoes a like change. On these two all-essential points there cannot be two opinions, so far as Böhme is concerned. Whether or not the reader is prepared to accept Böhme's statement, and comply with the conditions he lays down, is another matter.

The charge of obscurity has frequently been made against Böhme's expositions. He was fully aware of the difficulties that would beset his readers, and no one can charge him with neglecting to warn his readers of these, or with failing to point out, time after time, the way in which alone such obstacles can be overcome.

[1] Threefold Life, ch. ii., par. 51.

The following is a list of References to the chief autobiographical paragraphs in Böhme's Works, and paragraphs giving direct personal advice to the Reader. The latter are distinguished from the former by an asterisk.

Anno 1612.

AURORA:

Intro. 6*, 15-17, 39-42* ; **2**, 15-24*, 80 ; **3**, 1-3*, 27-29*, 82*, 104-105 ; **4**, 45* ; **5**, 27-30* ; **6**, 35-40* ; **7**, 1-5*, 17-19 ; **8**, 159-160 ; **9**, 1-2*, 19-20*, 85*, 86-87 ; **10**, 41*, 45-48, 65*, 92 ; **11**, 4-6*, 122-129, 135-136, 142-152 ; **12**, 146-151 ; **13**, 18-25, 26-33*, 80* ; **14**, 55-61, 142 ; **16**, 68, 124* ; **18**, 5-10, 93 ; **19**, 4-23, 50, 65 ; **20**, 70 ; **21**, 69-71 ; **22**, 1-4*, 9-20, 37-38, 47-49, 107-109 ; **23**, 48*, 75, 92-93 ; **24**, 7* ; **25**, 1-13, 45-59, 60-64* ; **26**, 142-150.

1619.

THREE PRINCIPLES :

Pref. 16, 18-19 ; **2**, 1*, 5-6* ; **3**, 3* ; **4**, 1, 6, 8*, 16-17*, 30*, 43* ; **5**, 1-2* ; **7**, 16 ; **9**, 9, 45-47* ; **10**, 1 ; **11**, 30* ; **12**, 1, 24* ; **13**, 1, 5, 22, 61 ; **14**, 50-53 ; **16**, 1-2 ; **17**, 14, 115 ; **18**, 60-62 ; **20**, 1-2 ; **24**, 1-3, 8, 14, 16-20, 27-32* ; **25**, 51, 53, 69, 84, 100, 107* ; **26**, 11-12* ; Appen. 23-24*.

1620.

THREEFOLD LIFE :

1, 20, 22*, 41 ; **2**, 4*, 65-67* ; **3**, 4-7*, 25*, 29-38*, 45*, 92 ; **4**, 1-4 ; **5**, 1-2, 33-35 ; **6**, 5-8, 9*, 35 ; **7**, 53-54, 8, 7-8 ; **9**, 1-3, 4*, 30, 31* ; **11**, 52 ; **12**, 35-36* ; **14**, 55.

FORTY QUESTIONS :

1, 58-66*, 293-296 ; **17**, 19, 21-22 ; **26**, 2-3 ; **30**, 2-5 ; **35**, 42-43 ; **38**, 1-6 ; **14**, 11-13.

INCARNATION, I. :

1, 16-21 ; 3, 1-2.

INCARNATION, II. :

6, 6 ; 7, 2, 20-25, 33, 34-57*, 51 ; **10**, 24-28, 67.*

INCARNATION, III. :

3. 32-41*.

GREAT SIX POINTS :
Preface*.

SMALL SIX POINTS :
Preface*.

1621.
SIGNATURA RERUM:
  7, 1*, 6*; 8, 50; 9, 61-66; 10, 1; 11, 73*; 12, 9-18, 29*, 36-37*;
  14, 1*; 16, 40*.
FOUR COMPLEXIONS:
  2, 113-114, 133-137*.
FIRST APOLOGY (TYLCKEN):
  Part I.: 14-42, 54, 62-63, 96-98.
  Part II.: 127, 254, 300-301, 429, 432, 435, 438, 473*, 532*, 585-586*, 587-588, 591, 594, 597-599, 617, 629*.
SECOND APOLOGY (TYLCKEN):
  Pref. 8-9, 12-14, 16-18.
  Part I.: 11-12, 53, 72-78, 165-167, 171-175.
  Part II.: 257-258, 270-271, 295-299, 306-307*, 308, 326-327, 328*.
CONSIDERATION UPON E. STIEFEL'S "THREEFOLD STATE OF MAN."
  Pars. 6-10, 112-117*, 161-163.

1622.
THIRD APOLOGY (STIEFEL).
  Text IV., Point I.: 49-51.
TRUE RESIGNATION:
  Pars. 15-17*.
OF REGENERATION:
  Par. 133.

1623.
ELECTION OF GRACE:
  Pref. 8-9, 17*, 3, 37-38*; 4, 1-5*; 6, 1*; 13, 56-57, 78-84.
A SHORT COMPENDIUM OF REPENTANCE:
  Pars. 24, 50-55.
MYSTERIUM MAGNUM:
  Part I.: Pref. 14-16: 18, 1; 26, 40*; 30, 31; 32, 19*; 33, 36*.
  Part II.; 35, 67, 36, 1-2*; 37, 2; 39, 10; 47, 1*; 51, 56-57*; 52, 27*.
  Part III.; 64, 30*; 76, 49*; 78, 9*.

1624.
ON DIVINE CONTEMPLATION OR VISION:
  3, 83.
OF CHRIST'S TESTAMENTS:
  Part I., Baptism: Pref. 1-4*, 26*.

PREFACE   xix

FOURTH APOLOGY (RICKTER):
Pref. 3, 5-6.
Part I.: 12-17, 50-53.
Part II.: 76-78, 84, 91, 105, 110, 145-147, 149, 156, 159, 163-166, 173.
Part III.: 182-183, 188-190.

177 THEOSOPHIC QUESTIONS:
Pref. 1-5*; 3, 1*; 5, 25*; 12, 1-3*, 19-20*, 28*.

HOLY WEEK: OR A PRAYER BOOK:
Pref. 32.

CLAVIS:
Preface*.
1618-1624.

EPISTLES (1649):
1, 23-24, 74-76; 2, 5-21, 45, 64-65, 74-80; 3, 1 et seq.; 4, 38, 74-86; 5, 50-51, 55, 87-88; 9, 27-28; 11, 23-29; 12, 8-10; 15, 15-34; 16, 6-7, 12; 17, 8-9; 18, 2, 8; 19, 3-6, 25-31; 20, 5-6, 20-22; 21, 14; 22, 5-7; 23, 14-15, 18; 25, 2-5, 25-28; 26, 5-11: 27, 5-18; 29, 2-3; 31, 1 et seq.; 32, 9-11, 15; 33, 2-5, 15-20, 25; 34, 2-8; 35, 8, 12-19.
A warning from J. B.: 1 et seq.

EPISTLES (1661):
9, 1-2, 5-7; 13, 1-3; 26, 8-12; 27, 4-8: 46, 4 et seq.; 49, 5; 51, 5; 52, 1 et seq.; 53, 1 et seq.; 54, 2-5, 15; 59, 1 et seq.; 61, 1-2.

C. J. BARKER.

FIR LODGE,
  ROSE WALK,
    PURLEY, SURREY.
November 28, 1911.

The Cottage, Cullompton, Devon.

MRS PENNY[1]

OLD readers of *Light*, who interest themselves in the deeper aspects of the spiritual problem, will have observed with lively concern the brief announcement, last week, of the removal of Mrs Penny from the earthly scene. We were not, indeed, unprepared for it. More than three years ago a painful crisis made death seem, even to her medical attendant, so imminent that she herself, and all her friends, were in daily expectation of the end. She rallied; but, for a long period, with scarcely abated suffering. Then there were some months of considerable relief; she was able to correspond with friends (though usually by an amanuensis) and even occasionally to see them. More than one of these travelled long distances for the privilege of a few (broken) hours of conversation with her. Brief articles by her appeared again, though rarely, in *Light* and elsewhere. But the activity of her life was over; she had parted with most of her valuable books by gift to those she thought most likely to appreciate and use them; even her own manuscript notes went to aid students of her favourite authors and subjects. Early in the now closing year the discipline of almost ceaseless suffering was re-imposed. Nothing is spiritually indifferent; and we may well hold, however vaguely, that from the purgatorial fire of the past twelve months this excellent life extracted the final uses of its incarnation. Through-

[1] *Light*, 30th Dec. 1893, vol. xiii. p. 618.

out it she could not cease to think, and my latest letters from her are largely concerning "the mystery of pain." Ideas are a more potent resource, even in physical torment, than is commonly supposed ("Give me a great thought," cried the dying Herder), and it was characteristic of her mind and moral nature that she would entertain with interest the suggestion—upon the principle of the solidarity of the race—that the pain of one may in some obscure way, and in some minute degree, draw off and localize a diffused element of disease in the whole society, or in some related section of it. But to one of her intellectual temperament it was weary waiting in disablement for the long-deferred release. Just before it happened there was the usual merciful relief from pain. Consciousness was apparently retained to the last. On Sunday, the 17th, she was heard to murmur, ": To-morrow—only till to-morrow." And so it was. On the morrow, soon after mid-day, she was liberated.

There has never been a more ardent, seldom, perhaps, a more intellectually qualified, student of spiritual and religious mysteries than the accomplished lady who has just passed away. With literary capabilities which in her youth had borne fruit in a novel declared by good judges to have been a production of uncommon merit, she was early initiated into the old theosophy by a husband[1] who had himself abandoned the pursuit and prospects of wealth in order to devote himself to a study which became thenceforward the passion of their joint lives. This gentleman, Mr Edward Burton Penny, was the first to introduce to the English public the works of the celebrated French mystic of the Revolution period, Claude de St Martin ("le Philosophe Inconnu"), by his translation of two profoundly interesting books, the *Theosophic Correspondence* of St Martin and Kirchberger,

[1] In this statement I believe Mr Massey was mistaken. See p. vi.—ED.

and that entitled *Man: His True Nature and Ministry*. It was to the first of these books (which has an indescribable charm for every lover of mysticism) that I owed the privilege of my introduction to, and long following correspondence with, Mrs Penny. During the long years of her widowhood, crippled and suffering often and much from a painful spinal affection, she led a secluded life of study in a picturesque old house ("The Cottage") in the town of Cullompton, in Devon, where she was greatly esteemed and loved, especially by the poor.[1] In a little wing of this dwelling was her "Book-room," containing, perhaps, one of the choicest theosophical libraries to be found; works in different languages (she was an excellent linguist), many of them very rare, and now only to be obtained by a collector's persevering efforts; works, the names of some of whose authors are scarcely known even to persons of literary research, but from which this devoted student was constantly extracting golden significance for the recondite circle of her thought. Prominent here, of course, was her great master in theosophy, Jacob Böhme—Böhme, of whom even the most adventurous readers may say — substituting his name — what Hutchison Stirling's German teacher said when questioned about Hegel: "Other writers may be this, may be that; but Hegel! one has to stop! and think! and think!—Hegel! Ach Gott!" But scarcely less arduous study is exacted by other and less known writers of this school whose works were here collected—by Franz Baader, Oetinger, Hamberger, Dionysius Freher, Gichtel, Fabre D'Olivet, Greaves, St Martin, and others. William Law is the easiest, but even Law—an English classic—is hardly known to the general literary public except by one, and

---

[1] I remember well the spontaneous testimony to her beneficence and kindliness by the driver of a conveyance I hired to take me to her house on the occasion of my first visit to her.

that by no means the most impressive, of his works—
the *Serious Call*. Here was a mine of hidden treasures,
which has never, perhaps, been so thoroughly explored
as by Mrs Penny—certainly never by an intelligence
more eager and docile, or more apt to penetrate difficult
meaning. Nor were her studies in this region confined
to one school. Her own writings shew the catholicity
of her reading whenever mysticism is in question. Her
knowledge of Swedenborg, for instance, was extraordinary, and her assimilation of his principles she found
easily reconcilable with the dominant influence of
Böhme. It rarely happens that the devotees of one
particular master are able to enlarge that ideal territory,
while the literary critic, though he may be omnivorous
for his purpose, seldom assimilates anything. Mrs Penny
was necessarily an eclectic, in speculation at least, just
because her principal studies had laid in her intelligence
so deep and broad a foundation for her faith that
thought was free from many a barrier which a narrower
or more traditional orthodoxy would have set up. Herself a Christian from profound conviction, she was
patient with modern scepticism, which she regarded as a
transitional state, naturally consequent on the dryness
and superficiality of the Church, and containing more
sincerity than ecclesiastical and conventional religion,
of which, if of anything, she might be called almost
intolerant, so greatly did it vex her soul. She hoped
that infidelity, in seeking to stamp *out* Christianity,
would really stamp it *down* to a deeper foundation, to
a natural philosophy of Divinity and Man. That she
found the groundwork, and even the complete plan, of
such a philosophy in Jacob Böhme, scarcely needs to
be stated.

It was occasionally suggested to Mrs Penny by a correspondent that Böhme required to be *translated*—rendered
into modern modes of thought and expression—rather

than to be *cited*. But she had her own method of interpretation, and that, for a patient reader, perhaps the best, viz., *collation*. She would bring passages from very different parts of his writings to bear on one another, till half-a-dozen several obscurities sometimes seemed to blend into a common luminosity. Her best analysis was always through synthesis. And she would give her readers or correspondents—at least I can answer for one of them—so firm a grasp on certain leading conceptions in the old theosophy, that these are henceforth recognized as main beams in the edifice, and one sees how great is the ideal weight they can support.

Mrs Penny's numerous articles in various publications, here and in America, have a special value. Without attempting systematic exegesis, she aimed at helping students through the difficulties she had herself encountered. And she never shirked a difficulty, or tried to conceal it in verbiage. If she could not understand a doctrine or a passage she said so, and at least made her readers see where the difficulty lay. But she rarely, if ever, quitted a subject without throwing some light upon it, or at least directing one to some pertinent idea. And no one knew better how to distinguish clear thought from what she happily designated "mental fumbling." The collection and reprint of her various writings, by a competent and sympathetic editor, would be no slight service to those who understand the spiritual significance and value of the old "theosophers."

In a seventeen years' correspondence with Mrs Penny I have seldom had a letter from her which I did not feel constrained to preserve for the sake of some thought or expression of more than momentary interest.[1] Her

[1] The letters here referred to by Mr Massey are, fortunately, still in existence, and have been kindly placed at my disposal by their present owner. Should a demand arise for more of Mrs Penny's writings, I hope to print selections from them at some future time.—ED.

lively and penetrating intelligence found, perhaps, its readiest and most spontaneous utterance in these unpremeditated compositions. But not the thinking intelligence only, the whole character spoke in them, and made their peculiar interest.

Mrs Penny was, I believe, under seventy at her death. *Light* has lost in her a contributor whose value some had learnt to appreciate, and a constant reader whose sympathetic intelligence could extract from even conflicting lines of thought whatever was best in each. Her Christianity and "Spiritualism," for instance, never prejudiced her against the modern "Theosophy," to whose exponents she gave willing attention. But to the last her ruling desire was to promote study of the profundities of Jacob Böhme. And for her own considerable attempts in this direction she will ever be held in esteem by initiates of that master mystic.

C. C. MASSEY.

CONTENTS

	PAGE
WHO WAS JACOB BÖHME?	1
JACOB BÖHME'S WRITINGS	12
WHY ARE NOT JACOB BÖHME'S WRITINGS STUDIED?	51
BÖHME AND SWEDENBORG	75
THE POWER OF IMAGINATION	86
EXPERIENCES IN OPEN VISION	92
EMANATIONS OF THE WORLD-SOUL	97
COMMUNICATING SPIRITS	99
THE WORLD-SOUL	143
ON THE WORLD-SOUL	146
THE DOCTRINE OF VICARIOUS SUFFERING	169
DEITY ANTERIOR TO CREATION	172
ON INFLUX	177
WHO ARE OUR SPIRITUAL ENEMIES?	186
NATURAL OBJECTS EXISTANT	228
THE SECOND ADVENT	233
THE USES OF PAIN AND EVIL	247
MARTENSEN'S "JACOB BÖHME"	261
THE DURATION OF EVIL	305
REINCARNATION	318
READY-MADE CLOTHES	322
ETERNAL BODIES	329
BURIED TREASURES	338
CREATION BY THE WORD	354
IMAGINATION AND PHANTASY	368

	PAGE
ALCHYMISTICAL PHILOSOPHERS	380
BÖHME AND THE "SECRET DOCTRINE"	383
ATMOSPHERES	388
JESUS AND THE CHRIST	390
UNCONSCIOUS CREATION	392
SPIRITUAL EVOLUTION	404
ILLUSIONS IN LIFE'S TRANCE	417
FORM	420
THE ADVANTAGES OF CHRISTIANITY	434
BÖHME AND RÂMA PRASÂD	438
PLANETRAY INFLUENCE	447
RESURRECTION BODIES	456
THE IMAGE	461
APPENDIX	474

ILLUSTRATIONS

PORTRAIT OF MRS PENNY	*Frontispiece*
THE COTTAGE, CULLOMPTON	*facing p.* xxi

WHO WAS JACOB BÖHME?[1]

ONE of the most remarkable cases of spiritual mediumship, in the highest sense; a man chosen by God for revealing knowledge that he himself had never sought, and did not understand, while at the urgent dictates of an invisible guide he wrote what was communicated to him. The saying of our Lord that as "the wind bloweth where it listeth, and thou hearest the sound thereof, but canst not tell whence it cometh and whither it goeth, so is every one that is born of the Spirit," is true of the *knowledge* born of the Spirit also: it was never more strikingly proved than in the case of Böhme. To this unlearned shoemaker, living more than two centuries ago in an obscure town of Germany, we owe revelations so profound, so various, and so divinely central, that while in nothing do they contradict the Holy Scriptures, in many points they supplement, in many more they explain and emphatically confirm, its teaching. The Bible would not have for me half the depth of meaning it has if this more recent messenger of God had not poured light on some of its most perplexing passages: a light to which human reason could never have won, but for which he had unconsciously made himself ready by intense singleness of purpose in seeking the one only refuge for the soul of man. "I never desired," he says in one of his letters, "to know anything of the divine

[1] Light and Life, August 2nd, 1886.

mystery, much less understood I the way how to seek or find it; I knew nothing of it, as is the condition of poor laymen in their simplicity. I sought only after the heart of Jesus Christ, that I might hide myself from the wrathful anger of God and the violent assaults of the devil; and I besought the Lord earnestly for His holy spirit and His grace that He would be pleased to bless and guide me in Him."[1] So seeking he found. With that ardent and humble approach to "the Centre"—to which he so often invites others—he won access to the unsearchable riches of Christ, in whom are hid all the treasures of wisdom and knowledge. These were opened to him in such unwonted measure, that to this day they have not been even approximately estimated at their true value: and a future generation will wonder why, when such writings were extant, any one could think that inspiration from on high ended with the writers of the New Testament, or that the promise of guidance into all truth, far more than the immediate followers of Jesus Christ were able to bear, had been broken, and eighteen centuries had passed away with no further utterance of the spirit of truth.

But for facts. Born in 1575, Böhme was as a youth apprenticed to a shoemaker at Görlitz, in Saxony; married to a daughter of a butcher in 1594, and had four sons, all of whom he brought up to some trade. While still a lad, alone in his master's shop, busily sweeping it out, we read of his having an interview with a mysterious stranger, who, after buying a pair of shoes, spoke very impressively to him of his duties and his future; and this is supposed by his biographers to have influenced his conduct, making him more zealous in all religious exercises, more studious of the Bible, more earnest in striving to live blamelessly. The natural consequence

[1] Epistles (1649), Ep. 2, par. 6.

of such endeavour was a keener sense of sin, with that tumult of conflicting desires and reactionary evil impulse which so often precedes the outburst of victorious light. Truly it is darkest before the dawning with very many, as Böhme seems to have experienced. But while he tells us of the fierce onsets of the enemies of the soul, he cannot find words glad enough or expressive enough to describe what followed. "I wrestled, in God's assistance, a good space of time for the victorious garland or crown of victory, which I afterwards, with the breaking open of the gate of the deep in the centre of nature, attained with very great joy."[1]

At the age of twenty-five he was first consciously overtaken by *the Spirit of the Light, which loved him exceedingly*.[2] Walking one day in the fields, the mystery of creation was opened to him suddenly, and, as he narrates, "in one quarter of an hour I saw and knew more than if I had been many years together at an university, at which I did exceedingly admire, and I knew not how it happened to me; and thereupon I turned my heart to praise God for it. For I saw and knew the Being of all beings, the *Byss* and *Abyss*,[3] also the birth or eternal generation of the Holy Trinity; the descent and original of this world, and of all creatures through the divine wisdom; I knew and saw in myself all the three worlds, namely, the divine, angelical, and paradisical world; and then the dark world, being the original of nature to fire;[4] and then, thirdly, the external and visible world, being a procreation or

---

[1] First Apology, Part I., par. 25.
[2] Ibid., par. 33.
[3] "*God*," Böhme has told us, "*is in Himself the Abyss without any will at all.*" . . . "*He maketh Himself a ground or Byss.*"
[4] "*Original to fire*" is a translation which proves either imperfect grasp of the meaning of the writer, or want of sympathy with the reader's mind.

extern birth; or as a substance expressed or spoken forth from *both* the internal and spiritual worlds; and I saw and knew the whole being [or working essence] in the evil and in the good, and the mutual original and existence of each of them." . . . "I saw it (as in a great deep) in the internal, for I had a thorough view of the universe, as in a CHAOS, wherein all things are couched and wrapped up, but it was impossible for me to explicate and unfold the same."[1]

But it was ten years later, when, finding these unsought riches of revelation come to him more and more, that he first tried to record their purport. He wrote the *Aurora*—his first work—for a help to his own memory, in 1612. After a while he lent the manuscript to a friend, by whose agency it got into the hands of a gentleman who was so much impressed with its unique value that he had it unstitched and copied from end to end by many different hands before it was returned; and this transcript, getting abroad, fell under the eyes of the authorities of Görlitz. As a matter of course it was vehemently condemned, chiefly by the Primate, Gregory Richter.

A religious writer who presumes to teach more than contemporaneous religious teachers know, and to understand what they deem an impenetrable mystery, is sure to be denounced as a heretic, a heretic all the more dangerous if, as in this case, the bringer of new things is evidently devout, and impugns, not the words of Scripture, but the wisdom of its interpreters, in supposing current meanings to be all that are contained, or that are to be found in it. This—and an unsparing

---

Dionysius Freher only could *adequately* explain the justice of those words, exchanging *to* for *of*, which evidently it was meant *to* be, the *original becoming of fire* caused by the intense friction of astringency and mobility in the darkness which *precedes* its outburst.

[1] Epistles (1649), Ep. 2, pars. 7, 8, 9.

rebuke of evil wherever it was, high or low, decent or gross—was the unpardonable sin of Böhme: to this day unpardoned by every reader who is not, in good earnest, fighting against self with Christ and for Christ. To those who are not, his writings may be interesting; to every thinker they *would* be, for "if a man would satisfy the human mind so that it may give itself up into the eternal rest, then a man must shew him the root of the tree out of which spirit and flesh hath its origin."[1] And Böhme alone offers to shew it,—but with a repulsive severity of reprobation, an obnoxious thoroughness of unconventional Christianity, which lays bare the cunning of self-deception under every kind of "devout shows," and presses on unwilling minds the "rude uncouth message" that in all the world there is no such cruel evil beast as that harboured in the breast of every man and woman,—self-love. In saying this, I by no means assert the converse. The most sincere conversion of the will from self-seeking to the obedience of Christ does not secure a liking for books so obscure as his. They bristle with terms so unusual, and thoughts so unlike the accepted coin of the religious world, that for a large majority of readers repulsion *must* at first be far stronger than attraction. A little patience, a little passing over what has no meaning at first, and dwelling on the sublime intensity of clearest utterance which is to be found on almost every page, and vigorous intellects will be more stimulated than baffled. But all minds are not vigorous, neither have all leisure for such exercise.

What embitters ordinary Christians more than anything else in this old teacher, is that he takes ignorance as to spiritual Mysteries for proof positive of arrest in Christian life. Again and again he meets the charge of

[1] Considerations upon Esaiah Stiefel's *Threefold State of Man*, par. 23.

speculating beyond bounds of holy awe, with the counter charge that if we were led by the Spirit more and more would be revealed to us of the deep things of God, and that the going on unto perfection to which St Paul exhorts would include increase of knowledge as well as greater holiness of life. In his *Apology* or defence against Gregory Richter he justly says: "You say that I will search out the Deity, and [you] call it devilish; thereby you shew your ignorance to the daylight, that you understand nothing of the Book of Nature, and also do not read the New Testament, for St Paul saith, *The spirit searcheth all things, yea, the deep things of God.*[1] It is not of man's ability; but God's Spirit performeth that searching through man's spirit."[2]

Recognition of this was at once his own safeguard and his credential as a man sent by God. Speaking of his own writing, he said: "I cannot say that I have learned or comprehended it, but so long as the hand of God stayeth upon me, I understand it; but if it hides itself, then I know not my own labour, and am made a stranger to the work of my own hands. Whereby I may see how altogether impossible a thing it is to search out and apprehend the mysteries of God without God's Spirit." ... "If it be His will for me to know anything, then I will know it; but if He willeth it not, then do I so also. *I will be nothing, and dead*, that He may live and work in me *what He pleaseth*. I have cast myself wholly into Him that so I may be safe."[3]

It is doubtless owing to this attitude of deepest humility and self-abnegation that he was so absolutely free from all the unbalanced excitement of visionaries; and were it not for his strong sense of the sublime uses of the humblest business on earth, his knowledge of the latent

---

[1] 1 Cor. ii. 10.
[2] Fourth Apology, Part I., pars. 44, 45.
[3] Epistles (1649), Ep. 3, pars. 23, 24.

powers in man and perception of man's original greatness, might have tended to disqualify him for the details of practical duty; but while asserting that "the soul is a sparkle out of the great omnipotency of God,"[1]—that "by the will God created heaven and earth, and such a mighty will is hidden also in the soul"[2]—he never lost sight of the nothingness and impotency of man as he *now* is, until Christ is formed in him, and every imagination is brought into obedience to Christ. No exaltation of self, because of the abundance of revelations, was possible to one who so well understood that mortification of selfwill and recipiency of grace is *all* that a human creature can do in "working out its own salvation." "The soul hath free will to go out and in, but it cannot generate itself in Christ; it must only go out of its own evil will, and enter into God's mercy." . . . "I lie in imbecility," he adds, "as a dying man, but the Most High raiseth me up in His breath, so that I go according to His wind."[3]

Some of the most *learned* of his fellow-countrymen sought him out for instruction on the mysteries of the natural as well as the spiritual world; and it is notorious that from his writings Sir Isaac Newton in England, and Hegel in Germany, drew what the French call *les idées mères*, to which their own fame has been largely due; but Böhme himself lightly esteemed any knowledge that fell short of that which, as he expressed it, "opens to us the paradisical gate in the inward centre of our image, that the paradisical light might shine to us in our minds," adding: "Seeing that Christ the Son of God hath generated us again to the paradisical image, we should not be so remiss as to rely upon art and earthly reason; for so we find not paradise and Christ, who must become man

---

[1] Third Apology, Text I., par. 112.
[2] Threefold Life, ch. viii., par. 18.
[3] Third Apology, Text IV., Point I., pars. 47, 49.

in us if we will ever see God: in our reason it is all but dead and blind."[1]

Yet never surely did a holy man so much exalt the uses of art and reason when rightly employed; one of his greatest peculiarities is the stress he lays on the value of all earthly pursuits so long as they do not *fill* and darken the mind. "Indeed, the divine wisdom standeth not in art and reason, but it sheweth art the way, what it should do and how it should seek. Art is really the tool or instrument of God wherewith the divine wisdom worketh or laboureth; why should I despise it?" . . . "All profitable arts are revealed out of God's wisdom; *not* that they are that by which man cometh to God, but for the government of the outward life, and for the glorious manifestation of divine wisdom and omnipotence."[2]

"Man must labour and trade, for therefore he is created into the outer world, that he should manifest God's wonders with his skill and trading. All trades, businesses, and conditions are God's ordinance; every one worketh the wonders of God."[3]

How different is *this* aspect of *worldly* pursuits from that which pretends to contemn all interests and occupations of present life in order to throw into strong relief the glories and bliss of a future state! as if trying to denaturalize man was the best method for spiritual evolution! The result of this mistaken effort meets us at every turn, a spiritual *falsetto* being too often adopted when the old Adam has not been so much mortified as ignored; and the recoil from such unwholesome tension too often proves that heavenly-mindedness is *not* the usual effect of disdaining earthly good. Our old mystic held "the old ass," as he quaintly terms the natural

---

[1] Incarnation, Part I., ch. iv., pars. 6, 8.
[2] Third Apology, Text IV., Point III., par. 77.
[3] Threefold Life, ch. xvii., pars. 11, 12.

man, in wiser estimation, and insists on its uses with regard to the new man, who is to be formed in it as gold is formed in the rough ore of its matrix. The persecution that he underwent after Gregory Richter had denounced him from the pulpit resulted in his being severely condemned for heresy, though on no one point could his judges find him guilty, but vaguely passed sentence on his writings upon "hearsay censure." He was forbidden to write any more, and to this order, with characteristic meekness, he submitted for six or seven years, quietly carrying on his shoemaker's craft meanwhile, till at last the dictates of his invisible guide, and the urgency of friends, led him to disregard the prohibition. Between the years 1618 and 1624 he wrote in quick succession the rest of his works (he wrote 31 in all), each, as it seems, opening more deeply and impressing more earnestly the mysteries and lessons which he had been taught.

In his *Third Epistle* he gives a wonderful account of the "instigation of the Spirit," under which in nine months he wrote three of his most profound books.

The disturbance raised in Görlitz by his persecution obliged him to leave it for the sake of peace. He went to Dresden, where he resided until his death—after a short illness—in 1624. His last words were: "Now I go hence into Paradise."

We are told that he was a small man of low stature, and the written account of his features in no way contradicts the impression given by his pictured likeness, of harsh and homely outlines illumined by a singular look of settled peace and intense inward activity.

Böhme has many wonderful truths to tell us, and a solution to offer of many mysteries deemed inscrutable by most divines; but the most priceless truth and the most unfailing pass-key to a treasury of spiritual knowledge which he presses upon us, in his every book, with ever new fervency, is the necessity of *continued* dying to self, and keeping the soul plunged in humility, patience, and love. A hard lesson practically, but how simple and easy to understand are the terms in which he gives it! "Thou wilt ask, What is the new regeneration? or how is that done in man? Hear and see; stop not thy mind, let not thy mind be filled by the spirit of this world with its might and pomp. Take thy mind and break through [the spirit of this world] entirely: incline thy mind into the kind love of God: make thy purpose earnest and strong to break through the pleasure of this world with thy mind and not to regard it."[1]

"Seek you nothing else but the Word and Heart of God: . . . you need not break your mind with hard thoughts, for with such high fancies and conceits you will not find the *ground*: do but only incline your mind and thoughts, with your whole reason, into the love and mercy of God, so that you be born out of the Word and Heart of God in the *centre of your life*, so that His light shine in the light of your life, that you be one with Him."[2]

And now, having so far learned who and what Böhme was from his own evidence as well as from the reports of contemporary biographers, I think we can understand the accuracy of his prediction in the preface to his *Aurora*. "Now, if Mr Critic, who qualifieth or worketh with his wit in the fierce quality, gets this book" (any of his books) "into his hand, he will oppose it, as there is always stirring and opposition between the kingdom of heaven and the kingdom of hell."[3]

Yes, but as the King of Heaven is Omnipotent, all who resist His rule *must* yield at last: at last all-con

---

[1] Three Principles, ch. xvi., par. 48.
[2] Threefold Life, ch. iii., par. 30.
[3] Aurora, Contents of this Book, par. 8.

quering love will extirpate the venom of scorn, and prevail even on *Mr Critic* to know "the meekness of wisdom," and all its resulting blessedness. "In the time of the lily," said Böhme, "my writings will be much sought after." Some little buds of that lily may be descried among us already.

JACOB BÖHME'S WRITINGS [1]

"Seeing you have my writings in your hands, I give you to understand that you should only child-like and simply consider them; and so you may find the pearl therein; for sharp or acute searching alone doth it not; but to will and do well."—Jacob Böhme's Epistle to C. B., Sept. 12, 1620. *Epistles* (1661), Ep. 9, par. 15.

"If I might advise you for the furtherance of your soulish life, I would recommend you to procure the writings of Böhme, and diligently read them. For, though I have studied philosophy and theology from my youth, and also exercised myself in polemical writings, and studied Greek and Hebrew, yet I must acknowledge the above writings have been to me of more service for the understanding of the Bible than all my University learning."—J. G. Gichtel, 1698.

"'WHAT is truth?' said jesting Pilate, and would not stay for an answer." The turn of enquiry thus described by Francis Bacon is a marked characteristic of the present day. However ready and conclusive the answer may be, it is unheeded if it requires patient and prolonged attention; because it is not satisfaction of the mind that is sought for by questioners so much as utterance of doubt. Uncertainty as to every point, which our forefathers held to be fixed articles of belief, is the favourite attitude of modern intellects. In this sea of doubt a large majority luxuriate, just as the habitually irresolute enjoy complaining of perplexities which, they say, admit of no possible solution. To the impatient mind total uncertainty gives a fallacious sense of freedom, and to the irresolute mind perplexity as to every line of action supplies excuse for sloth. The quickened

[1] Light and Life, Nov. and Dec. 1885, Jan. and Feb. 1886.

thought of modern times necessarily unsettles a large class of intellects "that delight in giddiness and account it a bondage to fix a belief"; and to such as these it would be vain to speak of Böhme. But they in every age are followers, not leaders, in human progress. Of a very different order are those which are now both ready and able to lead, if only they could convince themselves *what is not untruth.* Too well aware of the vastness of spiritual science to expect a brief and summary clearing up of its hitherto inscrutable mysteries, all they attempt to define is the amount of error that has over-laid authorized dogma; and for them the process is often a long and bitter conflict, as every struggle to advance against current habits of thought must be. And the saddest part of the struggle is that it has to be made against modes of belief which are esteemed too holy to call in question, by people whose very goodness makes any lack of wisdom more injurious than it could otherwise be. The narrow-minded pietist unconsciously drives stronger brained men and women into scepticism, by simplest means effecting complex results: for instance, the future world is spoken of—the devout bigot reverts to the almost obsolete idea of everlasting fire and brimstone torments *external* to the sinner, of divine *vengeance.* There is the quiet smile or outspoken sarcasm in reply, such a speaker being obviously unprepared for argument; and these, inflaming the zeal and blinding the judgment of the other by anger, prompt the accusation that the truth of God's Word is doubted, that the hard heart of unbelief has to be touched by more earnest admonition. Probably the heart in question is not at all hard, nor may any unbelief have been felt except as to the accuracy of this conception of the fate of impenitent sinners; but it is clear that if any one is so unwise as to make this idea of it a test of Christian faith, he or she greatly lowers the claim of that faith upon any reasonable being; for, finding these material torments regarded as an integral part of revealed truth, naturally leads to suspecting that all religious doctrine is equally the outcome of superstition, and is too often followed by disbelief in any future that *need* be feared. The frequency of suicide gives terrific evidence of such disbelief. Even in our nurseries we might learn that a threat which does not intimidate emboldens a wrong-doer; so does much of what has been called sound doctrine. Men are told of God's never-ending punishment of sin—of torments intense and illimitable, but such alarms seldom take the least effect on cultivated minds. Thinkers *cannot* believe, while conscious of so much mixture of good in people deservedly called bad, and of the many extenuating peculiarities of fate which promote evil, that a God who pities as a father does his children, will seize on the soul as soon as it is hurried from mortal wrappings, and place it beyond remedy. I say they cannot, and I know they do not.

Again, it is impossible for thoughtful people to avoid seeing that those will never be deterred from sin by threats of imposed penalties, who are taught that God promises on certain conditions to deliver from the *consequences* of sin. To the last they will assure themselves that He is so merciful that He will surely forgive and save, understanding by forgiveness an arbitrary decision of will, and by salvation escape from suffering.

Now, it is for those to whom popular Christianity offers grave offence that Böhme's teaching will be what Franz Baader said it was, "the only means of deliverance from the prevailing destructive knowledge or want of knowledge,"[1] for, to use the words of a brave

---

[1] "*das einzige Mittel der Besserung gegen die herrschende destructive Wissenschaft oder Unwissenschaft ist.* Deswegen J. Böhme keineswegs ein Mann der Vergangenheit ist und bloss der Historie angehört, sondern als ein Mann der Gegenwart zur Aufbahnung einer besseren Zukunft anerkannt werden muss."—Franz Baader's *Brief an Dr W. Strausky,* 1838.

contemporary,[1] "the truth requires to be proclaimed aloud that modern Christianity, as generally received, does not represent the teaching of Christ, and is not fit to be charged with the task of teaching the world a suitable and satisfactory morality." This inability of professional guides to reconcile Christian dogma to profoundly searching intellects need not surprise us, seeing that they bind themselves by oath to follow prescribed lines of thought rather than the spirit of truth wheresoever that goeth, and take their credentials from external authority; but the fact remains, the scoff and triumph of unbelievers.

Jacob Böhme, a medium for the Holy Spirit nearly three centuries ago, will carry us farther towards central truths than any later seer, and will harmonize many a conflicting aspect of truth; widely as its rays of light may diverge in their outermost issue, in closer proximity to the centre they will be found nearly related.

"For whom," asked the late Mr Christopher Walton, "are Böhme's writings useful, and what is their intent? The writer would answer, if he knew of any honest enquiring minds, in a Christian country, that after a careful study of the Holy Scriptures, and much pondering upon the great mystery of things all around and within them, especially upon the seeming incompatibleness of the bloody cruelty, misery and shocking injustice which are daily and with impunity perpetrated, and likewise recounted in the Old Testament itself, with the nature and character of the Deity as described in the Christian revelation as an Omnipotent, Omnipresent, All-wise Being who is all love and goodness to His creatures;—if there are, as doubtless there are, many such who thus stand in a state of doubt and uncertainty respecting the Holy Scriptures, and the working wisdom

[1] The Rev. T. W. Fowle in *Contemporary Review*, May, 1872.

of Divine love, then it may be truly said that to such is the word of this revelation sent."[1]

For as William Law says, "There is not any philosophical question that can be put, nor advice nor direction that can be asked in regard to God, or Nature, or Christianity, but what Böhme has over and over spoke to, and that in the plainest terms." A saying that needs this qualification—The plainest terms in which subjects of such mystery can be spoken of. As his translator, John Sparrow, quaintly reminds us in his Introduction to Böhme's *Mysterium Magnum*—"Mysteries cannot be expressed in easy words; some things most excellent[2] cannot be uttered by any words, therefore 'tis happy some other[3] hard things may be uttered though by hard words, better than none at all."

"The chief cause," says Dionysius Freher, Böhme's great interpreter, "of all these suspicions which we many of us cast upon this chosen vessel of God, Jacob Böhme, is that we can so hardly elevate our thoughts above the sphere of this temporal principle and the forms and course of things that are therein, and always think that our apprehension of things in their present condition is a true measuring line, fit to measure the same things exactly as they were before they came into this fragmentary state."[4]

Before specifying the peculiar knowledge to be gained from his teaching, I will cite the testimony of some of Böhme's most distinguished students, and then his own, as to the worth and the source of his revelations.

Edward Taylor, writing about the year 1678 an answer to one of the *177 Theosophic Questions* proposed by Böhme, said:—"Whereas men have dark, confused

---

[1] C. Walton's *Memorial of William Law*, page 82.
[2] Romans viii. 26.
[3] 2 Cor. xii. 4.
[4] D. Freher on *Deity and Eternal Nature*.

notions of God, like those of Athens dedicating their altar to the unknown God; of Him, therefore, whom men ignorantly worship do Jacob Behmen's writings give a clear, certain, demonstrable, and distinct knowledge, and of all things and worlds; also of all creatures, from the most holy, angelical Princes of Eternity to the most despicable excrescence of time."[1]

J. G. Gichtel, advising a friend in the year 1698, said:— "I have searched through many mystics in my time, but found in none of these what, with great labour, prayer, striving and wrestling through many years, I have found in this enlightened shoemaker; and I can never sufficiently thank God for His grace who thereby enlightened me in many perplexities, and solved such desperate dilemmas as met me in the strife with the dragon. And I may with good ground affirm, that if there is in Scripture anything obscure, magical, or mystical, Böhme solves it all; and I wish with all my heart that you may find your peace therein."[2]

Speaking of him in the first year of the present century, Poiret said:—"J. Böhme est le seul, au moins dont on ait les écrits jusqu'à lui, *auquel Dieu ait découvert le fond de la Nature*, tant des choses spirituelles que des corporelles; et qui avec une pénétration toute centrale des choses théologiques et surnaturelles, ait aussi connu d'origine les vrais principes de la philosophie, tant de la métaphysique, que de la vraie physique."[3]

Writing to a friend in 1792, L. Claude de St Martin told him: "Je ne suis plus jeune, étant tout près de ma

[1] Jacob Behmen's *Theosophick Philosophy Unfolded*, p. 111.
[2] Theosophica Practica, Vol. I., Letter 88.
[3] *Translation.*—"J. Böhme is the only one, at least whose writings we have until his time, to whom God has discovered the basis of Nature, in spiritual as well as in corporeal things, and who, with a central penetration in theological and supernatural matters, has also known from their origin the true principles of philosophy in metaphysics as well as in true physics."

cinquantième année; et c'est à cet âge avancé que j'ai commencé à apprendre le peu d'allemand que je possède, uniquement pour lire cet incomparable auteur." ... "Je reconnais n'être pas digne de dénouer les cordons des souliers de cet homme étonnant, que je regarde comme la plus grande lumière qui ait paru sur la terre après Celui qui est la lumière même." ... "Je vous exhorte, si vous en avez le temps, à vous jeter dans cet abîme de connaissances et de profondes vérités." ... "Dans Jacob Böhme je trouve une aplomb d'une solidité inébranlable; j'y trouve une profondeur, une élévation, une nourriture si pleine et si soutenue, que je vous avoue que je croirais perdre mon temps que de chercher ailleurs."[1]

Speaking of Schelling's works, Schopenhauer, still more recently said, "Es ist fast nur eine Umbearbeitung von Jakob Böhme's *Mysterium Magnum*, in welchem sich fast jeder Satz und jeder Ausdruck nachweisen lässt. Warum aber sind mir bei Schelling dieselben Bilder, Formen und Ausdrücke unerträglich und lächerlich, die ich bei Jakob Böhme mit Bewunderung und Rührung lese? Weil ich erkenne, dass in Jakob Böhme die Erkenntniss der *ewigen Wahrheit* es ist, die sich in diesen Bildern auspricht, obwohl sie auch mit gleichem

---

[1] La Correspondance Inédite de L.-C. de Saint-Martin, dit Le Philosophe Inconnu, et Kirchberger, Baron de Liebistorf, 1862, pp. 9, 29.

Translation.—"I am no longer young, being near my fiftieth year; and at this advanced age I have begun to learn the little German I know, solely to read this incomparable author." ... "I frankly acknowledge that I am not worthy to untie the shoestrings of that wonderful man, whom I look upon as the greatest light that has appeared on the earth since Him who is the light Himself." ... "I exhort you, if you have time, to dive into this abyss of knowledge and profound truths." ... "In Böhme I find a solidity that cannot be shaken; a depth, an elevation and a nourishment so full and so unfailing, that I confess I should think it time lost to seek elsewhere."—*Correspondence between Louis Claude de Saint-Martin and Kirchberger.* Translated by Edward Burton Penny, 1863. Letters 2 and 8, S.-M. to K., pp. 7, 33.

Fug in vielen andern sich hätte ausprechen können. Schelling aber nimmt von ihm was er allein von ihm nehmen kann, dieselben Bilder und Ausdrücke, hält eine Schaale für die Frucht, oder weisst sie wenigstens nicht von der Frucht zu lösen."[1] Dionysius Freher, of whom it is recorded that he "read all Böhme's books in the original more than ten times through, *though not without the greatest disgust imaginable in the beginning*,"[2] gave this testimony among many others of greater length: "As to Böhme, it is with me, and I am sure with many others also, beyond all doubt and question that he verily had a true and deep understanding, not in his reason, but in his eternal spirit, of the *manner* and *process* of the whole creation; nay, that he really and fundamentally understood even the way and method of the *necromancy* itself, not in practice as the devil's agents do, but in the ground and depth thereof, wherein they are blind and ignorant."[3]

And only a few years ago Mr E. Paxton Hood in his Essay on *Boehme, the Evangelical Hegel*, sums up his peculiar value thus: "To those who would know how much is to be said to the reason and the understanding to strengthen and confirm the faith, to keep the frail spirit of the thoughtful man from reeling from its steadfastness, or plunging into an ocean or night of despair,

---

[1] A. Schopenhauer's *Handschriftlichem Nachlass*, p. 261.

Free Translation.—"It is almost only a revived make up of Jacob Böhme's *Mysterium Magnum*, to which its every sentiment and every expression leads one to recur. But why in Schelling are the same images, forms, and phrases unbearable and absurd, while in Jacob Böhme I read with admiration and emotion? Because in Böhme I recognize the perception of *Eternal truth* which expresses itself in these images, though it might have done so with equal propriety in many others. But Schelling takes from him what only he could take; holds the husk for the fruit, or at least does not know how to separate it from the fruit."

[2] C. Walton's *Memorial of William Law*, p. 206.

[3] Ibid., p. 467.

the works of Böhme are full to overflowing of light and strength."

Evidence equally strong might be adduced from other writers, such, for instance, as Oetinger and Hamberger, both German exponents of his teaching, but what has been given already will suffice to convince any one who intends to study his works, that there must be very solid ground for such exceptional value being attributed to them. I well know the incredulity with which modern students hear or read such praise of writings which have been before the world for more than two centuries and have yet been little read: the natural assumption is that if they were really all their admirers say, they *must* have taken higher rank in literary estimation.

This, however true as regards books of more external interest, is never true of those which claim concentrated attention for a world to which the majority, even of students, remain indifferent, until introduced to it by Death—that inner world where the spirit acts with spirits —into which few of us care to look till driven by pain or grief from the louder and coarser excitements of outer interests. And it needs but little observation of English character to convince us that to average men and women such writings as Böhme's must be at first distasteful. When English readers can call a book *mystical* they have usually sealed it, virtually, for themselves and for all whom they can influence, as unreadable. Some, like the late Mr Vaughan, may take up a volume of his as an historic curiosity, and pass judgment upon it with lively decision, quite unconscious of having failed to perceive its scope. In his *Hours with the Mystics*, the only point which that excellent man made good when professing to deal with Böhme's writings, is that to criticize them without right comprehension of their contents is to ensure self-exposure. Since that book was published, twenty-eight years ago, time and enlarged intelligence have modified literary fashions, and the incoming tide of interest in occult studies has placed him far higher in the esteem of learned men than people in the first half of this century would have expected; but at no period could his books be read without arousing the instinctive antagonisms between prophet and priest, and the dislike of those who rely on doctrines that have been long fixed, and which they *therefore* regard as authoritative and final, for people who accept direct instruction from the unseen world, and look for ever-widening views of truth. Add to this invincible suspicion of the *un*fixed in religious matters, resentment as inevitable under the censures of the innovator! When in the late Mr C. Walton's *Memorial of William Law*,[1] we read that Böhme was "a discoverer of the false anti-Christian Church from its first rise in Cain, through every age of the world, to its present state in all and every sect of the present divided Christendom,"[2] enough is said to account for clerical feeling about him. Each division of Christendom's Church may bewail what is anti-Christian in others, but to see so clearly mirrored the special errors and self-delusions of *every* sect, inclusive of one's own, and to find those besetting evils denounced with all the force of justice—this is what few can stand without making a counter-charge of fanaticism to invalidate his verdict. And this has been so successfully made, that condemning Böhme as a very "mischievous writer," without opening one of his books, has been as usual as it is convenient for the purpose of discrediting them. So it was in his lifetime. "The citizens here about me knew nothing of my writing." ... " It was proclaimed among them for heresy, which notwithstanding they never read, neither was it examined ever as it was meet."[3]

---

[1] Unpublished, but to be found in most of England's large Public Libraries.
[2] Page 86. See Law's *Way to Divine Knowledge* (1752), p. 107; Reprint, 1893, *Works*, vol. vii. p. 195.   [3] Epistles (1649), Ep. 3, par. 19.

The invariable complaint as to the obscurity of style—on which account so many excuse themselves from heeding what is only too plain on themes distasteful to self-love—will hardly be raised as an objection by any one who has just ideas of the teaching he had to deliver. It was such as his own mind had been in no way prepared for, beyond an intense longing for Divine grace, and total passivity under its influence. "I speak," he says, "not of and from myself, but from that which the Spirit sheweth, which no man can resist."[1] "I declare in the presence of God, as I shall answer it before His judgment, where all things shall appear, and every one shall give an account of his deeds, that I myself know not how it comes to pass with me, save only that I have a fiery incitement, or strong driving and instigation in my will. I know not also what I shall write, for when I write the Spirit dictates to me in great and wonderful knowledge." . . . "I am, verily, a simple man, and have neither learned, nor after this manner sought after, this high mystery, nor knew I anything of it: I only sought the heart of love in Jesus Christ, and when I had obtained that with great joy of my soul, then was this treasure of natural and Divine knowledge opened and given unto me."[2]

Also, as William Law observes, "What he saw and conceived was quite new and strange, never seen or spoken of before, and, therefore, if he was to put it down in writing, words must be used to signify that which they had never done before."[3] And as his translator, John Sparrow, says there is this advantage in phraseology so unusual and uncouth, "that those excellent notions which he layeth down might not be slipped over as men

---

[1] Epistles (1649), Ep. 3, par. 38.
[2] A Warning from Iacob Beem (1649), pars. 14, 16. [Compiled by the Translator. Usually bound at the end of *Epistles*, 1649.]
[3] Law's *Letters*.

do common current English, but that the strangeness of the words may make them a little stay and consider what the meaning may be."[1] He is surely right as to that; readers too often believe themselves in possession of an author's meaning only because every *word* used is intelligible. But how could language, however clear, make such themes as Böhme's immediately intelligible to *any* mind? He gives a summary of a few of them thus, in answer to his accuser, Tilken. "Learn first to understand the Centre of the Eternal Nature, and how to distinguish the clear or bright Deity from Nature; and learn how the Deity revealeth or manifesteth itself through Nature, and learn what God's Wisdom is, how it is the outspoken substance of the Deity, and what the Divine Life is, and then what Nature Life is." . . . "Also what Paradise and Heaven are, what Evil and Good."[2]

Truly so soon as we see the least glint of light in the depths of knowledge he opens, we assent to his old translator's quaint confession, "All that I apprehend not is *not* nonsense, though I may think so."

A graver objection to the worth of Böhme's revelations is, that the fact of being a *medium* in no way guarantees the validity of the message thus transmitted to us. A clear perception of this, which we owe to the experience of Spiritists (however much we may disapprove of their practice), might have saved past generations from many a fever of fanaticism, due indeed to inspiration, but not that of the Spirit of Truth; now the credentials of this messenger are not only his deep humility and freedom from all self-assertion,

---

[1] Preface to J. B.'s *Three Principles.*
"Truths must be barbed and hooked to cling to us in their passage through the mind: to make them smooth and easy is only to facilitate their escape."—Sewell on *The Cultivation of the Intellect.*

[2] Second Apology, Part I., par. 34.

but the perfect harmony of his teaching with that of Holy Writ. Not that it is restricted to what we learn from our Bible, but that it is never in opposition, and greatly elucidates parts of it, which without his further revelation *has* been, and ever must be, a stumblingstone to every reader whose faith depends mainly upon a *reasonable* understanding of Scripture. These elucidations of his shall be briefly noticed farther on.

Moreover, we find evidence of his veracity as heavensent, in the forcible simpleness of his style; his words fit the windings of human nature in its innermost resorts as perfectly as old Bible words; and before we have time to scrutinize the justice of his verdict, both heart and head feel its accuracy, and flinch from it or accept it, as the case may be.

"As a chosen servant of God," said William Law, "Jacob Böhme may be placed among those who had received the highest measures of light, wisdom, and knowledge from above.... He has no right to be placed among the inspired penmen of the New Testament; he was no messenger from God of anything new in religion, but the mystery of all that was old and true both in religion and Nature was opened in him. This is the particularity of his character, by which he stands fully distinguished from all the prophets, apostles, and extraordinary messengers of God. They were sent with occasional messages, or to make such alterations in the economy of religion as pleased God; but this man came on no particular errand, he had nothing to alter or add either in the form or doctrine of religion. He had no new truths of religion to propose to the world, *but all that lay in religion and Nature as a mystery unsearchable, was in its deepest ground opened to this instrument of God.*"[1]

[1] Animadversions upon Dr Trapp's Reply, Law's *Works*, 1762, Vol. VI., p. 322. Reprint, 1893, Vol. VI., p. 205.

He was himself quite aware both of the nature of the communications made through him, and of their exceptional value. After describing the process of his own enlightenment, he added: "I exhort and entreat you, for the eternal salvation sake, to heed and mind well the Pearl that God favoureth us with, for there will come a time that it shall be sought after and greatly accepted of." ... "Look upon it aright, and pray God the Most High, that He would be pleased to open the door of knowledge, without which no man will understand my writings, for they surpass and transcend the astral reason."[1]

And again, speaking of the time of the end, when "Babel burneth up in the zeal and anger of God," ... "at that time my writing shall be *very serviceable*."[2]

Let his use of the pronoun *we* be noticed. Thus he explained it:—"I give you to understand that in these writings[3] which are now sent you, the author useth sometimes to speak of himself *we* and sometimes *I*. Now understand by the word *we*, the spirit (being spoken in the plural) in two persons, and in the word *I*, the author understands himself."[4]

"My revelation reacheth even into the three kingdoms, like an angelical knowledge; but not in my reason or apprehension, or in perfection like an angel, but in part, and so long only as the spirit tarrieth in me. Further I know it not. When he parteth from me I know nothing but the elementary and earthly things of this world."[5]

But this he wrote in his earliest book. At a later date what knowledge had come to him by "the impulse and motion of God," was sufficiently assimilated for transmission through his own understanding *in some degree*; yet at no period did he arrogate to himself any knowledge

---

[1] Epistles (1649), Ep. 16, par. 8.　　[2] Ibid. (1649), Ep. 26, par. 16.
[3] The Forty Questions.　　[4] Epistles (1649), Ep. 3, par. 39.
[5] Aurora, ch. vii., pars. 17-20.

of transcendental truth. He speaks of it as "What God knew in him." A profound suggestion this of the relation that *all* divine knowledge bears to the human intellect. It was by virtue of this relation that he justified what the critics of his day, as well as ours, have censured for being a presumptuous search into themes too high for human thought. "Mockers and despisers who would say it doth not become me to climb so high into the Deity, and to dive so deeply thereinto. To all of them I give this for an answer, that I am not climbed up into the Deity, neither is it possible for such a mean man as I am to do it, but the Deity is climbed up into me, and from its love are these things revealed unto me."[1] "The Holy Spirit in the soul is creaturely, viz., the propriety or portion of the soul; therefore it searcheth even unto the Deity, and also into Nature, for it hath its source and descent from the Being of the whole Deity."[2]

He in his turn reproaches ministers of the Gospel with their unprogressiveness in the knowledge of spiritual facts, and complains of the insufficiency of authorized theology to satisfy the deepest needs of the soul. "If," he says, "a man would satisfy the human mind so that it may give itself up into the Eternal rest, then a man must shew him the root of the tree out of which spirit and flesh hath its original; a man must shew and open to him the centre of the Eternal, as also of the inceptive or beginning Nature, that he may apprehend the earthly and also the heavenly mystery. And then is the Eternal beginning and the Eternal end totally one, wherein the spirit of the soul layeth itself into rest, for it seeth the wheel totally."[3]

If the depth of that rest was known, and the continuous delightful activity of gain to the mind which that rest

---

[1] Aurora, ch. xviii., pars. 8, 9. [2] Ibid., Introduction, par. 22.
[3] Considerations upon Esaiah Stiefel's *Threefold State of Man*, par. 23. See also *Three Principles*, ch. iii., pars. 4, 5.

admits one to, even in the midst of the confusing discords of modern thought, access to that rest would be sought for as life's chief good. But, like the all-satisfying rewards of fairy-tale heroes, it can only be approached by toil, self-abnegation, and child-like docility; without these it will never be won. It remains to specify the nature of some of those revelations with which Böhme offers to satisfy the mind which "doth not leave off searching till it comes to the innermost ground. But if it reach not the ground, it sinketh down in the ground, and cannot apprehend it, and then cometh doubting, unbelief, and contempt into the mind."[1] To how many are these *come* for want of *any* help towards reaching the innermost ground!

Perhaps the greatest of all truths to be won from his pages is that all evil, sin, and misery, while contrary to and in every sense repugnant to the love of God, are nevertheless consonant with arrested evolution of the *Eternal Nature of God in Man*; for he proves that there is a *Nature* in the Eternal life, and that, apart from that Nature, *i.e.*, the interaction of the Seven Spirits of God (*forms to Nature* in his translated phraseology), the abyssal Deity could not be known nor any creaturely life exist.[2]

It would take a small volume to explain this central truth, and the student must work it out from Böhme's own words, bearing in mind the undeniable truth that if "we live and move and have our being in God," there can be nothing in us or in our world which did not primarily originate in Divine Nature; but this very word Nature, *a becoming*, indicates first the absence of absolute, unalterable finality, and the door by which contraries might enter; what is *coming to be* may, on the lower plane of creaturely life, degenerate or fall short

---

[1] Threefold Life, ch. iv., par. 60.
[2] See his treatise on *The Incarnation*, Part I., ch. xiii., par. 68.

of due evolution. The power of Evil, with all its subtlety and skill, is, and has been, and ever will be, a dismaying fact to account for in a world brought into existence by an Omniscient, Infinite Love and Wisdom; but if once we apprehend Böhme's doctrine of the difference of God unmanifest, apart from Creation, and manifested by His Eternal Nature, *i.e.*, the ceaseless action of the Seven Spirits of God, it becomes intelligible that all which obstructs their original harmony of action in Nature and Creature will produce evil, which is not done by God, the only *Good*, and yet is done by misuse of forces derived from Him; that "falling short of the glory of God" (which I am convinced is an equivalent term for perfected action of the six *forms* of Eternal Nature in the seventh—the heavenly substantiality) is in the highest sense an arrest of evolution; the creature destined to find bliss by manifesting the infinite virtues and glories of Abyssal Deity, seeking it in self, works for other and lower objects; the fallen angels for self-exaltation; human beings to gratify desires which debased what they once were, to mortal life as we know it.

Now, ideas such as these call for considerable modification of all that were previously held as regards creation. Theology has used us to thinking of this as a work performed by Divine *Fiat*, irrespective of the will of the creature; and we talk of the formation of all the worlds and their various inhabitants, as if they were made and set in motion by the immediate will of the One Omnipotent God. "Men have led us on," Böhme says, "in vain images of the essential will, as if the only God did will this or that; whereas Himself is the sole will to the [being of] Nature and Creature, and the whole Creation lieth only and alone in the formation of His expressed word and will, and *the severation of the only will in the expression.*"[1]

[1] Mysterium Magnum, ch. lx., par. 41.

An idea he utters with blunter force in his profoundly instructive treatise on *The Election of Grace*,—" Never dispute about the will of God. We ourselves are God's will to evil and good: which of them soever is manifested in us, we are that, whether it be Hell or Heaven." [1] (A saying which it is very important to guard by the addition, "Will of God's *Eternal Nature in us*.")

He makes us understand that *every* Spirit forms its own body by its own will and desire, that one being separates itself from the will and life and *creative word* of another, in countless gradations of existence derived from the one source of all being to the lowest form of creaturely life. And that thus *all* things are made by the Word of God, in the transmitted potentialities of life; that thus the desire of God, to manifest the unsearchable infinitude of Deific powers and glories, brought into being all that exists, and is still bringing forth. "Thus now even unto this very day, all things are yet in the *fiat* or creating, and the Creation hath no end until the judgment of God." [2]

This identification of the will of the Word of God with the will of the creature in the soul of man, is perhaps the most difficult part of his teaching to explain; and his own words must be cited in the attempt. But no amount of quotation can give an adequate glimpse of the light which streams from his works on *Election*, and on *Divine Vision*, when long and patiently studied.

"The living Word of God, which is God Himself," . . . "speaketh itself through Nature forth into a Spirit of the World, as a soul of the Creation." [3]

" Every power has an emanation according to the right of Nature in the speaking Word." [4]

"The Word of God, viz., the Speaking Word, was in all properties in *Spiritu Mundi*, in the spirit of the world,

[1] Ch. viii., pars. 287, 288. [2] Three Principles, ch. xxiii., par. 20.
[3] Election, ch. v., par. 47. [4] Ibid., par. 45.

and in the *Ens* or being of the Earth, stirring up *ex Spiritu Mundi*, from the Spirit of the World; and spake or breathed forth a life into every *Ens* or being; viz., the Fiat, or creating power, which is the desire of the Word."[1]

"Every thing's centre as a piece of the outspoken Word re-outspeaketh itself, and compriseth or frameth itself into separability after the kind and manner of the Divine speaking, and so now if in this outspeaking there were no divine or free will, then the speaking would have a law, and would stand or be in or under compulsion or subjection, and no desire or longing delight might exist. And then the speaking were finite and inchoative, which it is not. But it is a breathing of the Abyss."[2]

And so "every centre maketh its own out-breathing, Nature, and Substance, out of itself, and yet all originateth out of the Eternal *One*."[3]

Now, it is only thus that "*in divisibility God willeth good and evil*."[4] But "without Nature and Creature He is the greatest meekness and humility, wherein is no way, footsteps or prints possibly either of any will to good or evil inclination; for there is neither good nor evil before Him. He is Himself the Eternal only Good."[5] But, as we find in Scripture, "with the holy thou art holy, and with the perverse thou art perverse." . . . "For in the thrones of the holy angels God is manifest in His love, and in the thrones of the devils He is manifest with His wrath, viz., according to the darkness and torment;

---

[1] Election, ch. v., pars. 88, 89.

[2] On the Knowledge of All Things, pars. 12-14 (*Several Treatises*, 1662). See also *Epistles* (1649), Ep. 6, pars.12-14. Let believers in Evolution note this. How infinite must be progression from the Abyss of all Being! See on this theme Professor H. Drummond's admirable chapter on "Classification," in his book on *Natural Law in the Spiritual World*.

[3] Ibid., par. 19. [4] Election, ch. vi., par. 81.

[5] Ibid., ch. i., pars. 57, 58.

and yet there is but one only God, and not two. According to the tormentive Nature He willeth torment, and according to the love He willeth love; as a burning fire desireth hard brimstone like itself, and the *light* of the fire desireth only an open place where it may shine. It taketh away nothing, but giveth itself for the joy of life; it suffereth itself to be taken; it hath no other will in itself, but *to give forth itself* and work."[1]

I venture to affirm that these great truths firmly grasped, of clear distinction between God in *total* and in *partial* manifestation, and of man's freedom to generate the first tormenting forms of Divine Nature, or their full circle of blissful harmony, would relieve us of the darkest suspicions that weigh more or less on every thoughtful mind, and would give us a key to many mysteries which have utterly baffled human intelligence hitherto. The every-day wonder which meets us on all sides—if once reflection goes beyond the surface—is that life is just what we make it in the inner world, and consequently largely modified in external life by our own self-admitted fatalities.

From the Bible we learn how peculiarly man's existence was a desire of the Supreme mind: "Let us make man in our image." And Böhme explains, as I believe no one else ever has, *why* and *how* the reformation of regenerate man must exactly correspond with the origin of the first Adam, and how wholly worthless is any more superficial reformation as regards Eternal Life.

I must be pardoned if on this point also I adduce his own testimony.

"The life of man," he says, "is a form of the Divine will, and is come from the inbreathing into the created image of man" (*i.e.*, what the world-soul had built up by derived agencies in gradual evolution, the breath of God animated), but that "life's will hath imaged itself with

[1] Mysterium Magnum, ch. lx., par. 46.

the outward earthly object or representation of the mortal nature." . . . "The inward Divine ground of the good will and substance extinguished, that is as to the creature, became workless, for the will of the life brake itself off therefrom and went into the perceptibility, out of the unity into the multiplicity."[1] "It turned itself from the speaking of the Word into a peculiar self-willing and speaking in good and evil, that is, into its own lust and contrived imagination; then the first good will in the creature to the re-expressing did perish, and now he must enter again into the *first speaking* Word, and speak with God, or he is eternally *without* God."[2]

"In which re-outspeaking the new regeneration of the human life and will is understood. For the human life was in the beginning of man in the Word of God, and by the inbreathing of the Word into the human body was manifested and came into sensibility, perceptibility and willing. Where, then, the willing hath broken itself off from the Word wherein the life was *without creature*, and hath brought itself into a self-separability and visibility of its perceptibility of the five senses. In which sensibility it now at present runneth, and seeketh the seat of God therein, but findeth only a *measureableness* and natural and creaturely formedness; wherein now it striveth about its own centre. For the own will hath brought itself into an own centre, and broken itself off from the whole, and, as to the total, is become as it were dead."[3]

The context, too long for quotation, is most valuable for learning on this recondite ground. Now the great secret which Böhme incessantly presses upon our belief is, that to attain this lost power of being the mouthpiece of God, "man must seek and call upon the Holy Spirit

[1] Divine Vision, pars. 2, 6, 7.   [2] Epistles (1649), Ep. 7, par. 15.
[3] Baptism, ch. i., par 8.

in himself; for in *himself* is the place where God dwelleth in His heaven, and taketh in the soul's will with its desire."¹

"The right way into the Eternal life is *in* man; he hath introduced the soul's will into the outward world, and that [the soul's will] he must again *in* himself introduce into the inward world."² And this presupposes mortification of the will that lusts for outward good. Without this death to the will of corrupt humanity the new birth cannot be. If the Spirit "dieth to its selfhood and breaketh its will in death, then a new twig springeth forth out of the same, but not according to the first will, but according to the Eternal will; for if a thing entereth into its Nothing, then it falleth again to the Creator, who maketh that thing as it was known in the Eternal will before it was created to [be] a creature."³

(But with all the spoils of experience, and all the powers of raising other fallen souls added to it.)

"When a man yields himself *wholly* to God, then his will falls again into the unsearchable will of God, out of which he came in the beginning," ... "for if the creature willeth no more than what God willeth through it, then it is dead to itself, and standeth again in the first image, viz.—in that wherein God formed it into a life. For what is the life of a creature? Nothing else but a spark of the will of God, which creature now standeth still to the will of God," ... "then nothing can torment it more; its willing is its own life, and whatsoever willeth in and with God, that is one life with God."⁴

And so the soul "falls again into the Word wherein it stood in the Eternal speaking."⁵

---

¹ Considerations upon Esaiah Stiefel's *Threefold State of Man*, par. 116 and onward.
² Ibid., par. 134.   ³ Signatura Rerum, ch. xv., par. 46.
⁴ Mysterium Magnum, ch. lxvi., pars. 63-65.
⁵ Ibid., ch. lx., par. 33.

Thus Böhme harmonizes the paradoxical sayings of St Paul, that man is to "work out his own salvation," and "that it is not of him that willeth, nor of him that runneth, but of God that sheweth mercy." The great and anxious work that man has to accomplish is the breaking of his own will. "A true Christian forceth against the self-ful lusts of selfhood, and willeth continually so to do; and yet is many times hindered by selfhood; he breaketh selfhood as a vessel wherein he lieth captive." [1]

"If the soulish abyssal will yieldeth, applieth, or uniteth itself to the Spirit of Christ in the inward ground, then Christ taketh hold of it, and draweth it up into Himself, and *therein* the ability existeth that it *can* do this." [2]

It is only thus that man becomes "an instrument in the voice of God, upon which only the will-spirit of God doth strike to its honour and deeds of wonder"; for so he is "born from within, out of the speaking voice of God in God's will spirit." [3]

"It is not said that they can take the grace, but that they should sink down into the grace, that grace may give itself to them, for man's ability to take it is *lost*; self-will is rent off from God, it must wholly sink down into God, and *leave off willing*, that God may receive it again into his grace." [4]

Even to the soul most deeply stained with sin this ability remains. "He cannot convert himself, yet his soul hath might and power from its very original, out of the eternal science of the Abyss, to throw himself into the Abyss, *into the ground wherein God generateth and speaketh his Word.* In which abyss of the creature

---

[1] Signatura Rerum, ch. xv., par. 31.
[2] Election, ch. viii., par. 160.
[3] Signatura Rerum, ch. xv., pars. 20, 22.
[4] Mysterium Magnum, ch. lxix., par. 18. See also *Incarnation*, Part II., ch. ix., pars. 26, 27.

the free gift of the bestowed grace lieth *in all men*, and sooner inclineth itself towards the soul, than the soul doth [this] towards this deep grace." ... "If any will say it cannot demerse itself into the Abyss, he speaketh as one that understandeth nothing by far of the mysteries of God, concerning what a soul is, and what an angel is, and will needs break off the twig from the tree wherein the twig standeth. The soul is spoken out of the Abyss into a creature; Who will break or interrupt the *right* of Eternity, so that the Eternal will of the soul, which is come into a creature out of the One only Eternal will, should not dare to demerse itself with that same will of the creature into its mother again, out of which it proceeded? Into the light which is extinguished in it, it cannot demerse itself in its own ability; but into the cause of the light, wherein there is neither Evil nor Good, it can demerse itself; for *itself* is the ground. Now, therefore, if it demerse itself and fall down from its imagibility or imagination in itself, on to the Abyss, then it is there already. And in this Abyss lieth its Pearl."[1]

This is not only one of the most practically important, but one of the clearest depths of Böhme's teaching, or I should not venture to enter upon it so largely. As a rule, Böhme alone can expound his own words. The Quietists practically understood this advice as to *sinking down*; no one will ever try it, I believe, in total surrender of every grasping wish, and every anxious desire, without knowing that in the ground of the soul, man *has* access to the peace of God.

According to Böhme, the soul in its likeness to the Triune Deity *must generate the light*, and through the light, "the Spirit which becometh generated out of the soul's fire, out of God's meekness, and substance, that is also the Holy Spirit; it dwelleth in the Divine

[1] Election, ch. xi., pars. 139-146.

property, and taketh its seeing out of the Divine property."¹ "Man in respect of his external comprehensible or finite body standeth only in a flitting figurative shadow or resemblance, and with his spiritual body he is the true essential Word of the Divine property, in which God speaketh and begetteth his Word, and there the Divine Science doth distribute, impart, impress, form and beget itself to an image of God."²

This last assertion may, at first reading, seem almost profane in its boldness. In his pages it has no such appearance, because he so unfailingly and reverently distinguishes between man as he is, without this new birth, and *with it*, claiming for regenerate man—when come to full stature in Christ—no more than did the Apostles, when Peter wrote of his fellow-Christians as being "partakers of the Divine Nature," and Paul, "He that is joined unto the Lord is one spirit."

Even as regards regenerate man, Böhme is most precise in guarding against the common error of fanatics. "The creature," he says, "is not God; it remaineth eternally under God, but God blazeth through it with His desire of the love-fire, viz., with His light and shining, and that very light, the soul, viz., the man, retaineth so long for its own as the *will* remaineth in God's light."³

Fully recognizing the original greatness of man, thanking God that his mind is indeed a beam of His omnipotence, glory, and skilfulness, ..."a figure of the great name of God"⁴—he yet never exalts the human soul apart from its mediumistic office, regarding

[1] Incarnation, Part II., ch. vii., par. 27.
[2] Epistles (1649), Ep. 6, par. 41. See also *Way from Darkness to True Illumination*, 1648, p. 36; 1752, p. 310; 1775, p. 264; 1781, "Law's edition," vol. iv. p. 118; 1901, p. 143.
[3] Third Apology, Text IV., Point I., par. 63.
[4] Holy Week, par. 126.

it solely as a basis for Divine action, created for the manifestation of God, and—failing in this—a monster—an abortion. Hence his urgency of counsel to annihilate the selfhood, to bring himself "into the One, viz., into God's will,"... "and leave himself wholly in God's mercy, and bring all his learnings into this one only thing, that he in his teachings and learnings will not do or speak anything but what God willeth through him; and thus all images [opinions and conceits] do die in him, and the soul's life falleth into the only living Word, which hath manifested itself again in the humanity."[1]

So entirely does he recognize that man's only power is recipiency of Divine influx, that whereas other teachers speak of what we know, he affirms that *all* true spiritual knowledge is what *God knows in us*. "God's spirit," he says, "must become the knowing in us."[2] And again, "I know not myself, it is not mine, but God's spirit *knoweth itself in me*; He allures me therewith to Himself; when he departeth or withdraweth then I know nothing."[3]

It is remarkable that this, one of his capital doctrines, in no way infringes upon the prerogative of free will, or upon the claims of every-day duty, as regards cultivating our talents, to the uttermost of our ability, for service, for *serving to God's purposes*—a distinction St Martin has well pointed out, since the instrument cannot actively serve the agent.[4]

For those who question the free will of man, Böhme has the ever-recurring argument (conclusive as he

[1] Mysterium Magnum, ch. xxxvi., par. 50.
[2] Second Apology, Part I., par. 54.
[3] First Apology, Part II., par. 587.
[4] "J'entends souvent parler dans le monde de servir Dieu, mais je n'y entends guère parler de *servir à Dieu*, car il en est bien peu qui sachent ce que c'est que cet emploi-là."—*Œuvres Posthumes de St Martin*, vol. i. p. 109.

deemed it) that as a direct emanation from the source of all being, he *must* have it. He tells us that the mind of man is anterior to every source of the properties of Nature, and therefore to every *quality* due to temperament or astral influence: "for the fire-soul is a root proceeded from the Divine omnipotence, and therefore it hath free will, and nothing can deprive it thereof; it may conceive either in the fire or light."[1]

"The centre of the mind is come out of Eternity, out of God's omnipotence; it can bring itself into what it will and whither it will."[2]

And so far from counselling to any ascetic withdrawal from the occupations of this present life, he regards a diligent development of every faculty, of all skill and art as a main object of man's existence. "God hath given to man again to seek and to reveal or manifest the wonders of God in this world's substance to his, viz., man's own joy, delight, and longing pleasure, that God might be praised, known, and acknowledged in all works, substances, and things."[3]

"Man is, therefore, become created in this world as a wise ruler or manager thereof, that he should open all wonders, which were from Eternity," ... "and according to his willing bring them into forms, figures, and images, all to his joy and glory."[4]

"The deeper a man is learned concerning God, the deeper he seeketh, and seeth into God's deeds of wonder in Art; for all profitable arts are revealed or manifested out of God's Wisdom; not that they are that by which man cometh to God, but for the government of the out-

---

[1] Mysterium Magnum, ch. xxvi., par. 7.
[2] True Resignation, ch. iii., par. 20.
[3] Third Apology, Text IV., Point III., par. 88.
[4] Incarnation, Part III., ch. vi., par. 31. See also, on this subject, *Three Principles*, ch. xx., par. 10, and *Threefold Life*, ch. xvii., par. 12.

ward life, and for the glorious manifestation of the Divine Wisdom and Omnipotence."¹ It is this complete grasp of the scope of human life from the inmost centre of being to outmost circumference of existence, which gives to Böhme's teaching the aspect of an inexhaustible survey. With one sentence —this, for example, "God himself is the Being of all beings, and we are as gods in him"²—he makes us feel that the capacities of man are as infinite as his destiny. Yet never must the qualification be lost sight of that man does not necessarily reveal Him who "is called God only according to the light, viz., in the powers of the light"; but he *must* reveal either that holy one of God or the wrath of God, *i.e.*, the anguishing forms of eternal nature unatoned.

Any attempt to give an idea of the circle of light opened to the student of Böhme is embarrassed by perceiving the commensurate darkness of mystery thus made visible by the abundance of revelations within that circle. I hesitate to prolong the attempt, and yet something must be said about *the Wisdom* so often referred to by him. For many years of *unaided* study this remains an insoluble and obstructive enigma. The reader finds Virgin Sophia spoken of in a way that forbids every thought of allegoric meaning. It is under this designation that he reveals the Maternal Principle in Deity, sometimes calling it the "Corporeity of the Holy Ternary, the delight and playfellow of the most High"; the "Eternal Mother, the great Mysterium Magnum," through whom "the Eternal Word breathed itself forth into skill or knowledge, viz., into infinity of multiplicity";³

¹ Third Apology, Text IV., Part III., par. 77. See also *Incarnation*, Part III., ch. v., pars. 31, 32.
² Threefold Life, ch. vi., par. 4.
³ Knowledge of All Things, par. 21 (*Several Treatises*, 1662). See also *Epistles* (1649), Ep. 6, par. 21.

elsewhere the "*Substantial Power* of the great Love of God," and, "the *outflown Word*" in contradistinction to the speaking Word.

Into this most profound mystery I dare not enter further; the unpublished writings of Mr T. Lake Harris, and the beautiful *Morgenröthe* of the Rev. J. Pulsford, have a little broken to the public mind this unfamiliar doctrine. In dim foreboding or remembrance it has never probably been long absent from subconscious human thought. Jane Lead [1] had been anticipated regarding her *Great Goddess and Queen of all Worlds* [2] by W. Postel in the 16th century, who taught "*that the Word had become man, but that when it made itself woman then the world would be saved.*" A belief which some of our contemporaries warmly advocate at the present time.

This belief in Divine Corporeity tallies with one of those marvellously fruitful revelations which every unprejudiced student will find to be so numerous in Böhme's writings; his admission of *substance* as a *sine quâ non* of true spiritual life. "There is a nature and substance in the outward world; so also in the inward spiritual world there is a nature and a substance which is spiritual, from which the outward world is breathed forth." [3]

The grossness of matter has discredited our ideas of substance, and we are used to think of it as very far below spirit. He teaches that it is only inferior, as a

[1] Jane Lead's *The Revelation of Revelations* (1804), p. 61.

[2] To no subject would the following remark of the true meaning of the word revelation better apply than to this:—Je prie mon lecteur de réflechir que comme le mot Latin *Velare*, signifie *Voiler*, de même *Revelare* doit nécessairement signifier *re voiler*, ou voiler de nouveau ce qui auroit déja paru sous un Voile primitif." Words taken from an anonymous book, *Les Mystères du Christianisme approfondis radicalement ou La Vérité*, vol. i. p. 24, published in 1771.

[3] Regeneration, ch. ii., par. 31.

manifestation is inferior to the power manifested—that it bears to spirit precisely the same relation that body does to life. "No spirit," he says, "can bring anything to pass without essence." (*Wesen* in the original, which means substance also.)[1] "*Without substance no working can be.*"[2] And his account of man's loss in the Fall is, "Our substance, vanished and shut up in death, was signified by the dry Rod of Aaron, which substance grew," ... "where God's substance became man, in whom the holy fire *could* burn; for the divine *Ens* which vanished in Adam, which grew again in such kindling, was the food of this love fire," ... "and that same love-burning was the new life of the regeneration."[3]

"For Christ had also a soul and spirit out of Adam, and the precious dear Word of the Deity, together with God's Spirit, awakened and raised up again in Christ's flesh the *dead substantiality* of the Sulphur, viz., the body which in Adam was dead."[4]

And he insists very forcibly on substance as well as spirit having been brought into human nature at the Incarnation of the Word. "Not spirit without *substance*, but the *substance* of the spirit environed and inclosed with God's Wisdom, Christ's flesh, which filleth the light-world in every place; which the Word that became man brought along with it into Mary."[5]

Of which he notices the *necessity* elsewhere thus:— "Now where the Word is, there is also the Virgin or Wisdom of God, for the Word is in the Wisdom, and the one is not without the other, or else the Eternity would be divided."[6]

"But when I speak of the Virgin of the Wisdom of God I mean not a thing that is confined or circumscribed

[1] Baptism, ch. i., par. 16.
[2] Ibid., ch ii., par. 11.
[3] Ibid., ch. ii., par. 31.
[4] Incarnation, Part I., ch. vi., par. 13.
[5] Ibid., Part II., ch. ix., par. 31.
[6] Threefold Life, ch. vi., par. 78.

in a place . . . but I mean the whole deep of the Deity without end and number."¹

Without attempting to touch upon the as yet unexplored mystery of the—*so to speak*—chemical action of the heavenly body and blood entering the corporeal solidarity of our race—and that much lies there within reach of spiritual discernment I am well convinced,—the rectifying efficacy of this divine incarnation is made more intelligible to us by Böhme's teaching as to the formative effect of *all* imaginations. That "*Every imagination maketh substantiality*"² is one of his keynotes. "Where there is no substance there is also no *creating*; whereas yet a creaturely spirit is no palpable substance, but it must draw a substance into itself through its *imagination*, else it *would not subsist*."³

"A spirit out of nature is a magic fire source, and is desirous of substance, the desire maketh substance and bringeth that substance into its imagination, that is the magic fire's corporeity, whence the spirit is called a creature."⁴

"The soul in Adam is gone forth with its imagination [into earthliness] away from *true* substantiality," and since then "the soul hath no image or body which remaineth eternally, unless it be through Christ *regenerated* out of its first substantiality."⁵

Therefore "we must introduce our imagination and desire into him, that our tinder of the faded image in him may begin to glimmer or glow in the Spirit and power of Christ."⁶

Of all Böhme's doctrines this perhaps is the most needful to modern divinity, *i.e.*, that regeneration does not consist in a new spirit alone, but in a *new creature*, an

---

¹ Threefold Life, ch. v., par. 56.   ² Ibid., ch. x., par. 31.
³ Incarnation, Part I., ch. v., par. 88.
⁴ First Apology, Part II., par. 186.   ⁵ Ibid., pars. 373, 265.
⁶ Third Apology, Text II., par. 49.

everlasting body; that this new-born creature is not itself divine, but that God dwells in it substantially—that it must remain hidden under corrupt flesh and blood till "Christ is formed in us,"—Christ identified *as to that body* with the Lord Christ in whom Jesus, *i.e.*, all the fulness of the Godhead, dwelt bodily; Christ the anointed humanity, Jesus the Divine life anointing it with the holy oil which Adam's corrupt imagination, lusting after earthly things, had dried up.

It is difficult to turn away from the rich treasures which crowd upon one's memory when trying to select the most desirable specimens of Böhme's gifts to mankind. William Law did not overstate truth when he said that by him "the true ground of every doctrine and article of Christian faith and practice is opened in such a ravishing, amazing depth and clearness of truth and conviction as had never been seen or thought of in any age of the Church."[1] "His works being an opening of the Spirit of God working in him are quite out of the common path of man's reasoning wisdom, and proceed no more according to it, than the living plant breathes forth its virtues according to such rules of skill as an artist must use to set up a painted dead figure of it. But as the Spirit of God worked in the creation of all things, so the same Spirit worked and opened in the ground and depth of his created soul an inward sensibility of it."[2]

As testimony from a totally different point of view let the opinion of a contemporary be weighed—one whose talents and peculiar opportunities alike qualified him for forming a just estimate. Writing in the *Athenæum*,[3] Mr C. W. Heckethorn said: "Böhme's metaphysical system—the most perfect and only true one—still awaits

[1] Collection of Letters, 2nd ed., 1769, Letter 1 ; 1815, Letter 2.
[2] A Dialogue between Zelotes, Alphabetus, Rusticus, and Theophilus. A fragment. Prefixed to vol. i. of the *Works of Jacob Behmen*, London, 1764.
[3] January 26, 1867, No. 2048, p. 127.

a qualified commentator." ... "In Böhme is to be found, not only the true ground of all theology, but also that of all physical science. He demonstrated with a fulness, accuracy, completeness and certainty that leave nothing to be desired, the innermost ground of Deity and Nature; and, confining myself to the latter, I can from my own knowledge assert, that in Böhme's writings is to be found the true and clear demonstration of every physical fact that has been discovered since his day. Thus, the science of electricity, which was not yet in existence when he wrote, is there anticipated; and not only does he describe all the now known phenomena of that force, but he even gives us the origin, generation and birth of electricity itself. Again, positive evidence can be adduced that Newton derived all his knowledge of gravitation and its laws from Böhme." ... "Every new scientific discovery goes to prove his profound and intuitive insight into the most secret workings of Nature; and if scientific men, instead of sharing the prejudice arising from ignorance of Böhme's system, would place themselves on the vantage ground it affords, they would at once find themselves on an eminence whence they could behold all the arcana of Nature. Böhme's system, in fact, shews us the *inside* of things, while modern physical science is content with looking at the *outside*. Böhme traces back every outward manifestation or development to its one central root—to that one central energy which, as yet, is only suspected; every link in the chain of his demonstration is perfect, and there is not one link wanting. He carries us from the outbirths of the circumference, along the radius to the centre, or point, and beyond that even to the Zero, Nothing, with mathematical precision."

Nevertheless, had Böhme read these words it is certain that he would have challenged the truth of the expression, *Böhme's system*. He repeatedly reminds his readers that he had none; that when he described "the true ground and depth concerning what God is, and how all things are framed in God's being," . . . he only "gave way to his impulse and will," and adds, "I am but a very little spark of light." " This work comes not from *Reason*, but from the impulse of the Spirit. Only be thou careful to get into thy spirit the Holy Ghost which issueth forth from God, and He will lead thee into all truth."[1]

That this direct dependence upon a Teacher, unfettered by ecclesiastical canons, would virtually exclude his books from the public, Böhme well knew, and if now and then he allows himself a caustic remark on this subject we cannot be surprised. Authorities had driven him from his home, after energetic persecutions, solely because he proclaimed the lessons of a superior Instructor. Speaking of the "wiselings of outward reason," he says: "They have understanding already in the eyes of their Reason, and they cannot miss; they can judge all things; what the Spirit of God revealeth that must be a *heresy* unto them, albeit they do not understand it."[2] And in his preface to the *177 Theosophic Questions*: "Mr Wiseling will dare to account it a sin to question so very high things, seeing himself cannot understand them." His summary in the opening of the *Aurora* of what "*Mr Critic, which worketh with his wit in the fierce quality, will say when he gets this book into his hand,*" is an accurately true account of just what is said by both the Mr Wiselings and the Mr Critics of our own time. But claiming no superior wisdom of his own, he is careful to explain how he won all the knowledge he transmits. "Not through my understanding, but in my resignation in Christ: from Christ's Spirit have I received the knowledge—the great mystery."[3]

[1] Aurora, ch. ii., pars. 78, 80; ch. iii., pars. 1, 2.
[2] Mysterium Magnum, ch. xii., par. 22.
[3] First Apology, Part II., par. 301.

"Searching is not the chief or most especial means to know or apprehend the Mystery, but to be born of God is the right invention,"[1] and faithfully he warns us of what really prevents Divine light from penetrating to our minds. "Men go about to seek God in their own will and skill: men would find God in their own will, and He is not therein; for He dwelleth only in that will which resigneth itself up with all its reason and skill to Him. To such an one He giveth real living knowledge and power to understand His being. Therefore we shall be dumb, dark, and historical to every one that is not born of God." . . . "He that will not seek thereby to be a new man born in God, and wholly and unfeignedly apply himself thereto, let him let my writings alone and leave them uncensured. I have written nothing for such a seeker; also, he will *not* be able wholly to understand our meaning, though he exerciseth much about it, unless he entereth into the resignation in Christ, and there he may obtain and apprehend the Spirit of the Universal; and we will warn the curious critic, speculator, and rational artist, that he amuse not himself; he effecteth nothing in this way except he himself entereth thereinto."[2]

And in one of his prefaces[3] he tells us that he shuts and locks up his book with a strong bolt or bar from the understanding of those who cavil at his writings in a proud, haughty way. What this bolt is we discover in the following sentence of William Law's:—"Above every writer in the world he has made all that is found in the kingdom of grace and the kingdom of nature, to be one continual demonstration that *dying to self, to be born again of Christ*, is the one only possible salvation for the sons of fallen Adam."[4] This is really the insuper-

---

[1] Forty Questions (1665), Ques. 1, par. 254.
[2] A Warning from Iacob Beem, pars. 4, 7.
[3] Preface to his *Three Principles*, par. 18.
[4] Letters, 2nd ed., 1769, p. 92; 1815, p. 88; Reprint, 1893, p. 153.

able difficulty which his writings present to *all*, which *intellect* is powerless to overcome. Before that central truth there is, as Böhme says, "a strong lock and bar in the spirit of man that must be first unlocked, and that no man can do, for the Holy Ghost is the only key to do it withal. Therefore, if thou wilt have an open gate into the Deity, then thou must stir and walk in God's love."[1]

"And we admonish the loving reader to demerse himself in Divine humility into God and his fellow branch or brother, and so he may read and conceive our received deep sense and apprehension, and be brought from all error into the true rest wherein all things rest in the Word and power of God."[2]

How deep a rest they only know who have reached it; but the immersion into profound humility is very difficult to those who have been used to teach with authority; as Freher expresses it when touching upon the unwillingness of "some of the learned" to read and consider what Böhme offers; "they account themselves so full with their present wisdom and knowledge, that they have no room to desire any other, especially that which cannot be attained without casting away the high esteem of that which they have laid up as a treasure to themselves already; and so every little difficulty of uncouth words or phrases and expressions, which they cannot presently see to agree with their former opinions, makes them loath to be troubled about that which they think themselves to have more and better knowledge of beforehand. Neither can they in reason be blamed, save that they block up their own way to inestimable treasures which they know not of, and others not so learned attain."

"From the beginning of the world," said William Law, writing to Dr Sherlock, "nothing extraordinary in the way of instruction ever came from God, but met its

[1] Aurora, ch. xiii., par. 31.   [2] Election, Pref., par. 17.

chief opposition from that which was the reigning wisdom and learning of the time."[1]

But now, for such students as can free themselves from slavery to any "reigning wisdom," and seek it where no ecclesiastical finger-posts point out merit, it only remains to cite a few practical hints for the best mode of approach to Böhme's treasure. With his translator, John Sparrow, I can say, "I also, who have much and studiously traced his writings over, have found them difficult, but far exceeding in recompense the utmost pains that I could possibly bestow on them; I find also that the understanding of them cometh *by degrees*, and frequent loving conversation in all the parts and pieces he hath written."[2]

When William Law sent two volumes of Böhme's works to his friend, the Rev. Mr Neve, he wrote: "The time will come when such supposed mysteries in J. B. will no more lessen your opinion of that fountain of light which was opened in him, than the spots which are said to be discovered on the sun do make you suspect it not to be a body of light. Read these volumes through, without staying at that which you do not comprehend, and you will all along see both why you should continue reading, and why you must be content to learn very gradually, and also whence it is that the greatest and most concerning truths are such a mystery to us."[3]

But he best guides us himself as to such studies when he says, "If you have a desire and delight to read my writings, read them diligently, and especially apply yourselves to the Centre of all Beings, and then the Three Principles will be plain and easy to you, and I know, and am assured, that if you apprehend the Centre in the Spirit it will afford you such joy as far surpasseth the joy of the whole world, for the precious stone of the

---

[1] Letters, 2nd ed., 1769, p. 3; 1815, p. 7.
[2] Aurora, Preface to the Reader.
[3] Walton's *Memorial of William Law*, p. 217.

wise men lieth therein, which giveth the certainty and real ground of all things; it freeth man from all trouble and perplexive thoughts in the controversies of religion, and it openeth unto him the highest mystery that is in him."[1] And again in his preface to the *Clavis*: "When a man reads such writings, and yet cannot understand them, he must not presently throw them away, and think it impossible to understand them; no, but he must turn his mind to God, beseeching Him for grace and understanding, read again, and then he shall see more and more in them, till at length he is drawn by the power of God into the very depth itself, and so comes into the supernatural ground, viz., into the Eternal Unity of God, where he shall hear unspeakable words of God, which shall bring him back and outward again by the Divine Effluence to the very grossest and meanest matter of the earth, and then back and inwards to God again."[2]

Shall a teacher, from whom Sir Isaac Newton learned secrets of physical nature, and Hegel a whole transformation of German philosophy, remain unstudied by all but a few sequestered thinkers in Great Britain? Are we so befooled by precedent, have the narcotics of "*received opinion*" made our many searching intellects drowsy in "*the easie ways of ancient mistakings*"? It will not always be so. Freher was surely a true prophet when he said: "I am assured with Böhme that this knowledge and understanding shall be raised up out of the dust and darkness, in the due time of God, and shall not be further so hidden, unknown, and unintelligible to the children of men as it hath been to the generality thereof since the beginning of the world—(he refers to man's knowledge of 'Divine mysteries'); when another generation shall be upon the earth, they that then live

[1] A Warning from Iacob Beem, par. 20.
[2] Clavis, par. 8.

shall again bless and praise God that He hath unlocked His secret treasures, and poured out His spirit of understanding upon them that know Him, and are deeply rooted in true love and divine humility." Now, Freher's contemporaneous generation has long passed away; and many secret treasures of spiritual knowledge have been unlocked since he wrote—is it from want of charity and humility that Böhme's are still unopened? It may be so; "mysteries *are* revealed to the meek."

WHY ARE NOT JACOB BÖHME'S WRITINGS STUDIED?[1]

"Therein are revealed and laid forth the mysteries about which, since the heavy fall of Adam, the world hath contended and alway sought."—*Epistles* (1649), Ep. 3, par. 11.

"If you come so far as to apprehend the spirit and sense of the author, then you will need no admonition, but will rejoice and be glad in this light."—*Aurora*, ch. ix., par. 20.

IT is strange that the idea of Böhme as an eccentric enthusiast, bewildered by imaginary revelations, can remain current among those who have any acquaintance with general literature; for it can hardly fail to strike every unprejudiced reader that his works hold a very high place in the esteem of men least likely to mistake eccentricity for genius, or confusion of thought for depth of insight. Not to speak of Franz Baader and Hamberger and Gichtel, in Germany; and St Martin, in France; he has had disciples in England of no mean ability. And many an eminent writer besides Coleridge and Emerson, though far from accepting him as a teacher, have referred to his curious writings with a reverence that no counterfeit light could inspire; while William Law, notable for keenness of judgment and a strictly logical habit of thought, does not hesitate to speak of him as "the divinely inspired Böhme." With all his exalted piety, I suppose, the severe good sense of

[1] New Church Independent and Monthly Review, 1884, vol. xxxii. pp. 458, 503, 574.

William Law has never been doubted, yet for the public these admirable works in which he gives an exposition of the most important points of Böhme's teaching, remain almost a dead letter.

When, however, we come to look into Böhme's books, we can better understand why they are so little studied. No human authority vouching for their worth, could recommend them to the human mind in its ordinary mood;—say rather, could reconcile it to them. Both by their sublime simplicity, as well as by their sublime depths, it is commonly repulsed. He claims from his reader qualifications of character and intellect seldom found together; and he emphatically declares that without these his communications must be as a sealed book.

Evidently it is a natural mode of escape from difficulty to say, after slightly glancing through several pages, that the writer did not himself understand what he wrote :—he avers repeatedly that by the light of reason he neither did nor could,—that by the Spirit of God such and such things were made known to him, and that he could only put into language such parts of those revelations as he was *enabled* to communicate. And what better plea could be found for instant and final condemnation? All those who believe that *nothing* more can be revealed to man besides what is contained in the Bible, are shocked at such impious presumption, as well as convinced, by this one assertion, of Böhme's unsoundness of mind. If urged still to examine his writings themselves, and see how he makes good his claim, their natural feelings will answer, "What need we any further witnesses? for we ourselves have heard out of his own mouth." All those—alas! not a few—who believe that there is nothing more to reveal to them— that the unseen world is only peopled by the varying phantasmagoria of the human mind,—smile where the others sigh, and without hesitation pronounce the author mad, and those who give him credence, likely to become so. From either kind of intellect not even the most cursory reading can be obtained; it would seem to them a most foolish waste of time.

But let us suppose a student of greater enlargement of mind and more faith and reverence than these, taking up any work of Böhme's, he would at once find his powers of understanding put on the stretch; singularity of style, uncouthness of phraseology, and marvellous novelties of idea would rouse his intellect to its most vigorous exercise, and believing, may be, that light and truth were to be won in that dark mine, he would wrestle for the mastery of its secrets; and so wrestling, would not gain it. Reason alone cannot attain it; the brain in this province cannot supply the right implements; the treasures of truth hidden here are *not* to be *thought out*, or submitted to any scrutiny of logic. It is not a case for rational conquest, but for recipiency in the understanding.

For a reader to open for the first time any book written by Böhme with an idea of submitting its contents to the most acute scholarly judgment, is as much beside the purpose as for a child unable to cipher to pretend to form an opinion as to the best method of teaching algebra. That "mysteries are revealed to the meek" is verified here, for without the docile spirit of an industrious child, desiring to learn, and ready to learn just as much or as little as the master sees to be good for him, content to hear many a saying it cannot yet understand in hopes of a gradually growing intelligence, and willing to toil on patiently till more can be explained,—without these qualifications little beside provocation and contemptuous surprise will result from reading Böhme. And the more athletic the intellect that tries by its own force to master his meaning, the more fruitless will be its efforts. Not because he teaches what is *contrary* to enlightened reason, but what is beyond the province of this world's reason and the egotism which blinds it—as all egotism must blind—by arrogating to itself a pre-comprehension of all the human spirit can perceive. Able reasoners are the last to suspect that *being* is a more essential condition of *knowing* than any intellectual skill or power in the pursuit of knowledge,—that from certain defects of being they may be totally incapacitated for right knowing;—that natural reason at its highest pitch of refinement will not afford even a glimmering *apprehension* of spiritual states and spiritual beings with whom all men on earth are most intimately connected. Until they can be persuaded of these facts in human nature, they had better leave Böhme alone.

Were it not for the unfortunate assumption that every well-instructed Christian already knows by the Bible all that is knowable of the unseen world, and of the original state of man, his writings might be studied with as much temporary deference as we pay to any writer on a scientific subject; chemistry, for example. The nomenclature is strangely unintelligible to a novice in that study, but deficient understanding is not charged to the writer's account but to the reader's own ignorance, and while he seeks to lessen this there is a suspense of all judgment, and an honest avidity to apprehend all that is before him, *according to the meaning of the writer*, which obviates any collision with preconceived ideas: and could this same attitude of mind be secured for the reading of Böhme, *something* would be won; at least his devout absorption in matters transcendently high would be recognized; and if still he was called a fanatic, yet his sincerity and holiness and grandeur of thought would never be denied, and he would be deemed worth a hearing. But it would depend on the inclination of the *will* whether that reader could derive profit from such attention, for only a humble and teachable spirit can find out Böhme's credentials as an inspired messenger of Truth. Verily such a one receiving this prophet in the name of a prophet shall receive a prophet's reward. If to strong-minded and self-willed students Böhme is impenetrable, he is far worse, he is a scandal and an offence to a large class of amiable people who delight in calling themselves *simple-minded* Christians; and if the first tell you they *cannot* profit by his pages, these weaker brethren will say with an accent of self-congratulation that they would be sorry if they could. For them, the apostolic determination "to know nothing save Jesus Christ and Him crucified"—the pious ideal of not being "wise above that which is written"—the full assurance that "the secret things belong unto God," are texts in which human indolence and pseudo-humility find a convenient terminus, although Moses went on to say, "those things which are revealed belong unto us and to our children forever." Now to us have been revealed glorious promises of increasing light. The Lord Himself told His disciples, "the Spirit of truth will guide you into all truth, . . . He will shew you things to come,"[1] "He shall take of mine and shew it unto you":[2] all in the future sense. Surely these professors of Scriptural simplicity of faith are unconsciously committing the very fault against which they protest and are claiming a power to judge contrary to the Word of God, when they deny the possibility of the Spirit having guided others into deeper insight of truth than the immediate followers of Christ were able to receive. Is the Holy Spirit bound to any era of time? Can we believe its office of love restricted for so many ages to reiterations of the same formula of divine truths with no enlargements to assist the growth of the human

[1] John xvi. 13. [2] Ibid., ver. 15.

spirit? Or, as some maintain, can it never impart life and light to the individual as well as to the race, except by what are called "appointed channels"? Notwithstanding the respect due to every sincere religious conviction, such an idea cannot weigh with us. And when the terms of promise are so free and abundant—"I will pour water upon him that is thirsty, and floods upon the dry ground "[1]—is it possible to deny that the account Böhme gives of his revelations [2] is far more consonant to Bible teaching than a scrupulous suspicion of all that lacks the guarantee of established authority?

I would not speak slightingly of any conscientious persuasion, but ought we not all to take warning, against this exclusive tendency, from the reason given of old by the Jews against heeding His words "full of grace and truth" who spake as never man spake? "*Have any of the rulers or Pharisees believed on Him?*" It is not only in the Jewish Church that rulers have shewn themselves slow to acknowledge the dawn of greater lights than those to which they were accustomed.

Now a false judgment based upon ignorance is generally more tenaciously held than one which arises from misconception of known facts,—pride being usually in inverse proportion to light; and there are few things so dearly prized as voluntary privations; were it not so I might try to convince those worthy people who use the word *simplicity* as opposed to deep learning, that vast acquirements of knowledge are not incompatible

---

[1] Isaiah xliv. 3.

[2] "I declare in the presence of God, and testify it before His judgment, where all things shall appear and every one shall give account of his doings, that . . . I know not what I shall write; for when I write *the Spirit doth dictate the same to me* in great wonderful knowledge, so that I often cannot tell whether I, as to my spirit, *am in this world or no*, and thereat I do exceedingly rejoice, and therein sure and certain knowledge is imparted to me."—*Epistles* (1649), Ep. 27, pars. 11, 12.

with extreme simplicity of character and purpose;—that multiplicity of ideas is no hindrance to singleness of heart and greatly induces to humility, and that when they speak of the simplicity that is in Christ, they would do well to remember that in Him also was hidden all the treasures of wisdom and knowledge. In the last chapter of the Bible some find their strongest argument against fresh acquisitions of truth in spiritual matters, "If any man shall add unto these things, God shall add unto him the plagues that are written in this book";[1] and the very point on which they humbly pride themselves—an unexercised intellect—makes it almost impossible to convince them that the threat is inapplicable to writings *not* added to that book.

It is only by superstitions such as these that one can account for the fact that while, in almost every department of human effort there has been in our day advance, new acquirements, new discoveries, accompanied with the exhilarating sense of unlimited possibilities of progress, in one direction only it is prohibited. Theology refuses to believe in any new light coming to us by direct revelation: exegesis of Scripture may, it is supposed, elicit a clearer understanding of revealed truths, but to look for any more than is to be found *there* is deemed fanatical, not to say profane; and one need not stop to consider how many whimsical theories and arbitrary interpretations have consequently been forced *out of*, or *read into* the Bible. The mind of man cannot chew the cud of old crops forever; even weeds and thistles will be snatched at for variety in very limited pastures. Nor though the history of every civilized country justifies the saying that revolution in religion as well as in politics is brought about by impeded evolution more than by any other cause, need we look to the past for evidence of its truth: without growth

[1] Rev. xxii. 18.

there must be decay, and that we see on all sides of religious life.

But it is not theology alone that refuses credence to any bringers of new facts from the spiritual world. "The world holdeth it impossible to know such things; whereas yet a spirit born in God searcheth into the Kingdom of Heaven."[1]

This is the assumption which so much offends both layman and cleric, for "the unenlightened mind holds it for impossible to be able to know such hidden secret mysteries, in regard it cannot apprehend them, and thereupon reproveth and ascribeth it to the devil."[2]

A very common result, as we all know!

All whose aspirations for worship are satisfied by religious formula, and these in every age will be the majority, must dislike inquiry into "hidden, secret mysteries," for all have a suppressed consciousness that it might unsettle contentment with routine.

Again, wise men of the world are forced to think such inspired monitors as Böhme mad, if they would escape the inference that if he was not they are themselves demented; for while he asserts that because of our origin in the Divine Mind we must still be able to return to that centre, to see, and know and feel its eternal incomprehensible qualities, declaring that God has made Himself "*visible, perceptible,* and *inventible,*"[3] they persist in thinking such ideas either silly or blasphemous.

In truth, as to this central perception of Deity, we are all pretty much alike; we search eagerly into all creaturely life and devote any amount of trouble and patience to what is *outside* our being: all that is effected in creation by separation from the Centre, and which

---

[1] Three Principles, ch. xxi., par. 42.
[2] 177 Theosophic Questions, Ques. 12, par. 1.
[3] Knowledge of God and of All Things (1661), par. 75 (*Several Treatises*, 1662). Also *Epistles* (1649), Ep. 6, par. 75.

tends more and more to multiply broken images of true being, attracts us, and is thought a right study; but, with supposed reverence and real distaste, we avoid searching within. Our spiritual ambition seldom rises higher than to repress manifested evil, and, for this, outside religiosity offers valuable aid. But in a certain sense it is as true of instituted religion as of the flesh, that it lusteth against the spirit; and the quickened spirit lusteth against those formalized observances of religion which give the measure both of its growth in the past and its arrest of vitality in the present: just as the body at once protects and serves as an instrument for the uses of the spirit, but is a restriction also, localizing and limiting what is in its nature independent of place and limitless in scope; so religious institutions are indispensable to spirituality up to a certain point, but when this is more developed they become inadequate and impede growth; even as in old age what formerly served the spirit as plastic flesh becomes rigid and infirm, and at last proves so much of a hindrance as to be forsaken. Spiritual life can animate effete form no better than animal life a worn-out body: it is not a question of *willing* to vitalize, it is an utter impossibility; and quite inevitable revolt from stationary religious thought impels many a vigorous mind to outbursts of doubt, not necessarily irreverent though seldom free from scorn.

Even within the last ten years we have seen the sceptical disquietudes of a few daring thinkers lose all prominence in the fashion of Agnosticism,—have heard a cheerful unhesitating denial of there being any God to worship accepted as the ripest outcome of modern philosophy. For those who accept it fully there may be immediate satisfaction from the consciousness of force in snapping old fetters, but the result of such freedom on other people's minds is desolating; directly or indirectly suspicions are infused as to the worth of *any* religious faith; and even while old moorings are passionately defended, there is often an underlying thought, eagerly stifled but never extinguished, " *Can* it be that my belief is formed by limitations of intellect rather than by the irresistible cogency of truth? Is it not possibly true only in relation to my ignorance, and not to any absolute verity?"

Now apart from all mental distress arising from such misgivings, observe their effect on practice. While thought oscillates on questions of faith, the mind may plume itself on a wise suspense of judgment, but the inmost being, the *will*, is subject to perilous confusions of motive. Whoever resisted temptation on the strength of a peradventure, or learned to love an unseen being, who is one hour adored as the Father of spirits, and another refused any sort of homage, on the hypothesis that *It*, no longer *He*, is only a pervading universal principle, a flux of ceaseless life with no headspring, and no consciousness of the motes that live or die in its current? Habitual uncertainties of opinion must sooner or later produce startling certainties of immorality. And this well-known fact is the excuse alleged by all teachers who try to adjust truth to the mind of recipients rather than allow it free access to all that can be known, without abatement or prudential mixtures.

In every age, not only in the Romish Church, spiritual leaders have been solicitous to screen off every cross light that might divert attention from such truths as they deem essential. Almost all clergymen fear the influence of general literature as tending to neutralize the effects of religious dogma. Yet to avert this influence is about as impossible in these days as to exclude air by blinds and window shutters. The clergy know it and groan over the irreligious temper of the time. Is it irreligious so much as impatient of outgrown instruction? Franz Baader spoke hard words to his contemporaries on this head, when saying in one of his lectures fifty years ago, "The misuse of intelligence on the side of the opponents of religion finds its strength in the *no use* of it on the part of its professional defenders"; and "that speculation had only become irreligious in the proportion that religious teaching had become unspeculative and spiritless."

It is doubtful whether there is not sharp hunger for faith of some kind in every human soul, but if the objects of faith are not shewn to it in any aspect that can meet the requirements of its *present* stage of growth, that hunger is baffled, and the mind angrily turns away from what offers to satisfy it and *cannot*. Many that now scoff at revealed truth are spiritually famished; they need strong meat, and the milk offered is frequently diluted by human bigotry. Böhme's teaching would satisfy these seekers, in nine cases out of ten, if only it did not cut so unflinchingly against the grain of human pride: and if acuteness of reason alone could interpret his obscurities our *savants* would reap large harvests from his books, for by him no perplexing issue of inquiry is avoided, and leading boldly toward as much infinitude of mystery as human thought can plunge into, he yet confers definiteness of belief, grounded on so firm a basis that those who learn of him doubt no more. His teaching is scientifically precise at the same time that it is illimitably expansive. But as he says, "Those that be born of God will here have their eyes rightly opened" ... "none should conceive and think that such a thing hath been in the power of man; for it is the revelation of God."[1]

Nevertheless were this all, the neglect of such a writer would still remain unexplained; as spiritual guides could borrow from him most valuable reinforcements of

[1] Threefold Life, ch. iii., pars. 38, 39.

arguments: this with *very* rare exceptions they never do. What then is the reason? The extracts that follow will, I think, sufficiently answer; for so vital is the heat of his zeal, so penetrating the eye of his judgment, that even to-day his admonitions strike sharply on the distinctive flaws of every school of religionists. If priests could forgive him for this, they would not be slow to direct the attention of lay people to the writings of a reprover so severe.

Imagine the feelings of some ecclesiastical ministers on reading these words. "O thou blind world, . . . thou supposest [that] thou oughtest not to dare to meddle with the Great Mystery" (office of the ministry, a side-note explains) "and that thou art not capable of it, and that the priest only is capable of it: but if thou art in Christ thou hast all free unto thee, thou hast His covenant together with the baptism and the sacrament and the body and blood of Christ therein. . . . Christ's disciples and again their disciples and successors have baptized; and the believing church or congregation have broken bread in houses, and where they could, and have fed upon the body and blood of Christ: the Temple of God was everywhere, wheresoever Christians were met together. We do not mention this for the pulling down of churches in which Christ's office is exercised; but we shew you the hypocrites, who bind you wholly to them, that you may go out from them, and go to the congregation of Christ, into the temple of Christ, and that you may not rest satisfied merely with the *church of stone walls*, for they are only a heap of stones, which is a dead thing; but Christ's temple is living. Ye are all agreed about the Church, and go diligently thither, but none will enter into the temple of Christ. But pray go into the temple of Christ, and then of dead you will become living."[1]

[1] Threefold Life, ch. xi., pars. 76-78.

"Men set up ceremonies. O, if they had kept the true faith and had shewn people the divine way into the new regeneration; if they had shewn them the clear countenance of God, then people had departed from their sins into a divine life."[1]

"And then they built great houses of stone and called every one thither, and they said that the Holy Ghost was powerful there and they must come thither" . . . "and out of the testimony of the Holy Ghost a worldly law was made, but then the Holy Ghost spake no more freely, but He must speak according to their laws, and if He reproved their errors, then they persecuted Him" (in His human mouthpiece), "and so the temple of Christ in man's knowledge became very obscure; if any came that was born of God, and taught by the Holy Ghost, and was not conformable to their laws, he must be a heretic."[2]

"But the Spirit of Christ in His children is not bound to any certain form, that it need not or ought not to speak anything which stands not in the Apostolical letter, as the Spirit in the Apostles was free, and they spake not all one and the same words, but from one Spirit and ground they did all speak, every one as the Spirit gave him utterance; even thus likewise the Spirit speaketh yet out of its children, it needeth no form aforehand composed and gathered together out of the literal word."[3]

"If men had not introduced any exposition upon the Apostolical word, and brought or contrived the same into other forms, then the instrument had remained pure, but the unilluminated mind hath set itself up to be a master therein, and bowed the same according to its own imagination and well-liking" . . . "and thus the spirit is extinct and is turned to an antichristian order and custom; men have taken and formed the word as an

---

[1] Threefold Life, ch. xiii., par. 43.
[2] Three Principles, ch. xxvi., pars. 24, 27.
[3] Mysterium Magnum, ch. xxviii., par. 52.

organ, and so they have brought it into a fashion and custom that a man must play thereon and others must hear the sound and tune which he makes."[1]

"Your Laws, Councils, Decrees, Canons, and your singular Articles or opinions are but mere deceit: the Spirit of Christ in God will not be bound to any laws."[2]

And which of the so-called evangelicals could read with patience such indictments as these? "Babel taketh the mantle of Christ upon her and saith, Christ hath undertaken and suffered for all my sins upon the cross, I cannot purchase or do anything for myself: my works avail nothing before God: I need only believe that Christ hath done it, and comfort myself therewith, and then I am already justified and acquitted from all my transgressions. Thus she cometh before God, and thanketh God that He hath paid the score in His Son."—"But itself remaineth in the mind of the Cainical brother-slayer in pride, covetousness, envy and anger."[3]

"*Sin must always be brought into the judgment of God wherein it was born*, and the holy love-fire of God must drown it and wash it away, else there is no forgiveness; neither offering nor covenant doth avail anything without it, also no going to church, neither singing nor devout shewing doth attain it, nothing else at all doth it but only the hungry desiring faith through the alone offering in the blood and death of Christ, where the desire doth wholly die . . . to its selfhood, and arise in Christ's resurrection with a true faith and Christianity, not in a specious show of holiness, but in the inward essence in words and works."[4]

"God requireth the Abyss of the heart, and saith that not one jot or tittle of His law of righteousness shall pass

---

[1] Mysterium Magnum, ch. xxviii., par. 58.
[2] Threefold Life, ch. iii., par. 67.
[3] Mysterium Magnum, ch. xxvii., pars. 52, 53, 56.
[4] Ibid., par. 45.

away till it be all fulfilled. Wherewith wilt thou fulfill the righteousness if thou art without the divine substance *in thee*? Thou wilt say, 'Christ hath fulfilled it for me, and satisfied the law.' That is true; but what is that to thee who art and walkest without Christ? If thou art not in Christ in the actual operative grace, then thou hast no part in Him."[1]

"Justification is effected in the blood of Christ *in man*, in the soul itself; not through an outward, imputed, accounted strange show."—"Christ with His love-blood in us fulfilleth the righteousness of God in the anger, and turneth it into divine joy."[2]

"It is said to thee, thou titulary and verbal Christendom, in the zeal of God, that thou, in thy tattling mouth, *without* Christ's Spirit, flesh, and blood in thee, art as fully heathenish and a foreigner in the presence of God as they [the heathen] themselves. Thy supposed election, special acceptation, filiation and adoption *without* the new birth is thy snare and fall."[3]

"Comforting and setting the suffering of Christ in the forefront is not the true faith; no, no, it is only without and not within; but a converted will, which entereth into sorrow for its earthly iniquity and will none of it any more."—"Therefore, dear brethren, take heed of putting on Christ's purple mantle without a resigned will: the poor sinner without sorrow for his sins, and conversion of his will, doth only take it in scorn to Christ."[4]

To the same effect, and too beautifully eloquent to break by extracts, is the last half of the 5th chapter of the 2nd Part of Böhme's treatise on the *Incarnation*, beginning from par. 76, which I earnestly commend to the reader's attention.

"O thou supposed Christendom!" I am tempted to

[1] Election, ch. x., pars. 82–86. [2] Ibid., pars. 119, 122.
[3] Ibid., pars. 150, 151. [4] Signatura Rerum, ch. xv., pars. 27, 30.

say, using his words, how few among your professed followers of Jesus Christ will brook rebukes like these! Probably the first impulse will be to say, "That is what we all know and what our ministers of His Gospel teach." But do they teach it as clearly, as pungently to the mass of "nominal and outside Christians" that occupy the best part of our churches? "Why," asked Böhme, "do you not break the fair nutshell and expose the rotten kernel and heart that lieth hidden within it and tell the *superior* as well as the *inferior* of his abominations and wickedness? If you are the shepherd of Christ, why do you not as Christ did, who told every one the truth to his face? He doth bruise and heal not for favour or respect of the person of any, but according to the will of his Father; and the shepherd of Christ ought to do the same."[1]

And if this is not enough to account for the peculiar acerbity with which, as a rule, the clerical mind reverts to old "Teutonicus," it must be remembered that he upbraids the devotees of Reason with an equally vehement onset; and gives our broad churchmen and scholarly divines as many unpalatable truths as he has offered to teachers of misleading doctrine: for instance, "Reason is captivated and fast bound in a close and strong prison, that is to say, in the anger of God, and in earthliness."[2] "We know nothing concerning God, what He is; but God's Spirit must become the knowing in us, else our knowing is but fiction, a continual confusedness, a continual learning and understanding nothing in the ground of the Centre." . . . "God's Spirit must be in Reason, if Reason will see God; there belongeth a humble resigned heart to it."[3] "We attain not the true ground of divine

---

[1] Of the Mixed World, par. 22 (*Way to Christ*, Bath, 1775, page 298). Also *Threefold Life*, ch. xv., par. 22.

[2] True Resignation, ch. i., par. 2.

[3] Second Apology, Part I., pars. 54, 57.

knowledge by the sharp searching and speculation of our outward Reason, but the searching must begin within in the hunger of the soul."[1]

"Go out from your toilsome seeking in Reason into God's will, into God's Spirit, and cast the outward Reason away; then is your will God's will, and God's Spirit will seek you *within* you; and then finding your will in itself, it revealeth itself in your will, as in its own; for if you give up that, then that is its own, for it is *All*, and when it goeth, then go you forth, for you have divine power; all which you then search, *It is therein*, and nothing is hidden to it: thus you see in its light."[2]

"Man is blind in all God's works, and hath no true knowledge unless the Divine breathing or speaking be revealed in his internal ground." . . . "It is therefore declared to all lovers of Arts . . . that they *first seek God's love and grace*, and resign up their selves to and become wholly one with that, else all their seeking is but a delusion or the courting of a shadow, and to no purpose, and nothing is found of any fundamental worth."[3]

"It behoveth man, and his main happiness depends thereon, that he also die unto the images of the letters in him, and disclaim or depart from all Reason's scholarship, or knowledge of nature . . . and enter into the one only life, *Jesus*, and not at all dispute about the way, where it is; but only think [or consider] that it is *in him*, that he must forsake all whatever he hath, either art, wit or skill, etc., and become one barely and nakedly in himself, bring himself into the One, viz., into God's will . . . he must give himself up will-less, and leave himself *wholly* in God's mercy, and bring all his learnings into

---

[1] An Epistle, pars. 3, 4 (*Way to Christ*, Bath, 1775, page 304). Also *Epistles* (1649), Ep. 32, pars. 3, 4.
[2] Forty Questions (1665), Ques. 1, pars. 60, 61.
[3] Epistles (1649), Ep. 6, pars. 61, 71.

this one only thing, that he in his teachings and learnings will not do or speak anything but what God willeth through him: and thus all opinions and conceits do die in him, and the soul's life falleth into the *only living Word*."[1]

"Every one saith, 'I have the key'; yet none will unlock his own life's book: *every one* hath the key to God in himself, let him but seek it in the right place; but you would rather contend and dispute about the key than seek it in yourselves. Therefore you are all of you blind that contend or dispute: you do but go seeking, as before a looking-glass: why do you not go into the *Centre*, for with other seeking you will not find the key, be as learned as you will. It lieth not in Art or Reason but in an earnest purposed resolved will, to go out from self and forsake all own self, skill and knowledge, and with repentant humble desires to cast yourself into God's knowing, and desire only God's knowing, yet with or in this manner, that He in you may know what He will: thus you will put on Divine knowledge and find the key about which you contend or dispute."[2]

What would Edinburgh, Cambridge and Oxford say to such counsels! Their teachers and learners are well convinced of their *own* being, but as to Deity,—well, that with many of them is an open question. We can hardly expect *them* to study Böhme.

But even now his worst offence to average human nature in every class, of every calling, has to be named. It is his unsparing and reiterated condemnations of man's "potent and open enemy, self-love," as the Antichrist against which every one of us must fight to the last moment of existence. "If Christ," he says, "shall live in man then the spirit of self-lust must die, and yet it doth not wholly die in the time of this life, by reason

---

[1] Mysterium Magnum, ch. xxxvi., par. 50.
[2] Second Apology, Part II., pars. 306, 307.

of the flesh, but it *dieth daily and yet liveth*; and therefore there is such contest which no wicked man feeleth, but only those who have put on Christ."[1] Now the last part of this sentence explains why those who listen readily enough to warnings against the world, the flesh and the devil, feel impatient when it is urged that even while sincerely endeavouring to resist these, they are beset every hour by a foe far more likely to hold them in a deadly unrelaxing grip. It is as if one was accused of blindness when sight seemed perfectly clear and strong: for the *true* life buried deep in every human soul is, in the majority of cases, in such an embryonic state that its corrupt and antecedent associate occupies all our consciousness, and there is not yet enough of divine life in us to push *that* into the field of vision, where we might recognize its loathsome poisoned nature. And as has been truly said by one of Böhme's most convinced disciples, J. Pierrepont Greaves, "Nothing so wounds self-love as to turn it round upon itself, its own likeness. Self-love being forced upon itself, is placed in a very wounding predicament; it feels deeply the act and does not forgive."[2] The angry resentment thus incurred is Böhme's certain inheritance: those only who have begun in good earnest to long for release from the strong magnetic compression of selfishness[3] will read

[1] Epistles (1649), Ep. 13, par. 15.
[2] Theosophic Revelations, p. 109.
[3] "And we do here understand by selfishness the human nature as it is broken off from its right true and inward Centre; as it is entered into its own government of the divided and contrary properties of life, as it stands upon a ground and bottom of its own making, and as it hath settled itself as it were to rest only in and upon itself." . . . "This selfishness we own to be the deepest ground of our corruption, and compare it justly to the root of a tree firmly fixed, wide and broad, stretching forth itself, or rather comprising all in itself; but continuing always deeply hidden underground; and this tree we call the tree of death." (Dionysius Freher, quoted by Christopher Walton in his *Memorial of William Law*, page 630.) The whole passage, too long for insertion here, unsurpassed, as I believe, for its

without repugnance his powerful entreaties to break from it into the liberty of total humility and self-surrender.

And the force of his earnest warnings against self-seeking in *every* form is intensified by his being so unlike monitors who inveigh against the use, pursuit and enjoyment of the good things of this life. He is no ascetic. "You must not suppose that we undervalue the outward life, for it is most profitable to us."[1] "Thou art in this world, and if thou hast a lawful, honest calling or employment, without falsehood or wickedness, continue therein,—work, labour, trade and manage it as necessity requireth, seek wonders both in the elements and in the earth, be it in what art, science or employment it will, it is all God's work : seek in the earth silver and gold, make artificial works thereof, build, till and plant, it is all to God's deeds of wonder."[2] "But he should not set his willing therein, and esteem that for his treasure, but for his joy and ornament he may use it; but with the inward man, he should labour in God's mystery, and then God's Spirit helpeth him also to seek and find the outward."[3]

Nevertheless to every self-centred desire we must die, if true humanity is to be reborn. "Whosoever will see the Kingdom of God and attain thereunto, he must bring forth his soul out of selfhood." . . . "All that doth vex, plague and annoy thee, is only thy selfhood: thou makest thyself thy own enemy and bringest thyself into self-destruction and death. Now if thou wilt get again out of death, then thou must wholly forsake thy own self-desire (which hath introduced itself into a strange

penetrative exposure of our worst enemy, the unreformable and all-deceiving monster, self-love.

[1] Forty Questions, Ques. 16, par. 7.
[2] Ibid. (1665), Ques. 12, par. 26.
[3] Incarnation, Part III., ch. v., par. 33.

essence) and become in selfhood and self-desire as a nothing, so that thou wilt no longer will or desire to thyself but wholly and fully introduce thy desire again with the resignation into the Eternal, viz., into God's will, that the same will may be thy will and desire. Without this there is nothing but misery and death."[1] Who does not know this experimentally, as one by one the idols of self fall down, for *all* must go, "the idols God shall utterly abolish";[2] and yet before we let go our hold upon one, imagination seizes upon another with a grasp quite as strong—and so on till death wrenches all things from it! And even then we may still be so blinded by the evil magic of egotism as *not* to see, that in forsaking one miserable little centre to return to the universal heart and centre of every world, we should gain all possibilities of life and joy and wisdom. "The introverted spirit of man resigned up into God, when he forsaketh all that is his own, doth attain the divine eye to see and understand; so that he gets much more again than he forsook, and that he is much richer than when he enjoyed his own; for in his own will he had and possessed only a particular, but in the resignation he gets into the total, viz., into the *universal*, into All; for *all* is from the Word of God."[3] And "you are to know that the love of God is so humble that when it hath kindled the soul with itself, *itself is subject to the soul*, but no soul will enjoy that but those that are humbled in the love of God and constantly go forth from their desires, that the Spirit of God may live in them."[4]

[1] Signatura Rerum, ch. xv., pars. 14, 5-7. Let any one who has the privilege of owning Böhme's *Signatura Rerum* turn to its twelfth chapter and read from par. 8 to par. 17, and feel there the pure and triumphant joy of a spirit that could anticipate the gain consequent on the loss of the "*proprium*,"—the blissful life that begins even on this side of dissolution, as death to self becomes habitual.
[2] Isaiah ii. 18.   [3] Mysterium Magnum, ch. lxvii., par. 13
[4] Threefold Life, ch. xvi., par. 36.

One of the most striking peculiarities of Böhme is his continual stress upon the necessity of *meekness* for bringing the human soul into rapport with its source; for God, he tells us, "*so far as He is in himself is the greatest meekness.*"[1] While at the same time he claims for man a dignity so supreme, and a birthright so glorious.—Take for a few brief samples of this: "We are children of the omnipotence of God, and inherit His goods in the omnipotency."[2] "God is Himself the Being of all being and we are gods in Him, through whom He revealeth Himself."[3] "By the will God created Heaven and earth, and such a mighty will is hidden also in the soul."[4]

But in that he postulates in all his teaching a God,—not only a universal creative tendency, but a God that filleth all things, yet "humbles Himself to behold the things that are in Heaven and earth," he will appear to many readers unworthy of their esteem; for *they* have got beyond that antique mode of thought; they have expanded their own so far as to believe that nothing of God is knowable. Indeed, I fear not by them.

It is saddening after reading in Böhme's, to take up the writings of those who call themselves Agnostics: one pities them so heartily for seeking, what they profess to search for, where it never can be found,—for hunting with Reason only, in circumferences, for that which *must* be found in the *innermost* deep of the spirit; which Reason never sounded or can sound.

In the first chapter of his *Threefold Life of Man* answer will be found to almost every difficulty that has been brought forward as to the discordance between our ideas of the God in whom *all* worlds originate, and the facts

---

[1] Divine Vision, ch. iii., par. 75.
[2] Forty Questions (1665), Ques. 6, par. 28.
[3] Threefold Life, ch. vi., par. 4.
[4] Ibid., ch. viii., par. 18.

of our world; yet on first reading it will perhaps seem hopelessly unintelligible; so I found it twenty-nine years ago; and now I see that I have not yet won all the treasures of knowledge imbedded in its depths. "*Go with me,*" said Böhme, "*into the Centre.*"—Going as far as one can; little by little retreating from the conflict of opinions that puzzle and confuse in the intellectual world, toward the infinitude of central light and life, one wins a profound peace, while the *knowledge* there found is but initial.

"If," says Böhme, "a man would satisfy the human mind so that it may give itself up into the eternal rest, then a man must shew him the *root* of the tree out of which spirit and flesh hath its original; a man must shew and open to him the centre of the eternal as also of the inceptive or beginning nature, that he may apprehend the earthly and also the heavenly mystery; and then is the eternal beginning and the eternal end totally one, wherein the spirit of the soul layeth itself to rest, for it seeth the wheel totally."[1]

This spiritual rest is assuredly to be found in Böhme's writings by those who can study them as learners and not critics; who can absorb, before they begin to analyze, *passing over what they cannot take in,* without any attempt to bring it under the jurisdiction of Reason or authority, before apprehension of meaning has been possible. All other kinds of quite new branches of knowledge are thus received; why not the highest—theosophy, "the true science of the mutual relations and magical laws of Deity and nature, and of the essential constitution of the latter both exteriorly to, and interiorly in man, and all beings."[2]

I have endeavoured to make the great German theosopher explain himself by apposite citations from some

[1] Considerations upon Esaiah Stiefel's *Threefold State of Man,* par. 23.
[2] Christopher Walton's *Memorial of William Law,* p. 688.

of his works: so cogent, persuasive and eloquently instructive are many crowding still upon my memory, that lest I should yield to the temptation of quoting more, I am obliged to close his books, and as I do so I think, "I would not give the little grain that was" (thus) "sown in me for all this world's good."[1]

[1] First Apology, Part II., par. 591.

BÖHME AND SWEDENBORG [1]

"When I consider and think why I write thus, and leave it not for other sharper wits, I find that my spirit is kindled in this matter, whereof I write; for there is a living running fire of these things in my spirit. And, thereupon (let me purpose what I will) yet this thing continually moveth and swimmeth on the top, and so I am captivated therewith in my spirit, and it is laid on me as a work which I must exercise."—*Three Prin.*, xxiv. 1.

I WOULD not presume to enter the lists in contention with Mr Podmore about his recent critique on the late Serjeant Cox's ideas of Spirit and body, both because I very imperfectly understand these, and because the subject is far beyond my grasp. As a disciple of Böhme's I cannot, of course, for one moment agree to any theory which would identify *soul* with any kind of *body*. "Mr Cox tells us that the soul of man is a refined body"; [2] but as I read Mr Podmore's papers I felt eager to remind him that a body, such as Mr Cox spoke of in the passage he quotes, is not necessarily more akin to matter than the hand is to an inclosing glove; and while waiting for some more competent pleader of the cause, I wished to draw attention to the advantages and honours of *body*, and to shew that Spirit does not gain but lose by being disembodied. In saying this, I only verbally conform to what I believe to be one of our established misconceptions. Taught by Böhme, I understand it to be as impossible for *Spirits* to exist without bodies as for light to shine without the molecules which vibrate in its transit; for

[1] Light, 1881, vol. i. pp. 186, 195.
[2] Address delivered by F. Podmore, March 21. See *Light* for April 2.

"there is no understanding without a body, and moreover the Spirit itself does not subsist without a body." [1]

A *soul* can exist without a body; it is in a most literal sense its damnation if it be so bereft of substance, but if it be possible—there are fearful conditions of *impossibility*—"*the soul attracteth corporeity to it.*" [2] And this only through the agency of Spirit. But matter and substance are not identical, though like the bee imprisoned by a glass window-pane, we are all apt to mistake the one for the other; but when the bee does escape, he finds out that the hard, obstructive barrier against which he beat, buzzing angrily, was not air, though air-coloured; that the matter which could break deprived him of his natural element, while this, the imperishable air, was pervious, and in proportion to his scope of action, illimitable. So shall we find, if leaving behind our material life, we are, to use St Paul's expression, "clothed upon" by heavenly substance. In the appendix to *Hafed*, worth, to my thinking, all the rest of the book, a Spirit at one of the séances of Mr Duguid is reported to have said: "Spiritual bodies, though undiscernible by you, are just as truly matter as earthly bodies; only you have no power to perceive anything but the crudest condition of matter." [3] I do not question the truth of that statement within the limits of that Spirit's experience, but either he knew nothing of *substance*, or he spoke as if matter was only another name for it. Swedenborg knew better. To cite him as an authority is, I know, to row against the tide, though even at the present day I think I can detect a slight turn in the tide; but on this question he is, in my opinion, not only an authority for reason to accept, but an enormous benefactor to the Christian world—treated hitherto like most benefactors, with ingratitude; like all givers

---

[1] Threefold Life, ch. iv., par. 5.   [2] Ibid., ch. vi., par 86.
[3] Page 344.

of new truth, with derision or obloquy, according to the nature of those who refuse attention to it. Saying this, I am self-condemned, as for many years I regarded his works as a repository for curious *fancies*, never for an instant thinking they could be facts, or doubting that he had been duped by mendacious Spirits in his reports of the unseen world, and that his good morality was far beneath the reverent study of one who aimed at spiritual attainments.

I read St Martin's summary of the merits of his writings: "Ils donnent à l'homme une secousse utile dans sa léthargie. S'ils ne lui donnent pas les plans exacts de la région spirituelle, ils l'engagent au moins à penser qu'elle existe"[1]—with full assent: and felt no wrong done by these words of the late Mr Christopher Walton in his unpublished *Memorial of William Law*: "I have no doubt that if Mr Law had given his opinion of Swedenborg it would have put an entire extinguisher on Swedenborg's pretensions to the least regard from serious and enlightened Christians."[2]

And now I not only study his pages with growing belief in their value, but I feel convinced that neither the Christian world nor the world of deep thinkers have yet extracted from them half the treasure they contain. The conviction stole in upon my mind as gently, and as independently of any human influence, as morning light comes in. I had no bias in their favour except that which they themselves offered; the same sort of bias that a key gives when it opens a lock without effort. For many of the phenomena of Spiritist séances of which I read reminded me of long forgotten assertions of Swedenborg, and the more often I referred to these, the more plainly I saw that the everyday wonders of our time fall into intelligible sequence of cause and effect under the steady light of his long contemned vision.

[1] L'Homme de Désir, 1790, p. 268, par. 184.   [2] Page 598.

So much for my acceptance of him as a seer and a teacher; but this does not by any means include assent to all he teaches, or belief in all his deductions from what he saw. Not only was he a fallible man, but doubtless the Spirits he associated with were sometimes ignorant, and sometimes mistook a correspondence (*i.e.*, representative figure in worlds unseen by us) for absolute fact.

I observe a peculiar bitterness against him in the minds of those who most revere Böhme. Placing the two on a level of comparison, they exasperate angry incredulity by the evident discrepancies of the elder and the more modern seer. Surely such comparison is as unwise as trying to measure expanse above ground by central depths. To Böhme it was given to see into the abyssal depths of being in both a formative and prehistoric epoch; his knowledge of the process of regeneration is unique—I may safely assume that no one else in any age has so accurately expounded its essentials; whereas Swedenborg appears to me unconscious of the existence of soul as antecedent to spirit, and of all the tremendous issues which hang upon the evolution of spirits from souls he has not a word to say. His ideas of spiritual life are as calm and composed as the curls of his eighteenth century wig; but what he can and does tell us about are the dynamic laws of that life when its initial stages are overpast.

It is, I imagine, his constant insistence upon *law* in spiritual life which has offended a large class of Christians, enlightened or otherwise; we are used to think of it as so completely beyond accurate analysis that we allow the most momentous of its interests to remain under a soft haze of consecrated *somehow*; and from placing our whole hope of salvation in the Saviour have come to think it almost profane to inquire into the *modus operandi* of deliverance; much more so to believe that unless we take part in it instrumentally ourselves, for us His work is, until we do, made frustrate. On this ground Swedenborg's condemnation of current Christianity was unrelentingly severe, but, to my thinking, not in any degree unjust, though I quite admit that he never seems to have had any adequate notion of the profounder effects of the life and death of Jesus Christ.

With this, however, or any other of his shortcomings in Scriptural orthodoxy I have here nothing to do; what I claim our deepest gratitude for is just the doctrine of Spirits having a bodily life which has exposed him to so much contempt for materialistic ideas, gross conceptions of the happiness of another world, and the like. He startles us, maybe, when he says most people think of Spirits as "puffs of intellect, or mere thinking principles";[1] but I remark that in all popular views of Spirits and Spirit life the farther they are distanced from anything that the body knows, feels, or does, the more heavenly, the more Spiritual, they are supposed to be.[2]

[1] See also par. 456 in *Heaven and Hell* in his chapter on the theme "That man after death is in a perfect human form."

[2] Much as Swedenborg is supposed to differ from Böhme, their teaching wholly accords in direct contradiction of *this* assumption. While the one says, " It is manifest that the Spirit of man is in a form as well as his body, and that the form of the Spirit is the human form, with sensories and senses as perfect when separated from the body as when in the body, and that the all of the life of the eye, and the all of the life of the ear, in a word, the all of the sensitive life which man possesses, is not of his body, but of his Spirit in those sensories and in their most minute particulars" (*Heaven and Hell*, par. 434). The other, as usual, going deeper into causality, simply asserts, "*Out of the Spiritual form the corporeal is generated*,"—(J. Böhme's *Three Principles*)—and enlarges upon the senses, not only of the human Spirit, but of the divine source of all being. "He is an almighty, all-wise, all-knowing, all-seeing, all-hearing, all-smelling, all-feeling, all-tasting God" (*Aurora*, ch. iii., par. 24). Very pertinent to this saying of Böhme's, which would horrify many theologians and philosophers too—uniting for once in the battle cry of "Anthropomorphism"—is this passage from Pordage's *Theologia Mystica* : "But you will say that these faculties, as likewise the senses of hearing, seeing,

Swedenborg, at once clearing the ground of all such error by making it evident that matter is not substance, brings his readers face to face with a far more stringent and invariable reign of law in the inner world than religious teachers have been used to recognize. While they combat feelings and states of mind, he turns from anything so vague, so open to the manipulation of self-love, and incessantly harps upon the certain indelible effect on the whole being of every smallest spiritual transaction. That "thoughts are things"; that the body of the spirit must be moulded one way or other by every thought, by every admitted impression; that the connection between evil and suffering is inseparable, till evil is given up and hated—are his key notes; and would not truths such as these, if received, have worked out a far more spiritual state of mind—*i.e.*, a state of mind more ruled by eternal interests—than all the warmest emotions of a piety that, treating the body as a temporary bridge between this life and a condition quite unimaginable, leaves to the despised body all its earthly delights, securing, as it is thought, the alien interests of the soul by modes that ignore their interaction?

We may hear the rank materialism of Swedenborg's heaven denounced at a table where certainly the enjoyments of the body had not been in any degree despised,

tasting, smelling and feeling, are only attributed to God to comply with our weakness and to make Him intelligible to our understanding, not that there are any such faculties or senses in God, but only by way of analogy and likeness. To which I answer that all the forementioned faculties and senses are most really and truly in God, even far more really than they are or can be in any creature; for in Him they are originally and in truth, and in the creature only by way of participation, and by way of analogy and resemblance. So that understanding, will, wisdom, hearing, seeing, etc., are in God primarily, essentially, and by way of eminence; and in the creature only derivatively, and by way of resemblance, as the copy expresseth and resembleth its original" (*Theologia Mystica* . . . by a Person of Qualitie, J.P.M.D. London, 1683, p. 35.)

though its true well-being had, by people who groan and sigh a few hours later in hymn or prayer for deliverance from the burden of the flesh; but in the clear atmosphere of Swedenborg's thought we learn that material pleasures are regarded as "filth" among purified Spirits, and as Spirits ourselves, though still heavily weighted, may begin in some degree to adopt their estimates.

To become more *spiritualized* is the usual ambition of earnest-minded people, for the only mode of being with which earthly experience has made us familiar is so corrupt and infirm that we have naturally supposed that to be perfect a human being must become pure Spirit (not quite knowing what we mean by that); but, at all events, not trammelled by bodily limits. I suspect this is as great a mistake as it would be to think the perfectness of circulation of blood secure if once it had no veins and arteries to run in. "There must," says Böhme, "be an attraction and inclosing, out of which the manifestation appeareth."[1] The error lies in our ignorance of Spiritual substance, as to which Böhme is so precise that I must again use his words: "As there is a *nature* and *substance* in the outward world, so also in the inward Spiritual world there is a *nature* and *substance* which is Spiritual."[2] And once to apprehend this is, I think, to be quit of one of the commonest hindrances to belief in the Incarnation of the Divine Man. If manhood is conditional upon the corrupt matter of mortal flesh and blood, no wonder the taking our flesh upon Him by the Son of God is denied as incredible; but if our flesh and blood is, as I believe, the rough and gross monstering of the original humanity, "*the angelical image, viz., the substance which came from the inward Spiritual world,*"[3] it need not outrage reason, or reverence

[1] Threefold Life, ch. i., par. 33. [2] Regeneration, ch. ii., par. 31.
[3] Ibid., ch. ii., par. 62.

for Deity, to suppose that the Perfect Man clothed Himself in our prison garment when He came to deliver us from our bondage, and shew us the only means of escape.

Dr J. Garth Wilkinson, in his admirable *Life of Swedenborg*,[1] remarks very cogently: "If God can be *inspirituate* surely He can also be incarnate, for Spirit is more bodily than flesh"—an expression which only Swedenborg's greatest successor can duly explain. According to Mr T. Lake Harris our imperfection as Spirits is most proved by our defective corporeity, by the very imperfect organization of our inner man. But it is impossible to convey his meaning accurately without his own words. He speaks in one of his discourses of "the gradual re-construction of the human body from centres to circumferences. Now, when with internal and Spiritual eye you look at the human hand, you discover that although there is the actual form of a hand, yet, as you penetrate more deeply into the structure, it becomes more rudimentary, more incomplete; for all men on earth having been born in disorder, those disorders are perpetuated and embodied in the finer and invisible structures of the flesh, even when they do not crop out to the surface, as in cases of malformation and idiocy."
... "There are, so to speak, vast organic spaces left unfilled between the body and the Spirit. The difference between man organic, as he is on earth in his unredeemed bodily condition, and man as he should be on earth in his redeemed bodily condition, is almost like the difference between the statue and the human form. The cunning artist carves his marble image; it stands erect in the appearance of the man, but the human likeness is only on the outside. So with us, the human likeness is principally upon the outside, but the internal structures, the internal divine forms of the faculties, are mere hints and suggestions left imperfect, left unfilled,

[1] Footnote to page 133.

and where they are striving to be filled out, at best partial manifestations of creative form and power. Christ alone as to His visible organization, Christ alone, in the last stages of His stay on earth, exhibits what an organic man is."[1]

Now, the received idea as to St Paul's words, "the redemption of the body," is that of a postponed hope; of one that cannot be realized until we have first put off mortality, and awaited the general Resurrection. I have no doubt we must wait till then for the fullest glorification of the redeemed body, but I am thankful to our contemporary Seer for making me understand that the redemption of the body, the structural "*new creature*,"— (not only a new heart or new mind)—or, as St Paul put it, Christ "getting a form" in us, need no more wait for death than the house or church in building waits for the scaffolding and all adjacent materials to be cleared away to be in process of formation. Our mortal bodies are what corresponds to scaffolding and material, and just as these are unsteadily reared, or wrongly chosen, does the stone or the Spiritual structure suffer. Here again Böhme is most explicit and worth hearing. "The dead or mortal flesh belongeth not to the birth of life, as that *it* can receive the life of the light as a propriety, but the life of the light of God riseth up in the dead or mortal flesh, and generateth to itself from or out of the dead or

[1] The Millennial Age, pp. 140-142.

In quoting these words of Mr Harris, I am, it is evident, begging the question that the Spirit forms its own body (subject, of course, to conditions more or less advantageous in the process, over which the individual Spirit has no control). When I can for an instant entertain the idea that the husk of a chestnut produced the nut within, I shall be ready to weigh the arguments of a materialist. Materialists, finding mental or spiritual deficiency where there is corresponding organic defect, conclude that the organization originates faculty, whereas the imperfection of organic life, unless superinduced by external injury, proves to me defective spiritual power. A door or a window may be found wanting in a house because it is blocked up by some catastrophe, but it is far more likely that the builder omitted to make one.

mortal flesh, *another* heavenly and living body, which knoweth and understandeth the light. For this body is but a shell from which the new body groweth, as it is with a grain of wheat in the earth."[1] I submit that it would make a most important and beneficial change in the views of all Christian people if they could regard their mortal bodies in this light; the dangerous extremes of the ascetic would be as much condemned as the lowering infirmities of self-indulgence—the interests of Spirit and *true body* being in no sense antagonistic.

"All things," says Böhme, "are come to corporeal substance to the manifestation of God's works of wonder."[2] That object cannot end with time.

"Spiritual corporeity," says Hahn, "is the aim of the work of God, therefore the old creation is first completed by the new [regeneration]. The first creation was only a formation for establishing matter";[3] and again: "Spiritual corporeity is the aim of the new creation, which the angels shall attain by the humanity of Christ."[4] I must quote this writer once more, as he so exactly gives my feeling on this subject. "Thou hast convinced me that spiritual corporeity is perfect blessedness, and harmony with perfect spirits in the perfect delights of spiritual bodies. I do not desire to resign myself to being a holy—one knows not what—an inanity. Neither is it Thy will, my God, that I should desire that."[5] Now without real structural regeneration I see no escape from just what Hahn here deprecates.

---

[1] Aurora, ch. xxi., pars. 71-72. [2] Threefold Life, ch. v., par. 123.
[3] Die Lehre des württembergischen Theosophen, Johann Michael Hahn, p. 189.
[4] Ibid., p. 87.
[5] Ibid., p. 397. The original text, with all its German *naïveté*, had better be given for the last passage. "Du hast mir gezeigt, dass Geistleiblichkeit vollkommene Seligkeit sei und Harmonie mit vollkommenen Geistern in Geistleibern vollkommenes Vergnügen; ich will also nicht einem heiligen Weiss nicht was? wie ein Unding überlassen seyn. Es ist auch nicht dein Wille, dass ich das wollen solle, mein Gott!"

It is a striking instance of the unconscious agreement of men whose spiritual vision takes in a widely different area that Swedenborg, who so frequently reiterates that it is a mistake of theologians to suppose the Spirit waits after death for its resurrection body, because as soon as consciousness returns after dissolution, men find themselves in bodies with all their senses,—unaware, as it would seem, of any connection between regeneration and bodily perfectness,—is yet the one to tell us that there are seven degrees of regeneration, and that only in the seventh is perfection, very few people in this life attaining to the fifth or sixth.[1]

On this point I cannot hold him to be any authority, since he advances the quite untenable opinion, positively as doctrine, that "regeneration proceeds from the external man to the internal. It is thus the angels perceive the Word."[2] If they do, I think they will be better informed when they are enabled to look into this mystery with more illumination. But as to the seven states of regeneration, it is highly probable that they are the gradual stages of progress of all who "go from strength to strength" in the growth of an immortal life.

The "seventh form of nature," to use the language of Böhme, is the combined interaction of all the preceding six, duly evolved, and there brought to substance. Now this I conclude is the perfected body of regenerate Spirit, the full growth and organic development of that germ of Spiritual life which is latent in all, but inert and powerless till the will of man—man's one inviolable possession—is so touched, or turned, either by consciousness of Divine love, or by the shattering forces of contrition, that it yields to converting influences, and earnestly invokes Divine aid to subdue all internal opposition and unite it wholly and for ever to the will of God.

[1] Arcana Cœlestia, ch. i., pars. 6-13.   [2] Ibid., par. 64.

THE POWER OF IMAGINATION [1]

THE surprise which the correspondent who signs himself "Trident" has expressed at creative power being attributed to imagination, led me to think that possibly some gaps in the mind of your readers might be a little filled up, and many interesting lines of thought suggested, by the quotations I have selected from writers whom no one can suspect of "scientific freaks." In any degree to do justice to the subject, a carefully written and ripely matured volume of thought would be required. All I venture to offer are germs of thought gathered on widely different planes, and on suitable mental ground they will not be altogether fruitless.

From Jacob Böhme I find so much light thrown on the powers of imagination, that selecting the clearest of his many dicta on this point is my only difficulty.

"That which breaketh the divine image" (in man) "is the *essential* fierce wrathfulness, and it is done through the imagination; or false or wicked love and imaging; therefore, it lieth wholly in the imagination; whatsoever a man letteth into his desire, in that standeth the image." [2]

"There is nothing in this world that can touch or kill the soul, no fire nor sword, but only the *imagination*; that is its poison; for it is originally proceeded out of the imagination, and continueth eternally therein." [3]

[1] Light, 1881, vol. i. p. 227.
[2] Forty Questions (1665), Appen., par. 33.   [3] Ibid., Ques. 11, par. 10.

"All things are existed through *divine* IMAGINATION, and do yet stand in such a birth or geniture, condition, or regiment."[1]

This saying will be better understood if I place next to it the following from his answer to the sixth theosophic question :—

"Angels are mere imaged powers of the Word of God; for man's mind is an express, or reflex image, or antitype of the eternal power of God. For all senses, or meanings, or notions, come out of the mind; and out of the senses, meanings, or notions, come right thoughts, viz., a conclusion or *imagination*, from whence longing lust [wish] or delight existeth; which longing goeth into a being or substance, from whence the perceptible desire, and out of that the work springeth; thus also is God, in like manner, the eternal mind, that is, the understanding; and yet, there would be no distinction therein, if He did not flow out from Himself. His outflowings are the powers; as in man the senses and thoughts; and the *powers* bring themselves into an imagination, wherein standeth the angelical IDEA."[2]

"Now seeing the eternal abyss is magical, therefore that is magical also, whatsoever is generated out of the eternal; for out of the desiring all things are come to be; Heaven and Earth are magical, and the *mind* with the senses or thoughts are magical; if we will but once know or understand ourselves." . . . "*Whatsoever the Magia maketh itself, that it hath*; the devil made himself hell, and that he hath; and Adam made himself earth, and that he is." . . . "A creaturely Spirit is no palpable substance; but it must draw in substance into itself through its *imagination*, ELSE IT WOULD NOT SUBSIST."[3]

[1] Of the True and False Light, par. 78 (printed at the end of *Several Treatises*, 1661); also *Epistles* (1649), Ep. 6, par. 78.
[2] 177 Theosophic Questions, Ques. 6, pars. 2–4.
[3] Incarnation, Part I., ch. v., pars. 77, 82, 88.

"For the soul is out of the eternal magic fire, which must also have magic food, viz., *by or with the imagination.*"[1]

"The inward blood of the divine substance is also magical, for the Magia maketh it to be a substance; it is spiritual blood, and which *cannot* be touched or stirred by the outward substance, *but by the imagination only.*"[2]

"Hold fast to love in your imagination; nothing can take it from you but your own imagination. As soon as our imagination goes out of the love, darkness enters the imagination and the devil then has access."[3]

Having thus proved that Böhme—*not*, I believe, exceptionally, but with great vehemence—insisted on the unquestionable creative might of imagination, it will be interesting to see how far he explains the process by which "longing goeth into being or substance," and to compare his explanations with that of a contemporary expert in práctices which we can only describe as magical. When I say *explain* I only mean that he tells us on this subject all that can be told.

"The will is the *mysterium magnum*, the great mystery of all wonders and secrets, and yet it driveth forth itself, through the *imagination* of the desiring hunger, into substance. It is the original of nature; its desire maketh a representation; this *representation* is no other than the will of the desire, yet the desire maketh in the will such a substance as the will in itself is. The true *Magia* is no substance, but the desiring *spirit* of substance; it is an unsubstantial *matrix*, and revealeth or manifesteth itself in the substance. The *Magia* is a spirit, and the substance is its body. The *Magia* is the greatest hidden secret, for it is *above* Nature; it maketh Nature according to the form of its will." . . . "The Magia is the acting

[1] Incarnation, Part I., ch. iv., par. 46. [2] Small Six Points, par. 7.
[3] Gichtel's Letters.

THE POWER OF IMAGINATION 89

of the will-spirit; or the performance in the spirit of the will."[1]

Now let us turn to Mr Sinnett's *Occult World*, and see if the report of the old mystic is not both confirmed and elucidated by that of the modern adept there quoted:—

"The human brain is an exhaustless generator of the most refined quality of cosmic force out of the low, brute energy of nature; and the complete adept has made himself a centre from which irradiate potentialities that beget correlations upon correlations through Æons of time to come. This is the key to the mystery of his being able to project into and materialize in the visible world the forms that his imagination has constructed out of inert cosmic matter in the invisible world. The adept does not create anything new, but only utilizes and manipulates materials which Nature has in store around him, and material which, throughout eternities, has passed through all the forms. He has but to choose the one he wants, and recall it into objective existence."
. . . "Every thought of man upon being evolved passes into the inner world, and becomes an active entity by associating itself, coalescing we might term it, with an elemental—that is to say, with one of the semi-intelligent forces of the kingdoms. It survives as an active intelligence—a creature of the mind's begetting—for a longer or shorter period proportionate with the original intensity of the cerebral action which generated it."[2]

"Would not this sound to one of your learned biologists like a madman's dream?" asks the same informant from his Asiatic seclusion. If it would to *them*, there was but a few years ago in France a thinker and an adept—now withdrawn from our mortal life—to whom such ideas would have been far from strange: he who called himself Eliphaz Lévi. In the introduction to his *Histoire de*

[1] Small Six Points, pars. 66–70, 88.
[2] Occult World, 1881, pp. 129, 131; 4th ed., 1884, pp. 88, 89.

la Magie, he tells us, "qu'il existe un agent mixte, un agent naturel et divin, corporel et spirituel, un médiateur plastique universel, un réceptacle commun des vibrations du mouvement et des images de la forme, un fluide et une force qu'on pourrait appeler en quelque manière *l'imagination de la nature*" . . . " l'essence de la lumière vivante" (la lumière astrale) "c'est d'être configurative, c'est l'imagination universelle dont chacun de nous s'approprie une part plus ou moins grande, suivant son degré de sensibilité et de mémoire."[1]

The subject is fascinating, and I must not allow myself any additional quotations, lest I encroach upon valuable space or weary puzzled readers. But there are perplexities of abstract thought which seem to promise so much, and, even while still unsolved, to offer such grand vistas of enlarging knowledge, that one turns from them reluctantly.

On that especial effect of imagination referred to by C. C. M., "Trident" will find a very interesting and by no means scientific chapter in Lavater's *Essays on Physiognomy*, Lecture 8, ch. ii., "On the Influence of Imagination on the Formation of Man." Having spoken of the not uncommon appearance of a dying person in the presence of a far distant friend, he says: "The *how* of the question is inexplicable, I allow it; but the *facts* are evident, and to deny them would be offering an insult to all historic truth."

Again, farther on, "When the imagination is powerfully agitated by desire, love, or hatred, a single instant

---

[1] Pages 19 and 21.
Translation.—"There is a mixed agent, an agent both natural and divine, corporeal and spiritual, a universal plastic medium, a common receptacle of the vibrations of movement, and the images of form, a fluid and a force that one might call in a certain sense the *imagination of nature*" . . . "the essence of the living light is to be configurative, it is the universal imagination of which each of us appropriates a part, more or less great, according to one's sensibility and memory."

is sufficient for it to create or to annihilate, to enlarge or to contract, to form giants or dwarfs, to determine beauty or ugliness." . . . "This faculty of the soul, in virtue of which it thus produces creations and metamorphoses, has not hitherto been sufficiently investigated; but it sometimes manifests itself, nevertheless, in the most decided manner."[1]

[1] ["What is it that has acted thus at a distance on another's senses or imagination? Imagination; but the imagination through the focus of passion. How? It is inexplicable. But who can doubt such facts who does not mean to laugh at all historical facts? . . . Imagination, actuated by desire, love, or hatred, may, with more than lightning swiftness, kill or enliven, enlarge, diminish, or impregnate the organized fœtus with the germ of enlarging or diminishing wisdom or folly, death or life, which shall first be unfolded at a certain time, and under certain circumstances. This hitherto unexplored, but sometimes decisive and revealed, creative and changing power of the soul, may be in its essence identically the same with what is called faith working miracles, which latter may be developed and increased by external causes, wherever it exists, but cannot be communicated where it is not."—*Essays on Physiognomy*, 1800?; 1827; 1866, ch. xxviii.; 1878, pp. 378, 379.—ED.]

EXPERIENCES IN OPEN VISION [1]

WHILE thanking "Student" very heartily for his extremely interesting communication in *Light*, October 29th, I am eager to point out that he has strong corroborative testimony as to the existence of the creatures he has seen, and that seeing them must indicate extension of faculty rather than any mental delusion. My memory does not serve for bringing forward all the evidence I have met with, but that which I can now recall may interest both this seer and some of your readers. At page 310 of Vol. I. of Madame Blavatsky's *Isis Unveiled*, she says, speaking of elementary Spirits (I pass over her first division of these "*larvæ of beings who have lived*," which, from the characteristics given, I cannot fancy to be identical with "Student's" anomalous creatures): "The second class is composed of the invisible antitypes of the men *to be* born. No form can come into objective existence—from the highest to the lowest—before the abstract ideal of this form—or, as Aristotle would call it, the *privation* of this form—is called forth." ... "Forms pass; ideas that created them and the material which gave them objectiveness, remain. These models, as yet devoid of immortal spirits, are 'elementals,'—properly speaking, *psychic embryos*—which, when their time arrives, die out of the invisible world, and are born into this visible one as human infants, receiving *in transitu* that divine breath called spirit which com-

[1] *Light*, 1881, vol. i. p. 358.

pletes the perfect man. The third class are 'elementals' proper, which never evolve into human beings, but occupy, as it were, a specific step of the ladder of being, and, by comparison with the others, may properly be called nature-spirits, or cosmic agents of nature." . . . "This class is believed to possess but one of the three attributes of man. They have neither immortal spirits nor tangible bodies, only astral forms, which partake, in a distinguishing degree, of the element to which they belong. They are a combination of sublimated matter and a rudimental mind. Some are changeless, but still have no separate individuality, acting collectively, so to say; others, of certain elements and species, change form under a fixed law which Kabalists explain. The most solid of their bodies is ordinarily just immaterial enough to escape perception by our physical eyesight, but not so unsubstantial but that they can be perfectly recognized by the inner or clairvoyant vision." [1]

These are but selected samples of several pages bearing upon the subject and well worth "Student's" attention.

Mr T. Lake Harris, in his unpublished *Arcana of Christianity*, tells of vision which he terms "aromal sight." "Aromal sight comes first. This is a perception of the emanation forms of natural objects. It reveals within the imponderable realms of nature an unsuspected universe." [2] But as this, according to him, is the result of attaining a certain stage of "open respiration," *i.e.*, breathing from spiritual lungs as well as physical, it may not at all answer to the phenomena in question.

As usual, when puzzled in such matters, I refer to Böhme, and find in his mine of causes clear recognition of facts that exactly correspond to these appearances,

[1] Page 311.
[2] Arcana of Christianity : The Apocalypse, ch. ii., p. 130, par. 242.

and I quote from him at some length because his writings are not always easy to get at.

"The spirits of the external world are not all eternal, but some are only inchoative which take their original naturally in the spirit of the external world, and pass away through nature and only their *shadow* remains."[1]

"For every form in the Matrix" (created Heaven, as he elsewhere explains the term) "hath its visible creatures, and such as are invisible to human eyes; which creatures in part as to us are as it were but mere figured spirits; as the fire hath spirits and creatures that are invisible to our material eyes, and we cannot see them: there are also in the air invisible spirits which we see not; for the air being immaterial, so are also the spirits thereof. The water hath material creatures which are not visible to us, and because they are not of the fire nor air, they are of another quality, and are hidden as to the fiery and airy spirits, except they will manifest themselves."[2]

"Every element has its own inhabiting spirits, according to the quality of that element, which are a *shadow*, *image*, and resemblance of the Eternal, but yet having a true and perfect life out of the science [root] of nature from the outspoken or expressed formed word, out of the Great Mystery. Not out of the true divine life, but out of the natural: which spirits have their dominion in the fire, in the air, in the water, and in the earth, in courses, orders, and polities."[3]

The term, "Great Mystery," needs some clue for the understanding, which part of Böhme's preceding context may supply:—

"When God had created the earth and the firmament of the stars, and had appointed in the midst the planetary

[1] Mysterium Magnum, ch. viii., par. 13.
[2] Three Principles, ch. vii., par. 31.
[3] Election, ch. v., pars. 50, 51.

orb of the seven properties of nature, with their regent the sun, then the spirit of the world opened itself out of all the properties of the powers, out of the stars and elements."

"For every power hath an emanation according to the right of nature in the speaking Word: which Eternal Word hath here included and comprised itself in the Mysterium Magnum, into a *time, as into a figure* of the spiritual Mysterium Magnum, as a great clockwork, wherein a man understands the Spiritual word in a work or manufacture [formation]" . . . "The formed Word of God speaketh itself forth into a *spirit of the world as a soul of the creation.*" [1]

(Be it remembered here that according to Böhme's shewing and the belief of many a more modern philosopher, the *soul is the instrumental factor of the body by the agency of the Spirit it evolves*; so that, in a certain sense, calling *Spiritus mundi* soul of the creation is no loose application of words.)

Now my groping guess would be that what "Student" saw were emanations of the world soul. I avoid using the word *creation*, because by the *Fiat*—the Word of God—all existence, all nature and creature originated, but that *Spiritus mundi* was the executive agent of the Divine Creator for producing our *material* world, I am too old a disciple of Böhme's to doubt.

As regards the unhappy human Spirits seen in the woods, J. M. Hahn has a dark saying, which an English translation will, I fear, obscure still further, as to the mode by which the Spirit of the world affects disembodied people who have not, by regeneration, attained to the new creature of heavenly substance. I give the passage for as much or as little as it may be deemed worth. Hahn is discussing the interim state between death and final judgment.

[1] Election, ch. v., pars. 44-47.

"The Spirit of the great world, the Spirit of the world and Spirit superintendent, or whatever one may call it—I call it the Spirit of formation and conservation—is present in all nature and creature. If now imperfected souls depart from the visible world, and are seized in the process of making, supposing they have not given themselves up wholly to the Holy Spirit, to the Divine Maker, their Magia lays hold of that same Spirit, that same Maker" (Spirit of the world), "and it seizes upon them. Hence come the monsterings and transformings of souls after death, and it is in this Scheol and place of transformation, where souls are after death, that this Spirit is present and at work throughout the whole of nature. Mark well, I have not said, this Spirit is present in the whole realm of creation, but only in the whole of temporal nature."[1]

[1] "Der Geist majoris mundi, der spiritus mundi und spiritus rector, oder wie man es nennen mag (ich nenne es den Geist des Machens und Erhaltens), überall in aller zeitlichen Natur und Creatur gegenwärtig. Wenn demnach unvollendete Seelen aus der sichtbaren Welt scheiden und sind im Machen begriffen, haben sich aber dem heiligen Geist, dem göttlichen Macher nicht ganz ergeben, so ergreift ihre Magia denselben Macher, denselben Geist, und er ergreift sie. Daher kommt das Umgestalten und das Verwandeln der Seelen nach dem Tode, und ist also dieser Scheol und Verwandlungsort, wo derlei Seelen sind, da ja dieser Geist in der ganzen Natur gegenwärtig ist und wirket. Merket aber wohl, ich habe nicht gesagt: dieser Geist sei im ganzen Schöpfungsreich allgegenwärtig, sondern nur in der ganzen zeitlichen Natur."—*Die Lehre des württembergischen Theosophen, Johann Michael Hahn*, p. 509.

EMANATIONS OF THE WORLD-SOUL [1]

HAVING no *knowledge* on the subject it may be absurd to offer any opinion in answer to "Student's" question in to-day's impression of *Light* as to the emanations of the world-soul; yet since both ignorance and faith are notoriously apt to have a belief quite independent of knowledge, I assume none when stating what I believe, viz., that the world-soul creates—by formative imagination—multitudes of bodies, which I call astral because I know no better designation for them; that these are animated by the outbreathing of the derived Spirit of the world-soul; and that they emanate from this sub-creator as necessarily as those thoughts of the Abyssal God which create *Spiritual* beings.

I suppose these forms to have their being in the life and nature of the world-soul, as certainly as our ideas have in our nature and life. And I feel convinced that a firm and patient apprehension of such an entity as this vice-regent in our *material* world, would not only give us nearer approach to hitherto impenetrable mysteries, but would greatly relieve the strain put upon reason by the supposed requirements of faith. If no longer trying to believe that God designed the whole of the creaturely world *as we now see it*, we should be more ready to worship the "Father of Spirits" with adoring love.

One other good effect I anticipate from a return to the old belief in the world-soul—a revival of reverence

[1] Light, 1881, vol. i. p. 399.

for astrology as a science. Regarded by the vulgar as a means of fortune-telling, it is naturally scorned by savants and reprobated by the religious; but a silly abuse of partial knowledge proves nothing against this source of occult truths. When once we are used to think of the agency of a world-soul in our own planet, the inductions of astrology as to other orbs, and the interacting influence of *their* world-souls, cannot be far off.

COMMUNICATING SPIRITS

THEIR CLAIMS TO RECOGNITION [1]

"IN Genesis ii., ver. 7, we read that when man was formed, Jehovah God 'breathed into his nostrils the breath of lives.' It was not *life* but *lives*—natural and spiritual. When we remember that breath is both spiritual and natural, we understand these expressions. While the bodily lungs breathe the natural air, the spiritual lungs inhale the aura which is the outer sphere of God Himself. And in this sphere all Spirits must live, whether embodied in nature or freed from matter. We may cease to breathe the outer air, and our bodies die. But we still breathe the more vital air of the inner life, and hence we merely leave the body, and our life is essentially unchanged. The medium of communication, then, between Spirit and Spirit, whether the Spirits be in the flesh or out of the flesh, is this subtle spiritual air or æther, which is as substantial to the Spirit as our air is to the body. It has its own laws and properties, the counterparts of the laws and properties of the natural air." . . . "We can thus understand the intimate connection which must necessarily exist between men still in the flesh and Spirits now disembodied. Existing together with us in the same spiritual atmosphere, which is the soul of the natural atmosphere, they have everything in common with us

[1] Light, 1882, vol. ii. pp. 27, 39, 51, 63, 75.

except the matter in which, for the time, we are enshrined."[1]

When I chanced to light upon this passage, looking a few days ago into a number of the *Spiritual Magazine* for 1864, its simplicity and clearness of thought as to the condition of those who have undergone dissolution, roused in my mind a great wish to have the question of the identity of Spirits with the people they profess to be, reconsidered.

Often as it has been discussed by persons most able to give an opinion worth heeding, it seems to me that something more of proximate truth might be gained by approaching the subject from an opposite side; asking ourselves not, Can those who claim to be the Spirits of departed men and women be indeed what they say they are? but, What is the supposition that we accept as an alternative? What theory have we so adequate for disposing of the so-called dead as to justify our very strong disinclination to believe that they are close at hand, and under certain conditions able to manifest their presence? Reasons for feeling slow to credit the statements of communicating Spirits are too many and too notorious to be worth dwelling upon: the mendacity of a very large class of Spirits, and the apparent weak-mindedness of others, as well as the occasional merging of individual Spirits into a society of which all the members call themselves by one name, tend to baffle attempts at identification in nine cases out of ten. I speak from hearsay, having never wished to be present at any séance, but of secondhand evidence I have had an abundant supply, and for some years past my thoughts have been swaying to and fro on this theme under influence of opposing testimony.

Such authorities as Dr G. Wyld (in *some* of his

[1] No. 3 of "Libra's" papers on "Spiritual Spheres and Atmospheres" in *Spiritual Magazine* for 1864, vol. v. pp. 69, 71.

arguments), Colonel Olcott, and Madame Blavatsky, would have brought my indecision to rest on the negative side if ingenious theory and very powerful argument could overbalance a mass of evidence all pointing the other way; and my object now is to confront the question, "Where do we suppose the dead to be, and in what circumstances?" with such witness as I can collect from a few writers whom I believe qualified to answer—writers, I mean, not accredited as inspired in the religious world, and therefore only considered to be authorities by those, fully as devout, to my thinking, who look for inspired teaching, *i.e.*, influx of eternal truth, from mediums who have lived *since* the first century after Christ. And I subject myself to suspicion and ridicule for referring to them as authorities all the more willingly that, less than thirty years ago, I should have thought any one who did so surprisingly credulous and unorthodox. To the inspired writers of our Bible, I do of course primarily refer in my own mind, but so various is the interpretation put on those passages which bear on the subject, that I could not be at all sure of their meaning the same to other students as they do to myself. For instance, the usual deduction from the text, "In the place where the tree falleth, there it shall lie," *I* could not for one moment accept, in all its everlasting despair; nor could I share the doubt many say they feel as to whether the Spirit of Samuel was evoked by Saul, or only a delusive representation. It seems to me one of the most unquestionable cases of a "revenant."

It may, I suppose, be assumed that every thoughtful mind has outgrown the extremely childish notion of there being one place for good Spirits and one place for evil,—gradations of each unaccounted for, either sort being removed at death as if to a separate box; yet this, I am persuaded, lies at the root of much popular incredulity as to communication with the departed. And probably even more deeply rooted than this is the obscure scepticism as to what we call individuality of character surviving so great a catastrophe as death. Swedenborg, to whom I refer, fully convinced of the veracity of *his* transmundane report, gives a tolerably accurate account of current opinion among ourselves when he says: "Philosophers who wish to have the credit of possessing more discernment than the rest of mankind, speak of the spirit in terms which they do not themselves understand, for they dispute about them, contending that not a single expression is applicable to spirit, which is derived from what is material, organic, or has extension. Thus, by abstracting from spirit every conceivable quality, it vanishes from their ideas and becomes to them as nothing."[1]

And again: "In the case of one person not long after his decease, I perceived, what he indeed confessed, that although he had believed in the existence of the spirit, yet he had imagined that it could only live an indistinct life; for he had regarded the life as being in the body, so that on the life of the body being withdrawn, there would remain scarcely any perception of individuality." Another Spirit after death "acknowledged that in the life of the body he had been perplexed with this phantasy, that the spirit was a mere thinking principle, without organization or extension."[2]

And in his *Heaven and Hell* he tells us that Spirits and Angels indignantly "charged me to declare that they were not minds without form nor ethereal spectres, but that they are men in form, and that they see, hear, and feel as perfectly as men in the world."[3]

Throughout this most interesting book Swedenborg repeatedly asserts that the Spirits of the departed are

[1] Arcana Cœlestia, ch. iii., par. 196.   [2] Ibid., ch. iv., pars. 443, 444.
[3] Heaven and Hell, par. 77.

still in the human form, and from thence concludes that no future resurrection is to be looked for; yet incidentally mentions in another of his works, *Of the Last Judgment*, that the Lord alone arose as to his body, "as well as to his Spirit," ignoring, as it would appear, the Christian's belief that he was the forerunner of redeemed humanity, and that in the resurrection of *his* body we have a pledge of man's ultimate resurrection in the body.

Jacob Böhme makes us to understand very clearly that *no Spirit can be altogether bodiless*; the soul can be, not the Spirit proceeding from the soul, and by soul I mean here of course the first emanation of the human being, which, originating in eternal nature, cannot pass away with time—*not* what so many writers seem to mean by the words, the *animal soul*, a very other and more recent contingent of humanity. But it is evident alike from Scripture, and all we gather from the testimony and habits of unquiet Spirits, that whatever kind of body they still act and feel by, it is a very unsatisfactory tenement; that they long for the coarse old sheath, having failed to attain to the new life of a perfect and imperishable body. For surely it is not uncharitable to conclude that those who have won to a better organization are unlikely to cling to the worse, reproducing it as vividly as they can in the old haunts of past existence. As to the nature of those uneasy bodies, I attempt to allay my own curiosity by accepting what Böhme tells of the astral body, and modern writers of nerve-spirit. May not the nervous system be the body left to us when cumbrous flesh and bones are done with? If it be so, its defencelessness from external influences for want of the protective, pain-dulling, enclosure of a less sensitive organization, is terribly imaginable. And no one who sees or reads much of Spiritists' researches can fail to have observed the seeming weakness of individual Spirits as to maintaining their line of thought or of communication, uninterrupted by aggressive or impertinent intruders. An acute witness of many a séance says: "We have felt amazed, too, at the mercuriality of spirit nature passing from one feeling to another under the slightest provocation, with a rapidity inconceivable to us phlegmatic and skin-coated mortals."[1]

And this is one of the common experiences that shakes faith in Spirit identity. A friend or relation may be giving a solemn admonition, and all of a sudden some nonsense is abruptly jumbled in by another Spirit; and the thought is natural that no Spirit worth heeding could be subject to suppression by immeasurably inferior beings; but till we know more of that strange existence where the *inner state* alone forms circumstance and body, place and outlook, are we justified in that decision? A thought, a moment's apprehension of disturbance, may displace that attitude of feeling which makes *rapport* with the communicating medium possible. This passage from Swedenborg's treatise *Of the Last Judgment*, gives, I think, some notion as to the cause of this: "Man's spiritual things which pertain to his thought and will, inflow into his natural things which pertain to his sensations and actions, and in these they terminate and subsist; if man were not in possession of them, that is, if he were without these boundings and ultimates, his spiritual things, which pertain to the thoughts and affections of his Spirit, would dissolve away, like things unbounded, or like those which have no foundation."[2]

Agreeing with Jacob Böhme[3] as to the comparative

---

[1] I. F. Emmett's *Spirit Dialogues*, 1860, p. 42.

[2] An account of the Last Judgment, p. 8, par. 9.

[3] "No Spirit can subsist in its perfection without the body, for as soon as it departeth from the body, it loseth its government or dominion. For the body is the mother of the Spirit in which the Spirit is generated, and in which it receiveth its strength and power; it is and remaineth a Spirit when it is separated and departed from the body, but it loseth its rule, dominion or government."—*Aurora*, ch. xxvi., par. 52.

powerlessness of disembodied Spirits, Eliphaz Lévi observes: "L'âme sans corps serait partout, mais partout si peu, qu'elle ne pourrait agir nulle part."[1]

I have myself a quite unsupported idea that in losing the mortal body, we lose not only the restraining enclosure which gives reactive force, but the combined co-operation of a multitude of subordinate Spirits necessarily disbanded at dissolution. But be this as it may, it is certain that the little we gather from communicating Spirits, as to "fluidic life" after death, fully bears out the expression a Hebrew Prophet attributed to a speaker in Hades to a potentate newly arrived there: "*Art thou also become weak as we?*"[2]

Again, the tenor of the messages brought to the living from invisibles is often so pompously trivial that we think it impossible for our once sensible and keen-witted old friends to offer such truisms in weakly turgid phraseology. But let us imagine for a moment what we should find it possible to say if we could only speak with old friends on the other side of the world from time to time by telegram—letters impracticable, and the intervening history of both parties unknown to each other. I fancy the most seriously-minded, eager for edification, would be apt to say something of well-known warning, or some generality that had nothing novel but strengthened emphasis, while the less grave would content themselves with a merry common-place, and those who suffered more than they chose to avow, would exhibit that anxious averseness to giving any direct information which characterizes so many an answer at séances.

One of the most common solvents for the hope that relations and friends recognize and communicate with inquirers is based upon a well ascertained fact duly

---

[1] "The soul without the body would be everywhere, but everywhere so little that it could not act anywhere."—*Histoire de la Magie*, p. 111.
[2] Isaiah xiv. 10.

announced by Swedenborg: "When Spirits come to man they enter into all his memory and excite thence what best suits themselves."[1] . . . "This Spirits can do most dexterously, for when they come to any one they see in his memory every particular it contains."[2]

But, while admitting this, let us also attend to what the same seer has to say about man's own memory after death: "It is evident that man carries all his memory with him into the other world."[3] . . . "When man passes from one life into the other, or from one world into the other, it is like passing from one place to another; for he carries with him all things which he possessed in himself as a man, so that it cannot be said that death deprives man of anything truly constituent of himself, since death is only the separation of the terrestrial body. The natural memory also remains, for Spirits retain everything which they had heard, seen, read, learned and thought in the world, from earliest infancy to the conclusion of life; but, since the natural objects, which are in the memory, cannot be reproduced in the Spiritual world, they are quiescent, as is the case with man in this world when he does not think from them: nevertheless, they are reproduced when the Lord pleases."[4] . . . "Everything which man thinks, wills, and speaks, or which he has done, heard, or seen, is inscribed on his internal or spiritual memory: but whatever is received into the spiritual memory is never blotted out, for it is inscribed at the same time on the Spirit itself, and on the members of its body, and thus the Spirit is formed according to the thoughts and acts of the will."[5]

One need not pause to think *if* the love of parents for children, of wives and husbands, and brothers and sisters, or strong affection for any human being is inscribed on

---

[1] The Earths in the Universe, par. 13. [2] Ibid., par. 11.
[3] Heaven and Hell, par. 462. [4] Ibid., 461.
[5] Ibid., 463.

the spiritual memory: surely if anything is, that must be. But Swedenborg further explains: "The external or natural memory, so far as regards all ideas which are derived from materiality, time, space, and all other things which are proper to nature, does not serve the Spirit for the same use which it had served man in the world; because when man in the world thinks from the external sensual principle, and not at the same time from the internal, sensual, or intellectual principle, he thinks naturally and not spiritually, but in the other life he is a Spirit in a spiritual world, and therefore he does not think naturally but spiritually. To think spiritually is to think intellectually or rationally. Hence it is that the external or natural memory, as to all material ideas, is quiescent after death, and that nothing which man imbibed in the world by means of material things is any longer active, except what he has made rational by reflective application to use. The external memory is quiescent as to everything material, because material ideas cannot be reproduced in the spiritual world."[1]

Now when we find repeated well authenticated instances of unseen beings who claim relationship with present people, communicating facts to prove it which *could* not have been found either in the memory of the medium or the thoughts of any one present, is it not going out of our way in the search after truth to refuse such evidence and say, "Still it *cannot* be the one we have lost! it must be some deluding Spirit"? The delusion, as it appears to me, is effected by our own obstinate superstitious belief that death entirely changes character, and removes as much from presence as from sight.

The theory by which I reconcile the assertions of Swedenborg, quoted above, is this: for want of a plane suitable for the continuance of its earthly impressions,

[1] Heaven and Hell, par. 464.

the memory of a departed Spirit is quiescent, closed up in his interior life; but the peculiar nature of a medium, re-intromitting the Spirit's perceptions to an earthly plane, may restore consciousness of past conditions, and reopen the hidden store of material impressions by which alone he can communicate with beings still involved in matter; just as a forgotten dream is occasionally recovered by the chance mention in society of something which gives the clue to its effaced pictures.

This wonderful power of mediumistic men and women to serve as a channel for intercourse between the visible and invisible worlds has been simply and forcibly described by Swedenborg: "Neither Spirits nor Angels, by their own sight, can see anything that is in this world, for to them mundane or solar light is as thick as darkness. In like manner man by his bodily sight cannot see anything that is in the other life, for to it the light of heaven is as thick darkness. Still Spirits and Angels, when it pleases the Lord, can see things in the natural world through the eyes of men; but this is not granted by the Lord, except to those whom He permits to speak with Spirits and Angels, and to be together with them. It has sometimes happened that through me they have seen their friends, with whom they had been intimate when in the body, altogether present as before, at which they were amazed. Wives have seen in this manner their husbands and children, and have wished me to tell them they were present and beholding them, and to inform them of their state in the other life. This, however, I was prohibited from doing, for the reason that they would have called me insane, or have thought my information a delirium of the imagination. I was well aware that, although they admitted with their lips, they yet denied in their hearts the existence of Spirits, the resurrection of the dead, and their living among Spirits, and these being able to see and hear by means of man." [1]

There is another statement of Swedenborg's which I cannot but think qualifies his assertion as to the effaced memories of material life, or rather postpones its validity until some time after dissolution. He tells us that "man passes through three states after death before he enters either Heaven or Hell." . . . "The first state of man after death is like his state in the world because he is still in externals." . . . "He knows no other than that he is still in the world, except when he adverts to the circumstances which occur to him, and remembers that at his resurrection" (from death) "the angels told him he was then a Spirit." [2] The context, interesting as it is, exceeds the limits of quotation, and concludes thus: "The first state of man after death continues with some for days, with others for months, and with others for a year; but it seldom endures with any one more than a year, and the duration is determined in every case according to the agreement or disagreement of the interiors and exteriors." [3]

The testimony of Mr T. Lake Harris is somewhat similar. "When a man enters the world of Spirits, after the old fashion of physical decease, it is but leaving one room for another; his earthly memory remains as before, there being a continuity of recollection; but when he is finally fitted for the heavenly eternity and enters into the light of Heaven to behold its beauties and feast upon its joys, the old natural memory sinks into entire quiescence; there is no continuity of recollection in the conscious memory, from present eternity into the past earthly time." [4]

[1] On the Earths in the Universe, p. 135.
[2] Heaven and Hell, pars. 491, 493.
[3] Ibid., par. 498. See also Swedenborg's treatise, *Of the Last Judgment*, p. 17.
[4] The Holy City, p. 10, par. 10.

When we come to visible manifestations at a séance, however strong the likeness may be to deceased friends, there appears to me to be no ground whatever for supposing that in those simulacra the persons themselves are seen; and yet, to my thinking, there is quite as little ground for supposing that such individuals are not present. What is called materialization *may* be the work of Spirits skilled in deception, fond, as Böhme[1] assures us all evil Spirits are, of "jugglery," but I cannot see why it may not be quite as possible for friendly Spirits, wishing to convince us of their presence, thus to represent it. That it is an effect of formative imagination on their part (not ours), I have long supposed from the transiency of such appearances.[2] We know that we can conjure up a face or a scene in our chambers of imagery for a few minutes, but to retain it there is not possible; the incessant movements of thought efface such ideas as quickly as one wave overflows its precursors. So, I fancy, do the vivid imaginations of the dead, when with matter abstracted from the medium, or other people present, they depict their former similitudes. Something, too, may be affected, as Madame Blavatsky says (*Isis Unveiled*, vol. i. p. 70); by deputy elementary Spirits effecting the same purpose.[3]

---

[1] "Indeed, this is still to this day their greatest joy that they can transmute themselves, and bring themselves into many images; and thus achieve or make phansie."—*177 Theosophic Questions*, Ques. 10, par. 1.

[2] See par. 14 of ch. xiv., "Sur les Fluides" in *La Genèse* of Allan Kardec, for a very interesting and instructive account of this process.

[3] "Every so-called 'materialization'—when genuine—is either produced (*perhaps*) by the will of that Spirit whom the 'appearance' is claimed to be but can only personate at best; or by the elementary goblins themselves, which are generally too stupid to deserve the honour of being called devils. Upon rare occasions the Spirits are able to subdue and control these soulless beings, which are ever ready to assume pompous names, if left to themselves, in such a way that the mischievous 'spirit of the air,' shaped in the real image of the *human* Spirit, will be moved by the latter, like a marionette, and unable to either act or utter other

In the context Madame Blavatsky repudiates the idea of the disembodied manifesting themselves because "their *divine essence cannot materialize* what is matterless and purely Spiritual." To which I readily agree, but she assumes a great deal more than I can even suppose when she talks of the disembodied being *matterless and purely* "spiritual." I fear that is a condition few attain immediately after decease—if they do long afterwards.

Now, as it is probable that the element in which the disembodied live is as impossible for us to occupy consciously with our bodies as for birds to live under water, or fishes in the air, one can understand why anything like *tangible* nearness is out of the question —unless for a very short time; but the soon dissolving image that is touched may be as real an indication of nearness as the shadow on the surface of the water is to fish of the nearness of birds.

"Il est certain," says Eliphaz Lévi (*L'Abbé Constant*), with all the positiveness of a man who thinks he has seen to the end of a mystery, "que les images des morts apparaissent aux personnes magnétisées qui les évoquent; il est certain aussi qu'elles ne leur révèlent jamais rien des mystères de l'autre vie. On les revoit telles qu'elles peuvent être encore dans le souvenir de ceux qui les ont connues, telles que leurs reflets sans doute les ont laissées empreintes dans la lumière astrale."[1]

But in the very same book, at page 184, he gives a detailed form of evocation, which could only, one would

words than those imposed on him by the 'immortal soul.'"—*Isis Unveiled*, vol. i. p. 68.

[1] "It is certain that images of the dead appear to magnetized people who evoke them ; it is certain also that they never reveal to them anything of the mysteries of the other life. People see them again such as they still are in the memory of those who have known them ; such as doubtless their reflections have left them impressed in astral light."—*Dogme et Rituel de la Haute Magie*, Tome II., p. 182.

imagine, appeal to a living heart within reach, and he assures his readers that the "revenant" will ultimately be seen! Are impressions left on the astral light that surrounds us likely to be revived by tender tones and affectionate observances? Truly, it seems to me that this mode of disposing of the phenomena in question is far more in need of explanation than the world-wide theory it is intended to displace.

Colonel Olcott is even more ingenious. After giving a most wonderful account of personified phantoms following each other in sequence, at the house of the Eddys, at Chittenden, Vermont, United States, he asks "If it can be shewn that the soul of the living medium can, unconsciously to his physical self, ooze out and by its elastic and Protean nature take on the appearance of any deceased person whose image it sees in a visitor's memory; if all the phenomena can be produced at will by an educated psychologist; if in the ether of science the *Akâsa* of the Hindus, the *anima mundi* of the Theosophists, the astral light of the Cabalists, the images of all persons and events, and the vibrations of every sound are eternally preserved—as these occultists affirm and experimentally prove—if all this is true, then why is it necessary to call in the Spirits of the dead to explain what may be done by the living?"[1]

My answer would be, even while ready to accept his assertion of possible feats of magic, that the Spirits of the dead *must be somewhere*; that the belief of every people in all parts of the world, before learning smothers intuition, is that the Spirits of ancestors keep near their descendants;[2] and because the idea of

[1] Spiritualist Newspaper, Jan. 21, 1881, vol. xviii. p. 27.

[2] Swedenborg says the same: "The Spirits of every earth are near their own earth, because they are from its inhabitants; for every man after death becomes a Spirit; and because they are of a similar genius, and can be with the inhabitants, and be serviceable to them."—*The Earths in the Universe*, par. 47.

a medium producing in one evening seventeen perfect likenesses of totally unknown men and women—from his physical *matter* delineating, "unconsciously to his physical self," copies of what he found in the memory of the spectators—appears far more difficult to believe than that seventeen Spirits availed themselves of William Eddy's strong mediumistic powers to recall their likeness, and prove their nearness to those they still loved.

"The will of the Spirit of the soul," says Böhme, "that the soul carrieth with it when the soul and body part."[1] Now, what can we be more certain of than that the will of most disembodied Spirits is to speak again with those most dear to them, or most familiar as companions? And a strong medium being, as Swedenborg has explained, one through whom departed Spirits can see back into this mortal life, is it not highly probable that many should take advantage of that opening—not very likely the *most* blessed Spirits, but numbers of the thousands who are hurried out of the body with all their earthly desires strong and eager, and no new body yet, even in the embryonic form?[2]

What theory have those to offer who disbelieve this, as to what follows behind the veil when the dreadful silence of death suddenly stills all the feverish vivacity of *this* life? (Of course I except such as are so amazingly credulous as to suppose *this* life the limit of human existence.) What has become of the love that day and night merged all self-interest in devotion to the happi-

---

[1] Threefold Life, ch. xii., par. 1.

[2] I mean here the true substantial body that results from regeneration, not the *bodily shape* assumed by Spirits,—well distinguished by Böhme in this passage, speaking of the soul: "Its own substance is altogether crude without a body, and yet it hath the *form of the body in its own spiritual form*."—*Three Principles,* ch. iv., par. 18.

ness of another; of ambition that pursued its objects, noble or ignoble, with unresting energy; of intelligence ardently bent on applying some discovery of truth to the good of the human race?

To think that the severing of flesh and bones and blood from the focus of forces like these alters their direction, is surely to stultify the mind with a superstition quite as gross as any that leads to terror from the proximity of disembodied Spirits. I have under my hand many score of detailed communications from Spirits inter-audited—if one may coin a word for the occasion,—and the concurrence of their testimony is overwhelming as to the eagerness with which they make themselves known, the evidently characteristic peculiarities of habit and thought they betray, and the life-like simplicity of their revelations :—revelations of what had happened to them before death, or in dying, never beyond the vaguest generalities as to present state. Eliphaz Lévi is quite justified in saying that revelations as to the unseen world are not gained by evocation of Spirits: and this I think is explained by what has already been cited from Swedenborg regarding memory. When that which in the Spirit-world is quiescent rouses again, the conditions of consciousness are probably as different as those of a person in trance and out of it. The secrets of death are kept from age to age, and by these very people who have most importunately clamoured at the threshold of the hidden world for some faintest intimation of what befell those who went before. One by one all pass beyond the ken, and the mystery remains; no doubt because its key is *incommunicable*.

Again Eliphaz Lévi says: "Les âmes des morts ne sont donc pas autour de nous, comme le supposent les tourneurs de tables. Ceux que nous aimons peuvent nous voir encore et nous apparaître, mais seulement par mirage, et par reflet dans le miroir commun qui est la lumière."[1]

Leaving on one side for the moment the question of *where* they are, I accept this conclusion of his only so far that, unless our spirits are in harmony with theirs we probably do not fall within range of their vision. For instance, if in loving peace themselves, they cannot, I suppose, perceive us in our angry, troubled moods (though they may miss our unison with their dominant feeling); and this on the same grounds that Böhme declares evil Spirits to be unable to see ours when they are quieted by love and humility, because, as a rule, Spirits have no perceptions beyond their own "principle" or internal world. But when we approach the question of *where they are* who have vanished from our life, dogmatism is peculiarly impertinent. Few writers have indulged in it with more impressive weight than William Law, on precisely this point—the fate of the dead; and I must confess that his revered teacher Böhme occasionally supports the hypothesis I find so untenable, that at the death of the body no light of our sun can remain to the Spirit—that unless the light of the eternal life is kindled by regeneration *before* decease, the Spirit finds itself in darkness.

"The light and spirit of this world," Law says, in his admirable *Appeal to All that Doubt*, "can no more be the light and spirit of immortal souls than grass and hay can be the food of angels, but are as different from the light and spirit of Heaven as an angel is different from a beast of the field. When, therefore, the soul of a man departs from his body, and is internally cut off from all temporal light and spirit, what is it that can

---

[1] "The souls of the dead are not then about us, as the table-turners suppose. Those we love can see us still and appear to us, but only by mirage, and by reflection in the common mirror which is light."—*Histoire de la Haute Magie*, p. 113.

keep such a soul from falling into *eternal* darkness, unless it has in itself that light and spirit which are of the same nature with the light and spirit of eternity?"[1]

By pressing home the horror of this sole alternative, Law really drives a thoughtful reader to seek some escape from his conclusions. It is found in the pages of his "blessed, inspired Böhme," though, as I have said, he now and then speaks of this alternative with as little qualification; for example, in his *Three Principles*.

"The soul hath no light in itself of its own, it must borrow its light from the sun; which indeed springeth up along with it in its birth; but that is corruptible, and the worm of the soul is not so; *as it is seen that when a man dieth it*" (the light) "*goeth out, and if then the divine light be not again generated in the centre, then the soul remaineth in eternal darkness.*"[2] But in another of his books he says: "All things of this world have a *twofold body*, viz., an elemental from the fire, air, water, and earth; and a spiritual body from the astrum; and likewise a twofold spirit, viz., one astral, the other elemental. Man only among all the earthly creatures hath a *threefold* body and spirit." ... "This [third] body is from the *water of the holy element* which died in Adam, that is, disappeared as to his life, when the divine power departed from him, and would not dwell in the awaked vanity. Which holy body must be regenerated if his spirit will see God, otherwise he cannot see him,"[3] adding a few lines farther on: "The *sidereal* body is the highest excepting the *divine* in man; the elemental body is only its servant or dwelling-house."[4] Now what reason is there to conclude that this "sidereal body" is

---

[1] An Appeal to All that Doubt, 1768, ch. i., p. 101. Reprint, 1893, vol. vi. p. 103.
[2] Three Principles, ch. xiv., par. 11.
[3] Mysterium Magnum, ch. xi., pars. 19-21.
[4] Ibid., par. 23.

necessarily shut off from the light of the sun by losing its external husklike organization? The very name given to it by Böhme would suggest that in our planetary system it was in its proper home; and in our total ignorance to speak as if this inner body died at the crisis we call death, for the sake of impressing the conscience, is as inexpedient for what is called "edification" as in the abstract it is rash and unwise, and to my thinking most dishonouring to the Creator and the Redeemer of man; for if William Law's conclusion be accepted, that total, hopeless darkness is inevitable after dissolution for the unregenerate, then Christ has *not* been victor over sin and death. For as we all know, true regeneration in this life is not the rule; it is most obviously and undeniably the exception.

Surely nothing more discredits religious argument than rhetoric, and to try and enhance the value of present blessings by ignoring the possibility of their continuance for a period after death, is perilous to even the faith it is employed to support. Especially must it be so when, as of late years, a series of destructive catastrophes have swept hundreds of our fellow creatures at every age out of this life without an instant of premonitory warning. To surviving mourners it must be almost *impossible* to believe that to all of these the *immediate* alternative was the light of the heavenly world or the darkness of a state which has neither the sunlight of our own, nor that Light by which every created sun is kindled.

Now I submit that an astral body is presumably open to astral light, and that so long as this lasts the light of sun, moon, and stars would reach it. And believing this, I in no wise make light of the loss of eternal light, but I am spared the horrible and amazing fancy that the thousands who hourly slip away from the fragile outer body, totally blind to that supernal light, are at once plunged into irremediable darkness.

Still, the alternative is but *put off;* and is so terrible, that once duly to apprehend all it means of possible damnation (no torments inflicted by an external Deity, but the infinite woe of a godless immortal) would be to give priceless value to every hour of present life. Here we can still break the evil will; we have instrumental means: we can coerce and restrain the body, so often hostile to the Spirit; but when nothing more external to us than our own thoughts and feelings remain, and these all averted by habit from the only sources of undying joy, how shall we recover lost ground? "For a Spirit without a body hath not that might or power as that Spirit which is in the body."[1]

So ready are our contemporary thinkers to look upon all conditions of time and space as the result of spiritual obscuration, that they are apt to insist on the almost certainty of these being at an end for purified Spirits. They produce strong reasons for this, but it is not yet evident to me why all that we call phenomenal impressions should end with our elevation to a state of real being. I cannot understand why the transiency of time and evanescent illusions of space should not remain in a purer state, still surrounding spiritual senses; fully known to be phenomenal, yet leaving to these *seemings* that cannot deceive: just as our knowledge of the laws of perspective underlies enjoyment of beautiful landscape. We do not think the near shrub larger than the distant tree, but in our present fallen state we do feel our little arena of action more important than the fate of the next county, and a few years of time more momentous than eternity.

It is quite clear from all Swedenborg's reportings that the circumstances of Spirits are self-evolved, are the outcome of their own internal state; and I feel almost over-bold to admit that I cannot believe this to be the

[1] Forty Questions (1665), Ques. 21, par. 16.

normal condition of *perfected* Spirits. To me it seems just what would necessarily characterize an intermediate state, when one stage of existence in an ultimated body was ended, and the Spirit had to await the general resurrection till the body of the human race, being made ready for its glorification, each least member of that body will enter upon its individual as well as its universal perfectness. I was, therefore, very much pleased when I met with this declaration of Mr T. L. Harris:—

"There is a region positive and primitive to the sun; arch-nature in superiors and antecedents, which serves as the sun of the sun. The solar elements thence derive vitality and potency. Our solar globe forms into an inconceivably magnificent world, of which the visible orb is the centre, co-extensive with the system. The inhabitants of this luminous expanse, in one degree, are the ripened and translated men and women of the peopled planets. Objectively they are in times and spaces, but subjectively out of space and time. In this latter they were visible, by their interiors, to the wise and virtuous Swedenborg, who saw them by the opening of his interiors, and was with them by the *rapports* of interiors with interiors. Still, having no arch-natural basis in his earthly constitution, he was unable to divine or cognize the luminous world; unable, in a phrase, *to realize Heaven by its objectivity.*"[1]

Of this objectivity Böhme spoke with equal emphasis more than two centuries ago:—

"The true Heaven is everywhere, even in that very place where thou standest and goest." . . . "But that there is assuredly a pure glorious Heaven in all the three births or genitures aloft above the deep of this world, in which God's Being together with that of the holy angels riseth or springeth up, very purely, brightly, beauteously

[1] The Concept of the Word (the 5th Part of *The Golden Child*, p. 9, Sec. 92, pars. 16–18). The italics are my own.

and joyfully, is undeniable, and he is not born of God that denieth it."[1]

And it is to be observed also when he writes of the unhappy Spirits "who have lost their first image," that he refers to a *place* as an advantage:—

"Though, indeed, the place of this world was given to Lucifer for a kingdom, for he was created therein, yet he is now *thrust out from place and space*, and dwelleth in the abyss where eternally he can reach no place of the angelical kingdom."[2]

I can myself hardly doubt there being distinct localities for different orders of Spirits when Divine harmony is re-established in the vast universe; but, as yet, until the final separation, I suppose the place of human Spirits, good and bad, to be conterminous with our earth and its surrounding atmosphere. That we can only see human beings in flesh and blood proves nothing more than that our organs of vision are adapted for the world we live in, and for no other. The prism shews us what colours are in space where we only see diffused light; and science, by spectrum analysis, has detected pencils of darkness, which, in the midst of brilliant colour, the common prism could not reveal. As near and as imperceptible are the inhabitants of light and of darkness to the world of mixed good and evil through which we fight our way.

Böhme's works are comparatively rare, so that references to them would not answer my purpose; I must therefore be excused for quoting largely from them. To my readers his dicta will not seem so conclusive as they do to my own mind, but they will probably interest; and being carefully sifted from much confusing context, are for the general reader better read in selection than in the blinding obscurity of a first approach to his books.

---

[1] Aurora, ch. xix., pars. 26, 27.
[2] Great Six Points, Point VI., ch. ix., par. 58.

"The whole deep between the stars and earth is inhabited, and not void and empty. Each dominion hath its own principle, which seems somewhat ridiculous to us men, because we see them not with our eyes, not considering that our eyes are not of their essence and property; so that we are neither able to see nor to perceive them; for we live not in their principle."[1]

"The whole deep between the constellations, so far as the Word gave itself in unto the creation, is nothing but a *life* and stirring of Spirits."[2]

"The paradise which the souls of the holy children of God go into (when the body deceaseth), is in the very place where the body deceaseth; it is also in the earth, it is in all the four elements; not divided but *entirely* everywhere."[3]

"Paradise hath another principle, for it is the Divine and angelical joy, yet not without the place of this world. Indeed it is without the virtue and source of it, neither can the spirit of this world comprehend it, much less a creature."[4]

"Reason, which is gone forth with Adam out of paradise, asketh, Where is paradise to be had or found? Is it far off or near? or, when the souls go into paradise, whither do they go? Is it in this world, or without the place of this world, above the stars? Where is it that God dwelleth with the angels? And where is that desirable native country where there is no more death? Being there is no sun nor stars in it, therefore it cannot be in this world, or else it would have been found long ago. Beloved Reason: one cannot lend the key to another to unlock this withal: and if any one have a key, he cannot open it to another." . . . "There is noth-

---

[1] Mysterium Magnum, ch. viii., par. 11.
[2] Threefold Life, ch. x., par. 20.
[3] Ibid., ch. v., par. 125.
[4] Three Principles, ch. ix., par. 4.

ing that is nearer you than heaven, paradise, and hell; unto which of them you are inclined, and to which of them you tend, to that in this lifetime you are most near: you are between both: and there is a birth between each of them; you stand in this world between both the gates, and you have both the births in you."[1]

"As little as God is alterable, so little also is paradise alterable; for it is a part of the Deity: when the outward dominion shall pass away, then will the place where this world now standeth be mere paradise, for there will be an earth of heavenly substantiality, which we may be able to dwell in through and through."[2]

"We shall be in paradise again and eternally rejoice therein and enjoy the fair bright springing of all manner of flowers and variety of forms, as also of trees and herbs and all sorts of fruits; but not so earthly, thick, or gross and palpable."[3]

"As we have all sorts of fruits in this world which we feed on in an earthly manner, so also there are all manner of fruits in paradise."[4]

All this will sound very "unspiritual" to many, but Böhme speaks of the state when man, the image of the Triune God, is perfected in all three principles. *Now the third is the world of substance, or ultimates.* Of Spirits not yet regenerated he reports a very different and varying state.

"Now seeing the departure of souls is various, so also is their condition after their departure various, so that many of the souls departed are indeed for a long time in purgatory, if the soul had been defiled with gross sins, and hath not rightly stepped into the true earnest regeneration, and yet do hang a little to it."[5]

---

[1] Three Principles, ch. ix., pars. 25-27.
[2] Forty Questions (1665), Ques. 40, par. 1.
[3] Ibid., Ques. 32, par. 2.   [4] Ibid., Ques. 21, pars. 7, 8.
[5] Three Principles, ch. xix., par. 38.

"It is with the soul which thus hangeth by a thread, and yet at the last end entereth into sorrow, and so layeth hold on the kingdom of heaven by a thread, where doubting and believing is mixed; it is with such a soul in this manner, that a hearty prayer and wish cometh to them, which, with total earnestness, presseth to the poor captive soul into its source, quality or pain. For that soul is not in hell, also not in heaven, but in the gate in the midst, in the source or quality of the principle where fire and light part, and is detained by its *Turba*, which continually seeketh the fire, and then that comprehended little twig or *branch*, viz., the weak faith, sinketh down in itself, and presseth after God's mercifulness, and giveth itself patiently into the death of the sinking down, out of the anguish, and that sinketh down out of the source, quality or pain into the meekness of heaven. And though many a soul be detained a competent [tedious] time, yet can the anger not devour that little faith, but must at last let it go."[1]

"There is little remedy unless the will-spirit have in the time of the outward life turned itself about into God's love, and reached or attained *that* as a sparkle in the inward centre, and then *somewhat* may be done. But in what source, quality, or pain and irksome tediousness that is done, the sparkle of love experimenteth well enough, which there is to break the dark, fierce, wrathful death; it is purgatory, or purging fire enough to it; in what kind of enmity the life standeth in terror and anguish, till it can in the sparkle sink down to rest in the liberty of God, he experimenteth very well who so *nakedly* with small light departeth from this world; which the present too wise world holdeth for a jesting matter."[2]

And not without some excuse, because of the mistaken

---

[1] Forty Questions (1665), Ques. 24, pars. 7-9.
[2] Great Six Points, Point III., ch. iv., pars. 29, 30.

notions that generally attach to the idea of purgatory,—as of a state in which God afflicts from without, and not, as it is in truth, the state in which the soul *discovers* and undergoes the torments its own unharmonized nature contains. Let Böhme try and explain some of these:—

"The soul's Spirit hath no woe done to it when the body departeth, but woe is done to the fire-life; for the *matter* of the *fire* which hath generated the fire, that breaketh away, but only in the substance. The figure remaineth standing in the will, for the will cannot break, and the soul must continue in the will and taketh the *figure* for matter, and burneth in the will."[1]

"For what the soul doth here, in this life-time, into which it involveth itself, and taketh it into its will, that it taketh with it in its will, and after the ending of the body cannot be freed from it; for afterwards it hath nothing else but *that*, and when it goeth into that and kindleth it and seeketh with diligence, that is but an unfolding of the same thing; and the poor soul must *content itself with that*: only in the time of the body it can break off that thing which it hath wrapped up in its will."[2]

How many of what we call ghost stories afford instances of precisely this state of arrested ideas, of an anxiety that might have been transient lasting through centuries! And if such a state is but faintly imagined, we shall be ready enough, I think, to accept another saying of Böhme's: "Every one hath his own hell; there is nothing else that layeth hold of it [the soul], but its own venom, or poison."[3]

Even a few days of solitary helplessness in undistracted pain would give ample exposition of that text.

[1] Forty Questions (1665), Ques. 18, pars. 9, 10.
[2] Threefold Life, ch. xii., par. 27.
[3] Forty Questions (1665), Ques. 18, par. 25.

And, again, what is the terrible fire which is to be the purging element in every soul of man? Fully to explain Böhme's teaching on this point would be impossible here; but a few more lines of his will *indicate* its drift. "At the end God will awaken the fire in the centre, which is the eternal fire, and will purge this floor; understand, it is the soul's fire," [1]—that fire which, immediately and originally derived from Deity, is the immortal part of man; which, arrested in its due development of light, and the heavenly body with which light clothes itself, for ever,—with unappeaseable want of light and love and Divine substance,—consumes every attempted substitute, and is in itself unquenchable. (Be it remembered, while using this word, that even in the souls of the blessed it is not and never can be *extinguished*, but in them the light swallows up the dark and fiery root of immortal being, and is itself everlasting.)

Now as to the state of those who on separating from the fleshly body have not even a "thread of faith," or "sparkle of love" of God, one could cite from the same seer many a statement, but these are so positive in detail that they may be justly suspected of taking colour from the usual mental furniture of the seventeenth century, largely borrowed from mediæval legends. The following passage appears free from that objection, and shall conclude my quotations from him on this theme:—

"Outward reason supposeth that hell is far off from us; but it is near us, every one carrieth it in himself, unless he kill the hellish poison with God's power, and sprout from thence as a new twig or branch, which the hellish source or quality cannot comprehend or touch." ... "Every man carrieth in this world heaven and hell in himself, which property soever he awakeneth, that burneth in him, and of that fire the soul is capable: and

[1] Threefold Life, ch. xi., par. 28.

so when the body dieth and departeth, the soul need not go any whither, but it will be cast home to the hellish dominion; whatsoever property it is of, those very devils which are of those properties wait upon it, and take it into their dominion, even till the judgment of God. Though indeed they are bound to no place, yet they belong to the same dominion, and that very source or quality they have everywhere."[1]

In fact the law of like to like acts in the world of Spirits without exception, and by an awful necessity evil tendencies, as well as good, intensify and strengthen themselves by consequent sympathy.

The whole of the twenty-sixth of Böhme's *Forty Questions* in which he tries to answer his friend as to "whether the souls of the deceased take care about men, their children, friends and goods, and know, see, like, or dislike their purposes and undertakings," is peculiarly pertinent to the subject before us, but being much too long to quote, will be referred to, I hope, by any one who has access to the book.[2]

It is evident that the habit of regarding the crisis of dissolution as a terminous to probation—a habit which religious teachers naturally insist upon—accustoms us to think of any condition not blessed or not full of torment as simply purgatorial, as solely occupied by reformatory suffering: yet the simile of this life being the time of seed-sowing so often used by such teachers, might, I think, suggest a less *immediate* result of either good or bad conduct; for even in a plant like wheat the fulness of the ear is at some months' remove from the time of sowing, and analogy would justify us in letting these periods in the existence of short-lived plants represent centuries, at least, in that of an immortal being.

---

[1] Great Six Points, Point VI., ch. ix., pars. 52, 55, 56.

[2] For a letter on this subject by C. C. Massey, see *Light*, vol. ii. p. 67 [ED.].

If such deferred expectation of final reaping acts as a soporific to any conscience, it is from a total misconception of what that delay involves. Let such an one consider for a moment the common facts of a germ, a sprout, a plant in leaf, flower, and fructification,—the properties of its life strengthening in each progression of growth. The germ may be soon trodden down, the tender blade easily eradicated, but the rooted plant must be removed by hard effort if it is to be done at all. And, meanwhile, supposing these properties to be productive of poison, as their evil similitudes in spiritual life are of anguish, that poison, that anguish must be intensifying with every stage of growth. The only hope is for those who do *not* believe "that eternal issues are irrevocably decided in a brief flash of existence,"[1] that after dissolution Divine love may prevail on the soul of man to have mercy on itself, and submit to the extermination of all the poison plants which have been sown on this side of death.

Believers in Reincarnation cherish this hope, of course, and have extremely powerful arguments for its support; but my quarrel with them is that they seem to think the human body, as we now wear it, the *only* possible vehicle that *ascendant* Spirits could exist in for repeated terms of probation. That many of them, little advanced by this life's experience, should so long for the old corporeal husk as to seek and gain readmission to a former phase of being, appears quite possible, but with so many worlds crowded in sight does it not argue some poverty of imagination to conclude that in this alone our spiritual schooling can go on?

"Man," said J. Pierrepont Greaves, "has seven stages of existence here or elsewhere; and in the eighth he will be perfected."[2] Why suppose all these seven to be in one corner of the universe?

[1] Links and Clues, by Vita, p. 153.   [2] Theosophic Revelations, p. 170.

Again, St Martin says: "Ce n'est qu'à la mort corporelle de l'homme que commencent les quarante-deux campements des Israélites; sa vie terrestre se passe presque entière dans la terre d'Egypte."[1]

Now supposing this comparison of his to be true to future fact, the trials of the Israelites out of Egypt were of an entirely different kind from what they endured before they were set free from its bondage; and probationary as we are told those trials were, they came to them at intervals, and in the midst of much that we must believe to have been an interesting if not an agreeable life.

The anonymous writer of *Le Mystère de la Croix* (published in 1732, second edition 1786, and by Williams and Norgate 1860), while sparing us no severity of supposed truth as to the crosses after death, takes a view of the state of the unregenerate dead far more rational to my thinking than those commonly entertained. After saying:—

"Il y a aussi d'autres temps après cette vie, d'autres siècles et éternitéz, dont les unes succèdent aux autres: car on n'a pas tout fait dans cette vie." . . . "Quoique après la mort, elle n'aye point tant de liberté, ni de pouvoir que dans cette vie, elle trouve néanmoins, après la dépouille de son corps, bien plus à combattre qu'ici."
. . . "Elle y fait la rencontre de tant et tant d'esprits, dont elle doit subir le jugement, et goûter les essences et propriétéz, bien souvent contraires aux siennes, si elle n'y est point passée pendant cette vie, de sorte qu'un esprit y combat contre l'autre, l'un juge et goûte l'autre, l'un condamne et afflige l'autre, jusqu'à ce que l'âme en soit victorieuse." He adds: "*Or elle y trouve aussi des alternatives de réveillement, d'acquiescence, de paix, de tran-*

---

[1] L'Homme de Désir, 1790, p. 298, par. 208. "Man only begins the forty-two encampments of the Israelites at the death of his body. His earthly life is passed almost entirely in the land of Egypt."

quillité, pour reprendre haleine et pour se préparer à de nouveaux combats." [1] I am loth to appear presumptuous, but in truth I cannot see why so long as the Spirit *is* able to fence itself with any suitable body after death its conditions need be intolerably severe. The doubt with me hangs upon just that point, What sort of body has the sensitive Spirit to make shift with when the new creature of spiritual regeneration is not formed? Böhme's idea of the astral body [2] outlasting the flesh and blood body by years or ages, according to the constellations dominating the time of birth, is shared by J. M. Hahn, whose opinions I quote, not as an authority but as those of one of the few writers known to me who venture to enlarge on the obscure topic of post-mortem prospects.

"There are souls," he quaintly says, "who are not so bad that they go into Gehenna or hell fire immediately

---

[1] "There are also other times after this life, other ages and eternities which succeed each other; for one has not done all in this life. . . . Though after death the soul has not so much liberty or power as it has in this life, it nevertheless finds much more to combat than it does here. . . . It encounters many Spirits, to whose judgment it is subjected, whose essences and properties it must test (often repugnant to its own) if it has not during life passed through them, so that one spirit makes war upon another, one judges and tests another, one condemns and afflicts another until the soul gains the victory." . . . "Now it finds also alternations of refreshment, of acquiescence, of peace, of tranquillity in which to take breath and prepare for new combats." [Not very unlike our present life this!] —*Mystère de la Croix*, 1860, pp. 160, 162, 163.

[2] I suspect even Böhme of confusing the astral Spirit and astral body in the following passage. He is speaking of unquiet Spirits: "Therefore many of them come again with the *starry Spirit*, and walk about in houses and other places, and appear in human shape and form, and desire this and that, and often take care about their wills and testaments" . . . "and if their earthly business and employment stick in them and cleave to them still, then, indeed, they take care about their children and friends, and this continueth so long, till they sink down into their rest, so that their starry Spirit be *consumed*; then all is gone as to all care and perplexity, and they have no more feeling knowledge thereof."—*Forty Questions* (1665), Ques. 26, pars. 12, 13.

after death, and, in my opinion, they never would go if they let themselves be reformed." ... "Where do those souls go before the judgment-day? and where are their judicial prisons and purgatories? They are partly in the earth, partly in the planets belonging to our solar system, partly in the upper region of the air. We read clearly that it is appointed to man once to die, and after that to undergo his own particular judgment. But not all, oh, no! the smallest number attain the appointed limits of life. For one shortens his temporal life in one fashion, one in another. Now those who have shortened their life have not yet released themselves from the ties of the starry region, and are therefore bound with their astral body and life to the astral band, and therefore are not judged immediately after death, because they have not reached the destined goal. They are therefore, as I suppose, in the atmosphere, or else become attracted by the properties and powers of nature in the planets, so that they there find their place for purification."[1]

Désbarrolles attributes a very different fate to those who resort to the planets under happier conditions of

[1] "Es gibt Seelen, die nicht so böse sind, dass sie gleich nach ihrem Tode in die Gehenna oder Feuerhölle fahren, und meines Erachtens auch nie darein fahren sollten, wenn sie sich bessern liessen." ... "Wo kommen also diese Seelen vor dem Gerichtstag hin? und wo sind die Gerichtskerker und Reinigungsörter? Sie sind theils auch in der Erde, theils in den zu unserem Sonnensystem gehörigen Planeten, theils in der oberen Luftregion. Dass dem Menschen gesetzt ist, Einmal zu sterben, hernach aber sein Particulargericht, lesen wir ja deutlich. Aber nicht Alle, O nein! der wenigste Theil erreicht sein bestimmtes Lebensziel. Denn der Eine verkürzt sich sein zeitliches Leben auf diese, der Andere aber ebenfalls, auf andere Weise. Solche nun, die ihre Leben abkürzen, haben sich noch nicht losgerissen vom Bande der Sternregion, sind also mit ihrem astralischen Leibe und Leben an das astralische Band gebunden und werden also nicht gleich gerichtet werden nach dem Tode, weil sie das gesetzte Ziel nicht erreicht haben; sind also entweder, so vermuthe ich, in der Luftregion, oder werden von den Naturkräften und Eigenschaften der Planeten angezogen, dass sie allda ihre Reinigungsörter finden."—*Die Lehre des württembergischen Theosophen Johann Michael Hahn*, p. 504.

spirit. Speaking of a soul that has been all that is humane, just, and loving, he says:—
"Then on the day of death it leaves its earthly envelopment, and flies away following the attraction of its star, and goes to live again in another universe where it makes for itself a new vestment analogous to the progress of its beauty; leaving on the one hand on the earth the material corpse seemingly inert, but which by its decomposition already conduces to new creations, and on the other the sidereal corpse, which rises like a luminous mantle to carry into the sidereal light, where all things diffuse themselves, the image, the reflection, the phantom of the body on the earth.[1] If, on the contrary, the mind has allowed itself to be subjugated by the gross passions of the body, if it has permitted falsehood, impure pleasures, injustice, all that is low, all that is evil, then on the day of death, the astral corpse made strong by the condescensions of the spirit, retains it prisoner as it did during life, and surrenders it to the Sidereal System, which drags it into the whirlpools of astral light.'[2]

Such a generality as that would fall powerless on my inner ear had not Hahn supplied me with some little

[1] Readers of Mr T. Lake Harris's unpublished writings will find here agreement with his account of the *Geist* of man as distinguished from his spiritual individuality.

[2] "Alors au jour de la mort elle quitte l'enveloppe terrestre, s'envole en suivant l'attraction de son étoile, et va revivre dans un autre univers, où elle se fait un nouveau vêtement analogue au progrès de sa beauté, en laissant d'une part, sur terre, le cadavre matériel inerte en apparence, mais qui déjà travaille par sa décomposition même à concourir à des créations nouvelles, et de l'autre le cadavre sidéral qui s'élève comme un manteau lumineux, pour aller porter dans la lumière astrale, où tout s'imprègne, l'image, le reflet, le fantôme du corps sur la terre. Si, au contraire, le mens s'est laissé subjuguer par les passions grossières du corps, s'il a permis le mensonge, les voluptés crapuleuses, l'injustice, tout ce qui est bas, tout ce qui est mal, alors au jour de la mort le cadavre astral, rendu fort par les condescendences de l'esprit, le retient prisonnier comme pendant sa vie et le livre au corps sidéral qui l'entraine dans les tourbillons de la lumière astrale."—Désbarrolles, *Les Mystères de la Main*, p. 54.

hint of what this domination of astral influence may mean.

"A magnetic force penetrates the whole creation, by means of which each creative sphere, and every outbirth from it, attracts to itself what is homogeneous. Hence every soul after the death of the body must pass by gradual stages through different places and conditions, either for separation and cutting asunder, or for purifying and being matured."[1]

Having now brought forward the best and clearest opinions I have been able to gather on this difficult subject—the state of those we call dead,—it only remains for me to point out that, for the most part, the evidence of people on this side of death, such as it is, in no way *contradicts* the reiterated and emphatic assertions of those who speak or write from behind the veil. Even the Reincarnationists, who believe that one life in this mortal body is followed by others in a similar perishable investiture, admit that in the intervals Spirits are in the Spirit-world, and if so, free—if Swedenborg's information does not mislead—to be present where their thoughts and affections are. Allan Kardec says: "The incarnation of the Spirit is neither constant nor perpetual; it is but transitory; in quitting one body it does not take up another immediately; during a lapse of time more or less considerable, it lives in the Spiritual life, which is its normal state; so that the amount of time passed in

---

[1] "Durch die ganze Schöpfung hindurch geht die magnetische Kraft, vermöge der jeder Schöpfungskreis und jede Geburt das Gleichartige an sich zieht. Desshalb muss eine jede Seele nach dem Tode des Leibes entweder zur Scheidung und Auseinandersetzung, oder zur Reinigung und Ausreissung durch die verschiedenen Orte und Stände stufenweise durchpassiren." Hahn's *Lehre des württembergischen Theosophen*, p. 499. *N.B.*—What ideas he attached to the words "*Scheidung*" and "*Auseinandersetzung*" applied to the soul, I am at a loss to imagine, but Mr Harris's speaking of the "*disintegration*" of lost souls for the ultimate rescue of the immortal germ will perhaps a little elucidate the dark saying.

different incarnations is trifling, compared to that passed in the condition of a Spirit at liberty."[1]

Merely to cite the strongest testimony of the proven presence of recognized friends and relations would be to take it from almost every book written on Spiritist themes during the last thirty years, as well as from a host of unimpeachable witnesses *vivâ voce*. One would have thought, if one did not know otherwise, that such books as *Spirit Identity*, and *Psychography*, by "M.A. (Oxon.)," and the late Mr Epes Sargent's *The Scientific Basis of Spiritualism*, would have set all doubt at rest in any candid mind. Yet they fail to do so. Readers will allow that here and there cases occur which admit of no doubt, and yet they will say, "I cannot quite believe that our dead are still conscious of the trivialities of this world! It must be some deluding Spirits that simulate their presence!"

Now if the *possibility* of a Spirit having been identified beyond all chance of error is proved even in half a dozen cases, we have no longer to question what is possible but what is *probable*, and there of course our judgment is necessarily at fault for want of data.

"I have dreamed that we are not to be changed so much, nor the law of us changed."[2] My dream proves nothing; nevertheless, a dream that has outlines is more effective than formless, in curious ignorance—cherished as the only position wisdom can warrant our taking with regard to a future certain for all of us, very near for some: and a hypothesis, however false, has at least

---

[1] "L'incarnation de l'esprit n'est ni constante ni perpétuelle ; elle n'est que transitoire ; en quittant un corps, il n'en reprend pas un autre instantanément ; pendant un laps de temps plus ou moins considérable, il vit de la vie spirituelle, qui est sa vie normale ; de telle sorte que la somme du temps passé dans les différentes incarnations est peu de chose, comparée à celle du temps qu'il passe à l'état d'esprit libre."—Allan Kardec's *La Genèse Spirituelle*, ch. xi., p. 232.

[2] Walt Whitman's *Burial*, W. Rossetti's selected edition.

this advantage, that it gives the mind a temporary footing in the world that must be entered, that encompasses us every moment, and suddenly from time to time engulfs in its black silence our nearest and dearest companions.

The cry "Memento mori" uttered from age to age by all who have preserved spiritual sanity in this hallucinated state of being, testifies to the wonderful negligence with which we toil, dance, or drowse on the brink of life's precipitous boundary, ever veiled and ever ready to shatter without an hour's notice the all-important interests of our present state. There is no stronger mental opiate than a resolve not to think. I dread its effects both as regards myself and those I have lost.

As to those gone before, they seem to me to run some risk of cruelty who assure us that all perceived of their presence is but the effect of our own imagination, like the reflections seen in a darkened window, which for a moment may be taken for objects beyond. We might faintly guess what sort of cruelty if, when unable to do more, we have called and beckoned to friends seen out of reach, and yet failed to catch their eye; when we think, "Oh! Why cannot they look round! how can they be so engrossed as not to turn this way!" I am the last person to wish that any one should so turn that way to *seek* for communications with the dead, believing as I do that the infinite love of the Father of Spirits would have made such intercourse natural and habitual had it been best for us; and that Perfect Wisdom must know, as we *cannot*, the danger attending it; but if such communications come, sought or unsought, free from any possibility of delusion on our side, I hold it to be unkind, as well as foolish, to treat them as untrustworthy.

It is quite in accordance with the dogma that death frustrates Divine power in any after method of saving, that we should, as virtually we do—Roman Catholics excepted—no longer attempt to give any succour to the dead. What Omnipotent Love cannot do, it seems, of course, idle mockery for any man to pray for; and hence, as I believe, we act with most unreasonable inhumanity. On what grounds? Apparently on the strength of these words in Holy Scripture, "No repentance in the grave," "After death the judgment," and *our* interpretation of the parable of the rich man and Lazarus—concluding that when the immortal part of man is severed from the corruptible, we have no further duty to discharge towards him or her, no scope left for the efforts of still hopeful love and still effective pity.

Alas! we use the Biblical image of death, speaking of it as "the land where all things are forgotten," and I think it might be almost as appositely applied by the dead to our hurrying, ever-occupying life in which they have not only been put to silence, but too often gradually effaced from thought. The earnest entreaties of unhappy Spirits for intercessory prayer are eloquent on this point: ought they not to have weight with us? We might need them ourselves—where we cannot transmit the request. And if we reflect on our omissions in this particular, I believe we shall find them due to the difficulty of ardently desiring anything that imagination cannot lay hold of, or experience draw results from, rather than to any sort of belief for which we can pretend to have a warrant.

Now as to self-interest; I can imagine some say, who have spared me a little time and more patience, finding as usual that the attempt to discover a gleam of light in thick darkness only wearies the mental eye: "But after all what is the use of trying to find out before the time what we shall all know sooner or later by experience?" My thought is that we shall only then discover how much we have lost for want of some *conceivable* notions of the after life; for unquestionably a state that can never be imagined is sure to be habitually absent from remembrance. No doubt we shall find out all that now baffles curiosity as regards the *rapports* of the disembodied with the living; but if we go even to a distant hotel or lodging-house and find a book or a desk on which our work or enjoyment partly depends left behind, we regret it with some pungency of chagrin and self-reproach. Let us for a moment try to imagine what it would be to find ourselves in the close-by, ever imminent "other world," with the wrath of God—*i.e.*, the original root-fire of our own souls—still unappeased, with a will no longer able to direct or control spiritual force by the help of our present bodily organization (which gives the contracting limits needful for the expansive impetus); out of sympathy with Divine meekness because of our pride; incredulous of Divine love because of our hate; and longing vainly for poor sensuous enjoyments then beyond our reach. I feel sure that such imaginings would affect present conditions more than all the crude, positive teaching about death which is so common, and, as I believe, so fearfully delusive; assuring people of perfect bliss all at once secured by the faithful after death, or the hopeless, *interminable* torments they are threatened with as the only alternative—teaching which assumes that dissolution can remove us not only from the embrace of Divine love and pity, but from the action of every known law of human nature!

Ah! who that believes this human nature to be something more awful than a breathing, eating and drinking, and digesting machine, crowned with a brain for its guidance during a short term of years, can think it will be time to understand something of the condition of departed Spirits when among them! I can well see that to inquire "What becomes of the dead?" may be as foolish as if an unborn embryo were to ask, "What happens after birth?" Yet to the unborn life we might truly answer: Concealment of spiritual sensations under many a fold of mortal flesh and conventional usage. So, truly, can we now answer the first question so far: All *those* modes of concealment from self-consciousness and self-betrayal must end with death. Is it wise to wait till then to prepare for the inexorable laws of the unseen life, where *all* the seemings of this world are to be destroyed as surely as the structure left behind in the grave?

"Men," says Mr T. Lake Harris, "are accustomed to expect Divine possessions not in the sequences of law but by the overruling of law."[1] That expectation ends with death; and what I therefore fear is, no punishment from any other being, but the sequences of the law of my own. I desire the godlike possessions of love, peace, and joy; and not Omnipotent Mercy can bestow them if I leave my mortal body with an unloving, vindictive, disquieting habit of nature. "*The planes formed in the mind on earth determine for cycles the conditions of eternity.*"[2] This makes for me the terror of death, for surely to be powerless to form the indispensable conditions of bliss, when every lower degree of comfort or illusory pleasure is beyond reach, must be supreme misery, even were there no fellow contributors of woe.

But I suppose few thoughtful people can doubt that powers hostile to man—call them by what name we will —have a subordinated dominion in the world unseen as well as in this: if, therefore, I am severed from material defences while my will and imagination work in accordance with their malignant desires, it is certain that I

[1] Wisdom in Council, p. 35, sec. 63.
[2] T. Lake Harris's *Arcana of Christianity*: the Apocalypse, pp. 393-394, ch. iii., par. 718.

must in some degree become their victim. I greatly fear that: not for a minute doubting the love and providence of the Father of Spirits after death, but what my spiritual insanities may bring upon me: for when they are, so to speak, fortified by the sympathy[1] of more powerful alienated Spirits, that merciful love *must* bring me to reason by severer treatment than any previously undergone. And this I imagine is what constitutes purgatory.

The habit of concluding that after death we shall be under quite a different dispensation, and in all respects unlike what we were in the flesh, necessarily fosters incredulity as to the dead still interesting themselves in the life left behind—a habit which must dull the action of conscience; for if death is to alter every usual turn of thought and force of affection, there will be a tacitly accepted theory that ideas of right and wrong may then be comfortably altered also. Any way, for such a totally transformed individuality, who will care to forego much of present enjoyment? And this habit, while robbing us of strong incentives to goodness, and great consolation and hope, has also led us to entertain most unworthy notions of God's wisdom and economy of forces. There seems something preposterous in the thought that He permits all the various and exquisite powers of the human spirit, enriched by daily increments of knowledge, to be suddenly thrown into disuse; inaction being not only a torment, but sure to deteriorate every power. Such a doom amounts to immense loss to the whole universe. A man dies in whose brain may have been

[1] "They know only of what they here conceived or took in, and the souls sink down in that opinion into the *deepest ground*, much deeper than they have here conceived, for that which was known in many of them of the same opinion, what any or all of them know in the same opinion, that *one soul alone* knoweth : for it is one body with all those that are of the same opinion, and they have one heart in many members."—*Threefold Life*, ch. xii. par. 28.

forged influences that alter the fate of nations; and in the wide blank that spreads through his former sphere of action, we feel as if all his plans had been annihilated. He no longer speaks, or counsels, or commands; audibly and visibly, no; but are we so unreasonable as to think his absorbing anxieties at an end because a flesh heart no longer beats in his *mortal* body? If the distinguishing characteristics of human nature were flesh and blood we might suffer such a thought. But we know better.

Now if the interests and affections of this life are carried through the crisis of dissolution, and I can no longer doubt it myself, it is very possible that the influence is extended by release from his material burden. He has entered, if Swedenborg does not mislead, into conscious association with the Spirits of whose society he has been in this life a member, and can probably act in concert with them (though weakened as an individual) more effectually than he did with embodied instruments of his will in the seen world. The course of modern history after the deaths of Cavour, John Brown in America, and Thiers, for instance, impressed me strongly with this conclusion: they were withdrawn from life with hopes unfulfilled and aspirations unsatisfied, but how soon after the death of each did their principles triumph, gaining permanent success!

My rambling, and I fear somewhat inconsequent considerations, must not be allowed to run on. In conclusion I would bring them to a point thus: If there is solidarity in the human race, which is, I suppose, an undisputed tenet of philosophers (Materialists excepted), there must be constant interaction; were this suspended by death it would amount to what in the individual body is paralysis. The steady advance of the present human generation as to knowledge and power sufficiently disproves anything like that. Now granting interaction of the living and the dead in the mass, we must admit its certain possibility as regards individuals. One need not stop to notice how much greater worth, interest, and moral safeguard the belief in that virtual oneness imparts to earthly life. In the words of Allan Kardec:—

"With the thought that activity and co-operation of individuals are limited to the present life,"—what does the ulterior progress of humanity matter to man? " How can it concern him whether in the future the peoples are better governed, more happy, more enlightened, mutually the better for each other's lives? Since he is never to draw any result from it, is not this progress lost to him? What is the use of working for those who will come after if he is never to know them, if they are new beings who soon after will themselves return to nothingness? Under the influence of denial of an individual future, all necessarily narrows itself to the mean proportions of the moment and of personality."[1]

(Kardec is here arguing for belief in Reincarnation, but these words seem to me quite as cogent with regard to belief in the solidarity of the human race in the body and out of it.)

Neither need I point out how consonant this tenet is with what all Christians verbally profess to believe, however little meaning they may derive from the words, "seeing we also are compassed about with so great a

[1] "Avec la pensée que l'activité et la coöpération individuelles dans l'œuvre générale de la civilisation sont limitées à la vie présente" . . . "que lui importe qu'à l'avenir les peuples soient mieux gouvernés, plus heureux, plus éclairés, meilleurs les uns pour les autres? Puisqu'il n'en doit retirer aucun fruit, ce progrès n'est il pas perdu pour lui? Que lui sert de travailler pour ceux qui viendront après lui, s'il ne doit jamais les connaitre, si ce sont des êtres nouveaux qui peu après rentreront eux mêmes dans le néant? Sous l'empire de la négation de l'avenir individuel, tout se rapetisse forcément aux mesquines proportions du moment et de la personalité."—Allan Kardec's *La Genèse*, ch. xviii., par. 13.

cloud of witnesses," [1] and, "I believe in the Communion of Saints."

Affection, of whatever kind, let no one doubt it, is the tie death cannot break. Hear Swedenborg on this text :—
"The ruling love remains with man after death." "That man after death is his own love or his own *will* has been testified to me by abundant experience." . . . 'The experiment has been frequently made whether Spirits can act in any degree contrary to their ruling love, but they have tried in vain. Their love is like a chain or rope, with which they are, as it were, tied round, by which they may be drawn, and from which they cannot extricate themselves; and the case is similar with men in the world, for their ruling love leads them, and by means of that love they are led by other men; but when they become Spirits, the government of their ruling love is more perfect, because then it is not allowable to assume the appearance of any other love, and feign a character not properly their own." [2]

("*Allowable*"? surely he meant to say "*possible*"?) But the words which I find still more consoling in that book are these:—
"The life which remains with man after death is his love and the faith thence derived; not love and faith in mere potentiality, but love and faith realized in action." [3]

What can be compared to a "rope attached" to the departed spirit, except love for those left behind, and the ability to *realize love in action*; how should these *not* bring near to us the unseen presence of those whose long-felt affection we mourn? Doubting the possibility of that, bereavement has complicated anguish.

"That dear hugged thing *Identity*
Gone, and the dream that grasped it gone—
All's gone." [4]

---

[1] Hebrews xii. 1. [2] Heaven and Hell, par. 479.
[3] Ibid., par. 476. [4] Joseph Downe's *Proud Shepherd's Tragedy*, p. 66.

Yes, truly: if love and remembrance can have been quenched by death, the past is darkened almost as much as the present, for we may conclude that the one in whose strong attachment we believe was—to our hearts—a simulacrum fully as deceptive as any false representation at a séance: if not, if the attachment was true and real, I think the nearness of the loving Spirit is almost as certain as its invisibility, unless repelled by the objects of its affection. The question each one of us can best answer for him or herself would be, "Is our love to the dead so much a spiritual reality that—*if* or *when* they can 'look us through and through'—we do not appear to them deceptive shadows of what they once believed us to be?"

> "Do we indeed desire the dead
> Should still be near us at our side?
> Is there no baseness we would hide?
> No inner vileness that we dread?"[1]

When at last seeing us *as we are*, and our self-love what it is, may *they* not be tempted to think, "It cannot be those we left! they are only misleading Spirits!"

[1] In Memoriam.

THE WORLD-SOUL [1]

"THE doctrine of a Soul of the World, otherwise called the Mundane or Universal Soul, must be acknowledged of very ancient date, as old at least as the Ionic philosophy; and seems to have been generally embraced by the most eminent sages of antiquity. They held it eternal, immutable, completely wise and happy, extended throughout the universe, penetrating and invigorating all things, the maker of the world and all creatures therein, the fountain of sense, life, and motion, from whence the souls of men and animals were discerped, and after dissolution of their bodies, absorbed thereinto again, and they gave it the appellation of God.". . . "But I apprehend the Mundane Soul originally was not intended to be understood of the Supreme Being, but a created God, dependent on Him for its existence and faculties, produced from everlasting by His almighty power and good pleasure; and though it was supposed the maker, it was not supposed the creator of all things, but to have formed the world out of pre-existent materials according to a plan assigned it.". . . "I think offence cannot be taken against our ascribing the generation and sustentation of the world to a created Being, as it seems rather to raise than depress our idea of the Divine Majesty; and everything done by the deputy commissioned for that particular purpose is always esteemed the act of the Principal. The very expression

[1] Light, 1882, vol. ii. p. 33.

commonly used, that God made all things by His Word, warrants our supposition of an intelligent agent who should understand and obey the Word when spoken; and those writings which speak of supernatural effects many times declare them performed by the ministry of an inferior hand."[1]

I cannot attempt to explain mysteries which are far beyond my comprehension, but this most sober-minded philosopher of the last century may partly satisfy the demand of "Student." From seers, whose perceptions in the unseen world give more direct knowledge, I think I could gather information that might interest him more, and bring the subject into clearer light; but it takes time to select the most brief and intelligible quotations.

The question, "*Would there not then be a higher and a lower God?*" can only be met by the larger truth with which alone we can harmonize these conflicting statements in Holy Writ, viz.: "Is there a God beside me? yea, there is no God; I know not any";[2] and again, "I am the Lord, and there is none else; there is no God beside me";[3] with our Lord's re-assertion of David's, "I said, ye are gods; if he called them gods unto whom the Word of the Lord came, and the Scripture cannot be broken";[4] and St Paul's "For though there be that are called gods, whether in heaven or in earth (as there be gods many, and lords many)."[5] The pressure of this paradox cannot be relieved until we acknowledge God to be in every sense infinite,—the abyss from which every world, and every creature in all worlds, *primarily* originates, and from which nothing can sever as to creaturely dependence, though from felt sympathy and support,

---

[1] Abraham Tucker's *Light of Nature Pursued*, vol. i., chapter on "The Mundane Soul," pp. 400, 401, 414.
[2] Isaiah xliv. 8.   [3] Isaiah xlv. 5.   [4] John x. 34, 35.
[5] 1 Cor. viii. 5.

anything can—even an angry thought. Abraham Tucker, with the cheerful superficiality of his day, seems hardly to face the difficulties which this acknowledgment involves, his Mundane Soul being a submissive agent, only carrying out the Divine will. What dismays us, looking a little deeper into the animus of Nature, is the evidence of antagonism, of fierce rebellion, and the desire to frustrate the purposes of mercy *within the universal embrace of an omnipotent source of all being and all creaturely power.* And, to the best of my belief, Jacob Böhme alone can offer any adequate solution of this terrible enigma.

ON THE WORLD-SOUL[1]

WITH regard to this subject I consider myself to be merely in the position of a carrier. Asked to try and explain that which I do but dimly apprehend, I go to my favourite warehouse for spiritual truths, and putting together a few of those which I deem most valuable, I bring them to *Light* with a very clear address—" To those *only* who care for the toil of searching for obscure truth." My freight will be worse than rubbish to any other kind of reader—irritating, because when language fails to convey definite ideas, one of two facts is certain; either words have been misused, or the reader's mind is not able to grasp the thought or information offered; and it is not usual to accept this last conclusion. To those who, glancing at my pack of uncouth words, call them nonsense, I can only say that reproach may cut both ways; such people have *no sense* of their value. Those, again, who think it rash, presumptuous, or profane to dive into such an abyss of necessary ignorance in quest of some gleam of light, I would entreat to leave it unexamined: for to many minds such inquiry is hurtful rather than useless, because if no curiosity is awake, the attempt to gratify it must appear in a very high degree absurd. But it is not fair to sacrifice the interests of the few to the tastes or prejudices of the many; and there are those among us to whom the mystery of creation and all its tremendous problems of evil and pain are a

[1] Light, 1882, vol. ii. pp. 199, 211.

source of deep unrest; who cannot accept the solution offered by theology, because in truth this is more of an evasion than a clearing up; and who say they cannot leave untouched the fretting knots of doubt, while they wait in faith and patience till "the vail that is spread over all nations"[1] is lifted. How should *they* wait a Heavenly Father's good time for relieving doubt and perplexity who are so dismayed by the seeming mercilessness of fate in our present world that they question the existence of such a Father? This state of mind, and all its varying shades of despondency or "agnosticism," is too well known to need explanation: it is for the wants of a mind in such states that I bring to the most likely market these burdens dug out with no small effort from Böhme's mine. But for him I might have been as unsettled and unhappy,—finding ordinary theological teaching, in Bible phraseology, a "bed shorter than that a man can stretch himself on it,"[2] and plagued at heart by the discords so frequently made by history and experience in the deep underlying consciousness of an ever-present God.

In the following extracts I propose to give, as briefly as may be, Böhme's account of the origin of opposing wills in the life that derives from one God, and cannot exist *out* of that Infinitude of Being however much they conflict; and this will necessitate a glance at his interpretation of the *cause* of sin and evil in any shape. Then his frequent mention of the soul or spirit of the world (for he uses the words indiscriminately when speaking of the macrocosm) will fall into place. If these different aspects of the world-soul do not suggest some valuable germs of thought I shall be disappointed. My package does but contain samples; readers who appreciate these will find *much* more help in the context, and I shall be greatly surprised if those who will give a

[1] Isaiah xxv. 7. [2] Isaiah xxviii. 20.

little persevering study to Böhme's books, passing over all that lacks *any* meaning at first, and absorbing passively all they can understand, do not very soon become aware that they have found access to the roots of many a mystery; that "the law behind the law" in nature and spirit is here to be discovered.

It has long been an accepted belief—resting on the first chapter of *Genesis*—that the stars were called into existence before the creation of man. My assumption, for it is nothing more reliable, is that our World-Soul was one of the earlier emanations of the Most High God; but of a later date than the "throne angels," one of whom was the first rebel, the first dupe of pride— "Lucifer, Son of the Morning" (for I am old-fashioned enough to believe in a spiritual adversary of our God) —and that according to the law of Spirits[1] it produced, as the *executive* of the creative Word, this visible world, of which man afterwards became inhabitant. That this World-Soul was corrupted by the evil magnetism of the soul of another orb, Mr T. Lake Harris told us some years ago. At the end of my extracts from Böhme I shall add his report of this and the other world-souls of which he became cognizant in a trance of many months' duration; and venturing to add that being quite beyond our ken or previous guess does not make the facts asserted impossible or ridiculous, though the king of a tropical country who was first told of snow and solid ice found them so, I pass on to my business of porterage.

"In God all beings are but one being, viz., an eternal One or unity, the eternal only good, which eternal One

---

[1] "The soul is the principle or beginning of life, that contains the plastick power whereby the body is formed according to a spiritual idea (or pattern) in the mind, and thus acquires a distinct appearance. The soul is therefore the workman or framer of the body."—Van Helmont's *Thoughts on Genesis*, 1701, p. 78.

without severalty were not manifest to itself. Therefore the same hath breathed forth itself out of itself that a plurality and distinct variety might arise, which variety or severalty hath induced itself into a peculiar *will* and properties, the properties into desires, and the desires into beings." [1]

"The visible world with its hosts and creatures is nothing but the *outflown word* which hath introduced itself into properties, where in the properties an own self-will is existed. And with the receptibility of the willing is the creaturely life existed." [2]

"And yet if there must exist a receptibility, then there must be an *own desire* to the perceptibility of itself, viz., a self-will which is not, nor willeth like unto the one only will; for the one only will willeth nothing else but the one only good which itself is; it willeth no other than itself in the likeness. But the outflown will willeth the *unlikeness*, that it may be distinguished from the likeness, and be its own *somewhat*." [3]

Here we must turn to his exposition of "How Sin is Sin." "God dwelleth in All, and there is *nothing* that comprehendeth Him, unless it be one with Him; and if it departeth out of that One, then doth it depart out from God, into *itself*, and is *somewhat else besides* God; and that divideth or separateth itself. And hence the law doth exist, that it must go again out of itself into that One, or else be separated from that One. Thus it may be known what sin is, or *how* it is sin, viz., the human will which separateth itself from God into its own selfness, and awakeneth its own self and burneth in its own source." [4]

Now for the understanding of this passage one need

---

[1] Epistles (1649), Ep. 6, pars. 8, 9.
[2] Divine Vision, ch. iii., pars. 22, 23.
[3] 177 Theosophic Questions, Ques. 3., pars. 9, 10.
[4] Small Six Points, Point III., pars. 42, 43.

only remember that discord can be made by sounding musical notes not in harmony and yet *within the octave*: the self cannot leave the *All* of God, but in contracting its self-ful "somewhat" it severs part of that all from the rest, and dissonance results. The comparison may suggest the thought that occasional discords increase musical harmony: even so; in the resolving of those discords a well-trained ear finds most subtle delight. But if those discords were to ache on the sense of hearing for a long time together, the effect would be painfully different. The discords in the human soul last so long that we need vast stretches of eternity for their return to harmony, and for these souls' release from anguish and unrest. Nevertheless, I dare believe that ultimate extensions of good will be educed by the Master's hand from the seemingly eternal misery of sin, and one sentence in the page next to that I quote from last supplies a hint full of meaning for those who can follow it out:

"Therefore there must a *new will* grow out of this opposite will, that so it may give up itself again into that one only union, and the contrary opposite will must be broken and slain, ... and so the will that is thus departed" (from self) "dwelleth in God, ... and is then known to be a new birth, *for it re-assumes all again into itself*, in *that One, but not with its own self desire*, but with its own love which is united with and in God, so that God is *all in all*, and his will is the will of all things, for one only will subsisteth in God."[1]

And that, too, is St Paul's account of the final issue of man's earthly tragedy. Now will not all that is *re-assumed* be of inestimable value? A simile may elucidate facts, but never satisfy in lieu of a reason, and it may be asked, How can any properties derived from perfect good cause evil? A question that cannot be

[1] Small Six Points, Point III., pars. 50-52.

evaded; and though to answer it fully, as Böhme can and does answer it, would be impossible here, I must give in fewest words the best idea I can of his solution of the enigma. He tells us of the seven Spirits of God, of the seven forces ceaselessly interacting in eternal nature, which form the base of *every life*. To name these is not to explain but to puzzle; and in the slight variety of his account of two or three of them one finds additional perplexity; yet these, *astringency, mobility, anguish* (consequent on the effort of these two first to escape from each other), *fire*—struck up from the violence of the contest;—and then *love*,—equivalent in his system to light—*sound* and *substantiality* are the roughly indicated names he gives to the seven activities of the Eternal Spirit. (And we must remember that the uncouth and insufficient *designation* of a seer of such agents as these, proves nothing against their actual existence.) Now on the due evolution of these all good depends, the first three being the root of the perfect blissfulness arising from the last three; but if the fire caused by the struggle of the first three does not develop light and *its* consequences, then evil begins, for—"The four first forms in *themselves* are the anger and the wrath of God in the Eternal Nature; and they are in themselves nothing else but such a source or property as standeth in the darkness, and is not material, but an originality of the Spirit, without which there would be nothing. For the four forms are the *cause* of all things, as you may perceive that every life hath poison, yea, the poison itself is the life."[1]

[1] Threefold Life of Man, ch. ii., par. 44.

I am so little satisfied with my own attempt to give any just idea of this doctrine of Böhme's, that I am fain to give Franz Baader's, which seems to me to make it more intelligible, even in rough translation:—

"The number seven contains a double ternary and a centre number."
"Self-hood arises in disseverance; own-will perceives and desires to

It will be easily understood what sort of anguish and of unsuccessful strength must result from a fierce hunger for getting and keeping—due to dominant astringency, or from a bitter, restless striving for advance—when the second form rules, or to intense susceptibility to the influence of such contending impulse, when love has not softened and enlightened, or the true "intellective understanding" which Böhme ascribes to the action of the sixth form—sound—been opened;

establish itself, and hereby places itself in a contradiction. This is urged onward through the second and third form of nature to its climax. Hence the three first forms make up all that is negative—the perverted ternary. But when the contradiction, whilst pushing on to the furthest point, or climax, has exhausted itself, then subjection takes place in a flash (Böhme's *schrach* or *skreek*), and now arises the other ternary in love, joy, and substantial being. One must begin the arrangement of seven forms of nature by fire, because it is the middle, where self-hood originates. Jacob Böhme began from the first, and therefore his representation and development of them are not quite successful. In fire the self-hood originates, and can go forward or backwards to the first or second ternary. Whoever desires to manifest *himself* impedes the source of his right manifestation, and evokes pain to himself." . . . " In the fourth form the spirit has not yet *sound* or *scent* or *seeing*; it is the Father, the formative will, the yet unactuated magic spirit. From the fourth form it can go, imagining, into the fifth, from whence it can mould itself in the sixth, and in the seventh become perfected as *body*: or it can go backwards out of the fourth form into the third, when it will be formed into the second, and completed in the first. The first and seventh, the second and sixth, the third and fifth forms, correspond to each other. The first form is merely excluding, denying; the seventh is also that, essentially, but softened and tempered. The first and seventh together are the includers of all conformable essences. The second is the dividing, pulverizing, destroying principle; this in the sixth form develops itself as the rightly *moulding* principle. . . . In the third is a mere fulness of conflicting atoms, in the fifth form they are united, and the mutual dependency of fellow members and self-life comes into play. In the third form multiplicity was without unity, and unity without multiplicity; in the fifth all is in one and one in all. It is always radically the same principle which rules in the first and seventh, in the second and sixth, in the third and fifth forms, but in one case the destructive principle is dominant, in the other light." (I am not so sure of this elucidating, but at least it is the explanation of a powerful *man's* brain, and so I hope it may serve.)

nor the rest or perfected bliss of heavenly substantiality been attained. Necessarily such conflict would kindle heat in that awful abyss of fire which *is* the soul; and the *will* of man,—the immortal part which was anterior to time—roused more or less by every provocative from within or without—*must* make unharmonized natures what every day shews us they are; nay! proves in some degree within each of us. Here then we get the meaning of the saying—" All whatsoever it is that liveth and moveth, is in God, and *God Himself is all*, and all whatsoever is formed or framed, is formed out of Him, be it either out of love or out of wrath."[1]

With more clearness than is usual to him, Böhme states the paradox, and answers it in the same book.

"Seeing God is *everywhere*, and is Himself *all*, how cometh it then that there is in this world such cold and heat, such biting and striking among all creatures, and that there is nothing else almost but mere fierceness or wrath in this world? The cause is that the first four forms of nature are one at enmity against the other without the light, and yet they are the causes of life."[2]

There is hardly a single work of his in which this origin of evil is not harped upon, so that any one who possesses either of his books can fill up this imperfect outline by reference to it; and I may proceed to the main topic of this paper.

"The living Word of God, which is God Himself,"... "speaketh itself through nature forth into a Spirit of the world *in Spiritu Mundi*, as a Soul of the Creation. And in the speaking forth or expression is again the

---

[1] Aurora, ch. xiii., par. 145.

Any one who can refer to Böhme's *First Apology to Balthazar Tylcken*, will find this mystery of good and evil most fully examined; in the first part he labours to throw light upon it, less systematically than in his *Treatise on Election*, but perhaps more effectually because of the many postures into which he throws the mind while confronting hostile criticism.

[2] Ibid., ch. ix., pars. 78, 79.

distinction or severation into the fiery astral root *in Spiritu Mundi.*" . . . "The Spirit of the World is now the Life of the outward World."[1]

"*In Spiritu Mundi*, many evil workings spring forth which appear *contrary* to God; also, that one creature hurteth, worrieth, and slayeth another; also that wars, pestilence, thunder, and hail happen. All this lieth in the Spirit of the World, and ariseth from the first three properties, wherein they break and frame themselves in their opposite will. For God can give or afford *nothing* but that which is good, for he is alone the only good, and never a whit changeth into any evil at all, neither can he, for he would then cease to be God. But in the word of his revelation or manifestation, wherein the forms, qualities, or dispositions arise, viz., wherein nature and creature ariseth, there existeth the working or framing into evil and good."[2]

I must here parenthetically observe how great a strain upon faith is removed by this explanation of evil. Every thoughtful child sees the contradictions of external nature to what he is taught of an all-loving Creator. He hears of sudden destruction from storms and earthquakes, and is told that these are sent in mercy for the chastisement of sinful man, or for the exercise of submissive faith, and *that* idea he can assimilate in some measure, his mother even having inflicted corrective trials now and then; but he sees the cruelty of animals tormenting and devouring each other—cats with mice, for example—and asks, "Why did the good God cause this?" "It was not so from the beginning; it is a consequence of the fall of Adam," is generally the pious rejoinder; which as soon as he is able to think a little longer upon the point he must feel to be a *put off*: what connection can there be in mercy or in justice between the sin of mankind and the sufferings of

[1] Election, ch. v., pars. 47, 48, 52.   [2] Ibid., ch. vi., pars. 63-65.

irresponsible beasts? Now in all Böhme tells of the World-Soul the connecting cause is found. To him also it was the key to those wonders of vindictive wrath in the historic books of our Old Testament, which scandalize so many of its benevolent sceptical critics in our day.[1]

"The other life" (the temporal life contrasted with the eternal life in this passage) "is an inceptive beginning efflux of the separator of all powers, and is called the soul of the outward world, which life in the outflown properties is become creaturely, and is a life of all creatures of the visible world wherewith the separator or Creator of this visible world imageth itself and maketh a similitude according to the spiritual world."[2]

"The stars and elements are a substance of the Spiritus Mundi."[3]

"The earth is a hunger as to the Spirit of the world, for it is sprung forth and divided from it."[4]

"Moses saith God made man of the dust of the earth, and breathed into him the living breath, and then man became a living soul. But we are here to understand that God did *not* in a personal and creaturely manner stand by like a man and take a lump or clod of earth and make a body of it; no, it was not so. But the Word of God was in all properties in Spiritu Mundi and in the *ens*, or being of the earth, stirring up from the spirit of the world, and spake or breathed forth a life into every essence."[5]

"Our first parents, with their spirit, are gone out of the heavenly paradise into the Spirit of this world, where then the Spirit of this world instantly captivated their body and made it earthly."[6]

[1] See *Three Principles*, ch. xviii., par. 29, and ch. xx., pars. 20, 24.
[2] Divine Vision, ch. iii., par. 30.
[3] Election, ch. viii., par. 4.   [4] Ibid., ch. v., par. 54.
[5] Ibid., pars. 86–88.   [6] Three Principles, ch. xxii., par. 16.

"The Spirit of the World had captivated Adam and introduced its substantiality into his imagination."[1]

"Adam with his mind was not in God, but in the Spirit of this world, and he became feeble as to the Kingdom of God, and so fell down and slept. And then God, by the Spirit of this world, through the Fiat, built or formed out of him the woman of this world. . . . In his sleep the Spirit of this world clothed him with flesh and blood, and figured him into a beast, as we now see by very woeful experience."[2]

"Adam must carry the untoward gross body that the Spirit of the world hath put upon him."[3]

"God the Lord, through the Spirit of this world, made them clothes of the skins of beasts, and put those on them, that they might see that according to this outward world they were beasts."[4]

"As this world breaketh and passeth away, so also all flesh which is generated out of the Spirit of this world must break and pass away."[5]

"As soon as Adam was overcome by the Spirit of this world, then he fell into sleep, viz., into the outward magia, which signifieth or resembleth death, for the outward kingdom hath beginning and end, and *must* break off from the inward; that is its death."[6]

"All whatsoever we think, do, and purpose in the outward man, that the Spirit of this world doth in us men, for the body is nothing else but the instrument thereof, wherewith it performeth its work."[7]

The same dislike which exists with regard to belief in planetary influence on the fate of human beings will undoubtedly be felt for this idea of a great Spirit ruling

---

[1] First Apology, Part II., par. 577.
[2] Three Principles, ch. xvii., pars. 54, 55.
[3] Ibid., ch. xxv., par. 31.
[4] Ibid., ch. xx., par. 6.
[5] Ibid., ch. xix., par. 7.
[6] First Apology, Part II., par. 215.
[7] Three Principles, ch. xxv., par. 1.

in material nature. It is an empire within that of the Supreme Ruler which is claimed, and as such it is eagerly denied, both because it runs counter to preconceived notions, and because godly jealousy takes alarm. And though other gods than *the* God are recognized throughout the Bible, as for example "against all the gods of Egypt I will execute judgment," and "Worship him, all ye gods," devout people will unhesitatingly maintain that the gods spoken of thus are only idols of wood and stone.

"The wise heathen," says Böhme, "have understood that subject and have honoured them" (throne angels) "for gods, yet they missed the true ground of the inwardness; but among the Christians it is altogether silent or dumb except to some few, to whom God hath manifested or revealed it." [1]

Surely this anxiety to prove the non-existence of other spiritual potentates in the universe arises from an estimate far too low of man's superiority of origin and ultimate destiny!

The second birth of regeneration restores his latent powers in possibility; and when these are fully developed neither the stars, nor elements, nor Spirit of this world will be able any longer to rule over him; for "we are children of the omnipotency of God, and inherit His goods in the omnipotency." [2]

It is a little singular that the fate-forming influence of *unseen* powers should be ignored as being incompatible with free-will, when the power of parents to mould their children's fate is so unquestioned. Yet by free-will we do not understand a will free from bias or obstruction, but one which is free, *within the narrow limits of temporal fetters*, to choose between the good and evil left open to choice; that decision in a restricted scope lead-

[1] 177 Theosophic Questions, Ques. 6, par. 18.
[2] Forty Questions (1665), Ques. 4, par. 28.

ing to unlimited consequences of *self-formation* either for good or ill.

"The Spirit of this world hath so very much longed after man and hath drawn him to it, that it might shew forth its wonders in him, that man should produce all arts and languages in it" (the Spirit of this world). . . . "We declare unto you that the Spirit of this world is created with such an inclination; and that it hath a natural will to reveal itself and all its mysteries, as we see before our eyes, by what it hath built or brought forth, how it hath erected a dominion and kingdom upon earth. Do but look upon the doings of man from the highest to the lowest; the Spirit of this world hath thus built the whole order of them and God hath permitted it." [1]

Yes, for in *every* case the terrible truth holds good that "Whereinto a Spirit introduceth its longing imagination the essence and property of that it receiveth is the great mystery of all Beings." . . . "The Will-Spirit is free, it is the eternal original, let it do what it will." [2]

But out of the great mystery of all Beings, One has entered into the soul of the human race, whose longing imagination is to save it from all bondage, and meanwhile the multiplicity of self-ful wills are in their unhappy servitude correcting and limiting the hurtful agencies of each other.

"The Heart of God with His desiring standeth towards us with His imagining." [3]

A digression must here be made with regard to the soul of man. When Böhme speaks of it without qualification, he always refers to the "*fire Spirit, the true essential soul,*" of which he affirms over and over again, "*it hath had no beginning: also it will have no end.*" [4]

[1] Threefold Life, ch. ix., pars. 7, 9, 10.
[2] Signatura Rerum, ch. xvi., pars. 25, 26.
[3] Incarnation, Part III., ch. vii., par. 20.
[4] Ibid., Part I., ch. iii., pars. 52, 54.

But of another that had beginning and must end he tells us the World-Soul was the deputed originator:—
"The outward created life from or out of this world, viz., from the sun, stars, and elements, which God, with or by the Spirit of the great world, breathed into Adam's nostrils, wherein then he became also an outward soul." [1]

It is this "outward soul," so far as I can learn, that is sustained by the World-Soul on its lower plane, precisely as the true soul of man lives in and by the Supreme Being; and I should suppose from analogy that at dissolution, or at any subsequent period when the spirit of man is released from the magnetic attraction of animal life, the animal soul became one with the World-Soul. [2] Before this merging of the individual in the universal, there is no doubt a possibility of gaining access to the forces of this "Cosmic Spirit," and subordinating them to the purposes of man. Mr Sinnett's friend, Koot Hoomi, refers to this power when he speaks of a process yet unknown to the people of the West for "strengthening and refining those mysterious links of sympathy between intelligent men—the temporarily isolated fragments of the universal soul, and the Cosmic Soul itself; bringing them into full rapport." [3] And by such full rapports I suppose most of the miracles of Oriental adepts are performed. I neither question the power nor its results, but while maintaining that this is not the *highest* exercise of human powers, I see that these last have so much fallen into abeyance that to the majority of minds this co-operation with the Cosmic Spirit would appear the highest, and its danger would not appear. Until it is understood how much the mediumship of man

[1] Incarnation, Part III., ch. v. pars. 74, 75.
[2] I account for the infallible wisdom of animals' instinct by their undivided union with the World-Soul; were we as wholly surrendered to the will of Him in whom our spirits have their being, sin and folly would not so strikingly distinguish the human race.
[3] Occult World, 1881, p. 145; 4th ed., 1884, p. 98.

is coveted by that great Spirit of the world, its ability
first to fascinate and then to subdue to a lower range of
power and less abiding results would never be suspected;
for while we are in mortal bodies every unseen spiritual
agent has a sort of prestige; we cannot see its limits,
and our own are constantly felt.

Yet it is no empty boast to say that the soul of man
is potentially incomparably superior to the spirit of
this outer world; it was made in the likeness of God;
it has ability to be made one with Him to whom is given
all power and all dominion both in Heaven and earth;
it is to be instrumental for opening the infinite wonders
of Divine wisdom, which as much exceed those of the
mundane soul as eternity surpasses time. And it is
this sense of latent power, coupled with faith in the
promises of God, repeated from century to century,
which leads many people to shun access to the ambiguous
agents of the mundane soul, in séances for instance,
lest a lower attraction should divert them from the
higher, and various and conflicting testimony of finite
spirits drown the still small voice of the spirit nearest
of all, who speaks to us from the centre of our being.

I am quite conscious of the offence that will be given
to many whose faith I most sincerely respect by the
notion of anything less than the *direct* action of the
God of all gods in creation, and in all subsequent human
agencies. To such people the idea of a "Cosmic Spirit"
acting as vice-regent in the outer world will be shocking;
a similar shock is given to the devout ignorance of an
uneducated person if one says that thunder results from
such and such well-understood processes of nature, or
that the cause of a rainbow is explained by the laws
of refraction of light. Impossible; thunder is the voice
of God; is it not said so in *Job*, chap. xl. 9? and in *Genesis*
that God would set his bow in the cloud? In vain one
speaks to such readers of secondary agents; they may

listen and keep silence, but will think your views profane—and be "of the same opinion still."

On minds better instructed I would fain press the consideration that intermediate powers in no wise diminish the supreme majesty and infinite power of the One from whom all existences derive; and that the action of subordinate wills being wholly dependent on the measure of life and ability *taken up* from the all-permeating efflux of Eternal Nature, it may be truly affirmed, though it sounds paradoxical, that all that happens in creation is done by Divine forces, but not all according to the will of God; which *only* Böhme can adequately explain, therefore he must be quoted from again:—"We know that God is a Spirit, and His eternal will is magical, that is, desirous; He always maketh substance out of nothing, and that in a two-fold source, viz., according to the fire and light. Out of the fire cometh fierce wrath, climbing-up pride, willing not to unite itself with the light, but a fierce, wrathful, eager, earnest will, according to which He is not called God, but a fierce, wrathful, consuming fire. This fire becometh also *not* manifest in the pure Deity, for the light hath swallowed up the fire into itself, and giveth to the fire its love, its substantiality, its water, *so that in God's substance there is only love*, joy, and a pleasant habitation, and no fire *known*. But the fire is only a cause of the desirous will and of the love, as also of the light and of the majesty, else there would be no substance: as it hath been largely expounded in the former writings." [1]

It is only thus that we are enabled to understand many a discrepancy in the Bible between the emphatic announcements of Divine mercy and exceeding pitifulness,—the unconditional "God is Love," and commands and transactions which outrage every instinctive sense

[1] Incarnation, I., ch. xi., pars. 44–47.

of pity. These disagreements are usually passed over as what are beyond the scope of human judgment. To the faithful the submissive inquiry, "Shall not the Judge of all the earth do right?" is a sufficient quietus; but now that faith ebbs apace, is it not well to remove from the scoffer's range any difficulty for which we can *apprehend* a possible mode of reconciling reason to faith? Comprehension is quite another phase of knowledge; and on this subject unprejudiced study has hardly begun.

Extracts from Mr T. Lake Harris's *Arcana of Christianity* should be prefaced by the reminder that they were communicated in a state of trance; and are not the result of cogitation or derived opinions. This fact may give them more or less weight, according to the tendencies of the reader. Ten years ago I confess to having looked upon these books as a stupendous instance of unbridled fancy: but much study of very different writers, and principally of Böhme, during these ten years, has brought to light so many wonderful agreements with, and confirmations of, the statements they contain, that I read in them now to learn and not to judge.

"Every sun has a solar spirit." . . . "Every planetary orb of the terrestrial sort a terrestrial spirit. The spirit of every orb is diffused into, and lives throughout, its mineral, vegetable, animal, and human kingdoms, and is an immortal entity, a living, indivisible, and instinctively conscious existence, but is without human personality, and so abstractly conscious of pleasure or pain, but without power to determine its own sensations. Insphered in every solar, aromal, or terrestrial planetary world, is an appropriate World-Soul, living in the life of all its distinct creations, and permeating alike its atmospheres, its waters, its material crust, and its electro-igneous centre. These World-Souls comprise the first

family of God, and their number is as that of the stars."
. . . "They are absorptive organs for the Divine Spirit; and pervading each its own world, and living in all its parts, they distribute throughout matter the Divine vitality." . . . "I was given to understand that the World-Soul of one planet had become inverted from light to darkness, in consequence of the abandonment of its race to moral evil; that the external body of that orb had long since been dissipated; but that the psychical form of the planet still adhered together, and was the abyss spoken of in ancient days." . . . "The lost Spirits from that orb were the first tempters and deceivers of our own human race." . . . "The World-Soul of our orb is exceedingly afflicted, and suffers in all the inversions of Divine order upon our globe."[1]

"The World-Souls of the universe exist in pairs, male and female. They maintain a vast impersonal consciousness throughout the electrical natural spheres of the orbs to which they respectively pertain. The World-Soul of our own orb is feminine and its masculine counterpart is that of the planet Mars, through which it is supported in its fearful struggles at the present time."[2] . . . "The nature and the direction of the affinities of the World-Souls determine, to a large extent, the industrial and social harmonies of the human races. The grouping of the planets, in psychical relations growing out of these affinities, determines the genesis of ideas in individuals." . . . "When the World-Soul is deranged or disturbed the disturbance and disadjustment of human society is inevitable, as it is through the World-Soul of each orb that the Divine harmonies are distributed."[3]

"The associations of the World-Soul determine the typal varieties of animals; and new races and varieties

---

[1] Arcana of Christianity, Part I., vol. i. pp. 100, 101.
[2] Ibid., The Apocalypse, ch. ii., par. 98.
[3] Ibid., Part I., vol. i. pp. 102, 103.

of races will appear among us as the result of the disenthralment of our own World-Soul from the slavery of the hells. The origin of subversive instead of harmonic types of lower life, quadrupeda and reptilia, together with the unsolved problem of the first cause of the state of universal antagonism which marked the ancient pre-Adamic periods of our own world's development, was in the magnetization of the World-Soul of this orb, through the means of the inverted World-Soul of that corrupted planet which has ceased to exist."[1]

"It may be objected that this view is false because Creation belongs alone to the One Divine Spirit, and that all the wonders of nature are attributable to Him. There is here, however, no reality but simply an appearance of difficulty; subversive creations are *through* the hells, but not *from* the hells, as a first cause. The ultimate form which a creation will assume depends upon the channels through which the creative influx shall descend in its approach to the plane of ultimates. If that influx, which is invariably Divine, is through mediums which have become perverted, an organic perversion is the extreme result."[2]

I wish to draw special attention to this saying about the magnetization of the World-Soul, because I think it points to a hitherto unworked vein of knowledge. The every-day marvels of magnetism, animal magnetism as it is called, will give us, I believe, something of a key to the mystery of evil. To all who think, I conclude it is a mystery; most of all, one would suppose, to people who regard the idea of a spiritual tempter as an outworn superstition. But if there is no powerful adversary behind the scenes, urging, prompting, and alluring to evil practices, how are we to explain conduct which opposes every instinct of self-interest? If human weakness accounts for much crime, it leaves much more that

[1] Arcana of Christianity, Part I., vol. i. p. 105.   [2] Ibid., p. 106.

is laborious and self-restraining unaccounted for: the delusions of vain women, of world-worshipping men, have more the effect of cruel bondage than of self-indulgence. Now if we examine the curious process by which a magnetizer induces in his patient every feeling which he wills to establish, and the completeness of consequent sensation in that patient, I fancy we may begin to understand how it is that men and women believe they will find happiness in an evil course, and success in habits which must land them in ruin.

In the sixth chapter of the first part of Böhme's *Treatise on the Incarnation*, from the first to the sixth paragraph there is a wonderful description, if I understand it aright, of the process of biologizing a mind reduced to a perfectly passive state in the case of Adam. I hope those who can refer to this will do so. No quotation in part will do justice to his meaning, but this much I must cite: after saying that Adam "lay as dead but was not dead, *but the Spirit stood still*," it is said that "all whatsoever the starry heaven bringeth forth stood magically in the mind as a looking-glass *on which the Spirit of this world gazeth*"; and, "when the earthliness wrestled with Adam, and that he imagined thereinto, he became instantly infected thereby."

Now the earth with its animals, birds, fishes, etc.,—outcome, as I suppose, of the delegated powers of *Spiritus Mundi*—had, according to Mr Harris, been *infected* by the mighty Spirit of a superior orb, and man coming to this world was open both to a direct and indirect magnetic influence adverse to that of the Holy One; for he drew his *animal* soul from the World-Soul, and this was already in partial subjection to the dethroned angel whom man was created to supplant—and if the teachings of some wise seers does not mislead—in the long reaches of eternity to *restore*, at the time of which St Paul spoke, when God shall be *all in all*; when as Hahn naïvely observes, evil *cannot* remain in any thing or any being.

"The poor soul is poisoned through a false imagination, and through its own compression of its desire is come to be such a hungry fire-source, which is only a shutting in of the true life."[1]

"Now the Spirit of this world is by the devil's kindling and poison, which he hath *darted* thereinto, become perished (*i.e.*, corrupted)."[2]

Are not these expressions as apposite to a man or woman whose wrath or malice drives on to murder as to a magnetized subject who is told he cannot move, or that the cold is intolerable while standing in the heat of a crowded room? There is the same "compression of the desire" on a fixed imagination, the same "shutting in of the true life." And so long as the delusion is not one that subjugates our own will and imagination, we can look on amazed and feel the truth of those Bible words, "he that committeth sin is the servant of sin"; and "where the Spirit of the Lord is there is liberty"; but when *we* receive into ourselves the devil's poison, how confident we are of our view of facts being correct; and so is the victim of a controlling magnetizer, till "the hard compression of the false magnetic desire is broken in sunder, and opened in that manner as a man strikes up fire."[3]

Now Böhme further tells us with reiterated emphasis that the kingdom of phantasy is the peculiar appanage of the fallen angel of light; that "Lucifer hath willed to domineer in the might and properties of the central fire, viz., in the changing and phantasy."[4]

If anyone who reads this has the good fortune to

---

[1] Testaments: Baptism, ch. ii., par. 4.
[2] Incarnation, Part I., ch. xi., par. 21.
[3] Testaments: Baptism, ch. iii., par. 7. See also par. 8.
[4] 177 Theosophic Questions, Ques. 5, par. 6.

possess his treatise on the *Election of Grace*, let it be referred to for most curious information as to what he means by this kingdom of phantasy; in chap. iv., par. 100, to the end of the chapter, the fullest account of this will be found. In chap. vi., par. 31, he says: "The kingdom of phantasy grasped after Adam, and would be manifested in the image of God."

This no doubt was the triumph aimed at by the envious rebel; to rivet the imagination of man by any means was enough for his purpose, for—"Every imagination modeleth only its like in itself and manifesteth itself in the similitude."[1]

But—"The Spirit of God goeth with the willing into the soul, it desireth the soul; it setteth *its magia towards* the soul; the soul need only to open the door."[2]

The brief mention of the World-Soul by two other writers will complete my consignment. Madame Blavatsky says: "The Astral Light, or Anima Mundi, is dual and bi-sexual." . . . "It is the life-principle of every creature, and furnishes the astral soul, the fluidic *perisprit* to men, animals, fowls of the air, and everything living."[3]

"The Anima Mundi proper was considered" (by ancient philosophers of whom she was speaking), "as composed of a fine igneous and ethereal nature spread throughout the universe—in short, ether."[4]

Eliphaz Lévi describes it thus: "A natural and divine agent, bodily and spiritual; a plastic, universal medium; a common receptacle of the vibrations of movement, and the images of form; a fluid and a force that one might call in a certain sense the *imagination of nature*. By means of this power all nervous systems secretly communicate with one another; from it arise sympathy and

---

[1] Incarnation, Part II., ch. iv., par. 9.   [2] Ibid, Part III., ch. v., par. 8.
[3] Isis Unveiled, vol. i. p. 301, foot-note.   [4] Ibid., vol. i. p. 317.

antipathy, from it dreams, and by it the phenomena of second-sight and supernatural visions are produced."

"Un agent naturel et divin, corporel et spirituel, un médiateur plastique universel, un réceptacle commun des vibrations du mouvement et des images de la forme, un fluide et une force qu'on pourrait appeler en quelque manière *l'imagination de la nature*. Par cette force tous les appareils nerveux communiquent secrètement ensemble; de là naissent la sympathie et l'antipathie; de là viennent les rêves; par là se produisent les phénomènes de seconde vue et de vision extranaturelle."[1]

[1] Histoire de la Magie, p. 19.

THE DOCTRINE OF VICARIOUS SUFFERING [1]

THAT your correspondent, Mr J. J. Meyrick, immediately after quoting these words, "if when we were enemies *we were reconciled to God* through the death of His Son," should add "if language have a meaning at all, their plain meaning is that God could not forgive us our offences until His anger was pacified by His sinless Son being punished instead of us," proves how blinding long authorized misinterpretation of Scripture can be: (his *inserting* "of God" after wrath, which is not in the text, in the 9th verse of *Romans* v., proves it also). Surely the words would have run "*God was reconciled to us*" had this view of Divine anger been the right one. The most superficial reader of Jacob Böhme knows that it is not—knows that the wrath which has to be pacified is that part of Deity in which the original life of man's soul consists;—that fire without which it could have neither being nor will. It was inevitable, and if so, one would conclude expedient, that in earlier times the purpose of the vicarious sufferings of the Redeemer should have been misconstrued. It *must* have been while pain seemed far more terrible than sin, and man thought of God as little differing from such a one as himself. The hard legal notion of a victim satisfying the claims of an offended God completely hid the *remedial*

[1] Light, 1882, vol. ii. p. 286.

process of a sinless being accepting the conditions of a fallen race that he might bring it back to eternal life. And even now to comprehend the whole bearings of this process—this transcendent mystery of love—is far beyond the deepest reach of thought; yet, little as we can tell of all it *is*, we are able to see quite plainly what it is *not*. It is *not* the means by which *God was reconciled to man, for "in this was manifested the love of God towards us, because that God sent His only begotten Son into the world, that we might live through Him."* [1] And again, "God so loved the world, that He gave His only begotten Son, that whosoever believeth in Him should not perish." [2]

But it is an old and easy device, when wishing to attack a religious doctrine, to identify it with its most commonly misrepresented aspects; and it is wonderful how much killing errors of this sort take before they are dislodged from the popular mind. No abstruse study is needed to prove the absurdity of this time-honoured stumbling block; William Law, in the last century, put it before the public in clearest light and with most cogent eloquence. While so doing, however, he dishonoured our national idol—*Compromise*—veiled as it ever is by so-called moderation. He pushed the standard of Christian conduct to the eccentric extreme of evangelical requirement, so that even devout clergymen found him "hardly safe"; nor, indeed, could it be expected of them to approve the theories of a man who took only a bunch of raisins and glass of water for supper. That alone bore out their suspicions that he was an enthusiast; and those who *did* read his books before they pronounced upon them generally added, "a *dangerous* enthusiast!" This was quite enough to seal his voluminous works to the general reader; and now, after nearly a century's industment on untouched bookshelves, rather than examine

[1] 1 John iv. 9.   [2] John iii. 16.

and accept his well-reasoned and irresistible teaching upon the Atonement, our clergy lament and marvel at the quick-growing infidelity of our times, and our laity still talk of Christians believing in a vindictive God! Only the most ignorant among them can hold such belief. When your correspondent says that the tenet of vicarious suffering "is not for true women any more than men, but for mean-spirited cowards who dare not face the consequences of their own acts"—that "it could only have originated in the heart of savages"— he must surely have been for the moment oblivious! What do not mothers, what the bringers to life of every *new* good thing, heroes, pioneers, and martyrs to every good cause, suffer for the benefit of others! and how, almost proverbially, the innocent for the guilty! The tenet, and—thank God!—the cheerful endurance, of vicarious suffering is from the divinest instinct in man's confused nature.

P. S.—Not having Law's works at hand now, I cannot refer to volume and chapter, but both in his treatise on *The Spirit of Love*, and in his *Way to Divine Knowledge*, if I remember rightly, he deals very fully and conclusively with the subject in question.

DEITY ANTERIOR TO CREATION[1]

"I conceive that the form of thought which considers Deity as a conscious existence outside and beyond its expressions is but a higher development of the Anthropomorphism that demands as its God a being shaped, fashioned, and embodied."

. . . .

"Thus God may be said to be neither personal nor impersonal *per se*, but as being the Absolute Totality of all things whose manifestation claims the worship of our souls, either as Mahommed, Buddha, Christ, or any other form of our highest ideal."—*Light*, June 17th.

I AM glad that the challenge thus thrown down has been taken up, and that some one has answered this in the interests of both faith and common-sense. The affront is offered to both. Miss Arundale need hardly fear being accused of Atheism, for the position of an atheist's mind is comprehensible, and I doubt if any "*ism*" yet formulated would correspond to this creed of hers—that an abstract idea of the Absolute Totality of all things should be worshipped in an individual human being as its manifestation (the choice of the "ideal" thus manifesting being left to the worshipper). But surely of the Absolute Totality of all things,—necessarily indifferent to any quality of any part—the only possible manifestation would be the totality of all things in the concrete; and how Mahommed, Buddha, or Christ, *could as individuals manifest universality*, passes thought; one being can manifest the will or characteristics of another, and in

[1] *Light*, 1882, vol. ii. p. 307.

One infinite being the totality of all things may indeed be latent; but manifested in one creature, no!

It is much to be regretted that when St Paul's saying, "In Him we live and move and have our being," was quoted by Miss Arundale, she did not pause to notice what that "expounder of truth" says in the context—in the four verses preceding and the three verses following that passage, in the seventeenth chapter of *Acts*. The very reverse of her conclusion is his; evidently he believed in a God of *conscious* existence, prior to creation and external to it as well as omnipresent and permeating every creature with life. St Paul would not have said anything so *flat* as what amounts to nothing more than "we live and move and have our being in the life of the universe," if by *Him* he only meant the absolute totality of all things; besides, the pronoun *him* would in that case have been strangely misplaced.

And again, how can she explain the terrible contradictions in this Totality if it represents the only God—cruelty and rapine in the animal world, gross selfishness among average mankind, and yet hundreds of men and women who find more joy in making others happy than they do in any self-ended pleasure! If human beings are conscious of this disinterested joy—not unfrequently inimical to self-preservation—surely we should apply to the emotions of love and pity David's argument regarding ears and eyes,[1] and say, He from whose universal life such emotions emanate, must not He feel our consciousness apart from creatural life? I feel ashamed of meeting any doubt of this so gravely. Is this what the enlightenment of the nineteenth century has brought—a confounding of the maker with the made, of the parent with the offspring, of the source with the stream proceeding from it! an attempt to prove that because God

[1] Psalms lxxiv. 9.

is everywhere, therefore everything in the universe is all that there is of God.

"It is impossible," says Mr Oxley, "to separate cause from effect, spirit from matter, God from man,"[1] and there all will agree with him—as difficult as to sever life-blood from the veins in which it runs; but as we know there was the cause of life acting before veins were formed, so we know they cannot be identical. Centuries ago an unlearned shoemaker knew very well that "the motion of a thing is not the highest ground of the power, but that out of which the cause of motion cometh."[2] Now, in the times when Böhme wrote those words, there was such gross ignorance of the truth, that he had constantly to deprecate the folly of supposing God to be in Heaven, afar off from the world; and he complained, "Reason speaketh very much concerning God and of His omnipotency; but it understandeth little of God and His substance, *what* and *how* it is; it severeth the soul totally off from God, as if it were *a sundry being or substance apart*."[3] And again, in his *Aurora*, ch. xiii., par. 145, he had said: "All, whatsoever it is, that liveth or moveth is in God, and *God Himself is all*, and all whatsoever is formed or framed is formed out of Him, be it either out of love or out of wrath." But he had been intromitted to depths of Divine Knowledge which made it impossible for him, while clearly perceiving this truth, to confound the effects of a life-giving power with their originating cause. And so precisely does he express revelation on this point, that I venture to submit his testimony to our modern philosophers as more *reasonable* even than this new mode of superseding Christian faith:—

"This world, with all that belongs to it, as well as man,

---

[1] Philosophy of Spirit, 1881, p. 210.
[2] Divine Vision, ch. iii., par. 55.
[3] 177 Theosophic Questions, Ques. 9, par. 10.

is created as an outbirth out of the Eternal Nature; understand, out of the seven seals of the eternal nature."[1] (The seven spirits of God are thus indicated.)

"The Eternal Centre and the birth of life, and the substantiality are everywhere. If you make a small circle, as small as a little grain or kernel of seed, there is the whole birth of the Eternal Nature, and also the Number Three in Ternario Sancto contained therein; but you include not, nor comprise, the Eternal Nature, much less the Number Three, but you comprehend the *outbirth* of the *Centre*: the Eternal Nature is *incomprehensible*, as God also is." . . . "The Eternity, as also the Deity, is in one place as well as in another, everywhere; for there is no place in the Eternity, but the outbirth maketh a place and room. Therefore God said, *I am Alpha and Omega, the beginning and the end.*' This world maketh a beginning, and God in the Number Three is the beginning; and it also maketh an end, and that is the Eternity, and also God: for before the time of this world there was *nothing but God* from Eternity, and after this world there will be *nothing but God* in Eternity: but the cause why we comprehend not this is because there is no comprehensibility in God. For where there is a comprehensibility there is beginning and end. And therefore we are shut up in darkness that we might labour and *manifest* God; as we have mentioned to you concerning the seven forms of nature, what an eternal labour there is therein, so that one form generateth another till they are all brought to light, and so the Eternal is manifest in a threefold form, which otherwise would not be known."[2]

"We have shewn you already concerning the seven forms of the *Centre* of the Eternal Nature, where every form is a several wellspring of nature: in like manner, out of every form, out of every wellspring, go forth

[1] Threefold Life, ch. iii., par. 40.   [2] Ibid., ch. vi., pars. 43-45.

Spirits, according to the multiplicity of essences and properties, every one according to its kind."[1]

I entreat Miss Arundale, and those who think as she does, to reflect upon this last significant saying, bearing in mind that all Spirits form their own embodiment; they will see that at least it answers the question why in the totality of all things there are so many contrary one to another.

[Miss Arundale's reply to the above article will be found at p. 326 of the same volume of *Light*, her original letter at p. 289.—ED.].

[1] Threefold Life, ch. iv., par. 37.

ON INFLUX [1]

A DOZEN years ago Mr George Barlow's remarks on unconscious mediumship in *Light*, for September 2nd, would have found strong re-echo in my mind. When he says, "I would rather at all costs develop my own originality than be indebted for inspiration to the greatest poets of the past; it is such an uncomfortable idea to my thinking to be perpetually open to the influence of all the unnumbered dead in this way," and again, "This idea of a constant river of spiritual influx is uncongenial to me because it makes of every created spirit a mere secondary and passive instrument, and leaves no room for that strong personal development of the individual soul of each, which I look upon as the highest prize of being," etc., he exactly expresses my past discontent with all the inferences of mediumship. It used to seem to me an easy cut-short method for explaining everything distinguished in human intellect, even if it did not loosen the very foundations of individual responsibility. I have come to a better understanding of influx since then, and would fain tell my present view of it to any one who still thinks of it as I did formerly.

I believe that a fallacy slips in with those words, "open to the influence of all the unnumbered dead." Our unseen spiritual associates are probably far more congenial and select than our circle of seen companions, for like seeks like in the Spirit-World; not like in power, of

[1] *Light*, 1882, vol. ii. p. 467.

course, but in tendencies, be they good or bad, in tastes
and turn of thought; and as the cultivation of these is
determined by our will, and promoted by circumstance,
I suppose the intrusion of alien minds—unless we have
allowed our own odylic sphere to be broken—is very
improbable.

If Mr Barlow will notice, I think he will find that
inspirations have generally, if not always, a conformity
with the thoughts of those to whom they come. Like
many another, as I suppose, observant of inner life, I
have proved the cessation of this sort of gift from the
unseen world when the taste to which it ministered
paled among more absorbing interests. At one time
quite *unsought* and *unexpected* verses have floated into
my mind, which were as certainly original as they were
superior to any I had intentionally written. After I
had outgrown that practice, for I was no poet, such help
was never again offered.

In the same way we find evidence given where there
is faith enough to accept, and withheld from those who
scoff. The old short-cut mode of accounting for this *was*
fancy, or self-deception, and still *is* for those who can
yet believe embodied human beings our only associates,
and all influence to be due to these and outward circumstances.

I fully share Mr Barlow's belief as to Shakespeare and
other notorieties among controls; and their claims of
being such may generally be accounted for by the well-
known mendacity of a certain class of Spirits; but at
the present time it is beyond doubt for hundreds, if not
thousands, of our best intellects that kindred Spirits out
of the flesh are as eager to promote the pleasure of like-
minded people in it, as those who are manifest to the
outer eye,—and quite as easily rebuffed, repulsed, and
distanced.

It seems to me most improbable that this law of influx should be so one-sided as for us to be only recipients. The natural, as Swedenborg has abundantly established, cannot flow into the spiritual degree, but inasmuch as we are Spirits I little doubt that we strongly influence others in the spiritual world before we lose our own material foothold in this.

In Fechner's admirable little book, *On Life after Death*, this is recognized:—

"Spirits draw near on all sides trying to make use of our faculties for themselves, in order to increase their own sphere of activity in a certain direction, and if they succeed in doing so, a new impulse in that same direction is given to our own mind in its development. Those ingrown Spirits in their turn are subject, though in a different way, to the influence of the human will. They influence and direct a man's mind, *they also receive new impressions from the store of his spiritual life.*"[1]

And thus I think we can understand how the influx must intensify rather than lessen originality, by which I here mean native disposition of mind or character; influx congenial to these is attracted, and if to a strong nature, this nature will probably fix and extend the habits of companion Spirits.

Now, within as well as without, it is possible for every sane-minded being to reject evil influences as soon as they are perceived: it is the sloth of self-indulgence that costs us that perception, and we must abide the consequences of that loss when it is incurred. St Martin put this very forcibly:—

"Voici donc comment il faut considérer l'homme dans son état actuel; la pensée ne vient pas de lui; mais lorsqu'elle lui est communiquée, il est susceptible de la concevoir; il faut donc qu'il ait en lui le germe où le principe de toutes les pensées, et que tout ce qui s'opère

[1] 1882, p. 30; 1906, p. 48.
The italicizing is my own, to draw special attention to those words.

sur lui, ne produise qu'un développement; ou plutôt l'âme humaine est un réceptacle sur lequel tout frappe, et elle n'a que la faculté d'adopter ou de rejetter. Qu'on ne croie pas cependant que cette faculté que l'âme possède de juger du bien ou du mal, soit inférieur à la pensée, il faut sûrement que l'âme soit encore au-dessus de la pensée, puisqu'elle a le pouvoir de la juger."[1]

And here he just supplies what I miss in Swedenborg's very convincing teaching about influx in his work on *Divine Providence*. He proves to his own satisfaction, and I suppose to most of his readers', an enlarged sense of the truth of the saying of Jesus Christ, "A man can receive nothing except it be given him from Heaven." He sums up part of his argument thus:—

"From all these premises no other conclusion can be deduced than that whatever a man thinks and wills comes by influx; and that, as all speech flows from thought as an effect from its cause, and all action in like manner from the will, therefore whatever a man speaks and acts comes likewise by influx, although derivatively or mediately. That whatever a man sees, hears, smells, tastes, and feels, comes by influx, cannot be denied; why not then what he thinks and wills? Can there be any difference, except that such things as are in the natural world flow into or impress the organs of the external senses or of the body, while such things as are in the spiritual world flow into or impress the organic substances of the internal senses, or of the mind? Therefore, that as the organs of the external senses, or of the body, are receptacles of natural objects, so the organic substances of the internal senses, or of the mind, are receptacles of spiritual objects."[2]

But he does not recognize as St Martin does, that the soul of man *must* in some sense be superior to all

---

[1] Œuvres Posthumes, vol. i. p. 377.
[2] Divine Providence, par. 308.

ON INFLUX

mediate influx in that he can refuse or accept it—a fact to which he testifies at page 210, *Ibid.*

"Moreover I perceive what flows into my exterior thought, whether it be from Heaven or from Hell; that I reject the latter and receive the former; and that still I seem to myself just as they do, to think and will from myself."[1]

And again:—

"Now, as a man does not desire to know that he is led to think by others, but is desirous to think from himself, and also believes that he does it, it follows that the fault is in himself, and that he cannot free himself from it so long as he continues to think what he does; *but if he does not love it, he dissolves his connection with those from whom his thought flows.*"[2]

When at page 226 he continues the passage quoted above with "since this is every man's condition, what then is his own?" one hopes for some account of what man *is* as well as what he is *not*, but he evades an answer, and goes on thus:—

"His self-hood does not consist in his being such and such a receptacle, because this self-hood is nothing but his quality with respect to reception, and is not the self-hood of life."

Here, as usual, I find that with all his vast embrace of wide reaches of truth, in more worlds than one, he falls short of Böhme in striking to central depths of causation. Böhme can tell us the cause of that "*quality with respect to reception,*" so obviously differing in all. Swedenborg leaves the mystery as much unnoticed as unexplained, both here and when he asserts that in hell "influent good is there turned into evil, and truth into falsity."[3]

Let me offer Böhme's key to those few who will have patience enough to let it hang up in their mental

[1] Divine Providence, par. 290. [2] Ibid., par. 294. [3] Ibid., par. 288.

laboratory until the time comes when they can see how perfectly it fits the lock in question. Nevertheless there is one beyond this for which even Böhme never attempts to offer a key.

"Everything doth bring itself from its own experience into form, feature, and shape, and likewise into life and operation as it standeth in its centre, in the Universal experience, namely, in the Great Mystery, in the Mother of all Beings."[1]

"And as the Spirit of every soul is constellated in the Eternal Mother, even so is its revelation, apprehension, and knowledge."[2]

"The inward property or disposition of the soul lieth now in the first created configuration of the stars or constellations, in the Eternal commencing ground that is not co-imaged or framed together in the outward bestial constellation or configuration of the stars."[3]

What does Böhme mean by the "Eternal Mother," the "Eternal commencing ground"? Undoubtedly the mysterious agent called the Wisdom of God both in his pages and in the 8th chapter of *Proverbs* in our Bible. See, for convincing proof of this, chapter viii. of Böhme's *Treatise on Election*, pars. 61 and 62; and this, for a briefer definition, from his *Second Apology to Balthazar Tylcken*, Part I., par. 69:—

"She is the highest substantiality of the Deity: without her God would not be manifested or revealed, but would be *only a will*; but through the Wisdom He *bringeth Himself into substance*."

"The Spirit of God maketh no new thing in man, nor doth it infuse any strange spirit into him, but he speaketh of the wonders in the Wisdom of God through man, and that not from the eternal constellation only, but likewise from the external constellation; that is

[1] Epistles (1649), Ep. 6, par. 15.   [2] Ibid., Ep. 2, par. 25.
[3] Election, ch. viii., par. 121.

through the spirit of the external world he openeth in man the internal constellation of the soul." [1]

"We find seven especial properties in nature whereby this only Mother worketh all things," (to wit, *desire* which is astringent, *bitterness*, cause of all motion, *anguish*, cause of all sensibility, *fire, light, sound,* and *substantiality*); "whatsoever the six forms are spiritually that the seventh is essentially." ... "These are the seven forms of the Mother of all Beings, from whence all whatsoever is in this world is generated." [2]

"The Creator hath, in the body of this world, generated Himself as it were *creaturely* in His qualifying or fountain spirits, and all the stars are nothing else but God's powers, and the whole body of this world consisteth in the seven qualifying or fountain spirits." [3]

(See *Treatise on Election*, ch. viii., par. 73, for detailed account of the action of these fountain spirits; "in a wheel or orb, like a moving sphere or clock-work, shut up with its generating life, wherein the properties are wrestling for the *primacy*; suddenly one is aloft, suddenly the other, the third, fourth, fifth, sixth, and seventh, as is also to be understood concerning the proceeding forth of the seven properties.")

Now, " the seed of man is generated in such a manner as the wonderful proportion, harmony or form of nature in its wrestling and rising up is generated from eternity; for the human flesh is and resembleth nature in the body of God, which is generated from the other six qualifying or fountain spirits, wherein the qualifying or fountain spirits generate themselves again and shew forth themselves *infinitely*, wherein forms and images rise up, and wherein the Heart of God, or the holy clear Deity in the middle or central seal generateth itself

[1] Epistles (1649), Ep. 2, par. 29.
[2] Signatura Rerum, ch. xiv., pars. 10, 14, 15.
[3] Aurora, ch. xxiv., par. 27.

above nature in that centre wherein the light of life riseth up."[1]

Observe that *fire* is the middle form of the seven, and that the soul without the soul's spirit is, Böhme tells us, a fire-globe, its original nature being the first three forms of eternal nature, which from the torment of their essential discord kindle the fourth—the fire—from which the *light* of life rises up and proceeds, in due evolution, to pacify and harmonize them all. When all seven forms are generated then first has the soul attained a spirit and a body too. And what goes on in the whole world of external nature has precisely the same cause and same effect in man.

"The life of man in this time is like a wheel where very suddenly that which is underneath becometh uppermost, and kindleth itself with every substance." . . . "and every form maketh substance in its desire,"[2] the prevailing "primacy" of one fountain Spirit determining this desire.

"For this is the right or law of the Deity that every life in the body of God should generate itself in one manner or uniform way; though it be done through many *various* imagings, yet the life hath one uniform way and original in all."[3]

"Man is created according to the qualifying or fountain spirits of God, and also out of the Divine Being" (*i.e.*, the *Spirit* of God and the *Wisdom* of God),[4] "*therefore* man's life hath such a beginning and rising up as that of the planets and stars was."[5]

"But that there are so many stars of so manifold

---

[1] Aurora, ch. xxvi., pars. 48, 49.
[2] Small Six Points, Point II., pars. 22 and 13.
[3] Aurora, ch. xxv., par. 51.
[4] "The Wisdom is the Holy Spirit's corporeity."—*First Apology*, Part II., par. 313.
[5] Aurora, ch. xxvi., par. 39.

different effects and operations, is from the infiniteness which is in the efficiency of the Seven Spirits of God in one another, which generate themselves infinitely,"[1] and "man's property lieth in sundry degrees, according to the inward and outward heavens, viz., according to the Divine manifestation, through the seven properties of nature."[2]

Add one more saying to all these—which I have tried to make intelligible by sequence:—

"Out of every separability of that which is separated or distinguished ariseth a Will according to the *property* or condition thereof; into whatsoever quality, condition or source the abyssal Will in the separability hath introduced itself, such a Will existeth."[3]

And I think it will be evident that Böhme takes us nearer to the cause of man's "quality with respect to reception" of influx being so different in different natures; for the wrestling wheel of nature before birth necessarily causes a predominant influence of one over the other at the time of the propagation of *soul*; and this effecting the future *will* and *desire necessarily* qualifies the Spirit.

The mystery that remains untouched is, why the soul of man should be held responsible for good or evil when its inward disposition lay in the "*Eternal commencing ground*"?

In the universal regeneration of future Æons this seal may be opened, but for the present, seeing how even our fallen world is saturated with love, the quietus of all my thoughts is that God is love, and our world and our life in Him.

[1] Aurora, ch. xxiv., par. 28.   [2] Mysterium Magnum, ch. xvi., par. 15.
[3] Election, ch. ix., par. 32.

WHO ARE OUR SPIRITUAL ENEMIES?[1]

"We are to consider how, out of the eternal good, an evil is come to be?"
—[J. B.'s *Mysterium Magnum*, ch. iii., par. 1.]

IF indeed mystical research is one of the objects which *Light* was intended to promote, ideas drawn from Jacob Böhme, the greatest of European mystics, cannot be out of place in its pages; very much out of favour no doubt they are. The majority of readers cannot care for them; but it is in the minority that pioneers of spiritual progress are generally found, and believing that to such Böhme's teaching is welcome, and that by such some adequate notion of its value will gain larger currency, I venture to plunge once more into a subject that must necessarily be abstruse—the nature of those enemies from which human souls have to be saved. I was going to say *desire* to be saved; but the characteristic of our time is that that desire is so faint in the majority as to be hardly perceptible. There must be some reason for this which the pulpit phrase, "a growing want of faith," hardly suffices to explain. The want is evident enough—its cause in contemporary *intellectual* life not so easily detected. Torpor of the will, stimulated externally by ever new varieties of allurement, and dulled, as to internal consciousness, by consequent preoccupation, is of course the main factor of coldness to spiritual interests; but the peculiar anomaly of our day is that often, with a very serious

[1] Light, 1883, vol. iii. pp. 480, 489, 521, 535, 544, 554, 564; 1884, vol. iv. pp. 2, 24.

attention to these, there is entire contempt for all that used to act on our ancestors, either as a religious check or incentive—the common attitude of many a highly cultivated mind as to this, being such as we take with regard to machinery that did its work well in the past, but has since been superseded by better inventions.

For example, when it is a question of belief in the Incarnation of the Son of God for the redemption of man, it is not vigorous disbelief that one generally discovers in unbelievers, so much as total indifference. Arguments and evidence miss their aim on minds quite incurious as to proof or disproof. When no need of salvation has been felt or perceived, the fact of a Saviour having come must be wholly unconcerning; and if, setting aside all apprehension as to a future life, it is urged that One came on earth "to save His people from their sins," the proffer is unheeded, not from ignorance of sin, or always from any lack of sincerest longing to be rid of its yoke, but from the conviction of powerful minds that human beings are able to be their own saviours; or in natures of an opposite mould, that sin is a fatality and not evitable.

This, so far as I can understand, is the fashion of modern philosophy, and it holds its ground by virtue of partial truth, famous as an amalgam for the rapid extension of error. Accepting such truth so far as it goes, —that by our own force if *we will* we can often resist temptation, and that organizations are frequently met with whose escape from sin would be little short of miraculous,—I appeal both to history and to present living consciousness when asking, Has sin no greater force than what self-command and self-culture can overpower? Have we verily no enemies worse than ourselves, promoting vice, urging us to evil?

It is very old-fashioned to admit any belief in the Satan of Holy Writ and the powers of darkness, against which it warns; by many people they have been consigned with Luther's devil to the lumber room of history, as obsolete superstitions; and so ignorant are we, for the most part, of the weakness of human nature, that in saying as some do, that they are not afraid of finding any worse enemy than self, they think it an assurance of comparative safety. But if in man's radical being there are realms of potential anguish and unguessed springs of torment, if, indeed, there is nothing in the universe which the soul of man does not comprise and share, what an idle boast it is! And if there are no evil beings alike the accomplices and the avengers of sin, why such terror in evil doers when death comes to shut them out in the unseen world? What do they fear if there are no powers of darkness? The wrath of God? Alas! it is not only belief in a devil, that has been dissipated in the crucible of modern thought!

Carlyle said truly, "The effects of optics in this strange camera obscura of existence are most of all singular. The grand centre of the modern revolution of ideas is ever this—we begin to have a notion that all this *is* the effect of optics, and that the intrinsic fact is very different from our old conception of it." From Böhme I learned what *is* the difference of the intrinsic fact and our conception of spiritual dangers; and I can see how extremely difficult it would be to rectify mistakes which run on a smooth, well-worn groove of habit, by recondite truths for which a road must be cut out through all oppositions of prejudice and sloth. Still this much must be granted, that hitherto no school of religionists has pretended to meet the root obstacle to religious faith,— *the power of evil in a world created by Omnipotent God.* It is invariably evaded: reason and philosophy are warned off *that* ground, and piety tries to fence off any approach to it, as the brink of a tremendous abyss of perplexity, lest there it should be maddened into Atheism.

Böhme challenged his contemporaries on just this point, asking, after many other questions, "What do you suppose *God's wrath* to be? or what is *that* in man which displeaseth God so much that He tormenteth and afflicteth man so, seeing *He* hath created him? And that He imputeth sin unto man and condemneth him to eternal punishment? Why hath He created that wherein or wherewith man committeth sin? Surely *that thing* must be far worse? Wherefore *and out of what* is that come to be? or what is the cause, or the beginning, or the birth and geniture of God's fierce wrath out of or from which hell and the devil are come to be? Or how comes it that all the creatures in this world do bite, scratch, strike, beat and worry one another, and yet sin is imputed only to man? Out of what are poisonous and venomous beasts and worms, and all manner of vermin come to be?" . . . "Give your direct and fundamental answer to this, and demonstrate what you say."[1]

No answer has ever been attempted—to the best of my belief—from his time to ours. It has been easier, and it was judged to be *safer*, to leave such mysteries alone; and as to attending to the one who did give answer to these questions, it was *much* easier to call him either a dangerous fanatic, or a wild dreamer, than to master one of his books. Only a few, and those of robust intellect, have accepted his teaching, at first as but a theoretic scheme; and at last as revelation that appeased all doubts.

But *was* it safe to leave these awful mysteries untouched? Did not such careful ignoring of their pressure on the mind cause suspicion that danger to faith lay there? When so many spiritual delusions have been ended by critical analysts of the past, it cannot surprise us that with this terrible excuse for doubt in the unexplained rule of evil (not to speak of any other excuse

[1] Aurora, ch. xxii., pars. 36, 37.

drawn from the lives of average Christians), reflective people begin to suspect *all* previous articles of faith of being accommodations to human ignorance. It is thus that every transitional epoch endangers the kernel with the husk.

Now, one often hears it said that all religions must undergo change and modification, as if that truth justified disbelief in the essentials of Christianity; a child when first conscious of the laws of perspective might as wisely say that these prevented his seeing some lofty hill conspicuous from all sides. Human ideas of Deity must expand, and so far alter with growth, but to try and efface the centre of structural life would be the very reverse of evolution; and to ignore a God is quite as much a retrograde movement.

Let me, as well as I can, sum up a few positions in which, apart from Böhme's solution, we must find ourselves when confronting the power of evil in this world. Either we must suppose evil and good to be alike the fortuitous outcome of impersonal will-less forces; or that evil originates in the will of some mighty Being *not* God, with whom God is in conflict, and so far as we can see in all our past and present here, *not* victorious; or to use the words of Mr St George Stock, "That evil is appointed in the good providence of God for some wise end." Had he said *permitted*, that statement might be allowed by the mystic, "but," he adds, "if all is to come right in the end, one hardly sees why it should have come wrong in the beginning." Now, it is precisely *that* which Böhme helps us to see.

I shall have to draw so much from Böhme in order to give his solution of the mystery of evil that my own words will be little more than connecting links for his. Earth-worms quote very largely from depths of earth which few eyes care to examine, and the little heaps of sifted mould which they bring up from the rough confusion of a lower soil serve to fertilize its more superficial plane. My ambition is to perform the office of an earthworm in another sort of ground.

When the creation of human beings is spoken of, it is as if a creature such as man could be willed into existence by Divine "fiat" without any possibility of defect (though that would make the derived being equal to its Creator), and without any formative constituents of nature. Any idea of means to this end is usually deemed unworthy of being connected with the work of Omnipotence; and this in a universe where, so far as we can judge, no end is attained without an enchainment of means that astonishes by its subtle niceties of adaptation, whenever it can be traced out.

"Many authors," says Böhme, "have written that Heaven and earth were created out of *nothing*, but I do wonder that among so many excellent men there hath not one been found that would yet describe the true ground, seeing the same God which now is hath been from eternity. Now, where nothing is, there nothing can come to be; all things must have a *root*, else nothing can grow. If the *seven spirits* of nature had not been from eternity then there would no angel, no Heaven, also no earth have come to be."[1] (*N.B.*—He means *eternal nature*, as all the rest of his teaching proves.) Further on he refers to these seven spirits again thus: "Thou must know that all the seven spirits of God are in the earth, and generate, as they do in Heaven. For the earth is in God, and God never died."[2] And in man, "for man's house of flesh is also such a house as the dark deep of this world is, wherein the seven spirits of God generate themselves."[3]

To explain by Böhme's own words what he means by these seven spirits of Eternal Nature, and the seven

[1] Aurora, ch. xix., pars. 67, 68.   [2] Ibid., ch. xxi., par. 78.
[3] Ibid., ch. xxvi., par. 81.

"forms" in the nature of our universe derived from that, would be to write a small volume, not very intelligible either. I must therefore hazard an attempt, roughly and briefly, to indicate what he tells about them, viz., that the Infinite Source of all being willed to manifest the infinite wonders of the Abyssal only God; that this will caused the magnetic (attractive) compression of desire, the darkness of an enclosure of a previously unseeking infinitude of powers and ideas which [1] he calls "*the nothing*"—in contradiction to any conceivable *somewhat*—and sometimes the "liberty." "The Lubet of the liberty doth introduce itself into Nature and essence, that it might be manifest in power, wonder, and being." [2] This enclosure of the desire, condensing power, so to speak, for concentrated purpose, is the *cause* of the second form of nature (itself the first)—the *mobility*, with its ceaseless wrestling to escape from that strong astringent force, and both together are the cause of the third—the *anguish* generated by such contrary action, and the divided sensibility it necessitates; this again drives on to such intensity of whirling motion as to enkindle *fire*, the fourth form; this again, by the secret influence of the *Lubet*, producing light and love, the fifth; *sound*, and resulting intelligence, the sixth; and all these finding in the seventh, *substantiality*, their completion and full appeasement. (This is, I am well aware, a very lame and crude representation of Böhme's revelation as to the origin of Nature; but this consoles me for my total inability to do justice to my theme; competent writers have admirably written about it—Dionysius Freher and William Law, for instance,—and what they

---

[1] "For the vast infinite space desireth narrowness and inclosure, wherein it may manifest itself, for else in the wide stillness there would be no manifestation. Therefore there must be an *attraction* and inclosing out of which the manifestation appeareth."—*Threefold Life*, ch. i., par. 33.

[2] Signatura Rerum, ch. xiv., par. 26.

wrote is unread. Inferior articles have in the present day a better chance of attention.)

It may be well to quote (abbreviated) one of Böhme's shortest summaries to justify my paraphrase; it can hardly be said to explain.

"We find seven especial properties in Nature, whereby this only mother worketh all things, which are these, viz., *first*, Desire, which is astringent, cold and hard and dark; *secondly*, bitterness, which is the sting of the astringent hard enclosure; this is the cause of all motion and life; *thirdly*, the anguish by reason of the raging of the impression where the impressed hardness falleth into a tearing anguish and pain by reason of the sting. *Fourthly*, the fire, where the eternal will [the Lubet] doth introduce itself into a darting flash"... "with which the hardness is again consumed and *introduced into a corporeal moving spirit*. *Fifthly*, the egress of the free will out of the darkness and out of the fire, and the potent desire which it hath sharpened in the fire, doth now in the light's desire draw into itself the essence from the fire, dying according to its hunger, the which is now water, and in the lustre it is a tincture from the fire and light, viz., a love-desire. *Sixthly*, the voice or sound. *Seventhly*, whatsoever the six forms are spiritually that the seventh is essentially, or in real substance."

"Thus these are the seven forms of the Mother of all Beings, whence all whatsoever is, is in this generated."[1]

I am painfully conscious of the obscurity of this passage; on first reading it will affect the mind as wonderful nonsense; but could any true explanation of creating life be *sensed* by the intelligence of man in his present state? I am sure it could not. The entirely ignorant must take something on trust, before any foundation of knowledge can be laid.

[1] Signatura Rerum, ch. xiv., pars. 10-15.

Readers who are fortunate enough to possess any of Böhme's writings will find in each of them abundant mention of these seven forces or forms of Eternal Nature. What I fail to make as intelligible as the subject admits, reference to his fuller account may make clearer. For instance, *Aurora*, ch. xviii., par. 28. But I must observe that had it not been for Freher's more lucid, though very profound treatise on *Deity as Manifested through Nature*, I should never, from Böhme alone, have been able to understand what he meant by the *Lubet*, or *how* the good pleasure of Divine love acted through the wrestling wheel of the seven Spirits of God. Those who have access to this very rare work or to C. Walton's *Memorial of Law* (unpublished, but to be found in most of our largest public libraries), which contains large extracts from other writings of Freher, will find the trouble of following his close line of argument richly repaid.[1]

Now, it is in the arrest of the right evolution of these seven forms of Eternal Nature that all evil begins, and before we deal with the question, "Who are our spiritual enemies?" we ought to learn how it is that in a world created by a holy God, anything can be antagonistic; and, as these "forms" are the seven Spirits *of God*, "generating God," as Böhme has it, the Scriptural saying, "I create evil"[2] is strictly true; though it is none the less true that God is love and did not will evil.

Let us try if by any possible analogy we can help ourselves to understand this passage ever so little. Suppose that an embryonic form of human origin was shewn to us, we should regard it with horror; it is an abortion, a comparatively formless and revolting approach to what, in its full growth, is a beautiful human shape, and yet it

---

[1] [For a catalogue of Freher's works, see *Memorial of William Law*, pp. 141-142, 679-688, and *Threefold Life*, 1909, Appendix B.—ED.]
[2] Isaiah xlv. 7.

is a requisite preparation for that matured excellence. All sinful beings, in our kind of bodies or out of them, are in this sense embryonic monsters; they have fallen short of right evolution; they act and feel in God and by the powers of God, and yet are contrary to God and remain in the wrath of God because good in them has not been wrought out to true being. And what is the cause of evil is equally the cause of the ceaseless unrest of human life. "Rest," Franz Baader tells us, "is unimpeded total activity. Every being acts restlessly so long as it has not attained the totality of its energies. The striving forces of Time seek rest, not to die but to be active without hindrance."

Perhaps Freher's image of the broken ring gives as good an idea of the cause of antagonism from breach of original sequence as any form of words could. After a long and careful exposition of the original good of the darkness which *must* underlie the production of fire before light itself can be manifested, he continues: "It belonged therefore essentially to God's eternal manifestation, of which it was—as to our weak apprehension—the first beginning that could have been made, if its end was to be attained; and which beginning having never been separated from its end, could not have been evil and stand in opposition to its end, which was good, and both together were but one thing. For this end found and took hold of its beginning and swallowed it up, so that they made together but one globe wherein they were inseparably within each other, the light manifested in the darkness and shining in it, and the darkness hid in the light, and not comprehending it; as we see in a simile, in every ring or circle in which the beginning and the end are united and combined, and which would never be called a circle or a ring if it had no beginning and end, yet so that the end always lays hold of the beginning and swallows it up into itself, and the beginning be lost and disappear in the end. Now, Lucifer, who, it is granted, is not a maker, still less a creator, but a destroyer, first broke the harmonious ring in himself—for inasmuch as he was a creature, inferior and posterior to Eternal Nature, he must necessarily have had it within himself—and thereby the beginning of it appeared by itself divided from its end, and was placed in strong opposition against it; just as when a ring is broken a beginning and end appear opposite to each other, whereas it was before but one entire thing."[1]

Lucifer, according to Böhme, first looked back into the strong first forms of Eternal Nature, in which he thought with his *fire* to prove superiority over the *meekness of light*; and in this process of imagining for himself self-chosen elevation, his light extinguished and his fire remained in the dark world.

To enlarge upon this portion of the subject would carry this paper beyond bounds, and is not necessary for its aim; only it should not be forgotten that any attempt to popularize doctrines of this vast scope *must* be at the sacrifice of all due proportion; many an adjacent branch of the subject must be ignored if minds unused to such themes are to be won to attend to them at all. The point I wish to make good without fatiguing by too copious extracts from my teacher, is that what we call *evil* took its rise when first Spirits of exceeding power, acting in God with all the Divine forces of the first four Spirits of Eternal Nature, "fell short of the glory of God," and broke the perfect sequence of right evolution. And that these mighty angels, with all their constituent Spirits, have for millions of ages remained in this state of tremendous opposition to light, to love, to all that is called in a special sense God—though nothing can have being out of, or apart from, the first Creator—God, the Father of Spirits.

[1] From D. A. Freher's Third Section of *Treatise on Deity*.

If I am told that all this belief in Lucifer and the fallen angels is the remains of superstition, an obsolete engine of priestcraft, I would request answer to this one question—since no philosopher will, I suppose, deny the truth of this dictum of St Martin's: "La mesure d'une erreur est en même tems la mesure de la vérité correspondante."[1] What can the truth be which corresponds to these old-world beliefs in a mighty tempter, a cruel adversary, a tormentor of evil men?

If both philosophy and theology are silent, surely the answer which during two centuries has satisfied some of the strongest intellects, might be accepted now for at least a working hypothesis.

"We have shewn you already concerning the seven forms of the Centre of the Eternal Nature, where every form is a several well-spring of nature; in like manner out of every form, out of every well-spring, go forth *spirits*, according to the multiplicity of essences and properties, every one according to its kind."[2]

It is curious how absolutely blind we may be to the freight of a sentence for which we have no prepared ground: it may be read repeatedly and yet lodge no idea in the mind. This is particularly the case when we read writings so loaded with obscurities as Böhme's necessarily are. (*Could* the riddle of the universe, if it were explained to us, be solved in simple language?) I suppose I must have passed over these words, "*Out of every form go forth spirits*," at least a dozen times before—only a year ago—they suddenly lit up a labyrinth of puzzles for which I had never found a clue. But I had found and held fast the Scriptural sayings that caused these puzzles, and so when the light flashed in, there was proof of its being true light, ready at every point

---

[1] De L'Esprit des Choses, vol. i. p. 88.
[2] Threefold Life, ch. iv., par. 37.

on which it fell. And just this is the advantage of the blind faith so often scornfully spoken of; it fixes words of revealed truth in the mind, and holds them there until intelligence can overtake belief: whereas if only what can be understood is retained, the measure of understanding is too likely to become the test of what we can believe to be true, and then the superstitions of ignorance stultify us more and more.

I read in the Bible of the enemies of the soul, of the powers of darkness, of spiritual wickedness in high places, and without any cavil, asked myself, How can God allow them to be powers? Why are they enemies? How did spiritual wickedness get into high places? and this tempting of the devil, even supposing that myriads of evil spirits form the enemy of mankind, how is it effected when, so far as self-consciousness goes, we are, for the most part, our own tempters? But having fully grasped Böhme's doctrine as to the soul of man being existent in the mutual interaction of the seven Spirits of Eternal Nature, having for the root of its *manifested* life the three first "tormentive forms" of that nature,—the fourth, *fire*, for its first essential life in nature; and the three last forms for the blissful evolution of that life, with a will acting in its fiery life free to allow either form or property of nature to elevate itself above the rest in its own abyss; free to "imagine into" either, to draw with all the magic magnetic strength of the will towards either,—then these few words "*Out of every form go forth spirits*," explained to me more than I had ever hoped in this life to understand.

To say that a man has no worse enemy than himself, meaning by such words that he permits and indulges what is evil in himself, is therefore to utter a very foolish, ignorant, and cruelly misleading notion. For what *is* man? A being who consists as to *nature* (of his anti-naturing original I do not speak) of these seven forms of Eternal Nature, which extend through all created worlds and cause all manifestations of spiritual life: hence his own abyss of being is in a very mysterious but terrible sense contiguous to that of *all* others, and limitless in potentiality. What is more awful still, man made in the likeness of God has no equal in the spiritual world in this prerogative—he alone among all creatures is a denizen of what Böhme calls the three principles, *i.e.*, the dark world, the world of light, and the world of ultimated essences; (corrupt and mixed in the nature of our earth, but pure and glorious and truly substantial in the region from which our world of nature derives); so that spirits native to those three principles all desire the agency of man, for "all would be creaturely"; even, so Böhme tells, "the Deity hath had a longing to see the wonders of the Eternal Nature and of the innumerable essences in substance and in corporeal things."[1] All seek the agency of a being who can represent their dominant desire in ultimates.

In the commonest instincts of human nature this longing to realize internal life by external shews itself; witness the efforts of an angry person to get some one else into a rage; of rough strong men to promote a fight; of greedy or frivolous characters to further the gluttony and vanity which they cannot themselves indulge. Now in the dark world where true substance is impossible to attain, this eagerness for *embodied* representatives is presumably very strong.

In the seventh form of Eternal Nature, the substantiality, all the other forms find their completion and rest, and this, one may suppose, is one reason for the effort of the spirits in each principle or property to find ultimation, *i.e.*, embodiment in man.

"The desire of the dark world is after the manifestation, viz., after the outward world, to attract and draw

[1] Threefold Life, ch. iv., par. 26.

the same essentiality into it, and thereby to satisfy its wrathful hunger."[1]

For every fire in the spiritual as well as in the material world needs substance to maintain its strength. Let us pause a moment to think what the will of an angry person is—anger, that so common ripple on the surface of life's tremendous depths!—in connection with the following passage: "The Spirit of God worketh in love and anger. For it is the spirit of every life; it is in everything, like as the thing's will and property is; for one property receiveth another; what the soul willeth, that willeth also the same into which the soul turneth itself: it is all magical: whatsoever the will of a thing willeth, *that* it receiveth."[2] Remembering also that "the original nature, first, and radical principle or constituent essence of the soul without the light of God is as mere a devil or infernal dragon as Lucifer himself is."[3]

Any one meeting the eye of man or woman when wrath bursts into utterance, must have instinctive consciousness of this, little as the oppressive or agitating influences of rage are understood. And not only one dragon in human guise confronts us then,—not *one* bosom devil animates us when our wrath blazes out: in either case, a multitude of spirits who go forth from the wellspring of nature in the property of wrath combine to emphasize the provocation and keep up the fire. This is quite as certain as that the least brawl in the street quickly attracts a circle of eagerly sympathizing spectators; and, if we but knew what we were about when we allow an angry look or word or gesture to escape us, we should suppress the first movement of indignation

---

[1] Signatura Rerum, ch. ii., par. 35.
[2] Great Six Points, Point V., ch. viii., pars. 48, 49.
[3] Way to Christ (Bath, 1775), p. 389, An Epistle from Jacob Behmen to a Person under Temptation and Trouble of Mind, par. 11. See also *Epistles* (1649), Ep. 13, par. 11.

as anxiously as we remove gunpowder from risks of accidental ignition.

"We have good and evil in us, into which we frame our willing, the essence thereof becometh stirring in us, and such a property we draw also from without into us." ... "If we lead ourselves to the good, then God's Spirit helpeth us, but if we lead ourselves to evil, then God's fierce wrath and anger helpeth us; what we will, of that property we get a leader, and thereunto we lead ourselves. And yet it is not the Deity's will that we perish, but His *anger's* and *our will*."[1]

The fall of Lucifer is described by Böhme as having been caused by this sense of power leading him to despise "the meekness and lowliness in which consisteth the Kingdom of Heaven, and the virtue of the heart of God." "He saw," Böhme tells us, "the greatest hidden mysteries of the Deity stand in such humility, he took offence at it, and entered into the fierce might of the fire, and would domineer with his own self, wit and reason over the heart of God: he would that God should be in subjection under him, he would be a framer and creator in nature, and therefore he became a devil."[2]

I am, of course, very far from thinking that by this crude statement, I convey any adequate notion of what these words were meant to indicate,—as far as I am from thinking that I fully understand them; but I understand enough for my immediate purpose, which is to shew how evil and enmity began among the "throne angels"; and let us hear Böhme's account of these before we go further. "Behold, when God set the Fiat in the will and would create angels, then the Spirit first separated all qualities after that manner as you now see there are many kinds of stars, and so the Fiat created them. Then there were created the princely angels and

[1] Great Six Points, Point V., ch. viii., pars. 52-54.
[2] Threefold Life, ch. iv. par. 61.

the throne angels, according to every quality out of the source of the Fire, a similitude whereof you have in the stars, how different they are." (Note that the three first forms of Eternal Nature and the darkness they move in are necessarily prior in action to the opening of the "source of fire.") "Now the throne and princely angels are every one of them a great fountain." . . . "Out of each fountain came forth again a centre in many thousand thousands." . . . "Every host which proceeded out of one and the same fountain gat a will in the same fountain which was their prince."[1]

Now, "when the moving to the creating of the angels was effected, then, . . . the properties stood in great working and did will to be creatural. In these properties did the creaturely will of Lucifer create; when he did apprehend the omnipotence therein, and found the wonder-doing power himself. . . . And instantly the properties in him became revealed or manifested, viz., the cold fire,"—(query, what we mean by negative electricity?)—"also the sharp, sour, hard, bitter, stinging painfulness or torment of the fire: thus became he an enemy of all love, humility, and meek gentleness."[2]

Why *thus*? Because "every property keepeth its own desire, for a property is nothing but a hunger, and the hunger doth form itself into such an essence as itself is." . . . "The dark hunger desireth essence according to its property, viz., earthly things; and the bitter hunger desireth bitter raging, stinging and pain; and the hunger of anguish desireth anxious hunger; also the melancholy taketh the desire to die, and continual sadness."[3] (Alas! we have not far to seek for proof of this; we find it in ourselves; we bewail it in other people!)

And, further, Lucifer "desired to be an *artist*. He

[1] Three Principles, ch. xi., pars. 1–2.
[2] 177 Theosophic Questions, Ques. 7, pars. 4, 5, 7.
[3] Signatura Rerum, ch. xiv., pars. 52–56.

saw the Creation, and understood the ground, wherein he would be an own self-god, and rule with the central fire's might in all things, and image himself with all things, in all forms, that he might be what he would, and not what the Creator would; as, indeed, this is still to this day their greatest joy" (the hosts of Lucifer) "that they can transmute themselves into many images, and thus achieve or make phansie [fantasy]."[1]

It was just this self-chosen application of power—this willing in opposition to the holy will of the *whole* of God's eternal nature, that brought the mighty rebel and all his hosts, in Böhme's language, "out of the temperature." "This is the very abomination before God that the life's forms are gone out from the equal agreement,"[2] for "nothing is evil which remaineth in the equal accord, for that which the worst doth cause and make with its coming forth out of the accord, that likewise maketh the best in the equal accord." ... "All was very exceeding good, but with its own elevation and departure out of the equality it becomes evil, and brings itself out of the form or property of the love and joy into a painful tormenting form and property." "King Lucifer stood in the beginning of his creation in highest joyfulness, but he departed from the likeness." ... "He forsook his order, and went out of the harmony wherein God created him; he would be lord of all, and so he entered into the austere fire's domination, and is now an instrument in the austere fire's might, upon which also the all-essential spirit striketh and soundeth upon his instrument; but it soundeth only according to the wrathful fire's property."[3] I think we have now sufficient data to understand why, if "out of every form as a well-spring go forth spirits" with the same will as that of their awakening

---

[1] 177 Theosophic Questions, Ques. 10, par. 1.
[2] Third Apology, Text IV., Point II., par. 66.
[3] Signatura Rerum, ch. xvi., pars. 6, 7.

Prince, the soul of man, which subsists in the perpetual interaction of the seven forms of Eternal Nature, *must* live among enemies to peace, externally as well as internally, constitutionally opposed to its welfare, until all are *atoned*, made one in *equal* action by perfected evolution. Now, by such unsuitable terms as outer and inner, which in a deeper sense no one could use regarding spirits, I only mean to indicate that enemies arise from the discords of other souls as well as from those beginning in our own.

Very significantly does Böhme say in his *Aurora*, to which I must refer the student for copious (and to a patient mind fairly intelligible) teaching about Lucifer, "In his pride he smote himself with darkness and blindness, and made himself a devil. He knew in God only the *majesty* and not the Word in the centre. He would needs inflame himself and rule in the fire over the meekness."[1] To the present hour how incessantly we make the same mistake! The dignity of pride, the superb stateliness of indignation, the forceful bluster of wrath, how much stronger and more availing they feel to every angry human heart! It knows the majesty, *i.e.*, the might of the kindled aching forms of nature, but not "*the Word in the centre*," the meek light of love escaping from the fire, and shining far beyond the lurid prison where only wrath and pain can be generated, and never the waters of eternal life and the imperishable substance which it forms. The forces of Eternal Nature are mighty, but to the Word in the centre alone was *all* power given in Heaven and in earth.

In the first book of *Kings*, ch. xix., the agency of the powers of Divine Nature, as contrasted with that of the Word of God, is marked emphatically. We read there that "The Lord passed by, and a great and strong wind rent the mountains, and brake in pieces the rocks

---

[1] Aurora, ch. xv., par. 12.

WHO ARE OUR SPIRITUAL ENEMIES? 205

before the Lord, but the Lord was not in the wind, and after the wind an earthquake, but the Lord was not in the earthquake, and after the earthquake a fire, but the Lord was not in the fire, and after the fire a still small voice." To this the negative is not added, and we are led to suppose that the God of Israel was in that voice made known. Again, when the disciples of Jesus proposed to bring fire from Heaven to punish the Samaritans, His gentle monition, "Ye know not what manner of spirit ye are of,"[1] suggests Divine knowledge of the evil source of a wish for exercising resistant *power* even with good intentions. "The devil sought great strength and power, as the present world doth great might and honour and despiseth the light of love."[2] And until Jesus Christ came to this earth and shewed the majesty of humble self-sacrifice, the power of meekness was unknown, and to this day so contrary is it to our natural ideas of greatness that very generally it is mistaken for defect of force.

"Learn of Me for I am meek and lowly of heart," was the new and wonderful teaching of Him Who gave for His last and all-embracing commandment, "*Love one another*." And now we know that "in love and meekness we become new-born out of the anger of God; in love and meekness we must strive and fight," . . . "for love is the devil's poison, it is a fire of terror to him wherein he cannot stay."[3] "Therefore it is that Christ so earnestly teacheth us love, humility, and mercifulness; and the cause why God is become man is for our salvation and happiness sake, that we should not turn back from His love."[4] In this passage the connection of ideas is not evident until we remember

[1] Luke ix. 55.
[2] Great Six Points, Point III., ch. iv., par. 31.
[3] Incarnation, Part II., ch. vii., pars. 44, 45.
[4] Threefold Life, ch: xiv., par. 71.

the office of imagination in re-moulding the attitude, and hence the "spirit of the soul," for, "*mark this, every imagination maketh an essence.*"[1] To say nothing here of the far less comprehensible effects of the Word taking flesh upon Him, we can easily see how much a fellow creature's example, greatly admired, tells upon the ideal of his admirers, and consequently upon their self-conduct. Jesus Christ gave the human race an absolutely new ideal. His forerunner announced that the Kingdom of Heaven was at hand, but He revealed the more important truth, "the Kingdom of God is within you." Into that Kingdom we enter so soon as we surrender ourselves to meekness and love; "in the love the fire dieth and transmuteth itself into joy."[2] Yes! and therefore is the joy resulting in proportion to the dying of the kindled fire.

But the habitual maintenance of love and meekness is, I suppose, a difficult achievement even to those who are constitutionally placable; to people of irascible nature so extremely difficult as to call for the Biblical proviso, "If it be possible, as much as lieth in you, live peaceably with all men."[3] With all men and at all times it is not possible, and for such exceptional cases Böhme gives a recipe which no one will ever try in vain. "If a fire riseth up in one qualifying spirit then that is not concealed from the soul. It may instantly awaken the other qualifying spirits which are contrary to the kindled fire, and may quench it. But if the fire will be, or become, too big, then hath the soul a prison, wherein it may shut up the kindled spirit, viz., in hard astringent quality" (which *here* I venture to explain to myself as *inaction and silence*)—"and the other spirits must be the jailers, till wrath be allayed and the fire be extinguished," . . . "but if the spirit breaketh out of prison, then put it in

---

[1] A Warning from Iacob Beem, par. 2 (*Epistles*, 1649).
[2] Third Apology, Text I., par. 58.　　[3] Rom. xii. 18.

again, *make good* thy part against it as long as thou livest." [1]

I must diverge a little from the main line of this chapter to call attention to the way Böhme here contrasts the power of the seven fountain Spirits with that of the soul, taking for granted its possible supremacy in every conflict. He here identifies the *soul* and *the will*; now as elsewhere the soul is spoken of as *one* with the seven Spirits of Eternal Nature, confusion of thought will result unless we carefully bear in mind that he has shewn that this Eternal Nature was, and is, the consequence of the Abyssal Deity willing to manifest itself: the original of the human soul also was prior to its manifestation, for we are told that God breathed into man the breath of life—a life that must have preceded all nature and creature since it emanated from God, and made man to be in the likeness of God. Hence the much contested free-will of man which now fights at such tremendous odds against what we call fate; *i.e.*, the forces of inferior beings raised by *his* fall, and insubordination to comparatively superior power, nay, in time, and as regards his external life to most undeniable superiority. Yet, notwithstanding all the opposition of the stars and the elements in his outer life, in the life within "all is possible; as soon is the good changed into evil as the evil into good. For every man is free, and is as a god to himself, he may change or alter himself in this life either into wrath or into light." [2]

An assertion that many will contradict, but one that should be taken as bearing upon the generality of human beings; not those who by long-continued indulgence of lowest instincts have lost, or by the hereditary penalties of ancestral vice have hardly ever attained, consciousness of their human birth-right.

In one short sentence Böhme sums up what is in the

[1] Aurora, ch. x., pars. 85, 86, 90.   [2] Ibid., ch. xviii., pars. 42, 43.

power of every human being whose spiritual degradation is not yet complete. "Man hath the death in him, whereby he may die unto the evil."[1]

Incapable as the deeply corrupted may be of doing or feeling anything right, *ceasing to do evil* remains possible, and when this—the whole of man's share in working out his own salvation—is persisted in, the Divine spirit begins and carries on the new creation of regenerate life. This habitual death to the instigations of the *divided* properties or forms of nature in us, is the indispensable condition of any true life. "The curse of God" (*i.e.*, the withdrawal of God's holiness—wholeness of action) "is come into the seven forms so that they are in strife and enmity, and one form doth annoy the other, and can never agree unless they all seven enter into death and die unto the self-will. Now, this cannot be except a death come into them, which breaks all their will; as the Deity in Christ was a death to the human selfhood."[2]

And had not Jesus Christ broken the rebellious will of the human selfhood in a true human soul, this death had not been possible to us: "For the soul being sprung out of the Eternal source, and having its originality out of the eternity, none can redeem it in its own root of eternity, or bring it out of the anger, except there come one who is love itself and be born in its own very birth, that so he may bring it out of the anger and set it in the love in himself, as it was done in Christ." . . . "We know very exactly that we could not be redeemed except the Deity did go into the soul, and bring forth the will of the soul again out of the fierceness in itself, into the light of the meekness; for the root of life must remain or else the whole creature must be dissolved."[3]

I hope that to any attentive reader of these attempts to explain the source of evil and sin, it may be said,

---

[1] Signatura Rerum, ch. xvi., par. 28. [2] Ibid., ch. xii., par. 30.
[3] Three Principles, ch. xxv., pars. 6, 8.

"Seeing now we thus know what we are, and that God letteth us know it, we should now look to it and generate some good out of us, for we have the centre of Eternal Nature *in us*. If we make an angel out of us, then we are *that*; if we make a devil out of us, then we are *that*."[1] The all-important question is *how* to make the angel. Let not our ability be doubted, if only the will be constant, for the spirit of man "is a son of the properties, and also a lord of the same, for in him consists the power; he may awaken which he please."[2] "For thou must know that in the government of thy mind thou art thine own lord and master, there will rise up no fire in thee in the circle or whole circumference of thy body and spirit unless thou awakenest it thyself."[3] . . . "In what quality soever thou excitest or awakenest the spirit, and maketh it operative, according to that same quality the thoughts rise up and govern the mind. If thou stirrest or awakenest the spirit in the fire then there ariseth in thee the bitter and harsh anger, for as soon as the fire is kindled, which is done in the hardness and fierceness, *then* springeth up the bitter fierceness or wrath in the flesh."[4] . . . "Be it in love or in anger, that which thou liftest up thyself towards or against, thou kindlest the quality of that, and that it is which burneth in thy compacted incorporated spirit." . . . "For when thou lookest upon anything which doth not please thee, but is contrary to thee, then thou raisest up the fountain of thy heart as when thou takest a stone and therewith strikest fire on a steel, and so when the spark catcheth fire in the heart then the fire kindleth. At first it gloweth, but when thou stirrest the source or fountain of the heart more violently, then it is as when thou blowest the fire, so that the flame is kindled, and then it is high time to quench

---

[1] Incarnation, Part II., ch. ix., pars. 12, 13, 14.
[2] Signatura Rerum, ch. ii., par. 25.   [3] Aurora, ch. x., par. 81.
[4] Ibid., ch. x., pars. 69, 70.

it, else the fire will be too great and then burneth and consumeth, and doeth hurt to its neighbour."[1]

A more wordy exposition of a notorious fact than the Apostle's "Behold how great a fire a little matter kindleth!"[2] But he spoke of the effect of sparks escaping in utterance; Böhme's object was to expose the forge on which they are first struck out. And here we have to remember that the kindling of wrath is not a mischief confined to one part of our being: in the words of St James, "it setteth on fire the course of nature,"[3] (wheel, or birth of nature, it is in the revised translation of the New Testament, and this precisely harmonizes with Böhme's account of it).[4] "If a creature which is like or as the whole being of God spoileth, elevateth, or kindleth itself in a qualifying or fountain spirit, yet it kindleth not one spirit alone, but all the seven spirits."[5] But how to prevent this kindling!—"For out of the essences go the senses or thoughts; they are and have their original out of the harsh astringency; for they are the bitterness and run always into the mind as an anguish wheel, and seek rest to try whether they may attain to the liberty of God. They are they which strike up the fire in the anguish wheel." . . . "They are the mind's servants and are the subtlest messengers; they go into God, and again out of God into necessity. And whereinsoever they kindle themselves, either in God or in necessity, viz., in falsehood or wickedness, that they bring home to the mind. Therefore must the noble mind often be lord over the evil and stifle it in its anguish, when the thoughts have entertained or loaden in false or evil imaginations into the desire."[6]

But the exceeding difficulty of that stifling! For while wrath lasts, we are animated by the eternal

---

[1] Aurora, ch. x., pars. 71-73.   [2] James iii. 5.   [3] Ibid., iii. 6.
[4] See *Aurora*, ch. xvi., pars. 11-13.   [5] Ibid., ch. x., par. 7.
[6] Incarnation, Part II., ch. x., pars. 12-13, 17-19.

nature of wrath, which is incessantly giving birth to and substantializing its own creations, by reinforcements of justifying fancies; and "in the eternal nature of the wrath, the light or the kingdom of Heaven is not known, and also in the eternal light, the kingdom of wrath is not known, because each kingdom is in itself. So is the soul of man also: it hath both kingdoms in it; in which it tradeth, in that it standeth. If it trade in the kingdom of Heaven, then the kingdom of Hell is dead in it, not that it is ceased, but the kingdom of Heaven is predominant, and the kingdom of fierceness is changed into joy; so also if it trade in the kingdom of wrath, then that is predominant, and the kingdom of Heaven is, as it were, dead; although, indeed, in itself, it doth not vanish, yet the soul is not in it."[1] And this trading of the mind is for the most part so blindly eager! "If one property or quality riseth and getteth above the other, then presently something followeth, so that the mind collecteth all its thoughts together and sendeth them to the members of the body, and so the hands, the feet, the mouth, and all go to work and do something, according to the desire of the mind, and then we say that form or property that driveth the work is predominant, qualifying, and working above other forms, wherein yet all other forms of nature lie yet hidden, and are subject to that one form; and yet the mind is such a wonderful thing that suddenly (out of one form that is now predominant, and working more than all others) it bringeth forth and raiseth up another and quencheth the form that was kindled before, so that it becometh, as it were, a nothing, as may seem in joy and sorrow."[2] And in what is technically called *conversion* also. Transition from a hopeless sense of being driven to commit sin, however habitual, to so strong a fear and loathing of it that it is shunned as

[1] Three Principles, ch. xxii., par. 90.   [2] Ibid., Appendix, par. 3.

the worst of evils, little as it is believed in by careless observers, is an historic fact in human nature, and is often as complete as it is sudden:—complete as regards a totally new starting point for the will, of course pitifully and most painfully incomplete as regards achievement of perfected conduct. Nor, when the dominion of each divided property is better understood, and the tyrannic power of rulers in their darkness more justly estimated, will the suddenness of conversion be so much a matter of surprise.

Just in that power of suddenly eliciting the influences of quite another world of thought and feeling, *i.e.*, another property of our nature, lies at once our greatest danger and our greatest ability to escape from it. As to the danger, let a lucifer box remind us how destructive a force may lie still and harmless while untouched,— force that, once kindled by the slightest accident, will suffice to destroy in a few moments the noblest handiworks of many a toilsome year. An angry word, a scornful look can as quickly set the whole mind aflame : and then one mind sets fire to another, and all former growth in love or holiness seems for the time as if it had not been; as we become calm we are ready to think all good-will and trust destroyed as well as present peace. But though much *is* lost, and future risk greatly increased, relief may be as sudden. The anger into which we have entered is God's anger, and must therefore scourge and plague us powerfully. "His anger is His strength and omnipotence and consuming fire; and His heart in the love is His meekness, and so now that which approacheth and entereth into His anger is captivated in the anger. But it is possible to go out from the anger, as His dear heart is generated out of the anger, which stilleth the anger and is rightly called the Kingdom of Heaven."[1]

[1] Three Principles, ch. xx., pars. 60, 61.

Go out? And how? "When the soul inclineth itself towards God's face and doth but a little *imagine* into God's love, then the Divine life becometh stirring."[1] And "then the anger of God sinketh down from the soul and so it is released or delivered in the love spirit from pain and liveth in God."[2] "Hold fast," said Gichtel in one of his letters, "to love in your imagination; nothing can take it from you but your own imagination. As soon as our imagination goes out of the love, darkness enters into the imagination, and the devil then has access." And again, "they knew from experience how easy it was to stumble and to fall by a thought from love into wrath, when the soul being plunged into a violent struggle has very hard work to recover its balance."

In this inquiry into the nature of our unseen foes, I am considering them as abettors of evil in man, rather than as his antagonists; for into the mystery of their enmity to man, as such, I have here as little cause to enter as I have capacity for its comprehension. This much, however, is no sort of mystery, that the evil always detest the good, and try to bring down comparative innocence to their own state. There can be no doubt that this instinct for promoting wickedness is strong beyond our bounded scope of vision. And, among all the tender mercies of the Father of Spirits, I suppose none to be much greater than the concealment of cruel enemies, whose power to intimidate, even if not allowed to harass us otherwise, would be fully equal to their malice. While we are in the flesh we have a veil which hides them from us, and, if Böhme did not mistake, many of us *from them*, unless fellow feeling gives them insight to us through our passions. Speaking of "a soul new-born in the light of God," he says: "The devil

[1] First Apology, Part II., par. 553.
[2] Election, ch. x., par. 102.

cannot see that soul, for the second principle wherein it liveth, and in which God and the Kingdom of Heaven standeth, as also the angels and Paradise, is shut up from him, and he cannot get to it."[1] And again, when speaking of covetousness: "It is the eye of hell; the devil seeth man therewith into soul and body."[2] But, quite apart from hostility to man, the "*wrath of nature willeth to be manifested.*"[3] And hence the terrific discord of the divided forms of nature tends to continual increase, for "know and observe that every life standeth upon the abyss of the fierceness." . . . "We all, in the originality of our life, have the source of the anger and of the fierceness, or else we should not be alive, but we must look to it and in ourselves go forth out of the source of the fierceness with God, and generate the love in us, and then our life shall be a joyful and pleasant habitation to us, and then it standeth rightly in the Paradise of God. For God calleth Himself a consuming fire and also a God of love, and His name, God, hath its original in the love where He goeth forth out of the source in Himself, and maketh it in Himself joy, Paradise, and the Kingdom of Heaven." . . . "But if our life stay in the fierceness, or in covetousness, envy, anger, and malice, and goeth not forth into another will, then it standeth in the anguishing source as all devils do."[4] In that anguishing source are countless tormentors; but they cannot approach us until we open what may compare to a sluice or dam of a river, rather than to a door, so great is the inrush as soon as it is made possible. "The devil continued in his own dominion or principality, not indeed in that wherein God created him, but in the aching, painful birth of eternity, in the centre of

---

[1] Three Principles, ch. v., par. 5.
[2] Great Six Points, Point VI., ch. x., par. 48.
[3] Election, ch. viii., par. 130.
[4] Three Principles, Appendix, pars. 28, 29.

nature and property of wrath; in the property which begetteth darkness, anguish and pain."[1]

Now the soul of man *necessarily* shares that property with him; it *is the root of all creatural life.* "The devil hath no authority or power over it, only that which is the source of anxiety in the soul is the very source or quality of his life."[2] And with this ocean of potential torment close about it, the soul is so lightly, quickly moved from one property to another, that a thought can do it. "The life of man in this time is like a wheel, where very suddenly that which is undermost becometh uppermost and kindleth itself in every creature."[3] We all know something of the daily marvels that result from this, and must have observed how entirely just, right, and inevitable anger and scorn, for instance, appear to us while they are felt; how they seem to take intensifying colour from all that is occurring at the time, and how actually false to the truth of things a companion appears who condemns such feelings as misleading. "I do well to be angry; I cannot but feel scorn!" is what we feel. Now as with the rise of anger a whole spiritual world flies open to us, and in that world every wrathful thought is strictly in its own element, this temporary hallucination is quite intelligible. "Alas," said Carlyle, writing to his mother, "why should I dwell in the element of contempt and indignation rather than in that of patience and love?" (For the mind that is prone on all occasions to kindle into wrath on the slightest provocation, often abhors the folly.) Why? Carlyle did not guess that in every element of contempt and indignation there are mighty confederates; that our *own* access to that element introduces us to their wrath, and this corroborates ours. As Böhme

---

[1] True Resignation (1775), ch. iii., par. 8.
[2] Four Complexions, ch. ii., par. 100.
[3] Small Six Points, Point II., par. 22.

has it, "The darkness graspeth the holy power" (*i.e.*, deific powers in human nature) "and bringeth it into malignity, and then it is as the Scripture saith,[1] *with the perverse thou art perverse, and with the holy thou art holy.*"[2] "Thou"—God in man. In precisely the same manner, and with the same plausibility, does every vice —covetousness, gluttony, lust, revenge—justify itself; and every indulgence of either propensity strengthens its hold on the will and its certain velocity of increase. For "the image of the spirit of the soul" (that which desire and imagination tend to form) "sticketh in the mind, and to whatsoever the *mind* inclineth and giveth up itself, in that is the spirit of the soul figured by the Eternal Fiat."[3] And if malignant or sensual properties have thus become *creaturely* in the human soul, the difficulty of opposing them by any properties that have *not* is, of course, tremendously increased; and when at last these evil properties rule, "l'horreur de la situation, c'est que c'est dans sa propre volonté que réside cette puissance là, et que sa volonté est soumise elle-même à cette puissance qu'elle s'est créée et engendrée."[4]

Therefore was our Saviour so stringent in requiring self-denial as indispensable to true life; "therefore Christ so emphatically and punctually teacheth us in the new birth love, humility, and meekness." . . . "For the desire of *Racha* or revenge ariseth in the centre of the dark fiery wheel of the Eternal Nature." . . . "And the soul's fiery form stands in the *Racha* as a mad, furious wheel which confounds the essence in the body and destroys or shatters in pieces the understanding."[5]

---

[1] Psalms xviii. 25, 26.   [2] Election, ch. viii., par. 83.
[3] Three Principles, ch. xvi., par. 43.
[4] *Translation.*—"And the horror of the situation is, that this power resides in one's own will and that one's will is itself subjected to this power, which itself has created and engendered."—L. C. de St Martin's *L'Esprit des Choses*, vol. ii. p. 315.
[5] Mysterium Magnum, ch. xxii., par. 62.

WHO ARE OUR SPIRITUAL ENEMIES? 217

Now when our Lord said, "Whosoever shall say to his brother, Thou fool, shall be in danger of hell fire,"[1] human reason naturally understood a fire that was both external to the soul in present time, and occupying space in a future world, and in earlier ages probably no ideas less childish could have taken hold on the gross intellect of unenlightened Christendom. But it is on the strength of such absurd and obsolete ideas that even now much ignorant talk about the disproportionate judgments of an "angry God" still gains a hearing. It is surely time for such false coin to be called in. Long ago Böhme taught *what* that hell-fire is,—latent in *every* soul,—making it obvious that if that consuming and indestructible fire does *not* generate light and the meekness of light, it must torment with a famished desire for the bliss it cannot find. Let him explain himself as well as passages taken from their context can explain. "No creaturely spirit can subsist in the creature without the fire-world, for even the love of God could not be if His anger world were not in Him. The anger or fire of God is a *cause* of the light, and of the power, strength, and omnipotency."[2]

In all Böhme's writings he explains with most varied iteration that *creaturely* life begins in the sinking down of fire, calling it "a birth of death, where yet not death, but the beginning of the life of nature doth exist."[3] The beginning of life everlasting, of the creature that is *new* in the old Adamic nature, takes its rise in precisely the same process; a death to the *kindled* fire of our evil passions, produces the light, and that ultimates its meek glory in the heavenly *substance* which is formed by the water of eternal life. The analogy is complete and exact. "In the outward world, in all creatures, every life, viz.,

[1] Matt. v. 22.
[2] Third Apology, Text I., par. 57.
[3] Election, ch. iii., par. 10.

the essential fire life, draweth substance to it, and that is its food to eat. And the fire of its life consumeth the substance, and giveth forth the spirit of the power out of that which is consumed, and that is the life of the *creature*. And you see, doubtless very rightly, how the life ariseth out of the *death*; it becometh no *life* unless it break that out of which the life should go forth."[1] Now, "the centre out of which evil and good floweth is *in thee*; that which thou awakest in thee, be it fire or light, that will be taken in again by its *like*, either by God's *anger* fire, or by God's *light* fire; each of them electeth or chooseth to itself that which is like its property."[2] "The wicked should not dare to say God maketh me evil; but the *God in him*, in Whose ground he standeth, maketh him what he can serve to be according to the utmost possibility."[3] "Power in the light is God's love-fire; and the power in the darkness is the fire of God's anger; and yet it is but *one* only fire; but divided into two principles; that the one might be manifest in the other, for the *flame* of anger is the manifestation of the great Love, and in the darkness the light is made known, else it were not manifest to itself."[4] I pray seekers for the *cause* of permitted evil to pause a little on that last sentence. In the third of the *177 Theosophic Questions*, from par. 26 to par. 45, this subject of the *fire of God* is made clearer, to my thinking, than in any other of Böhme's works.

That the common notion of hell-fire as a punishment inflicted on evil souls *ab extra* was allowed by the permissive providence of God, and for so many centuries, is a marvel, and must be a snare to those who receive the words of Scripture literally according to their

[1] Incarnation, Part II., ch. v., pars. 46-48.
[2] First Apology, Part I., par. 99.
[3] Election, ch. ix., par. 26.
[4] Mysterium Magnum, ch. viii., par. 27.

surface meanings; but it does not stand alone among the misunderstandings by which Divine revelation has been obscured. And considering that no truth for which the human mind at its *present* stage of growth is prepared, can be the *whole* truth on any given point of spiritual wisdom, nor *absolute* truth free from the modifications a finite recipient unavoidably gives to it, we should probably be wiser if we expected, as the Swedenborgians do, a continual opening of quite new meanings of Scripture, as the mind of the race opens more and more to heavenly influx.

But still, being ready to accept new meanings, and dismissing old interpretations, are very different postures of mind, and one does wonder at Divine love conniving, so to speak, at human error, by permitting the messengers of its Gospel to use language that could not but justify the horrible creed of Calvin; for example, St Paul's sayings in *Rom.* ix., which have notoriously led hundreds of men and women to causeless despair, or to confidence almost as unwarrantable. From the 15th to the 24th verse of this chapter, every sentence seems calculated to confirm the terrible doctrine of irresistible predestination. Words could not, one would think, more distinctly imply an arbitrary will in the Most High God to *cause* some men to be vessels of wrath filled to destruction, in order "to make His power to be known." Yet, as this contradicts the whole tenor of the New Testament, we know it cannot be a true interpretation; nor can all the ingenuity of theologians, by any strain of argument, reconcile this chapter with the recorded teaching of Jesus Christ. It would be possible so to underlie these words of St Paul's with Böhme's elucidation as to bring them into a sort of harmony with his oft-repeated phrase about God's desire to manifest all the wonders of Eternal Nature. "The Word hath created a will in the darkness to manifest the darkness with all its forms of the wonders of God the Father."[1] But this sort of process would not seem honest to me, since I think it quite clear that Paul himself as little understood the real meaning of the expression he refers to, "God hardened the heart of Pharaoh," as he understood the period indicated by Christ Jesus for his future visible return; and I, not believing that the Holy Spirit ceased to reveal truth after the time of the Apostles, accept Böhme's account of those words as revelation, and am thankful thus, and only thus, to understand "*whom He will He hardeneth.*"

Duly to appreciate the following passage, his whole treatise, *On the Election of Grace*, should be studied; it is, as a whole, quite irresistibly convincing. In it, commenting on *Rom.* ix. 21, he says: "The false, or wicked and evil soul and the holy soul come both out of Adam's soul, as out of one lump or clod of ground; which a man must understand to be spirit, or spiritually in the great mystery; but the one separateth or distinguisheth itself into light and the other into darkness. This potter maketh out of every separation or distinction a vessel, such as to which the separated or distinguished matter is useful and fit." . . . "As the Ens of the soul is, such also is the will of or to the making. God sitteth *not* over the will and maketh it as a potter doth a pot, but He generateth it out of His own properties." . . . "God worketh to the producing a life out of everything; out of the evil Ens an evil life, out of the good Ens a good life."[2]

"The spirit without a body must remain in the fierce, wrathful fire, for it hath *lost* its substantiality. But the spirit with a body which the *Turba* is not able to devour remaineth eternally in the substantiality, in God's body, wherein His spirit standeth, viz., the body in the love of

[1] Threefold Life, ch. iv., par. 21.
[2] Election, ch. ix., pars. 4–11.

God, which is the *hidden man* in the Old Adamical, which there hath Christ's flesh in the corruptible or fragile body."[1]

The nearness of the most opposite worlds *within* us is one of the most momentous facts to which we can become awakened. "All is nigh unto the spirit, but it may not see in any other world's property, but only in that wherein its fire burneth: that world alone is the spirit capable of," and—what is equally certain—"into which world now it uniteth itself and giveth up itself, from the same it getteth substance in its imagination."[2]

We can understand this better by a little recollection of our own experience than by any words of another person; this, and the possibility of being either inwardly transported or tortured, during the dominancy of any one property ruling in us. Who has not known the common effects of some strong emotion making one feel, while in close companionship with other people, worlds away from *their* life, either rapt in secret consciousness of incommunicable joy, or sinking deeper and deeper in dismaying gulfs of sorrow, or torn by conflicts of unsuspected passion! And in all these states we feel that we are both in a different phase of being, and a different phase of being *in us*,—that the emotion ruling within is reverberated from all sides without; every sight and sound, as well as every turn of thought, adding to its strength either by contrast or by harmony. This, I suppose, is but a rehearsal of that state of *self-determined* consciousness which must be ours after death. Dionysius Freher explains it thus: "Compacted bodies or palpable materialities are only those things in temporal nature which want, or rather are themselves, their own place, and make by their multiplicity and differences their distances from one another; their own proper and peculiar

---

[1] Forty Questions (1665), Ques. 1, pars. 307, 308.
[2] Great Six Points, Point V., ch. vii., pars. 8, 29.

corporeal extension in their only place. . . . Things, therefore, which have not, or have not yet, a compacted body, or are not yet limited to a certain extension, neither have nor require, or not yet, any place, but dwell only within themselves; and as their own visible extension is afterwards their own corporeal place, *so now their own invisible original root, or those radient properties out of which they have come into visibility and palpability, is their own spiritual dwelling place.*"[1] (It is in this sense, doubtless, that we are told of the traitor Judas that after he had hanged himself he went "to his own place.")

This original root of all human life being indestructible, we can thus understand Swedenborg's report of man's spirit after death being, so to speak, in a wholly subjective condition, and *yet* conjoined to the society of spirits of which it was unconsciously a member before death. Death cannot remove us from the realm of that property of Eternal Nature to which our own will in this life has made us subjects. Only by the previous formation of the new creature (the regenerate)—be it but in feeble nonage yet *existant,* in which all six first properties generate the seventh, the heavenly substantiality,—only in that *eternal life* can there be exemption from some over-ruling property of the un-at-one-ed "aching source of anguish which is called the anger of God."[2] And hence the terrors of death, for *that* wellspring "hath devils of such properties and names, which are also princes in their legions, for they have imaged themselves in the hellish property. This ground is their life, and holds them captive in itself; and as the properties of the hellish foundations are manifold, so also are such princes under them, ruling in the same properties."[3] Could those who dare to attempt dissolu-

---

[1] D. Freher on *Regeneration.*
[2] Regeneration, ch. i., par. 24.
[3] 177 Theosophic Questions, Ques. 11, pars. 7, 8.

WHO ARE OUR SPIRITUAL ENEMIES?

tion by suicide but faintly imagine how unspeakably more cruel are the tyrannies of unseen powers, than any under which they groan, suicide would be unknown. For "the dark world's substance and dominion standeth principally only in the first four forms of Nature, in a very exceeding strong and mighty potent dominion."[1] It is the agent of the terrific world whom the Saviour commanded His disciple to fear. "He that hath power to cast into hell: yea, I say unto you, *fear him*" (speaking no doubt of a collective spirit as one). And, again, "Give diligence that thou mayest be delivered from him, lest he hale thee to the judge,"—the incorruptible judge of conscience—" and the judge deliver thee to the officer,"— the executive property of torment inherent in sin—" and the officer cast thee into prison."[2] The horrors of that prison he knew, and how long a period of purifying anguish of spirit *must* be endured, before there *can* be any departing thence, before "the very last mite" of the wages of sin has been paid in the convincing torment of *self-condemnation.*

Though I cannot for one instant believe that the loss of our flesh-husk in any way interrupts the outflow of everlasting love from the heart of God towards man, I have begun to see why such alarming stress has been laid upon the *now* of earthly life by inspired teachers as "the day of salvation," "the accepted time," when we *can* work for it, before the after-period when we cannot. In this life we have a shelter, a hiding-place from the violence of mighty spirits deprived even of the external light we enjoy. Into our world these spirits of the dark world cannot look except through us; "and *therefore* hath God introduced the soul into flesh and blood, that it might not so easily be capable of the fierce wrathful substance," (with which wrathful spirits always strive to enkindle others; we have been taught quite recently to

[1] Great Six Points, Point VI., ch. ix., par. 33.   [2] Luke xii. 5, 58, 59.

apprehend that there *is* substance transmitted by all emotion). "Also it hath its joy the while in the sidereal essence,"[1] and thus the evil fires of the soul are outshone.

Again, we have in the fleshly body an external life of our own on which the will can act, and—action and reaction being equal—this outward life reacts on the will, modifies, appeases, and even breaks it as the case may be. If any one would duly estimate the helpfulness of a material body in this respect, let him just compare the different effects of a stinging recollection or angry thought occurring to the mind by night or by day. Even in the first case I think it will be found that generally the position of the body shifts as the painful impression recurs; we *turn round* as if merely moving thus lessened or changed it; and by day how many little distractions help us to manage anger better, to hold bitter thoughts in check. And not only does the activity of the body blunt internal feeling, but our rule over the body is so much more complete than our rule in the mind, that to prevent speaking angrily or acting unkindly is easy compared to getting rid of a vindictive wish or subduing a scornful impulse; for in that attempt the higher will can only oppose the lower with intensely concentrated self-coercion.

Now with full knowledge of the extreme uncertainty of our tenure of flesh bodies, and total ignorance of all the aggressive powers that may beset us when cast out of these bodies by death, would it not be the work of good sense to try and procure another body impervious to all possible assaults in any state of being? There is such a body. "There is an eternal in the temporal body, which verily disappeared in Adam as to the eternal light, which must also be born again through Christ."[2]

---

[1] Great Six Points, Point V., ch. vii., par. 28.
[2] Mysterium Magnum, ch. viii., par. 15.

"The new man is not only a spirit; he is even flesh and blood, as the gold in the stone is not only spirit; it hath a body, but not such a one as the rude drossy stone is, but a body which subsisteth in the centre of nature, in the fire; whose body the fire cannot consume."[1]

This gold, this heavenly substance, had been quite covered up by earthly matter, and no more *grew* in man; but "the heavenly Artist would not reject Adam's disappeared gold and make clean another new thing, but he took his own tincture of his own gold, out of which he had made Adam's gold, and tinctured it with his own gold, that is with the Word (viz., the power) of God and with the essence of the Word, viz., with the Heavenly corporality."[2] The translator thought good to render *Wesen*, which in German is both essence and substance—*essence*, but here undoubtedly substance was intended. And what an unexamined mystery lies here! No figure of speech, but a fact to which I suppose every advance in ontological research will testify, *i.e.*, that no spiritual life, even the Divine, can be existant without the interaction of an active spirit and a passive substance. Now in man's nature, while full of discordant properties, there could not be any *true* substance till the "temperature"— the perfect equilibrium of all the forms of Eternal Nature —was restored. Therefore until the incarnation of the Word or power of God, the *new man* was not possible. "Renew a right spirit within me,"[3] was David's prayer; but now "if any man be in Christ" (the Anointed humanity) "*he is a new creature.*"[4] The Holy Spirit did indeed act on, and influence and guide, the human will previously, but only with the new Adam could the new creation begin. Because wherever the Word is, there also is

---

[1] Incarnation, Part I., ch. xiv., pars. 22, 23.
[2] Mysterium Magnum, ch. xxxvii., par. 31.
[3] Psalms li. 10. [4] 2 Cor. v. 17.

what Böhme elsewhere calls "*the substantial Word.*" "*With the substance of the Word*, viz., *the Heavenly corporality*," the Word "came into the wrath of Eternal Nature, into the Father's property as to that nature, and regenerated the revolted human will in the same fire through the love-fire, and atoned God's love and anger, viz., the divided nature in the human will."[1]

"When the body deceaseth, then the sunlight is destroyed, and the soul standeth naked in the dark world." (This is why *the wrath* is spoken of in the Bible as "*the wrath to come*"; it is only fully felt then when all perishable light, the matter for the fuel of the soul's fire, is withdrawn.) "Therefore God brought Divine substantiality into the faded image of man."[2] "The highest love of the Deity in the name Jesu, did overcome the anger of God *in our soul* and inward Divine ground, proceeding from the substance of Eternity, and did turn it again into Divine humility, meekness, and obedience, whereby the rent, torn, and divided temperature of our human property entered again into the harmony and unity of the properties, viz., into Paradisical light, love, and life, that *real temperature where variety doth concentre and accord in unity*."[3]

"Wilt thou not have thy soul, which is given thee from the eternal highest Good, here in this time kindled again in the light of God, so that it becometh born again in the light out of the Divine substantiality; then it falleth in the mystery" (death) "to the *centre* of Nature, viz., home again into the anguish chamber of the first four forms of Nature. There it *must be* a spirit in the dark anguish source with all the devils, and devour that which it hath in this world introduced into itself: *that* will be its food and life. But being God would not have

---

[1] Mysterium Magnum, ch. xl., par. 10.
[2] First Apology, Part II., pars. 516, 517.
[3] Epistles (1649), Ep. 1, par. 12.

it thus with man, his similitude and image, therefore he himself is become that which poor man was come to be, after that he was fallen out of the Divine substantiality, out of Paradise, that he might help him again; so that man hath in himself the gate of regeneration, that he *can* in the soul's fire become born again in God." [1]

[1] Incarnation, Part II., ch. vi., pars. 38-40.

NATURAL OBJECTS EXISTANT [1]

WHEN "C. C. M.," Rev. G. D. Haughton, "Nöemon," and the Hon. Roden Noel, are discussing the meanings of Kant, of whom I know nothing except what other writers have quoted, it seems absurdly impertinent to venture an opinion, and I ask pardon in advance for being so presumptuous. But early in life I was introduced to the theories of Bishop Berkeley; and for several years tried hard to accept the views of the late Mr Hinton with regard to Nature, both in his books and from his patient teaching *viva voce*. The effort was quite unsuccessful: when most ready to be carried off my mental standing ground by his eloquence, an indomitable conviction reasserted itself within me that the objects we see externally are quite as much real things as our bodies (using "real," of course, in no supersensuous way) and no less independent of *our* perceptions for objective life than we are of theirs for our own. However satisfactory opposing arguments were to metaphysicians, I felt sure they were wanting in some link of fact which, once found, would invalidate their conclusions, and prove beyond further dispute that "what we call external things *are* 'something else' than mere presentations of our own sensibility." But what that link was I could not detect, and my stubborn *dis*belief in "*nothing at all that is perceived in space being a thing in itself*" remained undefended. It was, as usual, from Böhme that light

[1] Light, 1884, vol. iv. p. 96.

first came to me on this subject, for there is hardly any moot point of the kind which his books do not illumine. If nature is "the creation of the Divine reason in us," it will have acted by *means*. Our sacred books say, by the Word. Until I had studied Böhme some years, the expressions of the Psalmist, "He spake and they were made, He commanded and they stood forth," were very childishly understood. I regarded the creative fiat in the light of a *verbal command*, as a sort of "Hey presto" of Divine magic—the *immediate* work of Deific Omnipotence. Geological discoveries served to modify this foolish notion. And then I began to see the bearings of the obvious fact that with every spoken word, not only sound but breath goes forth, and by degrees learning that even for the highest spirit "*without substance no working can be*," I saw that what answered to breath is the æther which pervades creation. Oken, exactly agreeing with Böhme, describes it as "*the first matter of creation. Everything has consequently originated out of it. It is the highest Divine element, the Divine body, the primary substance.*"[1] With this basis of thought I could easily accept the following assertions of my master teacher, which I quote in close sequence, though from different works, that they may serve in some degree to explain each other:—

"We acknowledge that the will of the Abyss hath brought itself into a longing and imagination of itself, whence Nature and creature have their original: whence also the natural life hath its original, which now also *out of the partibleness of the exhaled will hath its own will and imagination*[2] *to form and image itself accord-*

[1] Elements of Physiophilosophy, p. 39, par. 169.

[2] Talking one day to a gentleman long experienced in cultivating variegated plants and shrubs, he told me that he produced new sorts by planting such as were spotted or diversely coloured in the leaf near others that were not. On my asking how he accounted for this strange effect, his answer was, "*The imagination of plants can be acted on* just as that of animals is known to be."

ing to its longing and desire. As we see such changing in Nature, how Nature imageth itself into so many kinds and properties, and how those properties do every one desire their like again."[1]

"The Word, viz., the efflux from the willing of God, was the Eternal beginning, and continueth so eternally."
... "This efflux floweth out from God, *and the outflown* [Word] *is His wisdom, the beginning and cause of all powers, colours, virtues, and properties.*"[2]

"Both work, viz., the speaking Word and the spoken. The speaking worketh in itself, viz., in the Eternity, and the spoken also in itself, viz., in the time."[3]

Now the power I claim recognition for in the minutest animalcule or the most microscopic vegetable is what Böhme calls elsewhere "*The Word of every life*," the self-creative imagination and desire by which *every* atom of life produces an objective manifestation. Because—

"The centre of everything, being a particle or spark from the expressed Word, doth again speak itself forth, and bringeth itself into a distinct particularity."[4] "For there is not anything substantial in the world, wherein the image, resemblance, and form of the inward spiritual world doth not stand."[5]

"The centre of everything is *spirit*, from the Original of the Word. The separation or distinction of the thing is own self-will of its own self-compaction; where every spirit introduceth itself into substance according to its essential desire. The formability of bodies existeth out of the experience of the willing, where everything's centre as a piece of the outspoken Word re-outspeaketh

---

[1] Baptism, ch. i., par. 17. (The sentences to which I want to draw attention most I have italicized.)
[2] Divine Vision, ch. iii., pars. 4, 6.
[3] Signatura Rerum, ch. xiii., pars. 2, 3.
[4] Epistles (1649), Ep. 6, par. 12.   [5] Clavis, par. 171.

itself, and frameth itself into separability, after the kind and manner of the Divine speaking." ... "*Every centre maketh its own out-breathing, nature, and substance, out of itself, and yet all originateth out of the Eternal One.*"[1]

It is on these grounds that I cannot believe it to be "the homogeneous constitution of our Egos that makes a uniform experience of the phenomenal world." I attribute a spiritual Ego to every cabbage; and so far from being able to think "*the order and regularity found in the phenomena of the lives*" (of those we call inanimate beings) "*what we could not find in them if we had not ourselves originally put it there.*" I can believe that from the soul of universal man in a previous Æon even smaller things than a cabbage or a rose got their souls, but never that they now win from ours a phenomenal appearance.

If it is not too silly a question to ask, I would fain know whether metaphysicians will attribute to the "homogeneous constitution" of dogs and cats their experience of the phenomenal world which is uniform with our own. We see a cat, and so does the dog who runs after it; so with the mouse that becomes visible both to ourselves and the cat; the impression of sense seems the same: how different the readings of that impression!

It is most probable that in making these ignorant remarks I earn for myself the disgrace due to people who break into an argument they very imperfectly understand; but when in our day the theories of Berkeley and Kant are cited as reasonable, I cannot but think of their comparative ignorance of the spiritual world, so continually opening itself to us. This deprived them of data which thinkers now possess, if they are honest enough

---

[1] Knowledge of God, pars. 11, 12, 19 (*Several Treatises*, 1661); see also *Epistles* (1649), Ep. 6, pars. 11, 12, 19.

to be clear-sighted. I suppose the idea of every plant or stone we see having latent spiritual life was as remote from the mental range of Kant as the workings of the telephone, and yet with that idea we have to reckon, and it must surely remodel our theories sooner or later if truth is aimed at more than philosophical *vraisemblance.*

THE SECOND ADVENT[1]

I

"Christ 'fills the universe, and in His second manifestation to His people, it will be in *their* bodies, for His body is His Church.'"

IN this quotation from "The Revealed Christ" in the first number of *Light and Life*, I find expression of a modern theory which, though held by people whose judgments I reverence, I have never been able to accept. If space can be allowed I am eager to explain why. On first reading that passage my thought answered, "Is there, then, to be no manifestation of the Head of that Glorious body? or does any one for a moment suppose that any *but* the man Christ Jesus can be this Head?" But the root of the notion quoted above lies, I believe, in the common error of using the words "Jesus" and "Christ" as if they were equivalents. It was this same Jesus whom the apostles were told should so come in like manner as He went. The importance of distinguishing between the two was first taught me by Böhme; and his words on this point may be of value to others. A careful examination of the different places in the Bible where these names are separately used, will justify his saying, "The name *Jesus* is divine, but the name *Christ* is God and man."[2]

Christ being the anointed humanity, and *the* Christ

---

[1] Light and Life, Oct., Nov., 1885.
[2] Third Apology, Text IV., Point III., par. 79.

the one creature in whom dwelleth all the fulness of the Godhead bodily. "The name Jesus, out of the Word of the Divine life, hath united itself with the woman's seed and given itself up into one person, which is called Christ. The name Jesus is the anointing of the woman's seed, and in the anointing He is called Christ the Son of God. The seed of the woman is beneath or under God as the body is beneath the soul, but the name Jesus is the giver." [1]

Hence it is evident that *Christ* may be formed in us, but that Jesus cannot be; and the one Person of Christ (through whom Jehovah speaks) cannot be said to fill the universe, though Jesus does: the coming again which the apostles undeniably looked for was the glorified creaturely Christ, in whose person Jesus would return: "in like manner." In what manner? Surely in the visibility and phenomenal limitations of a human body; and that St Paul said, "Henceforth know we Him no more in the flesh," in no way disproves this. He well understood that the spiritual body was substantial and creaturely; yet very different from the body of our humiliation,—the body of flesh which, by contradistinction, he calls the "natural body." A truth many divines seem to forget. Dr Holcombe, in America, maintains the consecrated error which I am now daring to combat. At page 23 of his *Letters on Spiritual Subjects*, he says, "The second coming will not be a coming from without as the Christian world expects, but a genuine coming or descent from within; nor special of one race, but universal, an influx of a divine human life into the body of humanity." No one can welcome the opinions of this writer more cordially than I, but this appears to me an amazingly untenable assertion to confront with the words of Scripture, "*every eye shall see Him*"; and with our Lord's significant question, "When the Son of

[1] Third Apology, Text IV., Point III., pars. 83, 84.

Man cometh, shall He find faith on the earth?" If the perception of His coming is conditional on states of spiritual receptiveness, no faithless or hardened sinner could see Him; and Dr Holcombe is too good a disciple of Swedenborg to forget that influx cannot be *forced* into closed interiors against the will; perhaps he believes with Thomas Lake Harris, that to such *averted* natures, the coming of the Lord will be immediate destruction of their mortal life. But he goes on to say, " Every coming of the Lord is therefore not a voluntary movement on His part, such as we imagine that He made, but a revelation of His presence always made, according to spiritual laws." What, His nativity on earth! was that not due to Divine *action*, but to be accounted for by the quickening of human perception? It is hardly fair to press hard upon words so unguarded; but I may answer with Böhme, when rebutting the same ideas—after quoting the words of Jesus, "I proceeded forth and came from God,"—he says, "Now the clear Deity needs no coming, for it is in all places beforehand; it needeth only to manifest itself to or in the place; and *all whatsoever cometh, that is substance.*" . . . "Therefore, when God would manifest Himself in Mary's disappeared substance, then came He with the substance, and manifested Himself in the united substance; He united His *coming* substance with the human substance; understand, with the heavenly human substance."[1]

It may be said the apostles' belief on this point was invalidated by their erroneous expectation of the Second Advent in their own life-time; so it is supposed did Eve expect the promised Helper, when at the birth of Cain she said, "I have gotten a man from the Lord." An eager outlook for the Messiah lasted for centuries, and generation after generation passed away with its hope unfulfilled; yet at last Messiah came, visibly present on

[1] Third Apology, Text IV., Point IV., pars. 27, 28.

earth, though only recognized by a few at first. Coming in glory as distinguished from that coming in humiliation surely implies such a revealing as not even the most obstinate doubter could refuse to see. There is a growing fashion of denying an *historic* Christ, while laying great stress on the spiritual influences of a *mythical* Christ, somewhat analogous to this rejection of hope in the Saviour's *personal* return among Christians. It is discarded as a childish conception, only fit for less enlightened times.

I venture to think this judgment is based on superficial ideas of what body is, and very indefensible prejudice as to the relation of size to force.

If by a human body we only understand the corruptible, we may well refuse to expect the Lord of glory in creaturely form; but if we remember our ignorance of the spiritual body, and that the first Adam was made in the likeness of God, we shall see that this is to confound the precious ore with the coarse matrix which enfolds it. The Word was made flesh; but the heavenly substantial flesh which, as Böhme has it, "faded in Adam," *i.e.*, became inert and lost to human consciousness, was that in which the second was, and is, a quickening Spirit. "Christ is a regenerator of that which is lost; He is not come for the sake of the earthly man, that He should keep that in its dominion, but that He might regenerate that in Adam which, when he awaked to sin, disappeared."[1]

"In this He was the express image of God from eternity, viz., in the figure of man, in which figure God created man with beginning and creature."[2]

In his day Böhme had many mistaken notions of Christ to repel, and on this particular point—the enduring creatureliness of the Lord Christ — he was emphatic and precise.

[1] Third Apology, Text I., par. 229.   [2] Ibid., par. 172.

"To our human substance the power and authority is given, but to the Divine nothing *can* be given. God will judge the humanity through the voice of the *humanity of Christ*, so that the humanity of Christ, according to *our* humanity, is the instrument to do it with."[1]

"Hath not Christ taken upon Him my creature? How, then, hath He in my flesh *slain death*, and quenched the anger of God?"... "God had not to do about a strange creature in that He became man, but about that which in Adam He created in Paradise."[2] "We know that we, according to the Paradisical angelical world, *have had* flesh and blood out of the heavenly essence and substantiality, which was the right body of the soul, and therein stood the image of Heaven."[3]

It is either disregard of, or total unbelief in, that glorious body which makes people, so to speak, nervously afraid of anything that tends to Anthropomorphic ideas of the risen Saviour, or of the regenerate in a future state of glory. And yet all use, seemingly without offence, St Paul's words, "In Christ Jesus neither circumcision availeth anything nor uncircumcision, *but a new creature*." What do they imagine that creature to be like when fully developed? Bodiless? Powerless? Speaking of our established superstitions as to this, Swedenborg said: "They can form no idea of their soul or spirit as of a man, but as of wind or air, or a phantom without form, in which there is yet some vital principle," ... "and do not know that it is the spirit of every one from which the body has its human form, consequently which is principally man, and in a similar form."[4]

To these apprehensive Christians the word *person*—so mistakenly, as I think, applied to each power in the

---

[1] Third Apology, Text IV., Point IV., pars. 84, 85 (see *Matthew* xxviii. 18).
[2] Ibid., pars. 103, 107.   [3] First Apology, Part II., par. 208.
[4] Earths in the Universe, par. 165.

Divine Trinity—is a scandal when applied to the Incarnate Word! In some way they must think that personality is swallowed up in the Father uncreate. To quote Swedenborg [1] again, "If you ask them *where* is His humanity? they will make no answer, for they separate in idea His divinity from His humanity, and make His divinity equal to that of the Father, and His humanity similar to that of another man; not knowing that in so doing they separate soul and body, nor seeing the contradiction that in that case He would have been born a rational man from the mother alone." [2]

Truly such believers do "separate His divinity from His humanity, placing His divinity beside the Father, and *His humanity they know not where.*" [3]

Böhme might have given them more consistent notions, and more agreeing with Scripture. "I must not say that in the person of Christ, viz.—in the man according to His humanity, that *He* has been taken on to the Deity, that the creature is ceased and taken up, or that the creature, soul and body from us men, is unmeasurable; no, for such a one is *not* our eternal High Priest, which I could never more see in the form of man; for the men when He ascended to heaven said, 'Ye shall see this Jesus come again as He ascended.'" [4]

The superstition as to size being anything of an indication of power is curious in a world peopled as this

---

[1] How much is yet to be learned from Swedenborg! While Oriental Theosophy is the reigning fashion among those who seek for occult knowledge, what treasures remain in his pages unnoticed! what a multitude of spiritual *facts*, opening to fruitful and expansive stretches of thought; for example, sayings like this, "Every civil, moral, and spiritual thing is not anything abstracted from substance, but all these things are substances. For love and wisdom are not abstract things, but are a substance."—*Angelic Wisdom concerning Divine Love and Wisdom*, par. 209.

[2] Divine Providence, par. 262.
[3] Ibid., par. 255.
[4] Third Apology, Text IV., Point III., pars. 15, 16.

world is from microscopic germs. In this week's issue of a paper professedly devoted to mystical research, I chanced to come upon these words, "Not the Christ of the popular Theology, where the idea shrinks and dwindles down to an isolated personality, but a larger, fuller, diviner Christ," etc., etc.[1] Does the oak tree shrink and dwindle down when its many centuries of age-enduring wood, and its yearly myriads of leaves are given forth to the future within the compass of an acorn cup? Perhaps in comparison with the illimitable worlds, seen by the supreme originators of all, ours is not relatively larger.

II

"Jesu, the Eternal Son, shineth through The Christ."—Böhme.

Impatience of the idea of our Divine Saviour reappearing on earth as a man is due to other habits of mind than this of forgetting that "man's self is not yet man," —that our present outer bodies are a monstrous and shameful burlesque of the true human form.[2] Modern minds crave for intellectual comprehension of what they

[1] Light, Aug. 29, 1885, vol. v. p. 421.
[2] St Paul's belief in the prolonged existence of the body, freed of its degrading adjuncts, is surely implied by his words in 1 Cor. vi. 13. It was not the *body* which God would destroy, but the corrupting receiver of corrupt food. Böhme, repeatedly asserting that this and all the "organs of shame" were superinduced by sin, and not essential constituents of the human body, explains in several of his works how food, in man's unfallen state, was, and how it will be, taken when his purification is completed: for instance, when in his *Election of Grace* speaking of man's state in Paradise—"The fruit was pleasant to behold, also good to be eaten, after a heavenly manner. Not to be swallowed down into a carcase for the worms, as now it is in the awakened bestial property, but in a *magical* manner. Indeed, to be eaten in the mouth; but then the centres of distinction and separation were in the mouth, viz., dividing each principle into its own, in that manner as it may be done in the Eternity" (chap. v., pars. 113, 114):
See also *Treatise on the Incarnation*, Part I., ch. iv., par. 50, and *Forty Questions*, Ques. 32, par. 4.

believe, and this leads some peremptorily to dismiss any thought as to *how* prophecies of the Second Advent are to be fulfilled, because such attempts at understanding would renew a baffled sense of their incomprehensibility; and others to eager acceptance of an hypothesis which connects known facts of spiritual life with all the glorious promise of an unknown future; and this suits the special liking of our time for trying to open every lock with one key—*subjective* experience. The knowledge that our ancestors mistook much that was within themselves for forces external to self, has been as variously applied and misapplied as any favourite nostrum for bodily relief, which having cured one pain is hopefully recommended for all. This acquisition of modern philosophy has been brought to bear on previous ideas, both of God and devil; and succeeds in effacing both from the creed of many hasty thinkers. Because God is recognized in universal existence as the life of all that lives, therefore, apart from the Universe there is no God, reversing thus the Biblical statement that "in God we live and move and have our being," and saying that God only lives and moves and has His being in us.[1]

Because we are evidently so often our own tempters, therefore the idea of a devil, a head centre of hostility to God is now—by how many!—derided as preposterous; the whole question set aside with catchwords of contempt: a "personal devil," "horns and hoofs," etc., etc. Undeveloped spirits is now the mild term for devils, and these and *human* weakness alone are supposed to account for the whole mystery of iniquity which thwarts both God and man. And, of course, so long as temptation, or sin and its consequent anguish, can be attributed to self-agency alone it is less feared; people think they can, sooner or later, adjust all that is wrong *in them-*

---

[1] An old heresy—as old as the times of Origen—revived from time to time.

selves; it is the spiritual wickedness in high places that is terrible; and for a time it may appear wise to consider that and the Prince and powers of darkness as an old wife's fable. Nothing could suit the enemy of mankind better.

Still further has occult learning, gathered from the East, helped to free the mind from old-fashioned belief. With a *transcendental self* to bring in as the agent of all that is unaccountable to reason in our inner life, beings of a superior order can be ignored as superfluous. The self that transcends my conscious self may be God-like in power, and however much I let some of my inferior selves sink in temporary degradation, the transcendental self, one would suppose, will be sure to set all right at last.

When I see the amazing claims made on our faith by well-satisfied subjects of their *unknown* highest self, there is within me an instinctive stretching out of the hands—in the language of the Psalmist—to the one High and Holy God, revealed to us by Jesus Christ. "Oh, set me up upon the rock that is higher than I," is the voice of my heart. "And that Rock was Christ." He still follows us unseen in life's perplexing wilderness—even those who do not own Him as their Shepherd. But *every* eye, we are told, shall see Him; and by Jesus Himself that "as the lightning cometh out of the east, and shineth even unto the west, so shall also the coming of the Son of Man be."[1] How then can the manifestation of the life of Jesus in the members of His mystical body be taken for *that* coming?

Is there not in the minds of people who so read it, some unconscious mixing up of ideas that belong to two different planes of existence?—the confusion of attributing accepted ideas of *spirit*-life to life on this earth? Time and space, all metaphysical thinkers will probably

[1] Matthew xxiv. 27.

acknowledge, to be phenomenal, *i.e.*, contingent on the perception of those who are subject to their laws; but while never dreaming of *such* laws being annulled for those in whose lives they look for the second coming of Christ, people will speak of any vision of the Lord Christ under conditions of time and space as absurdly derogatory,—as if time and space were earth-born clouds!

In all questions of this kind I refer to Böhme, because from his books alone have I gained satisfaction adequate to my demand: and from these I must quote several passages to justify my belief that except under these conditions God could never reveal Himself to *fallen* man. "We cannot say of man that he in the beginning was included in Time, for he was in Paradise included in the Eternity. God had created him in His image, but when he fell, then that *including in Time* caught him, wherein all things stand in a limit, measure, and weight; and that clockwork or machine is the outspoken word of God, according to love and anger, wherein lieth the whole creation; as also man according to nature and creature."[1]

"The Eternal Word hath here comprised itself in the Mysterium Magnum, into a Time, as into a *figure* of the spiritual Mysterium Magnum, as a great clockwork, wherein a man understands the spiritual word in a work or manufacture. The whole work is the *formed word* of God—understand, the natural word—in which the *living* word of God Himself is understood in the greatest inwardness, and that speaketh itself through nature."[2]

"The working word, out of all powers, hath expressed itself for a time, and brought itself into a substance, having beginning and end, and imaged it in the creation

---

[1] Election, ch. vii., pars. 120, 121.
[2] Ibid., ch. v., pars. 46, 47.

to a manifestation of itself." ... "This is thus manifested to the end that the Eternal Word with its working power might be creaturely and have an image."[1]

Now, the Word having, as Böhme says in another chapter of the same book, "compacted itself into a clockwork or machine included in time," there is surely nothing discordant with the timeless infinitude of that "living Word," if it acts according to the measures of time and space—limitations fixed for the express purpose of Divine manifestation. To deny the possibility of such restriction seems to me as unwise as it would be to question the illimitable potentialities of the human spirit, because it manifests itself in such a very small portion of matter as the human body.

Böhme often meets scruples as to believing in creatural limitations for the Word by comparing the *person* of the Lord Christ to our Sun. "The sun shineth or enlighteneth in the whole world, and so now if there were not in the deep such a substance as the sun, then it would not receive the glance or lustre of the sun; thus the *corporeity* of Christ is the fulness of Heaven, in the person creaturely, and without the creature living, in one spirit and power, not two."[2]

Again, "As the sun shineth in the whole outward world, and empowereth all and maketh it fruitful; and

[1] Election, ch. iv., pars. 42, 44.

"It was with a view to this first and most essential object that the Word was revealed, since no one can believe in a God, and love a God, whom he cannot comprehend under some form; wherefore they who acknowledge an invisible and thus incomprehensible principle, sink in thought into Nature and consequently believe in no God. Hence it pleased the Lord to be born on this earth and to make this manifest by the Word, that it might not only be known on this globe, but might also be made manifest thereby to spirits and angels from other earths."—Swedenborg's *The Earths in the Universe*, par. 118.

[2] Second Apology, Part II., par. 251.

the world is not the sun, so also the Christ shineth as a revealed or manifested sun, out of Jehova or Jesus, in the *creaturely* humanity of Christ. The name *Christ* is the manifested Sun out of the Eternal name JEHOVA or JESUS: Jehova is the Eternal Divine Sun, in which this great Love-Sun Christ, as a Heart in the centre of the Holy Trinity, hath been hidden to all creatures, and yet is through the Second Moving of the Deity, as a holy sweet *Love-Sun*, become manifested."[1]

Doubtless as time goes on the life of Jesus is more and more manifested in the members of Christ's *body*; and thus undeniably he draws nearer to our world; and if some of our most devout contemporaries believe *this* to be the coming predicted, it will not be the first time that a secondary sense of prophecy has been seized on by spiritually-minded men as the meaning foretold. And, indeed, to the mass of Christians, in whose minds a subdued thought must often arise of "Where is the promise of His coming," for—so far as any visible interference of heaven with earth can be discerned—"all things continue as they were," this notion of the Second Advent cannot but be agreeable. It is intelligible; and besides, human nature, at its best, recoils from liability to cataclysms, and is just now so much enamoured with the idea of evolution and all its gentle imperceptible advance, that it is peculiarly disinclined to believe that *any* sudden event will be allowed to arrest its course. Against this incredulity the Saviour warned mankind with most solemn emphasis. One among us still (Mr T. Lake Harris) has been for many years repeating the warning, that the generation existing when Christ comes will be overtaken with fire which will instantaneously consume all those who are not permeable to it, by reason of opened spiritual respiration, as an electric current shatters the tree which by non-conduction offers resist-

[1] Third Apology, Text IV., Point III., pars. 13, 14.

ance. But when Christ (*i.e.*, the anointed humanity) is formed in any human atom of His mystical body, that new creature is "*a body of light which is both like unto, and capable of Deity.*"[1] With such forecasts as this I have not the presumption to deal, even in thought; but as to the *objective* revealing of Jesus in the Lord Christ when He comes "to be glorified in His saints,"[2] I will add yet a few more samples of Böhme's testimony, because his works are too rare to be accessible to all readers. If it were not so, I would fain refer any one interested on this subject to chs. xxv. and xxvi. of his *Three Principles*: "My opponent will not permit that I should say *Christ is a creature*, and yet it is true so far as concerns the outward kingdom." . . . "He was a creature and he is one eternally; understand, as to the soul, and as to the substantiality which died in Adam."[3]

"He shall come again at the last judgment day, and manifest Himself in His own body which He had here, that all may see Him, be they good or bad . . . for in His divine glorified form we cannot behold Him before we be glorified, especially the wicked."[4] "We speak only of the comprehensibility and visibility of it to our eyes, according to which He is our brother; and He shall appear at the last judgment day in our fleshly form, in the power of God, as Lord over all."[5]

Böhme, who so cautiously refused to give any forecast as to the future on our earth, because it was unrevealed to him,[6] looked as to the eternal creatureliness of Christ, beyond the anticipated millennium, when saying, "Sin caused Jehova that He gave us the Christ out of the

---

[1] Böhme.   [2] 2 Thess. i. 10.
[3] Second Apology, Part II., pars. 247, 248.
[4] Three Principles, ch. xxvi., par. 7.
[5] Ibid., par. 9.
[6] See his letters to Paul Keym, *Epistles* (1649), Eps. 4, 5.

love; for in the eternity will be no Christ, but Jehova all in all; the whole human tree in Jehova. *Not that the person of Christ will cease to be;* . . . the creature remaineth, but Christ is then the Eternal High Priest in *all*, and the *creature* of Christ a King of men."[1]

And so shall Christ "*remain to be our brother.*"

[1] Third Apology, Text I., pars. 192, 193.

THE USES OF PAIN AND EVIL[1]

I

"If you wait till you can do a thing perfectly, or even according to what you may deem the lowest degree of propriety of execution, you will never do it at all. . . . You see your object clearly in view, and know your way to attain it; drive at it. If you persevere something valuable will be effected, though it may not be gratifying to your judgment and taste as to the manner of its performance."—Christopher Walton's Introduction to his *Memorial of William Law*, p. xiv.

THOROUGHLY dissatisfied with my own share in this attempt, the hope that in other minds something valuable may be effected, is my sole excuse for presuming to try and meet, with Böhme's words, the opprobrium of Divine government—the existence and power of evil. To a rapidly-increasing multitude of thinkers and talkers, it is either the real or the alleged cause for inability to believe in a Supreme Good God. And no one can gainsay the assertion that, so far as *we see*, evil, and its inseparable attendant woe, appear to have a generative force which goodness in all its agents seems unable to withstand. It is often said that evil exhausts itself, but if it does so in one sequence of events, in the course of that sequence it undeniably gives rise to new germs of new evil which seldom fail of similar extensive development. "In every will of every essence there is again a centre of a whole substance."[2] And those who believe the Scrip-

---

[1] Light and Life, March, April, 1886.
[2] Forty Questions (1665), Ques. 1, par. 115.

tural statement that "*God is Love*," and that from God *all* life derives, have truly a most difficult position to defend. Their assailants energized, some by despair, some by an agony of compassion, and some by contempt of what they judge to be a relic of mental slavery, press in vain for some solution of the tremendous enigma. I have never heard of any, except that offered by Böhme, which can reconcile facts with the faith professed by Christians; and even his solution one is obliged to supplement with a larger hope than his own times admitted, if one tries to justify the ways of God to men, as regards *bringing any creatures into existence who could remain rebels* even for a *seeming* eternity. The old-fashioned truism that the finite mind cannot possibly comprehend the purposes of the infinite wisdom of God, quiets the thoughts of a great many people, but when the finite mind has been quickened to such a new impatience of its old narrow conceptions (*e.g.*, of an angry God *punishing* the sin of a short life with unending torment, and thus glorifying His holiness and justice), as for ever to doubt the hard sayings of theology, surely some answer must be obtainable to meet the questioning spirit which does seek and passionately long for it.[1] Probably this growing impatience of darkness is due to some rays of light stealing in and rousing an eager desire for more. Glimpses of this light are to be discerned in Böhme's revelations, and these have brought so much peace to my mind on two points—the necessity of suffering, and the ultimate gain to the race from evil—that I long to share it with others. These two points I shall now try to make good in Böhme's words. He frequently speaks of the universe and all it contains having been brought

---

[1] "Men now, at the end of this time, do listen and long very much after the root of the tree, through which Nature sheweth that the time of the discovery of the tree is at hand, therefore the Spirit will shew it to them." —*Aurora*, ch. xxii., par. 65.

into existence for the sake of Divine self-consciousness—
that the Abyssal God might know the infinitude of
powers and glories which without limits are unknowable; "for, so long as a thing goeth forward externally,
there is no finding in the inward internally, only the
spirit which dwelleth in the inward findeth itself in
the outward."[1]

"God is the original of all beings; the beings are His
manifestation, and thereof only have we ability to write,
and not of the unmanifested God; who also were not
known to Himself without His manifestation."[2] "Therefore, the Divine understanding bringeth itself into spiritual properties that it might be manifest to itself, and be
a working life."[3]

This, according to our human understanding—thinking
of self, as in our *unwhole* state we must—seems a very
insufficient and scarcely a merciful reason for bringing
into existence myriads of beings able to agonize in mind
and body, able to sin to every depth of degradation: yet,
perhaps, the self-consciousness of a perfectly healthy
body might, as a figure, cause us to rectify that judgment.
In perfect health no part of the frame would, I suppose,
object against the sense of well-being, that it had been
born susceptible of damage. But the obvious reply to
that is that this vast universal body, which affords self-
consciousness to Deity, is never likely to be in perfect
health—that on earth, at least, we can answer for a large
portion of it being seldom free from "anguish of all

[1] Forty Questions (1665), Ques. 1, par. 285.
[2] Mysterium Magnum, ch. v., par. 10.
This, and similar expressions to the same effect, are objected to by Bishop Martensen as seeming to make God dependent on His creation for self-knowledge; but, as in other passages on the same subject, Böhme so guards his words as to preclude any possibility of such a misconception. I think an *implied* condition must be taken for granted here, such as "manifest to Himself *in finite existence.*"
[3] Ibid., ch. iii., par. 13.

sizes." Here, again, the flesh and blood body might serve, I think, to meet that difficulty. An inflamed part, or a numbed part—and all evil passions are an inflammation and all selfishness an arrest of vital action—causes much pain and uneasiness while it lasts, but as soon as the pain is over, the fever gone, or circulation fully restored, what a keen sense of comfort and enjoyment returns! and if the return of perfect well-being to Divine self-consciousness amounts to the everlasting life of every atom of perfected humanity (Böhme says, "*God only finds Himself in man*"), the misery that endures for some portions of time is *comparatively* no greater loss than any temporary ailment that befalls the body. My contention is that Jesus, the Heart of God, having desired the recovery of man from spiritual disease, will more certainly fulfil that desire than any human heart, while it beats, can send a vitalizing current to limbs half dead with cold; and I am persuaded that the less we think of this comparison as a figure, and the more we accept it as fact, the better we shall be able to apprehend the relations of God to man: this alone seems to me to solve the difficulty of holding fast the two ideas of God in man and God apart from man—in no wise to be thought of as identical. As the spirit can leave the body, and "*find itself*," or clothe itself in some other instrument of self-manifestation, so could Adam's race lose its *existence* if God so willed; whereas no spiritual life, either of evil or of good, of wrath or love, can exist without God—without the action of the seven spirits of Eternal Nature. Now, the fall and disease of man was the loss of their harmonious working in human nature. He became unholy by willing otherwise than God willed, which is always and for ever to generate light and love.

"As the sun hath but one only will, which is to give itself forth, and with its desire in all things to press forth and grow, and to bestow life, power, and itself on all things, so in like manner also is God, without Nature and Creature, the one only Good that cannot give or will anything but goodness."¹ And "Every willing of evil is a devil, a false compacted will for self, and a rent or splinter broken off from the entire Being."² But this rent acts as the prism acts on light; by breaking its perfect unity it reveals glorious colours, and shews us what in unbroken light could never have been discovered. Thus it is with these seven properties of Eternal Nature, "according to the outward created world, in evil and good, they are in strife one with another, to the end that the inward *spiritual* power might bring itself, through the striving root, into creaturely formations and generations, that the Divine Wisdom might be manifested in wonders or formations in the manifold life. For in the temperature *no creature* can be generated, for it is the one only God, but in the exit of the root of the one only will, in that it parteth itself into *particulars*, so a creature, viz., an image of the formed Word, may spring forth and exist."³ Here we have the secret of the *needs must* of anguish preceding joy: "Since God's love without the Eternal Nature had not been manifested, viz., without the anger fire; and the anger fire was the manifestation of the love fire, as the light cometh from the fire."⁴ Every candle we see burning exemplifies that truth; fire *must* precede light, though light does not necessarily shine out from fire; and as matter of some sort must be consumed to cause fire, so certainly can no true life begin without some previous death. The candle must lose itself, its substance, if it is to give light; the lucifer match must be smitten if it is to kindle it.

Now light can die down while combustion smoulders on, and just this happened in the human soul. "When the light in the creaturely, eternal, natural soul vanished

---

[1] Election, ch. i., par. 56.   [2] Ibid., ch. ii., par. 39.
[3] Ibid., ch. iii., pars. 98–100.   [4] Ibid., ch. vii., par. 80.

or went out" (as it must when self-will exalts itself to dominancy), "then the creaturely soul was only a source of God's anger, viz., a fiery nature."[1] And what the Word of God did to save us from our sins was most literally forgiveness; a *forthgiving* of re-awakened light from this fountain of aching wrathfulness. This was the quickening spirit which was brought into the universal soul of Adam, which is to make all alive. But on no easy conditions. "If a spirit is to subsist in the kingdom of joy, then it must have the *centre* in itself out of which the joy originateth, viz., the *centre* to the dark world, which is the sharp might, else it would be a stillness without moving."[2]

"Life ariseth out of death, it becometh no life unless it break that out of which the life should go forth; it must also go into the anguish chamber, into the Centre, and must attain to the fire-flash in the anguish, else there is no kindling." ... "Out of the greatest anguish existeth also the greatest life, as out of a right fire."[3]

II

"The anxious will must groan or pant after the liberty of the power of the Light, and totally give itself thereinto ... and thus the strong will goeth through the death of the darkness, quite through the essential fire, and falleth into the Light world, and dwelleth in the fire, without pain in the kingdom of joy."—*Incarnation*, Part II., ch. iv., par. 71.

To the ever-recurring thought of Reason, "Wherefore hath God created a painful, suffering life? might it not be in a better state without suffering and torment? seeing He is the ground and beginning of all things, why doth He permit the contrary willing; why doth He not break and destroy the evil that only the good may be in all things?" Böhme answers: "Nothing without contra-

[1] Election, ch. vii., par. 81.
[2] Second Apology, Part I., par. 90.
[3] Incarnation, Part II., ch. v., pars. 48, 49.

riety or opposition can become manifest to itself; for if it hath nothing that is contrary or opposite to it, then it continually goeth forward *out* and goeth not *in* again into itself, viz., into that out of which it is originally gone forth; then it knoweth nothing of its original. If the natural life had no contrariety or opposition and were without a limit, then it would never ask or enquire after its ground out of which it is proceeded, and so the hidden God would continue unknowable or unapprehended by the natural life."[1] "The evil or contrary will causeth the good, viz., the good will, that it presseth again after its original, viz., after God."[2] "Hence strife and anguish, also contrary or opposite willing in the mind originally ariseth, so that the total mind is *thereby caused* to enter again into a breaking or destroying of the thoughts, viz., of the natural *centres,* and to will to sink down out of the torment and paining of the contrary or opposite willing and striving, out of the anguish into the Eternal Rest, viz., into God, out of which it is sprung forth."[3] "At the end of this time," he continues, "it will be manifest wherefore God hath shut it up into a time, and subjected it to suffer under painfulness, viz., therefore that through the natural pain the Eternal power might become *together* brought into forms, conditions or shapes, and separability to perceptibility." . . . "So the Infinite Life thus becometh manifested."[4]

And we may not doubt that the created being who thus serves to manifest infinite life, to extend Divine self-consciousness, will for ever retain all it has won during subjection to the vanities of Time. On this head I must cite the judgment of Freher as opposed to a common mode of speaking of anticipated glory, as if perfected oneness with the spirit of God would be an effacement of individuality: just as many people persist

[1] Divine Vision, ch. i., pars. 14, 15.   [2] Ibid., par. 23.
[3] Ibid., par. 32.   [4] Ibid., pars. 51, 52, 54.

in understanding the Nirvana of Buddhists to be a state of extinguished self-consciousness. "Though they," (human spirits) "be in the completest union and communion, nay in a certain sense but one and the self-same thing, they must each stand in its own property and special qualification. Their oneness is a looking backward towards their only original which is One; their distinction or diversity is their looking forward into multiplicity, to bring forth which out of the original oneness they were themselves brought forth, and which they never could bring forth if they were not themselves distinguished and different from each other even in their own most intimate union and communion." . . . "Every particular brought forth out of Eternal Unity into Multiplicity shall be different from each other, and lie no more in the first Universal ground, but stand in its own particular essentiality."[1]

Arguments that may have proved to us the necessity of suffering fail to satisfy us as to foreknown evolution of sin. For, since a separate own will was essential to the life of a creature, and every will not that of the Holy God must have been open to the risk of deflection from holiness, it is evident that the fall was involved in the gift of creaturely existence. And the tremendous fact of man's nature, made in the likeness of God (*i.e.*, living simultaneously in three worlds, or Principles, as Böhme calls them), is that his will is *necessarily* free from Divine compulsion. "God's spirit and the soul's spirit are two persons; each is free from the other, and yet they stand both in the first beginning; each hath its will."[2] So that if any one say "God is omnipotent, and may He not do with man's will, what He will?" the answer is, "He is omnipotent, He maketh of thee what thou wilt; His love is omnipotent, and also His anger; that which

---

[1] Dionysius Freher.
[2] Forty Questions (1665), Ques. 6, par. 4.

getteth thee holdeth thee."¹ "For the fire soul is a root proceeded from the Divine Omnipotence, and therefore it hath free will, and nothing can deprive it thereof; it may conceive either in the fire or the light."² We can in no state be severed from the Universal Being who filleth all things. If we go down to Hell in our inmost being God is there also; for in good and evil man can only wield the terrific forces of Divine Nature, and only by their agency does he exist. "Here distinction is to be made between God's love and anger. They are indeed both called God, but God inasmuch as He is the Eternal Good is not the anger. The anger hath another principle; in the love fire indeed they are one, but in the separation they are two, and seeing that they are both eternal, without beginning, therefore they have also an eternal will wherein the one cannot kill the other, but each continueth in itself eternally, and they are two centres, yet come originally out of the Unity, out of one only ground." . . . "There is no other but one only God, yet the love would not be manifest and there would be no love known without the anger. Therefore the love yieldeth itself up to the anger fire that it may *be a* love fire; but if the anger severeth itself off from the love into own receptibility, that, doth *not* the love hinder with *force*, else it would follow that God would be at odds in Himself."³ A truth which makes us understand why, when the anger in a human soul has severed itself from the love, the consequences are not hindered with force. But it does not explain why, in the first instance, any being was by its very constitution empowered to rebel and alienate itself from good. We must seek further for any answer to *that* enquiry. And this is Böhme's: "Man was in equal accord in his properties;

---

[1] Second Apology, Part I., par. 184.
[2] Mysterium Magnum, ch. xxvi., par. 7.
[3] 177 Theosophic Questions, Ques. 9, pars. 3-5.

no property was manifest above the other, for he was God's image."[1] And in that unbroken state of harmony was innocent and glorious; but "a thing which standeth in equal balance or like weight hath no moving or desiring to anything; it is one and is of itself. But when it goeth forth from the temperature, then it is *plural*, also corruptible, and thus hath need of help, viz., of grace and compassion." . . . "If that be once done," (the work of grace by the Creator and the faith of man) "the first making findeth a new life in itself, that is existed out of the hope and out of the faith and the desire, and findeth that it is more spiritual than the first out of which the thing existed: therefore it cannot withstand or make resistance, but must suffer the spiritual life to dwell in itself. And here ariseth the restoration of the first substance that hath corrupted, or destroyed itself; so that the last body is better than the first, for that is wholly spiritual, generated out of faith, hope, and love."[2]

"God's holy life would not be manifested without Nature, but be only in an eternal stillness." . . . "Now, if it must be manifested, then there *must* be somewhat which hath need of the love and grace that is *not like* the love and grace, and that is the will of Nature, which in its life standeth in opposition and contrariety or adversity, that hath need of the love and grace that its pain may be changed into joy. And in that change or transmutation is the holy incomprehensible life manifested in the Word as a co-working life in Nature. For the painfulness of Nature causeth that the will of the Abyss, which in the out-speaking hath severed itself into self-singularity, uniteth itself again to the holy Abyssal Life that it may be softened, or allayed, or mitigated. And in the allaying or mitigating it is manifested in the *life of God*."[3] "For the painful work-

[1] Mysterium Magnum, ch. xxix., par. 12.
[2] Election, ch. ix., pars. 298, 303-306.   [3] Ibid., ch. ix., pars. 46-52.

ing of the creature in this life-time is the opening and begetting of Divine power, by which that power is made moveable or operative."[1]

"The Divine Ens which is spiritual *cannot* be manifested but through the strife of Nature."[2]

Now, here Swedenborg's teaching as to the three worlds, the Celestial, the Spiritual, and the world of Ultimates, comes to my help, enabling me by a rough application of his ideas as to the Grand Man—composed of *all* spiritual beings—to perceive how much vaster will be the extent of celestial life, *i.e.*, of absolute sinless blessedness, if it can be brought into ultimates.

We are told by Böhme that before Adam lost original glory,[3] this celestial life was ultimated in heavenly substance; and that he was then in God's likeness the occupant of all three degrees of Divine manifestation; but seeing that by corrupting imagination man clothed himself with *material* life also, there is clearly a more ultimate outbirth. If this is glorified in the course of vast periods of time there is gain to the universe from his fall. And his ascent will be, according to Scriptural intimations, fully equal to his descent. Franz Baader had something to say on this head (writing to Schubert in 1816), which will be better understood now, at least by readers of Mr Oxley's and Mr Sinnett's books, than it could have been in his own life-time. "The Divine leaven in man, once become active, helps us not only to lift ourselves up again from every evil association, but in re-ascending we take with us, in expiation, analogous virtues (for in every creature lies hid the seed of the Word or name of God which was sown in the first creation); these, like accursed and banished spirits,

[1] Supersensual Life, par. 49.
[2] Election, ch. viii., par. 226.
[3] By Adam I understand a *collective* unit, a race, not an individual fraction.

we emancipate from that region, even as the plant, appropriating to itself excellent properties from out the manure, raises them together with itself out of the dark earth, and clothes itself with them in the region of light." . . . "For when we come in contact with evil in this present time, it is not intended that we should merely avoid that contact henceforth, but that we should chemically separate the poison offered to us, and set free as our prey the good which it has absorbed."

This I suppose to be the object of Divine love in permitting all the woe and evil that is involved in our present material environment. The immediate influx of celestial life is obviously impossible; if it fall upon unprepared natures such influx is destruction: but while screened in some measure by astral light and elemental influences from the false and cruel magic of rebel spirits hostile to good, true heavenly substance can be formed in us, and our corruptible mortal life, by its very necessities, can release from the mysterious chaos we call matter, latent soul-germs for an immeasurably long uprise of spiritual evolution. And thus I understand Böhme's saying, that "when God introduced the spiritual world according to all properties into an *outward substance*, then the inward continued in the outward; the outward as a creation or creature, but the inward as a generating substance."[1]

"In that manner as precious pure gold lieth and groweth in a gross, drossy, dirty stone, wherein the drossiness helpeth to work, though it be not at all like the gold; so also must the earthly body help to generate Christ" (anointed humanity) "in itself."[2] "We shall, as to the heavenly substantiality, excel the angels, for they are flames of fire throughly illustrated with the light, but we attain the great source or quality of the

[1] Election, ch. iii., par. 92.   [2] Ibid., ch. viii., par. 253.

meekness and love which floweth forth in God's holy substantiality."¹

"The joy of the saints must arise in them out of death as the light ariseth out of a candle by the destruction and consumption of it in the fire; that so the life may be freed from the painfulness of nature and possess another world. And as the light hath quite another property than the fire hath, for it giveth and yieldeth itself forth, whereas the fire draweth in and consumeth itself, so the holy life of meekness springeth forth through the death of self-will, and then God's will of love only ruleth, and doth all in all. For thus the Eternal One hath attained feeling and separability, and brought itself forth again with the feeling through death in great joyfulness, that there might be an eternal delight in the Infinite Unity, and an eternal cause of joy, *and therefore painfulness must now be the ground and cause of this motion or stirring to the manifestation of all things.* And herein lieth the mystery of the hidden Wisdom of God."²

How glorious a hope! for this "exaltation is a mere pure divine forming and begetting in the Wisdom of God, where the Word of God is also thereby born in man, and that man also generateth God; so that he is a substantial God, viz., a harmony of the divine kingdom of God."³

The one perfect Man who by the total death of self-will began the universal reign of God's "*will of love,*" re-affirmed the same truth, "*I said, ye are gods,* and ye are all the children of the highest."

There is yet another reason given by Böhme for the miseries of this present state, which, until I had read Mr Oxley's *Angelic Revelations* and Mr Sinnett's *Esoteric*

---

¹ Incarnation, Part I., ch. v., par. 114.
² Supersensual Life, par. 57.
³ Election, ch. ix., par. 357. See *Galatians* iv. 19.

Buddhism, was a saying impenetrable even by a guess. "To this end the poor soul standeth in the prison of the astral and elemental kingdom, that it might be a labourer and re-unite the wonders of the external Nature with the light world and bring them into the beginning."[1]

I must not attempt to put into words such dim ideas as I have gathered from both these books as to the potential *spiritual* life of every atom of what we call inanimate Nature: other readers will find what suggests them; and for some approach to understanding how soul life became thus buried in what we call matter, I must refer them to the Baroness von Vay's little book on "*Geist, Kraft, Stoff.*"

[1] Epistles (1649), Ep. 5, par. 46.

MARTENSEN'S "JACOB BÖHME"[1]

THE appearance of this book[2] in the admirable translation given by Mr T. Rhys Evans must be a pleasure to those who are already acquainted with Böhme's works, and a window of hope for those who desire to be, but who, either for lack of access to them, or of spiritual conditions almost more rare than these, remain ignorant of their contents. Both class of readers will, I think, be gratified by Bishop Martensen's book, always supposing that they bring a keen appetite to his studies; for he enlarges on most obscure themes with surprising lucidity, and is free from any of that "insignificant nugatory prattle," which is the too common resource of English writers when they lay before an impatient public a burden of recondite instruction, conscious that it will be as little welcomed by the majority of their readers as it is *fully* comprehended by themselves. But even among ourselves this flippancy of tone, often adopted as a sort of implied apology for *expecting* intellectual effort, is happily much less common than it was; when, for example, *Hours with the Mystics* came out.

The Danish metropolitan, seeking first to meet the demands of his own high intelligence, never stoops

[1] Light and Life, Sept., Oct., Nov., 1886.
[2] Jacob Boehme: His Life and Teaching, or Studies in Theosophy, by the late Dr Hans Lassen Martensen. Translated from the Danish by T. Rhys Evans, 1885.

to compromise for the sake of propitiating less earnest thinkers. But in the attitude he takes towards Böhme, nevertheless we find him quite a bishop; not for a moment deigning to recognize anything of *inspiration* in his knowledge. "I undertook," he says in the preface, "the perusal of his complete works—no insurmountable task, seeing that they comprise only seven volumes in Schiebler's edition." To those who have gone through even two or three of those volumes several times, it will seem preposterous that one reading, however careful, should be supposed adequate for gaining any *just* idea of their freight; and to such readers the suspicion that this illiterate shoemaker wrote, "as he was moved by the Holy Ghost," will not probably seem strange; but a bishop would be apt to repress it as *unauthorized*. Evidently Martensen does his best to give an honest account of Böhme's teaching, but either missing or evading its aspect as *super*-rational, he gives it in the language of reason, when, as it stands in the original text, reason is out of court.

So little is he inclined to receive anything from him as revelation, that finding what he says on certain points unconfirmed by the Bible (though *not* contradictory or unacceptable to reason), he rejects, *in toto*, information offered, and averts his intelligence from most precious gifts with all the conscientious dogmatism of a theologian. For instance, when he comes to the question of Adam's fall before the production of Eve— to the account by which Böhme harmonizes the discrepancy between vers. 27 and 31 of *Genesis* i., and vers. 18 of chap. ii. of the same book, he dismisses it as an untenable theory because "Scripture does not give us the slightest indication that Adam's sleep was the result of a sinful fall"[1] and "we cannot discover his Scriptural authority for permitting the severance which now took

[1] Page 243.

place to be occasioned by a sinful fall, and for viewing the creation of woman as, at best, a counter-active measure, a remedial provision against a disturbance which had taken place. Scripture does not give the remotest hint that Adam was intended to propagate himself magically, but points out the sexual relation with which we are acquainted, as the original one."[1]

In order to judge of what Martensen thus rejects, I must put before the reader a number of quotations from the work in which this great mystery is most fully laid open, the *Mysterium Magnum*; to give any summary of their drift *not* in the Seer's own words is impossible; and placing only the most essential in close sequence, I leave *numbers of highest value* unquoted. Considering the interest lately roused by Mr Laurence Oliphant's *Sympneumata* in England, not to speak of the peculiar doctrines of Mr T. Lake Harris in America, bearing on the supersensual relations of man and woman, I cannot believe such passages as these will be found unworthy of the space they occupy.

"All that is earthly in man, that is bestial and corruptible, and *not* man; albeit God created man an external body out of the *limus* of the earth; yet it is not to be considered of us, as now it is; for the true human *body*, according to the *inward world*, is a *spiritual sulphur*, a *spiritual mercurius*, and a *spiritual sal.*" . . . "In no wise the gross beast which passeth away and returneth not again; the true, real body which is *hidden* in the grossness is a spiritual body in comparison to the grossness: it is created indeed in flesh and blood; but in a fixed, steadfast, incorruptible flesh and blood."[2]

"Adam was a man and also a woman, and yet neither of them distinct, but a virgin full of chastity, modesty, and purity, viz., the *image* of God; he had both the

[1] Page 242.   [2] Mysterium Magnum, ch. xvi., pars. 2, 3.

tinctures of the fire and light in him; in the conjunction of which, the own love, viz., the virginal centre, stood."
... "Such a man as Adam was before his Eve, shall arise, and again enter into, and eternally possess, Paradise."[1]

"These two beings, viz., the inward heavenly, and the outward heavenly, were mutually espoused to each other and formed into one body, wherein was the most holy tincture of fire and light, viz., the great, joyful, love desire which did inflame the essence, so that both essences did very earnestly and ardently desire each other in the love desire, and loved one another: the inward loved the outward as its manifestation and *sensation*, and the outward loved the inward as its greatest sweetness and joyfulness; as its precious pearl and most beloved spouse and consort; and yet they were not two bodies, but only one; but of a *twofold* essence."[2]

"If God had created him for the earthly, corruptible, miserable, naked, sick, bestial, toilsome life, then He had not brought him into Paradise; if He had desired the bestial propagation then He would instantly, in the beginning, have created man and woman, and both sexes had come forth in the *Verbum Fiat*, into the division of both tinctures as it was in the *other* earthly creatures."[3]

But "Adam in his *perfection*, while he was man and wife, and had the magical conception in him, did amuse himself, or imagine after the beasts, and introduced himself into bestial lust to eat and generate as beasts do." ... "Thus the image of God formed itself in the *Verbum Fiat* into such a beast as we are still to this day, and this same was done in itself, viz., man's own Fiat—viz., the first form of nature, which is the desire

---

[1] Mysterium Magnum, ch. xviii., pars. 2, 3.
[2] Ibid., par. 8. [3] Ibid., par. 5.

of God's manifestation, did effect it and none other maker from without him."[1]

The last sentence, wholly unintelligible to an unprepared reader, needs translation. *Astringency* is what Böhme calls the first form of nature: in his *Election of Grace* he uses the very significant phrase, "the *magnetical attraction is the beginning of nature*."[2] Now, it was the desire of God to manifest Himself that originated Eternal Nature, and from thence *all* natures; and it is one of Böhme's most capital doctrines that creation by the Word was caused by its *re-outspeaking* in all nature and creature. "The *beginning* of all and every substance or thing is the Word, viz., the outbreathing of God's substance; and God was the Eternal One from Eternity, and continueth the same also in Eternity; but the Word is the efflux or *outflowing* of the divine willing or of the divine knowledge."[3]

"The visible world, with its hosts and creatures, is nothing else but the *outflown Word* which hath introduced itself into properties, wherein in the properties an own self-will existed."[4]

This digressive hint, so to speak, of a profound depth in Böhme's revelations, was indispensable, because, according to him, the spirit always forming its own body, by the "*magnetic attraction*" of imagination and desire, Adam was his own "miscreator." "The desire," he repeatedly says, "maketh itself substance." "It was so done when Adam began to put his desire and imagination into the outward world."[5] . . . "He brought the

---

[1] Mysterium Magnum, ch. xix., par. 25.   [2] Ch. ii., par. 41.
[3] Divine Vision, ch. iii., par. 2.
[4] Ibid., ch. iii., par. 22. See also *Knowledge of All Things*, par. 12 (Several Treatises, 1662), and *Epistles* (1649), Ep. 6, par. 12.
[5] One naturally asks how could a creature so perfect as Adam put his imagination and desire into a lower plane? Böhme answers, "The crafty distemper or infection introduced by the devil was in the *Ens* of the Earth whence Adam's *outward* body was formed; into this earthly Ens the devil

earthly source or quality into the pure elementary flesh, which was created out of the Divine substantiality, so his light extinguished, that is, he went with his will spirit out of the Divine substantiality into the stars and four elements," and they, "the stars and elements, put on [1] to the body the fierce, earthly clothes of *their* essence and substantiality," . . . "and so God and the Kingdom of Heaven was lost, for the Divine image disappeared, and the earthly began to appear; the outward fiat gat the predominancy" (let it be understood, the outward fiat in Adam), "for as soon as Adam was overcome by the spirit of this world then he fell asleep, viz., into the *outward magia*, which signifieth or resembleth death; for the outward kingdom hath beginning and end, and *must* break off from the inward, *that* is its death." [2]

"Adam died in Paradise, as God said unto him: If thou eatest of the tree thou diest; he died to the holy, heavenly image, and lived to the awaked bestial image. For now when Adam did awake from sleep, he was still in Paradise, for the vanity in the flesh and soul did *not* yet actually and effectually work, and was yet dumb, still, and senseless, until they did eat of the forbidden fruit, and then the earthly dominion began to rise." . . . "The heavenly image at last quite disappeared, which in Adam's sleep, and also in his awakening, *did*

brought his desire." (*Myst. Mag.*, ch. xxvi., par. 67.) Elsewhere Böhme describes a process exactly answering to *animal magnetism*, practised by the dethroned angel Lucifer on Adam.

[1] *Put on.* This seems a contradiction to what has just been said above of the spirit forming its own body; but it is not so, the astral efflux and the four elements were the substance on which the magic of Adam's desire worked; the one pure element in which he lived before gave itself originally to the *fiat* of his will. "Car enfin, cette vérité doit sortir de l'ombre des Sanctuaires : la volonté était créatrice chez l'Homme Universel. Tout ce que cet homme voulait, était quand et comment il le voulait. La puissance et l'acte étaient indivisibles dans sa volonté."—(Fabre-D'Olivet's *La Langue Hebraïque restituée: Cosmogonie de Moyse*, p. 92).

[2] First Apology, Part II., pars. 212, 214, 215.

yet live, both in Adam and Eve, but in a very obscure and *impotent* manner."[1]

"Thus hath Adam's spirit by the imagination brought a power into the earth, and so the matrix of nature gave him what he would have."[2]

"Thus we understand what the woman or wife is, viz., a *half* Adam; Adam hath, in the superior might, the first principle, and Eve the second." . . . "In the man the spirit is fiery, that soweth the fiery tincture; in the woman the spirit is watery according to the light, that soweth the spirit's tincture; in the inward kingdom the image of the faded substantiality, and in the outward the air's property out of the abomination of the earthliness."[3]

Two very important points should be noted in this last passage. *First*, "*Watery according to the light*," senseless to any one unversed in Böhme's lore; but that *all* substantiality originates from light is one of his master keys to many a mystery; and again and again he points out how, from fire, light, and from light, air, and from air, water is *naturally* produced, taking the elementary fire, light, air, and water, as the visible representations of the Holy Trinity, speaking of *God the Father as fire, God the Son as Light, God the Holy Ghost as air*, and the water *of eternal life as the Wisdom, mother of all substance.*

It is noticeable that Swedenborg, seemingly ignorant of the earlier mystic, emphatically asserts that the *atmospheres* of the sun originated the substances and matters of our earth.[4]

Secondly, the woman's spirit's tincture is "the image of the faded substantiality." Why? Because her spirit's

---

[1] Mysterium Magnum, ch. xix., par. 24.
[2] Incarnation, Part I., ch. v., par. 103.
[3] Third Apology, Text IV., Point II., pars. 56, 93.
[4] See Swedenborg's *Divine Love and Wisdom*, Part IV., par. 303.

tincture *is* light, the second holy principle, and "every divine creature, as are the angels and souls of men, hath the Virgin of the wisdom of God as an image in the *Light of Life*, in the substantiality of the spirit";[1] but man having fallen, woman has *but an image* of God's image in her light tincture, till Christ is re-born in her, and has overcome what Böhme obscurely calls the *air's* property out of the abomination of the earthliness, *i.e.*, the body formed *externally* by *astral* influences to which the abomination of our animal condition has subdued man, who was made to rule over them. I thus understand "air's property," because Böhme as well as St Paul attributes the "*power of the air*" to the spirit of disobedience: telling us that between the earth and the moon rebel spirits have permitted sway.

But now for the last links of this long expository chain. The purposes of the Omnipotent God cannot be frustrated. "Such a man as Adam was before his Eve, shall arise again, enter into, and eternally possess, Paradise."[2]

"The heart of God moved itself, destroyed death, and generated the life again. Thus now to us the birth and becoming man or incarnation of Christ is a powerful and very weighty matter, that the total *abyssal heart* of God hath moved itself, and so therewith the heavenly substantiality which was shut up in death is become living again."[3]

"Understand, in the right human and heavenly sub-

[1] Threefold Life, ch. v., par. 57.
[2] Mysterium Magnum, ch. xviii., par. 3.
"First the heavenly substantiality had the predominancy, but afterwards when Adam went back with his lust into the earthly substantiality, then the earthly got the power and predominancy," ... "and therefore must God, with the heavenly substantiality, *in us become man*, and in the heavenly virgin, and in the earthly, God is become man, and hath put upon our souls the heavenly substantiality again, viz., his heavenly body."
—*Threefold Life*, ch. xiii., par. 19. See *Ibid.*, ch. vi., pars. 96, 97.
[3] Incarnation, Part I., ch. ix., pars. 20, 21.

stantiality, which in Adam was shut up in death, would God become man; not in the earthly, introduced into the noble image and soul; into the right human nature of the second principle, in which God dwelt before Adam's fall, into that very essence [substance] shut up in death is God's Word entered; *that is the seed of the woman, and the Word is God's seed.*"[1]

"Christ is that virgin-like image which Adam should have generated out of himself *with both the tinctures.*"[2]

"He brought again the *virginity,* viz., two tinctures into one unseparable, eternal conjunction in the love, no more in the desire after *substance* as it was in Adam, but only in the desire after power. The two tinctures generate *no more substance,* viz., a propagation, but holy power and God's holiness."[3]

For "the two loves, which in the temperature are *divine,* which were divided in Adam, when the imagination turned itself forth from the temperature, are *united* again in Christ."[4]

It is without scruple that I have so fully given the *clearest* expressions I could select of Böhme's teaching about this great mystery—the intense, mutual love of man and woman; because on one hand the grossness of animal passion has desecrated, and on the other total ignorance of its spiritual origin has lowered it in common habits of thought to the level of an earthly and transitory affection. Even by thoughtful and purest-minded Christians it is often so regarded. Misled by their preconceived ideas as to the relation of the sexes to each other, they read into the words of the Lord Jesus, "In the resurrection they neither marry nor are given in

---

[1] First Apology, Part II., par. 236.
[2] Incarnation, Part I., ch. xi., par. 29.
[3] Third Apology, Text IV., Point IV., pars. 64 65. See *Forty Questions,* Ques. 1, pars. 224, 225; also Ques. 36.
[4] Election, ch. iii., par. 47.

marriage, but are as the angels which are in heaven,"[1] tacit condemnation of any hope of heart-union in a blissful hereafter. But how could two once severed halves when for *ever united*, marry or be given in marriage? Surely that is a self-evident impossibility; asserting *that* our Saviour never said that being as the angels which are in heaven did not pre-suppose the restoration of original oneness.

As usual, human wisdom interprets divine promises by negations rather than by intensatives. Had the human mind—untaught—been tasked to make pure white, undoubtedly it would have begun by trying to exclude every colour from its manufacture; by divine wisdom, as science proves, the process is reversed, and purest white is the combination of all colours. It is far easier to think of a state of existence from which feelings seldom unmixed with frailty *here* shall be wholly banished, just because it is so very hard to imagine the pure gold that divine love can rescue from all our defilements of sin, and to understand that even in its most debased forms the self-ignoring passion of love must proceed from a higher source than human nature as it *now* is. It seems to me a very injurious effect of age-long arrest in theological thought, that our *prescribed* ideas of heaven have been so sedulously cleared of any connecting link with this life's supremest joy. The heart has thus lost its natural hold upon the eternal future. For I doubt if any one who *has* known perfectness of reciprocal love, whether married in life, or in heart and spirit only, will deny that descriptions of everlasting praise and adoration of the Redeemer, not only as supremely loved, but as the *sole* object of love, are inoperative as a lever of hope compared to such as admit of intense affection for a human being also. Saintly people who have *not* known the best of a fellow-creature's

[1] Matthew xxii. 30.

love may deny it, surely no others. For even now, with all the flaws of that *best* in our present state, it seems to the happy hearts which have felt it pure and holy enough for the heaven where the Lamb is followed in light, and quite inseparable from all we understand by *identity*. If this love is lost in just men and women, what *can* be left that is specially their own?

Böhme says, " All, whatsoever is in this world, is a type and figure of the angelical world"; . . . "of all whatsoever this world is an earthly type and resemblance, that is in the divine kingdom in great perfection in the spiritual essence; not only spirit as a will, or thought, but essence, corporeal essence, sap, and power; but as incomprehensible in reference to the outward world."[1]

We owe much to Dr John Pulsford for so bravely giving to the world his unconventional belief as to the future of human love in his beautiful book *Morgenröthe*. To quote from it would be as ineffectual as to detach a few petals from the rose to prove its sweetness; to be read aright, it must be read in its entirety.

It is very observable that those who, on religious grounds, repudiate any imaginable likeness to earthly bliss in the Christian's heaven constantly fall into modes of speech which appear to translate into devout language every human affection—seeming to appropriate the love of the Lord Jesus Christ in a personal sense, better suited to the exclusive attachment of wife and husband than to the adoring love of the redeemed for a *universal Saviour* —as tender in pity towards the sinner as towards the saint. Hymn writers are, in some degree, answerable for this; but neither writers nor quoters of *some* hymns can imagine the repelling shock they often produce.

It is also remarkable that the frequent reference in our Bible to the relations of husband to wife, and bride to bridegroom, by which these amorous pieties are

[1] Signatura Rerum, ch. xvi., pars. 16, 17.

justified, give—one would suppose—the strongest sanction for the hope of eternal union which ordinary religionists condemn.

But well does Dr Pulsford remind us of caution in proclaiming this hope even now. "Why has the gospel of our *whole* humanity been so long withheld? The impure would transmute heaven's purity into more impurity." . . . "Hitherto the unity has been only known on its fallen plane, and not as it was in God's beginning. The divine unity could not be conceived by the animal-human race. The gross conceptions and appetites of the race would have carnalized, profaned, and abused any testimony that could have been given of the essential oneness of the sexes. For the same reason that which is most holy should still be withheld from dogs, and the pearl of heaven's dual unity from swine."[1]

Equally regrettable as a hasty refusal of truth, most important in its bearings upon our second birth, is Martensen's positive tone about *essentiality*, which, as I have just shewn, is exactly that which the first Adam lost, and the second Adam, the "quickening Spirit," restored to our race. Thus Martensen *mis*understands it.

"When Böhme says that the '*essentiality*' which was dead in Adam, and was again quickened in Christ, cried 'My God, my God, why hast Thou forsaken me?' we believe that we can approximately understand this marvellously profound but obscure expression if we take '*essentiality*' to mean the spirit in distinction from the soul, that which is, in the most rigid sense, the divinely-imaged in human nature, that which makes it capable of love and of union with the Idea, the Virgin."[2]

Böhme's translators are answerable for the mistake of rendering *Wesen* essence, which, oddly enough, means in German both essence and substance; this was in accordance with the ideas of their day. Even John

[1] Morgenröthe, 1881, pp. 72, 66 ; 1883, pp. 95, 87.   [2] Page 273.

Sparrow, with all his reverent and diligent study, seems to have missed the point which Böhme reiterates with emphasis in almost all his works, that all spiritual beings have corporeity—even the Being of all beings. We are often blind to what we do not expect to see. The oneness and yet the difference of pure substance and pure spirit was not, and hardly now *is*, a received idea. Yet just upon *this* Böhme tells us regeneration depends. He says that the incarnation of the Word was necessary, because "the matter was not about forgiveness only; the soul wanted not only forgiveness, but a new birth."[1] "When Adam's will spirit imagined after earthliness, God let him fall down; for he brought the imagination of earthliness into the heavenly substantiality."[2] "This substance, vanished and shut up in death, was signified by the dry rod of Aaron, which substance grew in this awakening and introducing of the heavenly living love essence where God's substance became man, in whom the holy fire could burn"; . . . "that same love-burning was the new life of the regeneration."[3]

"Seeing man was earthly and elementary, there must also be an elementary medium or means for that purpose wherein the flowing forth of the Divine love in the covenant might take hold."[4] "And, therefore, God assumed the humanity that He might work in and with us, with the Deity, through the humanity."[5]

It is much to be wished that those who speak of the obsolete childishness of belief in an "historic Christ" could at all reach the depth of causation, where the coming of *the* Christ, the Divine Anointer, to the human race *at a given point of time* is seen to have been as necessary for its purpose—to employ a very homely

---

[1] Baptism, ch. ii., par. 2 : Böhme's revised text, 1652 ed., p. 10.
[2] Incarnation, Part I., ch. vi., par. 7.   [3] Baptism, ch. ii., par. 31.
[4] Ibid., par. 27.
[5] Ibid. : Böhme's revised text, 1652 ed., p. 18.

simile—as waiting for the right time of year to graft a tree. Its sap must be in a certain stage of flowing before this can be done with success; and the human stock had to be developed to a certain pitch of spiritual growth before there could be receptiveness for the quickening spirit. For this the Law was a most essential preparative; and when that had done all it could for men, "then came the fulfilling of the promise and put another new body on to thee; for thou canst not have another soul, for thy soul was out of the eternity."[1] [Fuller light on this point will be found in the *Third Apology*, Text IV., Point IV., par. 28 to par. 32, and *Incarnation*, Part I., ch. ix., par. 46; and *Ibid.*, ch. xii., par. 37.]

Why Martensen judged it suitable to speak of the Virgin Sophia as "the idea," when *all* ideas of the Abyssal God prior to nature and creature are said by Böhme to have been reflected in her as a passive mirror of the Divine mind,[2] I cannot understand. Yet I believe it must be admitted that in one of Böhme's writings he had enough to confuse him as to what conception *she* attached to the word. In the fifth of his *177 Theosophic Questions* we find him call "*the Idea the express image of God, a form of the Divine names*,"[3] and in the twelfth the expression occurs "which Spirit *the idea, Jesus, viz., an efflux from the Divine unity, came to help and relieve.*"[4] Martensen's very immature treatment of "Teutonicus" tempts one to a redundancy of criticism, and as a restraint upon this, I must only allow myself to enlarge on his *most* defective apprehensions; even thus I fear the patience of the reader may be too severely strained.

At page 110 we find it said that Böhme represents God

---

[1] Three Principles, ch. xxii., par. 85.
[2] In *Light*, Dec. 24, 1892, Mrs Penny acknowledged herself mistaken in this statement. See p. 463 of the present volume.—ED.
[3] Par. 3.   [4] Par. 24.

apart from Eternal Nature as "life and yet not life; only a figure or schema of life. God does not become the living God until the Eternal Nature arises"; again, "although it is spirit itself that posits Nature, it is permitted to borrow its life from Nature." A gross misconception; yet I grant it is easy in a *cursory* perusal so to misunderstand him; but no one thoroughly conversant with his writings could allow that this is his doctrine: very many quotations one could adduce utterly to disprove it; the only difficulty is to select one of the clearest on a theme so inevitably obscure. In his treatise on the *Incarnation*, Part II., ch. iii., from par. 17 to par. 27, the admission of such an idea is combated; and at par. 24 of the same chapter he says, "God is in Himself the Abyss, viz., the first world of which no creature knoweth anything at all, for it standeth solely and alone with spirit and body in the Byss or ground. Thus also God Himself, in the Abyss, would not be manifest to Himself, but His *Wisdom* is, from Eternity, become His ground or Byss."—*See Context.*

To quote detached passages of this kind about a mystery quite unsearchable would only perplex readers not used to Böhme; and as many sayings of his may be found *seemingly* contradictory, it might leave the balance even between the opinion of Martensen and that of his critic. It will be better to accept the judgment of Dionysius Freher, whose thorough mastery of the sense of "Teutonicus," after reading all his books throughout ten times, gives *his* verdict exceptional value.

It is much to be regretted that the Danish Bishop had not seen Freher's expositions: evidently he had not; for a student so candid could never have written as he does if these *had* been known to him. Those who have access to the late Mr Christopher Walton's *Memorial of William Law* (unpublished), must feel deeply grateful to him for putting such large portions of Freher's writings within their reach. But for these, this Bishop's version of Böhme's teaching as to the relation of Eternal Nature to the Eternal Spirit would have found me ill prepared to meet it, and I should have been induced to think the greatest of mystics in error, or, at best, rash in expression. Martensen's whole indictment is clear and forcible, but too long for quotation. This in brief is its outline. Böhme represents God, who is a Spirit, as needing Eternal Nature for His own perfected life; the source of all Being and all existences as needing His instrument of manifestation for *self*-consciousness and self-knowledge. What I now offer of Freher's anticipatory defence will sufficiently meet the misunderstandings exposed from page 110 to 127.

If, as I am fain to believe, the blessed dead retain their memory, and their interest in the pursuit of truth which occupied them in this world, I cannot but think this good man will, for truth's sake, be pleased to have his mistakings of an earlier teacher rectified.

"Concerning understanding, knowing and perceiving itself, both these are affirmed and denied of the first Abyssal Being by Teutonicus, and both are consistent with each other with respect to two different worlds."[1]

"As to the first Abyssal World, no affirmative saying from this world can be admitted into that, though never so much refined and exalted, because there is *no coherence, no analogy, and no mutual answerableness* between them, the one of them being in Nature, and the other without Nature."[2]

"This first world is deeper than any natural sense or thought can reach. But now, when such a sense is denied, the question is, What is then left, or what benefit can we reap from such descriptions? (as Böhme's). Answer.—There is left a deeper sense, excluding the generation

[1] Memorial of Law, p. 265. [2] Ibid., p. 268.

of Eternal Nature, and therefore not conceivable by creatures what or how, but only knowable that it is. The words of Böhme signify that all our ideas of this first Abyssal world must be negative; and that no affirmative one, truly to be called so, can be had thereof by any creature."[1]

"I know very well that, according to the principles of Teutonicus, in various senses, upon different accounts, and with several respects, that which is by him considered as before Eternal Nature, may be called both something and nothing; and may be said again to be neither nothing nor something; and truly he cannot be blamed for such variety and seeming contradictory expressions. He could not help it, and no man living on earth shall be found able to represent these things to the understanding of another, with such expressions as never should seem to cross and contradict each other. If the Spirit of God in the Revelation could have said of one and the same thing it was, and was not, and yet was, nay, could have added *here is wisdom*, etc., who can justly complain of Teutonicus?"[2]

"Wisdom, in the first world, is not an empty name, but it implieth not only a perceiving its abyssal state, but also a finding itself able and all-sufficient for per forming its intent, viz., for going through the first three properties of dark Nature into the fire, and through the fire into the light: for this is its going into the second world, and its becoming in this world, that which it will be, and not yet can be in the first world."[3]

"We do not deny that all the Divine perfections are in the Triune Being without Nature, yet we say that they are not yet exerted, and cannot become exerted but by the raising up and passing through the properties of Nature"; . . . "and so we cannot so properly say God is

[1] Memorial of William Law, p. 269.   [2] Ibid., p. 262.
[3] Ibid., p. 272.

Omnipotent without all Nature, but more properly we say, He is all-sufficient to shew forth His omnipotence in the generation of Nature. Which all-sufficiency cannot raise in us any idea of defect or imperfection, but rather of all and every perfection, only considered as still concentrated, and not yet out of that centre unfolded and displayed."[1]

It was after reading Freher's reply to objections similar to Bishop Martensen's that a Mr Pierce thus acknowledged its sufficiency. "I return many thanks for the sight of these papers; before which I did not distinguish between the Eternal generation and the Eternal manifestation, but conceived the Threefold Spirit in the Abyss to be ungenerate and hidden; but now I understand the Triune Spirit to be in the Abyss generate and manifest to itself before Nature. And that which pleaseth me much more is to see none of the former descriptions denied or laid aside, but reconciled with the latter, which I did not understand further than the Eternal Nature; but might well have expected more in them than in the former had I considered that the author (Böhme) *saith 'the descriptions are one deeper than another,'* and that he *saw more and more*; but I, not minding this, took the former to be complete, and thought he knew all at first, though not able to set it all down, and for that reason I laid by what I could not find in them, thinking it was enough to know as far as the Eternal Nature."[2]

Martensen's misapprehensions of Böhme on this point were due to just this arrest of thought. *Beyond* no creature can imagine, but to believe Eternal Nature the *all* of which the God of gods is cognisant, is to fall below rational thought. From page 126 to 132, commenting on what he terms "the dark-nature principle in God," Martensen is so wholly on the wrong track that to

[1] Memorial of William Law, pp. 296, 297. [2] Ibid., p. 286.

answer his assertions in detail would be unfair as well as waste of time. He writes on this subject as correctly as any one might who, while describing some chemical experiment, was ignorant himself of one of its main factors; and I do not believe that the most acute mind, studying Böhme without Freher's aid, could altogether escape a false conclusion here. Less powerful intellects may have been aware that the contradictions found in his teaching were *apparent* only, if convinced that Böhme spoke from a higher ground than Reason; but, to the best of my knowledge, Freher alone has faced these perplexing disagreements, and thoroughly resolved their discord. Until his Treatise on "*Deity, considered as manifesting Himself through Eternal Nature*" is placed by some benefactor of mankind within reach of an English public, I do not think Böhme's hardest knots can *ever* be loosened even to the degree they then might be—by every reader patient enough for close attention to the slow windings of an eighteenth-century style. With such attention this admirable Treatise is not at all hard reading.

On one point alone, the action of the *Lubet*—or, as Böhme sometimes calls it, the *Liberty* (because that Divine pleasure is free from all necessity)—in evolving the seven forces of Eternal Nature, Freher's elucidation is priceless. For many years, not perceiving what is *implied* in Böhme's own words, I foolishly supposed these forces would of themselves lead from the first harsh astringency to the striking up of fire, and all subsequent effects; unconsciously sharing the superstitions of the materialist, who attributes *life* to protoplasm, but from Freher one learns that without the Lubet, Eternal Nature could not be : it was and is the desire of Divine love that comprised and thus concealed its omnipotency in those first severe *conditions* of evolution, that Deity might be manifested—and oh! how infinitely much more than that form of speech implies!—let us say rather that the generation of the ever blessed Trinity in a lower world might be made possible in an endless *naturing* of souls.

How the right evolution of light in *this* Universe was arrested, and for a vast period of time hindered by the rebellion of the "throne-angel" called Lucifer, Böhme has stated, and Freher has explained, in the Treatise mentioned above, and this part of his revelations the Bishop seems to have grasped with great distinctness.

Instead of combating one by one such misconceptions of his as this at page 133, "If God, as the Being of all Beings, is to be conceived as the Union of Spirit and Nature"—and at page 144, "That God, as Spirit, is regarded as potential not actual, a life which is not a life, but a mere figure and schema of life," I venture for the satisfaction of *some* readers, at the risk of fatiguing others, to quote Freher again in reply.

"It is absolutely false that Böhme considereth God only so. For though he hath the same expressions that are in this objection mentioned, viz., that God is considered *only* in the second principle of light, yet it is as clear as the day at noon that this *only* is by Himself limited and confined to Eternal Nature, and especially to the three tinctured and harmonized properties thereof. So that it is to say that God, as manifested in Eternal Nature, is considered only in the second principle. And so this *only* doth not at all import that there is not a deeper and more central consideration of God, since it is notorious that he considereth God also as unmanifest, in that Abyss where there is neither darkness nor light, that is before Eternal Nature."[1]

To Martensen's saying "God as Spirit, or God in the still mystery, is for Böhme only universal will, or the will of Unity, the mystic freedom which at root wills

[1] Memorial of William Law, p. 260.

nothing, and can only become a definite will through the agency of Nature."[1]

Freher's words answer—"God will manifest Himself in Nature, which cannot be done without the desire; but having in Himself a Lubet, wherein the Eternal generation of the Trinity is implied, He is manifest to Himself before and without the manifestation in Nature, and cannot but know, perceive, and find Himself."[2]

The first few paragraphs of the 16th chapter of Böhme's *Signatura Rerum* are so explicit on this subject that it alone might have saved the Bishop from his mistaking there.

Freher's Treatise on *Regeneration* gives a fulness of satisfaction to every enquirer as to this profound mystery; to quote from it is to take but a drop of water as a sample of the *quality* of waters in a deep well.

When at page 140 of his *Studies* Martensen says—"God as a Personality *is* severity and self-exaltation, is holiness and righteousness, is the jealous God who vindicates His own honour, and is also gentleness, self-surrender, and love," with context to the end of that page, one feels very powerfully what Böhme's teaching has done to *relieve* the mind from any idea of the High and Holy God such as this; for surely here is the anthropomorphic concept of Deity which is rebuked by the saying, "Thou thinkest I am such a One as Thyself"; here the fountain source of the degrading barbarities man has attributed to God, and practised upon his fellow-creatures for "*the glory of God*"; here the justification of Puritans and Calvinists who, like "the renowned Dr Preston," when rebutting in the time of Charles the Second all arguments of hope for hardened sinners after death, declared that "never did strong man glory of his strength more than God doth of His sovereignty. Now if it fall that in the illustration and exercise of these His glorious attributes

[1] Martensen's *Jacob Böhme*, p. 112.   [2] Memorial of William Law, p. 282.

and excellences, some creatures smart, yet He delights not in their smart and sufferings, but in the demonstration of His Omnipotency."

I thank God the two centuries and a half which have elapsed since those words were uttered by a holy man, have raised our conceptions of Deity from that childish level!

But how does Böhme teach as to this? On what basis can *he* plant contrary convictions? On this, that all which is predicated in the Scriptures, and all we see and feel of severity, wrath, jealousy, and the like, is referable to the spirits of God's Eternal Nature acting in the world where their properties are in manifest distemperature *according* to that divided state. God Himself, he tells us —conformably to St John's repeated assertion—*is Love*, and *can only love*. "God loveth all His creatures, and can do nothing else but love; for He is the only Love itself. But His wrath is understood to be in the temporal and Eternal Nature."[1]

This very important key to all the discords of our present life would have taken the Bishop more fully into Böhme's meaning as to *necessity* of evil. "In all creatures there is a poison and malignity; and it must be so, otherwise there were no life and no mobility, nor would there be any colour nor virtue, thickness nor thinness, or any perception whatever; but all would be as nothing. In this high consideration it is found that all is through and from God Himself, and that it is His own substance, and that He has created it out of Himself. And the evil belongs to the forming and mobility, and the good to the love, and the *austere, severe* or contrary will belongs to the joy."[2]

Taking this assertion alone, one is not surprised that he was "stumbled" by it; and such expressions are in-

[1] Election, ch. v., pars. 75, 76.
[2] Preface to the *Three Principles*, as quoted in Martensen's *Studies*, p. 130.

cautious, as much so as many to be found of the Hebrew prophets in our Bible; but I submit that they are not fairly to be taken alone until we have discerned their truest sense. As I understand this passage, Böhme speaks here of the outcome of the properties of Nature, derived from Eternal Nature, but—in our world—broken off from the perfect harmony and *equality* in which they originally interacted. Now that their holiness (wholeness) is in discord, the poison and malignity are indeed as indispensable as the gall bladder to the animal body, but *not the manifestation* of this poison.[1] What can be meant by such an expression when he speaks of *colour*, virtue, thickness, and thinness, depending on that poison? Surely the same that he indicates when saying that *all* life must proceed from "the anguish chamber."

The first three "tormentive properties" of Nature that kindle and maintain life are those which the words *harsh astringency, mobility*, and *anguish* but faintly point to: these tremendous forces, he teaches us, *must* underlie life in every degree of creatureliness.[2] (The dread alternative is what he calls *the great still-standing death*, where astringency holds captive all the evolutionary forms of nature.)

"In this high consideration," he adds, "it is found that all is through and from God Himself, and that it is His own substance, and that He hath created it out of Himself."[3] Yes, verily, for the desire of the Abyssal God *imagined*, and thus formed the nature which is "His

---

[1] "The anguish, trouble, sorrow, and anxiety which are in man's outward mind and nature, being exterior to the depth of his eternal soul, are only a shadowy figure thereof, and quite unable to declare the inward essentiality of so deep a thing—a thing so transcendant to all external nature."—Dionysius Freher.

[2] "That is the poison source whence the fierce wrath and all evil and malignity originally arise, and yet is the right original of the perceptible life; the life findeth itself thus."—*Incarnation*, Part II., ch. iv., pars. 30, 31.

[3] Three Principles, Pref., par. 14.

somewhat"—"all things are arisen through the Divine imagination, and do yet stand in such a birth, station, or government."[1] "Every imagination maketh substantiality." How much more the imagination of the Supreme Spirit!

"And the evil belongeth to the forming, and mobility, and the good to the love, *and the austere, severe, or contrary will belongeth to the joy.*" In quoting this problematic passage, Martensen should have finished the sentence, "so far as the creature is in the light of God, *so far the wrathful and contrary will maketh the rising Eternal joy*, but if the light of God be extinguished it maketh the rising painful torment and the hellish fire."[2]

So far, inasmuch as the greater the fire the greater the light to arise from it, for "the fire of God is a cause of the light, and of the power, strength, and omnipotency. But in the love the fire dieth and transmuteth itself into the kingdom of joy, for at the end death originateth, which is as a dying in the fire; out of which dying the light as another source or quality originateth." . . . "Every angel and soul which will live in God's Light and Power must die to the selfhood of the fire's dominion in the desire."[3]

Who does not know what anguish it often is to die to the selfhood, in the fire of wrath, or any strong desire in the "Fire's dominion," *i.e.*, Nature *unatoned*; but let all who read this believe it! "If there were no anguish there would be no fire; if there were no fire there would be no light; if there were no light there would be neither Nature nor substance, and God would not be manifested."[4]

To apprehend this great fact in spiritual nature more clearly and fundamentally, the third chapter of Böhme's

---

[1] Epistles (1649), Ep. 6, par. 78.   [2] Three Principles, Pref., par. 14.
[3] Third Apology, Text I., pars. 57, 58, 60.
[4] Second Apology, Part I., par. 141.

treatise on the *Election of Grace* should be studied with care and patience.

At page 151, where his main error as an interpreter of Böhme is repeated, "Böhme views God in the still mystery as mere potentiality"—which he does not— Martensen seems to me to have stated his doctrine as to the efflux which makes up the Divine Quarternary with great clearness, but apparently without seeing that *so stated* the Heavenly Wisdom and the glory of God are identical. I believe they are closely related. I have been gradually led to that conclusion, during the last two or three years, by noticing the agreement of all Böhme says of the one, with almost every reference made in Scripture to the other in an *objective* sense.

Yet I scarcely like to express the strength of my convictions on this head, knowing that they must seem fanciful and presumptuous to any one who has not long and *carefully* examined all Böhme's intimations.

The Bishop seems to catch, and soon again to lose, this *glint* of light, for he proceeds to speak of God's glory in quite another sense than that of an "objectivity different from God, and yet inseparable from Him; prior to, and independent of, the created world: the first and eternal production" (emanation would be, I think, a fitter word) "of the Triune God, the mirror from which His riches are reflected upon Him."[1]

My belief is that by "glory" is meant that by which (through the medium of the Wisdom) the Holy Ternary becomes perceptible.[2] The Wisdom Böhme often speaks of as the "outflown Word"—inseparable from The Word from which all created existence derives, and so to speak, the passive recipient of Being from the Father of Spirits; and thus in a very exact sense the Mother

[1] Martensen's Jacob Böhme, p. 151.
[2] In his *Third Apology*, Text I., par. 213, we find this expression, "*The Eternal Wisdom, viz., the glance of His glory.*"

of all worlds. "For from the Eternal Mother the inceptive Mother came to be." ... "Out of the Eternal Nature God hath manifested or revealed His Wisdom; for in the Divine Wisdom hath the *substance* of the spirits and creatures been from Eternity; but with the moving of God the Father it passed into a *formed* creation, according to the property of the Essence in the word *fiat*, in the word of power."[1]

When Moses said on the Mount, "I beseech Thee shew me Thy glory,"[2] I suppose that *this*, the Heavenly Wisdom, was what he was permitted to see a glimpse of. When the shepherds were told by angels of the birth of the Saviour, and the glory of God shone round about, I understand the same. Again, when in *Romans* vi. 4, St Paul says, "like as Christ was raised up from the dead by the glory of the Father," I believe the "corporeity" of the Triune God—as Böhme calls the Wisdom—must be understood. Space cannot be spared for citing other passages of the Bible susceptible of the same interpretation, but these are enough to explain the bearings of the hypothesis. And in that oft-quoted and oft-misapplied injunction to *do all to the glory of God*, I find for it further support. Can the creature be supposed in *any literal* sense to increase or heighten what we *usually* understand by the glory of the infinitely great God? Surely it is but a puerile notion adapted to our ignorance to imagine it; but this is what the human creature *can* do to increase Deific glory; it can by meekness—by death to self—*produce* recipiency for the *water of eternal life*, of which "divine substantiality, Christ's heavenly corporeity" is formed; and just to the degree that Christ is formed in us, so is the glory of God extended.

It would require a volume almost as large as the one under review duly to scrutinize the Bishop's remarks

[1] First Apology, Part II., pars. 173, 184.   [2] Exodus xxxiii. 18.

upon the created and the uncreated Heavens, where I find it more difficult to get a thoroughfare for thought than in any page of Böhme's, just because of the intricate blending of true and false readings of his lore: I shall therefore pass on to what he says of the Wisdom, and believing its connection with the glory of God to be nothing less than that of the *unmanifest* with the *revealed*, I will venture to touch upon one branch of this great mystery which seems to me to admit of some degrees of apprehension.

If Martensen had not so wholly missed or refused Böhme's teaching as to "essentiality," by which word, in the original, *substantiality* was undoubtedly meant [1] we should not find him saying, "As Theosophy frequently reiterates, Wisdom, the Idea, can at the same time diffuse itself throughout all created space, can pervade and most subtilly permeate all things, and can also concentrate itself and dwell absolutely in one individual soul," without any reference to all Böhme says of the *formation of heavenly substance in the human soul.*

The difficulties surrounding this part of his writings are so very great that one cannot be surprised at any attempt at *thinking out* the subject failing utterly. For following Böhme's many and emphatic words about the Wisdom, we have to combine images that naturally conflict, viz., "the outspoken substance of the Deity," "Corporeity of the Holy Spirit," "the Mirror of the Abyssal God," and the Helpmeet—the woman of Adam before he fell and needed his Eve. This is the most confounding assertion of all! Thirty-two years ago I began to read Böhme, and only ten years ago could I attach the faintest apprehensible idea to such words as meet us again and again in one of his easiest and simplest writings—the *Way to Christ.* For example: "When Christ the corner-stone stirreth Himself in the

[1] See Martensen's Jacob Böhme, p. 273.

extinguished image of man, in his hearty conversion and repentance, then *Virgin Sophia* appeareth in the stirring of the Spirit of Christ, in the extinguished *image*, in her *virgin's attire* before the soul."[1] So repulsive and impossible to receive did I find this and similar phraseology even twenty years ago, that I passed it over unread, whenever the word *Virgin Sophia* warned me of the mental *impasse*. And to reduce their import to anything of an allegorical figure of speech was as impossible as to understand it literally. But I had learned from previous gains in Böhme's inexhaustible treasury of light that all he affirms to be a fact must be accepted as such, and not mistaken for any theoretic fancy of his own; so I was fain to let this tangle of nonsense (as it seemed) lie quiet in the mind till the Giver of all Good gave me any ray of intelligence about it; for I knew well that pulling hard at such knots only tightens them more inextricably. Such waiting for *unspoken* instruction, earnestly desired, is seldom disappointed. It was granted to me at length *as I believe*; but by a very gradual process. Thoughts of the ubiquity of the Lord Christ, and the *individualized* Christ in regenerate men and women in whom Christ is formed, gave me the first help; then the saying, "Where the Word is, there is also the Virgin, or Wisdom of God; for the Word is in the Wisdom, and the one is not without the other, or else the Eternity would be divided."[2]

In the *Third Apology*, Text II., par. 35, Böhme speaks of "In the Jesu, viz., in God's Love and Wisdom," I was further helped to fasten together a few ties of thought bearing upon the puzzle by what I read of the *Akâsa* of the Eastern Adepts, of an invisible substance in our

---

[1] Way to Christ, 1648, p. 57 ; 1752, p. 74 ; 1775, p. 55 ; 1781, p. 23 ; 1894, p. 30 ; 1911, p. 80.
[2] Threefold Life, ch. vi., par. 78.

lower atmosphere which—by force of long-exercised concentration of will—these Adepts frame into objects of external vision, nay, into tangible existence, and in connection with this the words of Jesus came to mind, "If ye had faith as a grain of mustard seed, ye might say unto this sycamore tree, Be thou plucked up by the root, and be thou planted in the sea, and it should obey you."[1] I could see that by this faith an attractive force of *desire* was indicated, the desire of a vegetable soul—but yet a soul—and that when the human soul was rebuked for lacking that faith, such energy of *will* and *desire* for creating their objects must have been man's original endowment. Then followed thought of how mentally we do still create, and that Böhme tells us that *all* substantiality, all creating, even God's, was by imagination: "all things are arisen through the Divine imagination, and do yet stand in such a birth"[2]; and I began to see what the Wisdom was *relatively to the Word*, and how exactly true are the words of *Proverbs* viii. from verse 22 to 31, that as an infinitely purer analogue of our Akâsa, "the Wisdom is God's manifestation and the Holy Spirit's corporeity, the body of the Holy Trinity; and this whole Name in one Eternal substance manifesteth itself through the Wisdom."[3]

And as the Akâsa is passive to the will of the Adept, and Eternal substance is to the outgoing Fiat of the Word, so we know in all generation is the feminine nature to the masculine, and in this sense would the Wisdom, while united to the human soul, be truly its wife and helpmeet; the fire and light tincture then united in Adam forming thus holy substantiality; which, as has been already explained, "faded" when the imagination of the first Adam fixed upon grosser objects. Until this perished *substance* was brought back

[1] Luke xvii. 6.   [2] Epistles (1649), Ep. 6, par. 78.
[3] Third Apology, Text III., par. 43.

into the human race the restoration of the Divine Image was impossible. J. G. Gichtel is in his letters (written between the years 1668 and 1701) a very emphatic witness to all Böhme had previously taught on this obscure theme, and as they have no published English edition, I think quotations from them will here be serviceable.

"I have been," he says, "driven to dig so much deeper in my soul, till at last, in the innermost ground, I found God's kingdom and the image of God which was lost in Adam." . . . "Sophia is a regenerate Christian's new spiritual body which can stand in the fire, and what the strong, gross, earthly bones are to the gross body, that Sophia is to the Divine Image in the new man—viz., strength, power, and might to fulfil the will of God." . . . "Sophia must be born from our two inward fires. The mystery is very great! as soon as we surrender our natural will of selfhood so that we become one will-spirit with God, then immediately the original *Ens* which faded away in Adam begins to stir in our soul." . . . "Only when you have obtained the victory will you understand what Christ is in us, namely, that He is the second Adam with both tinctures, the right bridegroom and husband of the Virgin and widow, and sweet bride and wife to the unmarried man, whom I have called Sophia." . . . "From this you can understand what true praying is, viz., to bring forth with Sophia, the wife of our youth,[1] Father, Son, Holy Spirit, and *Wisdom*, which is done by the will and desire. But the will is spiritual, a spirit as subtle as a nothing, and therefore it cannot work without a body." . . . "Therefore Christ teaches the new birth, without which we cannot enter into the Kingdom of Heaven. Now in the regeneration Sophia is our helpmeet, for Christ has restored the two tinctures which were by the craft of the devil severed

---

[1] Malachi ii. 14.

in the first Adam into a male and a female, making them one again—viz., a virginal manhood."

Now as to the Wisdom or Virgin Sophia, as Gichtel designates her, being as universal a potency as the Word, and at the same time to individual human beings an individualized entity, however strange it may be to our usual conceptions, the oneness of the Lord Jesus Christ with *the Christ formed* in every regenerate soul, might prepare us to accept the idea. It is in fact *necessarily* involved in the Scriptural doctrine of Christ, as Böhme words it, "getting a form" in us: Christ being alike "*the power of God and the wisdom of God*";[1] but a vagueness of thought has accompanied this belief as to the formation of a new *creature*, and the mind naturally recoils from any such definite image as Böhme and other mystics repeatedly present. If Böhme is to be believed as a trustworthy witness, this very important part of his teaching must be accepted. And truly did he say, when labouring to place it within reach of other minds, "here again we need an angel's tongue; for the mind ever asketh *how* and *where*; for when the Deep is spoken of, which is without comprehension or number, the mind always understandeth some corporeal thing. But when I speak of the Virgin of the Wisdom of God I mean not a thing that is confined or circumscribed in a place, as also when I speak of the Number Three, but I mean the whole Deep of the Deity without end and measure. But every divine creature (as are the angels and souls of men) hath the Virgin of the Wisdom of God as an image in the *Light of Life*, understand in the substantiality of the Spirit, wherein is the Number Three, dwelling in itself."[2]

"*In an image*," that is the special affront to reason, only reconciled to as much of holy mysteries as *Theology* can sanction. But Böhme insists upon that "unauthor-

[1] 1 Cor. i. 24.   [2] Threefold Life of Man, ch. v., pars. 55–57.

ized" idea, "She is the *substantiality* of the Spirit, which the Spirit of God putteth on as a garment, whereby he manifesteth himself, or else his form would not be known; for she is the Spirit's corporeity, and though she is not a corporeal palpable substance like us men, yet she is substantial and visible."[1]

Gichtel testifies emphatically to her visibility thus: "My beloved helpmeet looked down upon my childish shyness with mercy, and in 1673, as I was praying at mid-day, after the appearance first of a black cloud, then of a white one, opening before me, she appeared to me in the form of a Virgin, and assured my creaturely being mouth to mouth that she would sustain me, reminded me of all the promises of Jesus Christ, and put His faith into my heart, and thus armed me against all the assaults of the devil." Böhme is eloquent, though evidently cautious, in his disclosures to the same effect: so soon as "the soul be freed of the evil beast, *then* it hath the open gate in its beloved image, in which Christ hath opened Himself with the Divine love-fire. And then is the Union already there, the bride cheereth her bridegroom, viz., the Noble Virgin in the love of Christ, being awakened again, which taketh the soul, its loving bridegroom and man, into her arms of the divine desire; and what is there done I have no pen to write it with: it is more than human or natural to write that."[2]

Yet much more than natural at once to accept such reports! Nevertheless the records of all great saints in every age tell of visions such as Gichtel's; among Roman Catholics they are received as the appearance of the Virgin Mary, and while adoring her and offering petitions to her, unconsciously they worship that Eternal and Divine Virgin whom the Word brought

---

[1] Threefold Life of Man, chap. v., par. 50.
[2] Third Apology Text II., pars. 50, 51.

back to our race when it "was made flesh and dwelt among us."

Let me now try to suggest some way—dim and imperfect, I know—for understanding in what sense the Wisdom can be thought of as the *Mirror* of God, we must first dismiss all ideas of fixity; whenever Böhme speaks of "*looking-glasses*" he means the reflex objectivity of forms first imagined, as the ideas of Deity pass into the eternal substance of the Virgin Sophia. So we may suppose do our desires and resulting imaginations, energize and really *create* forms in the impalpable neurine of the brain, and that potential force becomes, so to speak, determined; a focus of action is posited, and by that centre magnetic attraction, with all its creative consequences, begins to act.

When I read in a paper of Mr Mohini Chatterji,[1] this sentence—" Eastern psychologists maintain that the physical body is merely the most condensed part of a vast nebulous mass which surrounds it as cometary matter surrounds its brightest part," and this quotation from Professor Haeckel in Mr Romanes' interesting book on *Mental Evolution in Animals*—"The general conclusion has been reached that in man, and in all other animals, the sense-organs as a whole arise in essentially the same way, viz., as parts of the external integument or epidermis. The external integument is the original general sense-organ,"[2] . . . "and all special senses are differentiations of the general sense of touch,"[3] I began to see that the one law of differentiation of a universal potentiality was the beginning of all such life, effected from the highest to the lowest plane of creation by what Böhme calls "*a will to the substance*"; and that "the mirror of the Virgin-like Wisdom of God whence the Eternal Nature doth always arise from Eternity"[4] has its

---

[1] Theosophist, vol. vi. p. 218, June, 1885.
[2] Page 104.   [3] Ibid. (Romanes).
[4] Epistles (1649), Ep. 5, par. 45.

earthly analogue in what our scientists term *protoplasm*. They can perceive *that* and descant upon it at large, but the *soul* life, i.e., the *will*, "*the severation of a peculiar self-will*," with its desire causing life—causing the wheel of Nature to revolve ceaselessly in every newly-formed centre, *that* science can never detect: but to deny or to ignore its presence as some *Savants* do is to wrong their own reason. "*Will giveth life, and substantiality manifestation of life.*" Wheresoever we see substance, growing, or matter of any sort, there we may be certain is a *will*, be it in a mollusc or a blade of grass.[1]

Now to apply this to the formation of the new creature in the human soul. It is an extremely hard task to put into words ideas so much beyond language, and I entreat for great indulgence when I try so clumsily to transfer my understanding of Böhme's to the mind of a reader. We must keep close to the central fact of man having been made in the likeness of God, and to *every* soul the unalienable right of free will being assured by reason of that likeness, however much obscured. The desire and *imagination* of man has consequently power to "compact itself into substance," and the life and teaching of Jesus Christ has been given us to fix the imagination on the highest ideal—the Divine Son of God, who, "*without Nature and creature, is the greatest meekness and humility.*"[2]

If we imagine after that example; if the will kindles the desire to follow it, and be of one spirit with our Lord Christ; we attract the heavenly substantiality which the universalized *spiritual* protoplasm, and *the Word and the Wisdom* generate in us. "Where our will is, there is

[1] There is yet a deeper cause than Will, but one that must arise in the unsearchable mind of God—*thought* which necessarily precedes both desire and will. Of course the thought of man or angel, and, for anything we know to the contrary, of lower orders of being also, sets the "Wheel of Nature" in motion on lower planes of existence.

[2] Election, ch. i., par. 57.

our heart also; God is in us, and when we enter into His will then we put His Wisdom on to us, *and in the Wisdom Christ is a man.*"[1] "The Word is *everywhere,* so is the substantiality (the body of the Word), though indeed without image; for the creature hath only the formation or image."

Why should the *phenomenal* difference of outside and inside soul life stand in the way of this conception? "Whatsoever can be thought to have a being anywhere in the creature, the same is likewise without the creature everywhere, for the creature is nothing else but an image and figure of the separable and various power and virtue of the Universal Being."[2]

"For all beings are but one only Being, which hath breathed forth itself out of itself, and hath severized and formized itself; and yet it proceedeth out of the same impressure, or formation, into a centre peculiarly distinct; that is, with each impressure and forming of the desire— where the severized, parted, and divided will doth impress and form itself into a peculiar particularity where a centre doth arise, and in the centre a *separator* or Creator of its own self, namely, a former of the *re-expressing* or re-spirating will."[3]

Böhme's own words have expressly dealt with this point. "In the creature is the newly-introduced substantiality, viz., Christ's heavenly flesh *creaturely;* but without, besides, or beyond the creature it is *uncreaturely;* for that very substantiality is the right, true, Divine Principle; it is as great as God's majesty; in all places, filling all in the Second Principle; and *that* in the body or *creature,* and *that* without the creature, is totally entirely *one* undivided, totally one power or virtue, might and glory, Paradise and pure element, wherein God's Eternal Wisdom dwelleth. As the sun

---
[1] Threefold Life, ch. xi., par. 72. See also *Ibid.,* ch. xiii., par. 24.
[2] Clavis, par. 96.   [3] Epistles (1649), Ep. 6, par. 65.

shineth or enlighteneth in the whole world; and so now if there were not in the deep such a substance as the sun, then it would not receive the glance or lustre of the sun. Thus the corporeity of Christ is the fulness of the Heaven, in the Person creaturely, and without the creature living —in one Spirit and power or virtue, *not two*."[1]

Leaving a number of important points untouched for lack of space—and fear of lack of interest in the reader —I can only attempt to qualify one or two more of Martensen's assertions. For example, at page 312, where he says that no *localized* Heaven is admitted by Böhme to exist. This, however, we find in his first book, after saying the true Heaven is everywhere, he adds in the next paragraph: "but that there is assuredly a pure, glorious Heaven in all the three births or genitures aloft above the Deep of this world, in which God's Being, together with that of the Holy Angels, riseth up very purely, brightly, beauteously, and joyfully, is undeniable, and he is not born of God that denieth it."[2]

Yet it must be owned that very few passages of like tenors, certainly none so decided, can be found in his writings. At page 318, after quoting what he calls many strange and baseless utterances on the subject of the salvation of heathen, Turks, and Jews, Martensen continues: "Böhme says in many places that heathen, Turks, and Jews, can be saved, even although they have not known the Christ who has come in the flesh, provided they have only stood in the *other* principle, in the Light-principle, and have sought God with earnestness. God then considers them as children who know not what they say. It does not depend on knowledge, but on the will." . . . "But . . . if it be sufficient to stand in the Light-principle (in the non-incarnated Logos), the ques-

---

[1] Second Apology, Part II., pars. 250, 251. See also *Epistles* (1649), Ep. 2, pars. 55, 56.

[2] Aurora, ch. xix., pars. 26, 27.

tion arises: Why is the incarnation necessary? a necessity which Böhme, in accordance with his fundamental view, most vigorously maintains." One is tempted to meet this question by another: Why attempt to pass judgment on a teacher whose lessons have been so hastily gone through that one of his most central doctrines has been missed? Martensen must have passed by unheeded all that Böhme has said with emphatic force about the *oneness* of the human race: here, for instance, is his treatise on the *Four Complexions*, "all souls have a communion or sympathy with that *one soul* of Jesus Christ. They come all out of or from one original root, and are all together but as one tree with many branches. Therefore His breaking open that enclosure" (that iron gate which was fast shut in the soul of man), "and the grace or benefit thereby obtained is derived from Him into and upon all souls, even from Adam to the last man that shall be."[1] And in his *19th Epistle*, "as the sin and wrath of Adam, being yet but *one*, pressed upon and into all; so likewise passed and pressed the motion of God's love in Christ's humanity, and out of Christ's humanity, *through the whole humanity of all men*. Christ is again become the heart in the human tree; the Divine sound which hath revealed itself in Christ's humanity effectually, that soundeth through Christ's humanity in the *Universal Human Tree*; and there is nothing wanting, or in the way, but that the twig which is on the tree will not draw the sap of the tree into itself."[2]

"The Deity or the Word which moved itself in Mary and became man, that became man also in like manner *in all men* that had died from Adam to that time, who

[1] Way to Christ (1775), p. 345: *Four Complexions*, ch. iii., par. 84. *The Remainder of Books written by Jacob Behme* (1662); *Four Complexions*, ch. i., par. 84.
[2] Epistles (1649), Ep. 19, pars. 16, 17.

had given up and commended their Spirits into God, or into the *promised* Messiah. And it passed upon all those which were yet *to be born* out of the corrupted, perished Adam, who would but suffer that Word to awaken them or arise in them; for the first man comprehendeth also the last. Adam is the stock, we all are his branches; but Christ is become our sap, virtue, and life."[1]

Now in all he says of the salvation of heathen, Turks, and Jews, Böhme assumes as conditional just that drawing of the sap, *i.e.*, the childlike obedience of the will to God, however ignorantly worshipped. See on this subject the effect of the incarnation on the patriarchs and saints before the coming of Christ, this significant saying in the *Third Apology*. "That very substantiality wherein God would become man was faded or disappeared in Adam, when he died to the Kingdom of Heaven and Paradise. This faded or disappeared seed became, in its *principle, co-propagated.* And in this seed stood the limit of the covenant, out *of which the* Spirit of God in the saints manifested itself, and not through the faded or disappeared substance; but with Christ's becoming man or incarnation, *the substantial manifestation proceeded,* where God dwelleth within in the substance, as a life of the substance."[2] Significant indeed, but to one new to Böhme's range of ideas so obscure, that something of a rough paraphrase may be serviceable. The "seed of the woman" was the dormant principle of the Wisdom; inasmuch as God had *inspoken* the promise regarding it, "*It shall bruise thy head.*"[3] The *operative* Word of God was assured to Adam's race—what is to be understood by this as a seed's *principle* being propagated from one generation to another I make no pretence of understanding, but I perfectly understand by all analogies that until

[1] Incarnation, Part I., ch. xii., pars. 56–59.
[2] Text IV., Point III., pars. 48, 49.
[3] Genesis iii. 15.

conditions of development are supplied no substantial manifestation can proceed. These conditions the Word and Wisdom combined brought to the human race when in Mary they *assumed the outward fleshly human substance*. Again, it is surely surprising that after reading his *4th* and *5th Epistles*,[1] any one summing up Böhme's doctrines as to the future, could render their meaning thus: "After the world has enjoyed a springtide in the 'thousand years' reign,' a season of 'peace upon earth' during which all religious dissensions are to cease, and when Christ is to rule over the Church like a shepherd over His flock, the Philosopher's Stone, by which we shall be enabled to know all things, and to extract from the metals their spirit and heart, will be discovered, and the world will perish by fire."[2] I wish Martensen had given references to chapter and verse for this; only constructively can I find anything like a belief in the millennium; these two are, I believe, the nearest approach to it. "Then he kindleth the Turba wherein the great fire burneth, which consumeth flesh and blood, also the stones and the elements, and then shall Babel drink her last draught. And after that Enoch hath peace a little time, and it is the golden year."[3] And, "Then is the time when Enoch and the children under his voice do lead a divine life, of which the first life of Enoch was a type; and then there is a blessed and golden year, till Enoch's last translation comes, and then the Turba is born (which, when it shall enkindle its fire) the floors shall be purged, for it is the end of all time."[4] Both

---

[1] These numbers refer to Ellistone's translation, 1649 (*35 Epistles*). They correspond to numbers 8 and 11 of the German *Theosophische Send Briefe*. For a table giving the numeration of Böhme's sixty-two Epistles in German editions and the corresponding Epistles in the English translations, see end of *The Remainder of Books written by Jacob Behme*, London, 1662.—ED.

[2] Martensen's *Jacob Böhme*, p. 328.

[3] Forty Questions (1665), Ques. 35, par. 38.

[4] Mysterium Magnum, ch. xxx., par. 46.

these passages are embedded in context so obscure that I could never feel sure that I understood their bearings; whereas in his *Epistles*, referred to above, he distinctly combats expectation of a thousand years' bliss on this earth. "*I have no knowledge*," he says, "*of the thousand years' Sabbath; I know not sufficiently to ground it with Scripture.*" I may miss his meaning as well as Martensen, but all he says of the time of the Lily seems to me to belong to life in the *New Earth*.[1]

But on one very material point I must agree with Böhme's critic more than with himself. The whole of sections 105 and 106 appears to me nearer what I suppose to be the truth regarding the fate of reprobate souls than Böhme's conception of it. He clearly declined to be considered illuminated by the spirit of God as to the times and seasons of this world's future. "I have no knowledge of it," he repeats, "seeing the Scripture doth not give clear evidence," and insists on his ignorance, "for the dark mysteries are no other way at all to be known save only in the Holy Ghost; we cannot make conclusions upon hidden things, unless we have the same in real knowledge, and *experimentally find in the illumination of God*, that what we aver is the truth and will of God; and that *it is also agreeable to His Word*, and grounded *in the light of nature; for without the light of nature there is no understanding of divine mysteries.*"[2] And that he had not this light of nature given him as regards the future on earth, he notices even in his first book, when saying that there the reader "will come to the true ground. It is true that from the beginning of the world it was *not so fully* revealed to any man, but seeing God will have it so, I submit to His will, and will see what He will do with it. *For His way which is before Him is for the most part hidden to me; but after Him the*

---

[1] See also *Threefold Life of Man*, ch. iii., pars. 80, 81.
[2] Epistles (1649), Ep. 4., par. 13.

spirit seeth even into the highest and profoundest depth."[1]

I venture, therefore, to think—with all my deep and grateful reverence for Böhme—that as to the future of our race he is not to be referred to as a trustworthy seer: the little he says about it is instinct with the prejudices of his era, and he never appears to outsee them. It would probably have been dangerous for his contemporaries to have had admitted to its grosser mind any such hope as that our generation is blessed with— a hope that can never *lessen* the terrors of the future for unrepentant sinners (because no *effective* imagination lays hold on endlessness of time), but which sees that their inevitable anguish is self-inflicted, and not imposed by a wrathful God as punishment, and hence must diminish as sin is purged; in fact, when the *horrors of sin as such* are better understood, such coarse torments as our ancestors imagined have necessarily lost credence, and we no longer mingle our thoughts of God as a Father who pities His children, knowing whereof they are made, with that of a vengeful executioner after death.

Martensen says very truly that Böhme's professed belief in the everlasting torments of the damned conflict with other parts of his doctrine. Not, so far as I have understood directly, but constructively, for instance, when he says: "Nothing subsisteth in Eternity unless it hath been from Eternity."[2] How, then, should sin and its consequent misery?

From the 101st section to the end of his book, I am more in accord with the Bishop and with Oetinger, Hamburger, and Baader, whose opinions on this momentous subject he gives, than with Böhme's: he might have classed with these that of J. Michael Hahn, not a commentator, but in singular agreement with

[1] Aurora, ch. ix., pars. 89–91.   [2] Threefold Life, ch. vi., par. 74.

"Teutonicus" otherwise. Hahn's "larger hope" included the repentance and ultimate restoration of the fallen angel and his host—a hope shared by L. C. de St Martin, though not so positively announced.

Again, when at page 280 Martensen speaks of the *locality* of Heaven, I find his argument more convincing than all inferences from Böhme's of an opposite tendency. One passage here well deserves quoting: "Scripture tells us that there is a spiritual and Heavenly body, from which it follows that there must be for this appropriate space-relations. If Christ has a transfigured and glorified corporeity (which is an *articulus fidei stantis aut cadentis*), there must also be a region that corresponds with this. Now, although this region or these regions must, in comparison with our material region, be called spaceless, superspacial, yet absolute spacelessness cannot be attributed to them."

It is in the Bishop's *Envoi* that I find his wisest words. Naturally, as an ecclesiastic, his eagerness to edify is somewhat in advance of his readiness to learn; and in going through his book I am often tempted to apply to him Böhme's mild rebuke, "You bring the opinion of others" (of "Teutonicus") "into suspicion as if they had not written aright of the mystery; it were better that had been left out, seeing you have not understood their opinion."[1] But in his last pages, when summing up the mistakes of the Church in its attitude towards Theosophy, he speaks with weight of one of the most rooted errors of our own clergy—their antagonism, as a body, to all that is not theologically defensible and fixed. If in this respect the tide has begun to turn, we may yet have our pulpits filled by men who *can* bring forth treasures, *new* as well as old—who will lead the laity to spiritual depths and heights to which at present there are no "authorized" guides.

[1] Epistles (1649), Ep. 4, par. 91.

Let Martensen's warning be quoted here, for words so unpalatably true are little likely to be cited elsewhere. "With regard to Theology I make the general remark, that in my judgment—a judgment which has been greatly confirmed by these studies—Church Theology is not wise in assuming a hostile attitude towards Theosophy and in endeavouring to exclude it altogether (a course, however, which has not been adopted by *all* the representatives of theology). It is not wise in this course, because it hereby deprives itself of a most valuable leavening influence, a source of renewal and rejuvenescence, which Theology so greatly needs, exposed as it is to the danger of stagnating in barren and dreary scholasticism and cold and trivial criticism." . . . "It must be obvious to every theologian who has a more than superficial acquaintance with Theosophy, that it has aroused and attracted attention to a circle of Scriptural conceptions which theology has disregarded, or to which it has devoted very slight pains, because it is not in possession of the categories which are requisite for their treatment. As one great instance, among many, may be mentioned the conception of the *Glory of God* and the *Uncreated Heaven*. No one will deny that these are fundamental conceptions in Holy Scripture, while in theology they are scarcely even accessory notions, and indeed are referred to in many theological systems as 'dark points' which it is best to avoid. And yet it will hardly be denied that it is the duty of the theologian to bring to light the fundamental conceptions of Scripture, and to offer some explanation of them." . . . " It is very illusory to suppose that scholasticism has any value of its own, when it lacks the emotion of the mystic or immediate intuition of that new and higher world of experience of the heavenly realities which Revelation unveils for us." . . . "And it must be regarded as a sign of retrogression, not of progress, that there should now be any who occupy a position in which they do nothing else but repristinate the old orthodox theology. It must undoubtedly be admitted as expedient that ecclesiastical tradition should be preserved, and ecclesiastical testimony maintained, in opposition to neo-rationalism and all its cognate systems. But in such circles there can be no real progress in the Christian apprehension of truth."[1]

[1] Pages 338–341.

THE DURATION OF EVIL[1]

I

"When we cannot establish a theory, we must satisfy ourselves with the amusing haziness of an hypothesis."—Dr ASHBURNER.

As to the duration of evil and the Divine sufferance of all its terrific consequences in this present state, I am a little helped to understand it by remembering that to "the Holy One who inhabiteth Eternity" there can be no divisional series of events: all must be seen and known in a timeless *now*, and the good to be educed from evil as present as the misery from which it is brought forth. While, on the other hand, transactions between the giver of life and the creature, that we think of as done, because a part of their process lies far behind our personal experience, are no more completed than the flow of life from that creative source. For example, we speak of the Creation as a past event, and yet manifestly it is incessantly proceeding, both as to matter and spirit (sharply dividing them as we do), and theology treats of the Atonement as a finished work, which, of course, in one aspect it is, but if completed the strife of nature in humanity would be at an end, the creature delivered from the vanity to which it was subjected by, in Böhme's language, "imagining after earthliness," and God would be all in all. For as "in Adam's soul the properties (of Eternal Nature) divided or distinguished

[1] Light and Life, Dec. 1886, Jan. 1887.

themselves," all exercising own self-will, so Jesus Christ, the Atonement for sin, "assumed our sins in the Adamical Nature, understand the fountain out of which sin floweth, viz., the divided forms or qualities of life in the human nature."[1] *Thus pacifying the wrath of God in man.* And while this is manifested in the human soul, the discordant working of the seven spirits of God *in it* remains unharmonized: a work only Omnipotent Love can effect and is effecting, but how gradually! For "the curse of God[2] is come into the seven forms, so that they are in strife and enmity, and one form doth annoy the other, and can never agree unless they all seven enter into death, and die unto the self-will. Now, this cannot be except a death comes into them, which breaks all their will and is a death unto them, as the Deity in Christ was a death to the human selfhood."[3]

Surely until there is universal death to the human selfhood the Atoning work is unfinished; and looking to what is to be seen of its life at the present time, one would say its vitality was unquenchable. What then can support the assurance of hope that "as in Adam all died, so in Christ shall *all* be made alive"?[4] Since the alienation of self from God is death, how shall even the Omnipotent restore it to life? There must be many an individual who has asked the same question in utter despair, groaning under the oppressive yoke of self-seeking, and who has yet come to a sense of comparative emancipation, who is conscious that his or her centre of action has been changed from self-love to that of a higher will. Many must have been aware that the same liberating process has taken place in another soul, and

---

[1] Election, ch. ix., pars. 149, 252.
[2] "By God's curse or withdrawing, the heavenly body was shut up and the anger source set open."—*Signatura Rerum*, ch. vii., par. 22.
[3] Signatura Rerum, ch. xii., par. 30.   [4] 1 Cor. xv. 22.

if asked how it was done, it is certain they would tell of no slight affliction, no gentle breaking down of the will, and that they would thankfully attribute that deliverance to the corrective force of an infinite mercy which is supremely powerful. If that sovereign love can conquer one rebel fast bound in deathly selfishness, may we not believe that it has modes of crushing down resistance, terribly commensurate to the obduracy of other wills, and equally successful?—whether in this world or another, in this Æon or another, is quite a distinct question; *possibility* and ultimate purpose is all I contend for. And on this ground, apart from all we gather from the Bible as to the success of the Saviour's agency ("He shall see of the travail of his soul and shall be satisfied"),[1] if, as Böhme says, "nothing subsisteth in Eternity unless it hath been from Eternity,"[2] it is unimaginable that the torments of sin should be endless. Seeing that the alteration of the "temperature" of the seven forms of Eternal Nature began in Time, is it not presumable that whatsoever evil has gone out of every *divided* form—not having arisen in the "Eternal fixity," to use Böhme's phrase, as the souls of men and angels have—it *must* come to an end when all forms of derivative Nature are atoned by the restored harmony of Eternal Nature in Man; which evidently they will be when God is "all in all." Speaking of the insect tribe, St Martin says: "Ce sont clairement des êtres apocryphes, par rapport à la Nature."[3] And so are evil spirits from the well-springs of the divided properties; these, I fear, find in the human soul just that suitable atmosphere which enables them to exist, to gain a body and power for concentrated action in the temperament to which they belong. But enormously as this "apocryphal"

---

[1] Isaiah liii. 11. [2] Threefold Life, ch. vi., par. 74.
[3] L'Esprit des Choses, vol. i. p. 164. "They are evidently apocryphal beings as regards Nature."

birth must extend the dominion of evil, yet as time-born it would necessarily end in Time. Böhme never admits such a hope as this for the host of fallen spirits which we conveniently comprise in the singular number—the devil; and he speaks of their interminable torments with all the cheerful confidence of a seventeenth century Christian; but it is not as a prophet of the future that his revelations are most precious: he very distinctly says, when answering a friend's inquiry as to the end of the world, "This knowledge is not given to me," and "it is not revealed to me, the Lord hath not commanded me to teach it. . . . I leave it for those to whom God would vouchsafe the knowledge of it."[1]

But, now, if we refuse to accept the creed of our forefathers on this point, how are we to understand the expression "losing his own soul"?[2] and what possibility is left for hope, if we believe that when death finds any soul dominated by the four tormentive properties, all ability to form a new will, and generate light and true substance by dying to the old, is irrecoverably lost?

Will any one dare say that we *ought not* to face this darkest of all enigmas? It cannot be altogether evaded if one feels for fellow creatures; and if the despairing answer of theology is invalid, what hypothesis can be offered?—that of ultimate annihilation, or of irresistible forces of spiritual progression as soon as the weight of matter is removed? This last is the favourite doctrine of spirit teachers in the present day: they assume that progress from bad to better and from better to best is as natural *after* death as the reverse appears before it. They speak as if there were a law of post-mortem spiritual levitation as invariable as that of gravitation in fleshly life. Yet Andrew Jackson Davis, one of the most

---

[1] Epistles (1649), Ep. 4, pars. 72, 34.
[2] Matthew xvi. 26.

notable Seers, has said: "Let it be perpetually remembered that the most interior part of man, his spirit *per se*, is an unparticled, indivisible, self-attractive, intermagnetic, perfect, absolute, unprogressive essence."[1] If it be perfect, of course there is no need of progress, but that seems a dejecting outlook for an immortal; and if all evil was only what could be sloughed off from the spirit as naturally as a snake casts its old skin, stationary goodness might be possible in other worlds—in this it is not; but that one expression, "*self-attractive*," points to tendencies very unlike casting off spiritual habitudes. A pupil of Böhme must anticipate just the reverse—a far stronger astringency of the "hard, magnetic self-compression"; and as the conflict of this, with desire for mobility, increases anguish, *that* is my immediate hope for ruined souls: such anguish as may, even after death, create a sinking down of the soul's fire to the abyss of Divine mercy, and a consequent rekindling of its light; feeble it may be, but initiating a new birth.

Let me for the time drop all conventional habits of speech, all decorous reference to received ideas, as well as all guard against ridicule for daring to enter upon this tremendous theme. It is rash and may be foolish, but whenever a life goes out near us which no stretch of charity can connect with hopes of bliss, thought *will* return to it again and again; and words that are but ignorantly conjectural may touch the darkness with faint gleams of partial elucidation, and suggestions almost too crude for coherent utterance, may rouse more powerful intellects to seize the longed-for clue.

[1] Pantheon of Progress, p. 75.

II

"C'est dans la terre que se prépare la substance qui sert de base et de premier degré à la ré-intégration ou à la renaissance de tous les êtres de l'univers."—St Martin.

In offering these tentative thoughts to any other mind, I feel as one who throws great, uncouth stones into a river where only a solid bridge could serve for ordinary travellers, but which some well-poised, adventurous bodies might find useful if determined to hazard the attempt of crossing over where no bridge was; only the river in this case is an unfathomed abyss, and the stones ill-defined notions, too unconnected, perhaps, to afford adequate support for a theory.

It is certain that Biblical sayings cannot always be taken in their most obvious, literal sense; but the longer our Bible is studied together with Böhme, the more evident it becomes that they have a literal sense drawn from facts which have not yet dawned in the world of received ideas. For example, the words "lake of fire and brimstone."[1] We know what our ancestors understood by them; the grotesque illustrations of some of their devout books force upon our notice the childishness of their conceptions of hell, and by a very natural recoil people who have not had their faith in Scripture sneered out, or scientifically scoffed away, explain such terms subjectively; the torments of hell, they say, are symbolized thus. Yes; but if my supposition is correct, it is as our mental sufferings are symbolized by bodily pain—what is left of existence to a reprobate soul will be both cause and effect of spiritual loss. The fire is that of the soul, which "never shall be quenched"; what is immortal cannot die. And the brimstone? I first caught any illumination as to that from this passage—

[1] Revelation xx. 10.

"the soul hath all three principles in it, viz., the most inward, which is *the worm or brimstone spirit.*"[1] (The whole context of this saying should be examined.) The *worm*? Doubtless so called from the incessant writhing motion of the first three forms of Eternal Nature that originate the fire—the immortal life; constringency and mobility, equally vehement, anguishing for escape the one from the other. This worm dieth not. Again, "The anguish, bitterness, and woe are like a brimstone spirit, *and all spirits in nature are brimstone,*"[2] and but a little further on in the same book these other words confirmed the guess, "The soul must enter again into the inward; if it remain in the outward it is in hell."[3] Then, perceiving that the words fire and brimstone indicate exactly that arrest of holy (whole) evolution of life which forms true substance, that captivity to the first four "tormentive sources," which Böhme assures us will constitute the *world to come* of the wicked; because only after the cessation of mortal life can their nature be fully revealed, I remembered these sayings in Mr Oxley's *Angelic Revelations—*"You have spoken to us, Angel, concerning the hells. Are the inhabitants there a further development of life, lower in degree than our own?" ... "They belong to still more external states."[4] Again, "by the hells we presume you mean the most external";[5] an impression confirmed by Mr Sinnett in his *Esoteric Buddhism*: "The worlds that are higher in the scale are those in which spirit largely predominates. There is another world ... in which matter asserts itself even more decisively than on earth."[6]

In connection with these words, Biblical sayings about "chains of darkness" and "outer darkness" offered other

[1] Three Principles, ch. xii., par. 56. [2] Ibid., ch. x., par. 47.
[3] Ibid., ch. xix., par. 65. [4] Vol. i. p. 329.
[5] Vol. ii. p. 156.
[6] Esoteric Buddhism, 1883, p. 32 ; 1892, p. 41.

links in the sequence of thoughts so loosely strung together. If in our present level of material existence we are blind to the spirit world around us, what must be the condition of lives more "deeply immersed in matter"? Would it not answer to such a descriptive phrase as being in chains of darkness?

Now, supposing that we try to imagine the state of desperately wicked souls; it is not surely conceivable that they should remain for cycles of ages in an unchanging state? or that the universal law of increase in every spiritual habit should be suspended after death? And it will be granted that all egotism is *contractive*; as age hardens character, the excess of that narrowing influence is very commonly visible; in the case of misers strikingly so—all natural feeling, all healthy play of thought seems restricted. Take now Böhme's account of the effects of sin in this life—"The poor soul is poisoned through false imagination, and through its own compression of its desire is come to be such a hungry fire source, which is only a shutting in of the true life and a ground of darkness, wherein there is no more any true *Ens* wherein the Life might bring itself into Light. As a hard stone is shut up, so the soul was shut up."[1]

And next let M. Roze be heard, when, as a medium in his *Revelations of the World of Spirits*, speaking of men and women too much retarded to follow transformed glorified beings after death, he says that they remain in the "Voirie"[2] "*Cataleptisés until they are attracted as*

---

[1] Baptism, ch. ii., pars. 4, 5.

[2] "Voirie, se disait autrefois pour grand chemin, il se prend aujourd'hui plus ordinairement pour le lieu où l'on porte les boues, charognes et autres immondices" (*Dictionnaire de l'Academie*). But M. Roze explains the word as "the place where all that is animate is born, lives, and transforms itself; thus the vegetable earth is the Voirie of animals and vegetables, which draw from it the elements of their material constitution, and lay them down there after death to serve for other creations" (*Monde des Esprits*, première série, p. 55). Monsieur H. J. Amiel seems to have had a

germs on a new orb."[1] Let us also remember the Baroness von Vay's report of fallen spirits who remain hidden, slumbering, "wrapped up death-like in electric fluid,"[2] and of others, "outcast adverse spirits divided into fluidic and atomic molecules rotating round their mother worlds,"[3] and gradually roused to renewed consciousness and service in the construction of other worlds. Is it not thinkable that "this compressed blind soul substance"[4] may so gradually lose itself in the fatuity of perfected self-concentration as to contract, age after age, to the sealed-up latent fire of a germ that lacks soil and elemental stimulus for the recovery of a working life? I submit that thus it would be emphatically in chains of darkness; its fire not quenched, its worm of life not dead but paralysed, all consciousness lost in what Böhme calls "the great still standing death."

In one of his wonderful books, T. L. Harris speaks thus of the destruction of the hells: "Each spirit in the hells, who sinned and fell among the sons of Adam, prior to this having ceased to be a human entity has yielded up the soul-germ of his separate existence to God who gave it. Then a new race of mankind shall appear to reinstate the lost of our world in which the extinct soul-germs shall be reanimated."[5]

singular gift for what he called *re-implication*; for imaginatively tracing backward his own previous development to just the germ-like state to which I suppose we should relapse if spiritual evolution had failed in the present life, he says that it was "possible to reduce oneself to the condition of a germ, a point of latent existence; to free oneself from space and time, from the body and from life, to plunge again from circle to circle even to the darkness of primitive being, to experience by indefinite metamorphoses the feeling of one's own new genesis, to withdraw and condemn oneself, in short, even to the actuality of Limbus." See Preface to Amiel's *Journal Intime*, vol. i. p. xxxviii. But the process, which would be of absorbing interest in the world of thought, in a world devoid of light must be full of horror.

[1] Page 55.   [2] Geist, Kraft, Stoff, p. 24.   [3] Ibid., p. 49.
[4] Baptism, ch. ii., par. 6.   [5] Arcana of Christianity, p. 400, par. 719.

And again Mr Oxley's teachers help to a congruous supposition. Speaking of redemption from the hells, "they have been redeemed from that outer state into which Jehovah propelled them."[1] "The dust, or the remains, will, of course, have to be taken up again, and passing through a superior incoming order of humanity, will of necessity become a higher and purer substance."[2] "Behold, those who were dead live again, and those who for ages have been lost to memory are called again into conscious existence."[3]

As to this bringing back into consciousness, Freher's singular narrative of Gichtel's access, after long and intensely earnest prayer, to the soul of a friend who had killed himself, is worth heeding. "This miserable soul he found in the first harsh astringent property of the centre of nature, in the figure of a little globe so contracted, astricted, and narrowed, that it had, as to appearance no life, and no ability to exert any of its powers and faculties. Like as a man exposed to a great intolerable frost contracts his hands and feet and all his members into the narrowest space, rolling them up as near as he can in the figure of a globe, so that he lieth as a dead immovable thing, for no life nor motion appears without, though there is still a narrowed life within which is shut up as it were in a narrow prison." From which the unhappy soul was at length brought out by many struggles through differing degrees of anguish to light and eternal peace. The narrative will be found in *Notes and Queries*, Nov. 21, 1863, Third Series, vol. iv. p. 406.

Putting all these suggestive touches together, I can harmonize the conflicting theories of those who expect annihilation for incurably evil souls, and those who believe in enormous cycles of purgatorial arrest of all

---
[1] Angelic Revelations, vol. iii. p. 55.
[2] Ibid., vol. ii. p. 122.   [3] Ibid., vol. iii. p. 54.

that is blissful in spiritual existence. For in one sense the human soul is annihilated when reduced to the unconsciousness of a germ of life that has to be evolved through mineral, vegetable, and animal states before blind instinct changes to conscious freedom of choice; and on the other hand this degradation from human liberty to the inertia of an unquickened seed can hardly come to pass without long preliminary periods of horrible despair and self-loathing; time enough for wailing and gnashing of teeth before stupor numbs sensibility. And this hope of an ultimate bringing back of every spark of life from the total damnation of its former existence, I find far more consonant with the dark sayings of Holy Writ than with man's terribly hopeless interpretation of them, which oblige us thankfully to remember that God's thoughts are not as our thoughts, nor His ways as our ways. And I remember, too, Van Helmont's warning against the ignorant finality of man's conceptions regarding evil and good. "That there must be many ages or periods for the subduing of darkness may be understood from the nature of seeds; for like as the seeds that are sown are, with the help of light and heat, at length ripened into a tree, which tree again at its full growth brings forth fruits and new seeds, the same is to be understood of this visible world, which must at length come to full ripeness, and then by divine virtue bring forth and shed the seeds of new worlds, in which there is a new working out to perfection, and a new war commenced betwixt light and darkness."[1]

When the darkness of our present Æon is wholly subdued, and in our solar system God is all in all, the soul-germs of the lost may be re-awakened, and gradually brought upward to His marvellous light, by those who seek and find it now.

[1] Thoughts Upon the Four First Chapters of the First Book of Moses, called Genesis, ch. i. 4, London, 1701, p. 42.

"Matter is as a jailor to spirits; this matter imprisons them; and to those who will be able to understand me it may be said that the arrangement of gross matter and of bodies such as we see would not have been produced if there had not been rebellious spirits." . . . "Though I have said above that matter is the jailor of these spirits, I must add that only a part of them are shut up in it, and not all; otherwise there would be no possibility of collusion of trials, assaults, and temptations from subaltern moral agents."[1]

"The chaos from which our globe at least, and perhaps many other worlds, has come forth, was composed of primordial elements, whose disarrangement was caused by the revolt of angels; it was even composed, too, of a great number among them who, from one descent to another, from one degradation to another, had been thrown down there in a state of disorder and discord corresponding to their moral rebellion; and thrown there thus, with the *chains of darkness* and opaqueness which this rebellion had placed upon their being, once so glorious, and now materialized and, if I may use the expression, grossly *physicalized*."[2]

"We have seen that this father of mankind, this first man or created heap of dust, was the terrestrial globe on which we are; and hence it is still our hell; and we know that our body is only a living *Earth*. It follows from this, the atoms forming our body, actually vivified by the Divine Jesus, would without Him have remained throughout Eternity in the same infernal place, and in the same inanimate condition which our Earth offers to view. Now it is evident that in this state we should have been damned or condemned by God to an eternal privation of His divine life, as well as having to share the sufferings of other terrestrial atoms, constantly trodden under foot by living beings, mutilated by the

[1] Dutoit's *Divine Philosophy*, vol. ii. p. 283.   [2] Ibid., vol. ii. p. 275.

ploughshare of the labourer and the spade of the gardener; constantly agglomerated in mineral and vegetable substances, which endure fresh mutilations and a succession of varied torments."[1]

"My reader ought to perceive that the interior of the Earth has always indisputably formed hells for men who inhabit its surface; he will undoubtedly recognize the souls of the wicked ones who have been damned or condemned from the beginning of the ages to remain eternally *in our hells* with all the other spirits of the Prince of darkness."[2]

[1] Truth, vol. ii. p. 47. Published in 1771.
[2] Ibid., vol. i. p. 116.

REINCARNATION [1]

ALMOST a convert to belief in Reincarnation, and a very reluctant one;—notwithstanding the powerful arguments that have been brought forward in its support, still *almost* and not quite convinced, I wish—since the subject has been reopened in *Light*—to submit to its readers an objection which I find to be insuperable: the limitation of human souls on which this doctrine is based. Though Kardec admits that spirits as well as worlds are ever newly created, yet if we learn to understand by birth only a fresh rebirth of old spirits, we can hardly escape the sense of our race being a much smaller one than we had before thought it. All limits, even imagined, thus affecting the mind. Van Helmont, one of the strongest believers in what he calls the "revolution of souls," was driven to support his belief by this process of limitation. "They are mistaken," he says, "who think that every day there are new souls created. All spirits are already created, and the souls are continually more and more elaborated until they arrive to the immortality of their bodies." [2]

If we believe that, we must also believe that there is no propagation of souls! But this would contradict every analogy of Nature. It is now an accepted fact that soul life energizes in the vegetable as well as in the

---
[1] Light, 1887, vol. vii. p. 32.
[2] Thoughts Upon the Four First Chapters of the First Book of Moses, called Genesis, ch. ii. 1, London, 1701, p. 99.

animal kingdom; and the increase of that life by propagation cannot be doubted. This may be answered by saying that the number of *animal* souls in mankind is thus constantly enlarged, and that these form an ever new basis for *receiving* a certain number of pre-existent spirits for progressive transmutations. Van Helmont's illustrations of this theory are a little too preposterous for acceptance,[1] but the ideas we gather from Kardec, the Baroness von Vay, Oxley, F. Hartmann, and many others, as to the spirit[2] winding itself into the necessary conditions of rebirth most suitable to it for another period of earthly discipline, are so plausible and so consentient in tenor, that my strong dislike to such prospects might have been overpowered if I had not been rooted and grounded in Böhme's opposing doctrine. Briefly and roughly stated, this is his unvarying and most precise teaching as to the genesis of the human spirit: the soul of man is a fire awakened by the *occluse* desire of God, originating in a thought of the Divine mind, and taking effect in the will to manifest itself in a creaturely form: this fire, kindled by the interaction of the first three forces of Eternal Nature, necessarily generates the light which is its revelation, and the true spirit of man *is* that light—if light evolution is not obstructed (in which case that ray of Deific light remains " workless," but not

[1] Paradoxal Discourses, Part II. Concerning the Microcosme, ch. iv.
[2] Kardec is very precise in his account of the method by which spirits introduce themselves to ante-natal circumstances. (See his *Genèse Spirituelle*, chap. xi., par. 18.) The spirits who communicate by the mediumship of the Baroness von Vay, speak of their plans for reformatory re-embodiment on earth much as invalids do of the health establishments to which they mean to resort; and now and then specify the character and position of the parents they have chosen for their début in a new outfit of flesh and blood bodies. One of these spirits said that his wickedness had been so great that in 300 years he had been re-incarnated ten times. Is it not possible that such wickedness may still lead him to tell fibs? Swedenborg has assured us that it is a habit to which the *dis*-embodied are peculiarly prone.

extinguished, in its own hidden principle), and it necessarily forms its own body for self-manifestation and organized efficiency on the plane to which it is born.

Thus, according to Böhme, it would be as irrational to think of a soul *not* producing its own proper spirit as to speak of a fire that had not been kindled by light and would not bring forth light. As he abundantly shews, *soul is generated* as unquestionably as the fire of life is kindled in every child that is born.

How, then, are we to dispose of these conflicting ideas— that of the soul's innate spirit, and that of a spirit that supervenes and attaches itself, like a parasitical growth, to a germ adapted to its own purposes? Of course no Christian who prays for the indwelling of the Holy Spirit can refuse belief in habitual association with other spirits than our own, but that is very different from two spirits being born simultaneously. The only possible way out of this dilemma that I can see—if the belief in rebirths is accepted—is one I greatly dislike even to name, the hypothesis that the *pre-existent* human spirit, by its thought, desire, and will, secures fleshly embodiment by first setting in motion those forces of nature (derived from the seven spirits of Eternal Nature) which conditionate birth. Yet, if this were so, how impossible it would be to call that offspring the child of its parents in any sense not degrading to humanity! All the notorious facts of heredity, of spiritual and mental, as well as animal, characteristics passing down from father to son for many generations seem to contradict such a notion.

Kardec's dogmas regarding Reincarnation give poor half-taught human spirits a wider range than later writers allow, for he speaks of migration from one world to another, after long intervals of what he calls purely spiritual life; but we are asked to accept the very repulsive idea of a repeated coming back of time-worn spirits to the old arena of endurance and combat and death. No wonder it is refused; even though some of our wisest contemporaries insist that it is the *needs must* of our immediate post-mortem future. Is it not possible that they may be mistaking the remedial exception for the invariable rule? Or can it be that we have such a complex multiplicity of souls in our seeming unity, under the headship of what Van Helmont calls man's "central life spirit," that some of our tributory Egos have to return for further development, while the Head of the tribe enters into its rest?

We shall all solve the riddle for ourselves by and by, but, unfortunately, it will be impossible to supply the right answer to those we leave behind, conscious remembrance of *this* stage of existence being forfeited when the *revenant* insinuates itself once more into a body about to be born. I do not pretend to form any opinion upon this unravelled mystery, but I expect to find that *enfleshed* life is by no means the only existence suited for spiritual progression.

READY-MADE CLOTHES [1]

PROBABLY most readers of *Light* have been puzzled at sometime or other by the well-known trick of communicating spirits announcing themselves as distinguished people, and have now and then felt, while reading some deeply interesting message from hidden spheres, what the French call a *retour sur soi-même*, when the unseen informant adds that it comes from Confucius, Plato, or Kepler, as the case may be. Indeed, one turns back rather sharply on such occasions to intuitive commonsense, feeling as if willingness to believe had carried one away a little too far. Yet very often communications so suspiciously endorsed seem otherwise to bear the impress of veracity How is it, one asks, that any gleam of truth can reach us combined with evident or presumable falsehood? Swedenborg's assertion that the habitual mendacity of spirits exceeds all that we are familiar with on our own plane of being, has never given me a satisfying key to the enigma: it only suggests another, *Why* are they so fond of fibs? Among ourselves fibs are seldom without motive; vanity, malice, or self-interest of some kind prompting untruth; and among the crowds which throng the accessible approaches to minds in the flesh, tricksy and malevolent spirits can hardly be so many as the boundlessly false appear to be; what, therefore, can be the temptation? Only a few days ago I chanced on a saying of Swedenborg's, in a book of his

[1] Light, 1887, vol. vii. p. 411.

not seen before, which gave me a glimpse of a reason. "It is," he says, "a peculiar circumstance in the spiritual world that a spirit thinks himself to be such as is denoted by the garment he wears, because in that world the understanding clothes every one." Now, it has long been understood that the contents of a medium's mind always more or less modify every utterance given through it; thus the informing spirit uses what he finds there. May there not be *unintentional* assumption of an ideal character found in the mind of a medium? The rule which this great seer tells us obtains in spirit-world is continually exemplified in our own: as regards the clothing of our bodies, the body's mimetic representation of feeling, and the dressing up by imagination of the *conscious* Ego, any one may prove it by observing what takes place within and without. A soldier in full uniform, a bishop in lawn sleeves and apron, an ill-dressed or well-dressed woman, all feel themselves to *be* what their garments denote in a much stronger degree than reason alone can justify; and both actors and painters know well that to simulate gestures of passion is to induce emotional excitement; of varying intensity, of course; but invariably attitude and gesture will—in some measure—confirm the state of mind which it interprets externally. A remark of the late Mr W. Bagehot exemplifies this very neatly. "Lord Chatham was in the habit of kneeling at the bedside of George the Third while transacting business. Now no man can argue on his knees. The same superstitious feeling which keeps him in that physical attitude will keep him in a corresponding mental attitude."[1]

Quite as certain it is that we all live up, or down, to our imaginations of what we are. With two such good authorities as Jean Paul Richter and Novalis to vouch for this fact, it is needless to try and make good the

[1] English Constitution, 1867, p. 108; 1872, p. 79.

point. The one says, "Whoever remarks to a man, and much more to a woman, 'you are certainly cross or angry,' will find such useless plain speaking verified, even if it be not true at first. One so easily becomes that which we are taken to be." And Novalis still more boldly tells us, "If a man could all at once verily believe he *was* a moral man, he would become such." In each case the ready-made garment of imagination dominates consciousness. Nor would this surprise us if we had any adequate idea of the creative force of imagination. By it, according to Böhme, the eternal and the temporal worlds came into existence: the imagination of the supreme abyssal Deity in the first case, and that of *spiritus mundi* in the other, *producing* all that is.

But what concerns us more practically is the warning he gives as to its momentous effects in the microcosm. "The soul," he tells us, "must have magic food, viz., by or with the imagination . . . it must draw in substance into itself through its imagination, else it would not subsist."[1] Can these sayings of his throw any light on the love of personation so common among those who speak behind the veil of our grosser embodiments? Is it that they, having lost material bodies and not attained true enduring substance for the soul's magic food, are like people trying on one suit of clothes after another, when assuming characters, in hope of finding some that can satisfy imagination? I think self-love in the flesh knows something of that process now and then; and what a weariness constant change of its imaginative clothing becomes as times goes on! One day it all seems so poor and trumpery—the next, its tinsel glitters like gold; the inflation of self-importance so occupying! the shrunken squalor of self-contempt causing so much dismay! We have all of us a strong reminder of the risks of desirous imaginations in our present bodies, for

[1] Incarnation, Part I., ch. iv., par. 46, and ch. v., par. 88.

it was "the will" of our first progenitor that "*did imagine into this monstrous property*"[1] of gross flesh and blood, and the worst of the danger is in the reaction of body on the spirit. "The form impregnateth its imagination"[2] as surely as that fashions the form, and as "the essence is in the body even so the spirit doth figure and form itself internally."[3] The imagination once established, "the phantasy receiveth nothing into itself, but only a similitude or thing like itself, and that likeness is the power of its life."[4]

Nor does the danger stop there. Adam's lapse of imagination (I speak as the convinced disciple of Böhme) brought all the race into what he so truly calls "the stage play of the self-hood of nature,"[5] and in every part of that play we have most accomplished prompters behind the scenes in the victims of an antecedent rebellion. "The devil," said Gichtel, "is anxious about our soul's imagination; he understands it better than we." If by any allurement of *other* magic he can famish our souls by hindering them from "imagining a little into the love of God," suitable sorceries for that end will be ever fresh and strong: and by the conventional *he*, I mean a host inimical to man from envy of his potential supremacy. The Father of Spirits knew how this would be, and has in mercy given us a perfect pattern of what man should be, and must be, to become wholly a man and no longer a confused creature, doubtful alike of his origin and his destiny, ready to believe himself the transient outcome of the forces of Nature—a passive irresponsible link in the chain of cosmic evolution. Especially in these days, when society echoes with a multitude of voices decrying all old phases of belief, and literature besets us with a

---

[1] Mysterium Magnum, ch. xxii., par. 19.
[2] Incarnation, Part II., ch. iii., par. 7.
[3] Mysterium Magnum, ch. xx., par. 37.
[4] Election, ch. iv., par. 122.   [5] Ibid., ch. iv., par. 60.

tangle of theories only agreeing in the destructiveness
of negation; when old habits of thought have been
torn to rags, and souls shiver in the comfortless wastes
of doubt.

Any one who has known what it is to feel in a chaotic
state of undefined purposes, driven here and there by
conflicting impulses and fruitless agitation of thought,
will understand the sort of help which is afforded by a
ready-made ideal of what one ought to be,—a firmly
settled mould into which thought can at once subside.
Roman Catholics will understand it; but we need more
than Papal authority can offer; we want clothing for
self which death cannot remove, nor sickness discredit.
It is just this which the example and counsel of our
Divine elder Brother supplies. Let us take it direct from
Him in its simplest principle of filial obedience and the
humility which is the *sine quâ non* of all persistent love
—("the throne of love is humility")—for verily all the
disguising modifications given to the character of the
Lord Christ by scores of small-minded zealots have done
much to disfigure it in modern views. The habits of
that Brother are ready for our ideal outfit at any moment,
and are such as all of us can adopt; for He having worn
the rough wrappings of our flesh knew what is in man
in that condition, and exactly measured our need,—need
of peace, and motive force that cannot fail of its object.
That "*the life of man is a form of the Divine will*"[1] was
the great truth to which His whole life gave witness.
Surely it would go far toward helping us to maintain
cheerfulness and fortitude, at all times, if we would
accept all that is unchosen and inevitable in our lot as a
manifestation of the *permissive* will of God, as the place
in life's battle where we are to hold the ground for Him,
and conquer by patience and meekness of wisdom. Volition *can* reach this much of the garment of the Christ;

[1] Divine Vision, ch. ii., par. 2.

at any time by exerting the *magic fire* of the soul it can compel itself to be dumb under insult and wrong, and refrain from accusation and threats while suffering. And if Böhme was not mistaken there is no time to lose in trying thus to clothe ourselves with humility—(the most comfortable and becoming wear if people would but try it!)—for he says: "In whatsoever essence and will the soul's fire liveth and burneth, according to that essence is also the *fiat* in the will-spirit, and it imageth such an image: so now when the outward body deceaseth, then standeth that image thus in such a source and quality. In the time of the earthly life it may *alter its will* and then also its *fiat* altereth the figure; but after the dying of the body it hath nothing more wherein it can alter its will."[1] Why not after the outer body's death? Because, as he and Swedenborg both assure us, with the loss of the body we lose the power of restricting our thoughts, wills, and opinions to ourselves; we become a part, so to speak, of a common-stock mind, that of a society unseen here, to which we have belonged—but unconsciously by virtue of our most interior life—while believing our spirits alone. I entreat attention to the inferential meaning of those words "in such a source or quality." Quality, according to Böhme, is an equivalent to the German word *Quell*, a spring or source. The outcome of every *source* is not confined to present time, is not limited, is not easily exhausted. If we carry with us into another world a *source* of misery in any vicious quality not transmuted, as in this life it may be, we must expect copious floods of anguish. If it is well now, it will be unimaginably, blissfully well beyond the short road across which we pass on earth, to have accepted the durable, close-fitting simplicity of the raiment of Christ. "*God's substance*," said Böhme, "*is humility.*"[2]

---

[1] First Apology, Part II., pars. 266, 267.
[2] Election, ch. vii., par. 152.

This explains a little how it was that while He Who came to rescue us from the masquerade of evil powers truly described Himself as *being meek and lowly*; He could announce, when quit of coarse flesh and blood disguise, that to Him was given " *all power* both in Heaven and earth."

ETERNAL BODIES [1]

"Understand us aright what we mean; we speak the precious and sublime truth, as we know and understand it. The new man is not only a *spirit*: he is even flesh and blood, as the gold in the stone is not only spirit: it hath a body, but not such a one as the rude drossy stone is."—Böhme's *Treatise on the Incarnation*, Part I., ch. xiv., pars. 21, 22.

MR LOCKERBY seems inadvertently to have blended ideas gathered from Böhme and Mr T. Lake Harris. Such words as "primates," "atomic forms," and "arch-natural" at once remind one of the *Arcana* of our great contemporary seer. They are not to be found in the writings of Böhme (his only use of *arch* in a qualifying sense is arch-shepherd). Neither can I recall in them any mention of a magnetic body, though he says emphatically that "the magnetical attraction is the *beginning of nature.*" [2]

But in claiming for him speciality of teaching as to the elaboration of an arch-natural body in the human frame, Mr Lockerby is wholly right, and I thank him for drawing attention to that most important point, and gladly seize the opportunity for trying to make it a little clearer than it can be while embedded in very obscure context. According to Böhme the necessity of regeneration bears upon *substance*; not a new state of mind or feeling, but the heavenly body which the first Adam lost and which only the second—Christ *in us* —can restore. A new soul we cannot have; it is an

[1] Light, 1887, vol. vii. p. 483.   [2] Election, ch. ii., par. 41.

organism suited to the soul's divine life that every child of man needs and cannot have without the "new creature" of the second birth. This he urges with importunate iteration, and he startles readers unused to his books by attributing to this new creature flesh and blood; here for instance, "seeing God hath created man in a substance, to be therein eternally, viz., in flesh and blood; therefore of necessity, to that willing which giveth itself up into the Eternal, must such flesh and blood be put on; *as it was*, when God created it in Paradise in the Eternal. Whereby then we clearly know that God hath not created us in such flesh and blood, as we now bear upon us, but in such *flesh and blood*" (those last words in his translator's largest capitals) "as to the willing, in the new birth, is put on."[1]

Unlike some of our modern seers, he could not flatter mankind with the hope of any other bodily existence behind the veil proving permanent, however real, pleasant, and lasting it may seem. He knew better. Listen to his earnest warnings as to this.

"Thou art so weak in the outward life that thou canst not prevent thy constellation or Astrum, thou must go into the corruption or breaking of thy body, when the constellation leaveth thee. And there thou seest undeniably what thou art, viz., dust of the earth. . . . Thou livest to the configuration" (of the stars) "and elements, they rule and drive thee according to their property; they give thee employment and art; and when their *seculum*, time or season is run about, that thy constellation under which thou wert conceived and born to this world is finished, then they let thee fall away. And then thy body falleth home to the four elements, and thy spirit which leadeth thee, to the mystery . . . thus must thou moulder away and become earth and a nothing, all but the *spirit*, which is proceeded

[1] Incarnation, Part II., ch. vi., pars. 15, 16.

out of the Eternal, which God introduced into the *Limus*: therein consider what thou art, even a handful of earth, and a source or quality-house or tormentive *work-house* of the stars and elements."[1]

Böhme never denies that after dissolution of its outward body, the human soul may still live on in the astral body, a short or a long time according to the periods of the stars ruling over its mundane existence; but he affirms that sooner or later this body must perish as the elemental body did before it, and leave the soul which has not attained to the new birth, or even to the "*little thread of faith in the new regeneration, which holdeth the Saviour fast* by that thread, though very weak, and *setteth its imagination or desire further into the heart of God*,"[2] "raw and naked," "without

[1] Incarnation, Part II., ch. vi., pars. 33-38.
[2] Three Principles, ch. xix., par. 42.

Böhme's account of the action of souls still clothed in an astral body after death will have, I fancy, intrinsic value for readers of *Light*, so I give one of his most graphic passages from the *Forty Questions of the Soul*: "Concerning the souls which have not yet attained heaven, which stick in the source, quality or pain in the principle in the birth, these have still human matters with the works on them, and they search diligently after the cause of their detention: and, therefore, many of them *come again* with the starry spirit, and walk about in houses and other places, and appear in human shape and form, and desire this and that, and often take care about their wills and testaments, supposing thereby to get the blessing of holy people for their rest and quiet. And if their earthly business and employment stick in them and cleave to them still, then, indeed, they take care about their children and friends; and this continueth so long, till they sink down into their rest, so that their starry spirit be *consumed*, then all is gone as to all care and perplexity, and they have no more feeling knowledge thereof; but merely that they see it in the wonders of the Magia. But they touch not the *Turba*, nor seek what it is in this world, for they are once sunk down from the Turba through death; they desire *that* no more, neither do they take any more care, for in care the Turba is stirring; for the soul's will must enter with its spirit into earthly things, which it would fain *forsake*, for it hardly got rid away from them before; it would not cumber itself to *let in* the earthly spirit again. We speak freely and certainly that this sort do no more, *after they are come to grace*, purposely, take care about human earthly matters: *but about*

government"—in short, a will devoid of all executive power, a hunger forever famishing and insatiable.

Among all teachers (I was going to say human teachers, but remembered how earnestly he protests that what he taught was revealed to him; that he was a medium for "that which the spirit sheweth, which no man can resist,"[1]) he is unique in revealing to us the process of regeneration, or rather attempting to do so. I use the word attempt with reference to the understanding of those who read him, for all the ideas he transmits on this theme are precise and consistent, invariably agreeing in purport though expressed in ever-varying modes of speech. It is not possible to give any adequate précis of these ideas, neither is this the place for them, but this much must be said. Mr Lockerby's expression as to "placing ourselves *en rapport* with the Divine Man for Him to clothe with His body by causing the new creative law, evolved by Him, to operate from soul to body," is a long way distant from the account *Philosophus Centralis* gives of the indispensables for "the soul attaining the Eternal Flesh again." It reads like an accepted inference from pages in the *Arcana of Christianity*; for to judge by his writings Mr T. L. Harris has never been intromitted to the same depths of regenerative experience, and in his school one finds no recognition of the tremendous spiritual throes which are known to so many in the crisis often called conversion; many, I mean, of those who can give any date to a process of which, I am persuaded, *not* all in whom the new creature is forming are distinctly conscious.

heavenly matters which come to them through man's spirit, they see them, and have their joy therein." Sparrow's translation, 1665, Ques. 26, pars. 11-15. I put in italics three sentences in this quotation, that thus attention may be drawn to implied beliefs which I find full of comfort, and far more credible than theologically orthodox.

[1] Epistles (1649), Ep. 3, par. 38.

It may be that the opening of internal respiration, on which he lays such stress, is as necessarily preceded by "a death unto sin," as what we call the new birth. This is the "new creative law of the Divine Man," and inexorably binding; a prolonged dying of the false and evil will of what Böhme terms our "*assumed* selfhood"; and a constant mastery of the "gross phantastical sulphur" of our material bodies. These hold captive the imprisoned supernal light that forms an imperishable body in the water of eternal life. For the full emergence of this light not only must self-will die to its rights, but contrition must break open its prison; and who can produce *that* at pleasure! Surely not our own polluted hearts, too much used to their firstborn darkness to feel or even believe how thick that darkness is! And therefore in one of his prayers Böhme cries out: "O great Holy God, I pray Thee *set open my inwardness to me*, that I may rightly know what I am; unshut, I pray Thee, in me what became enclosed and shut up in Adam."[1]

For Böhme and Mr Mohini Chatterji are in full agreement as to the nature of the true human spirit. "Regeneration," says this last, "is to be accomplished by Christos, the incarnated wisdom, the true human spirit,"[2] and Böhme says: "The most inward ground in man is Christus; not according to the nature of man, but according to the Divine property in the heavenly substance, which he hath generated anew."[3] Hence we can understand the two following clauses of his little creed about regeneration, formed, he assures us, "not from supposition or opinion, but from our own true knowledge in the enlightening given us from God. First, that the new regenerate man, which lieth hidden in the old

---
[1] The Holy Week, or a Prayer Book, par. 119.
[2] Man: Fragments of Forgotten History, p. 42.
[3] Election, ch. vii., par. 98.

as the gold in the stone, hath a heavenly tincture, and hath divine heavenly flesh and blood on it: and that the spirit of that flesh is no strange spirit, but its *own*, generated out of its own essence. . . . Sixthly, that the *possibility* of the new birth is in all men, else God were divided, and not in one place as He is in another."[1]

One who had evidently gone through the great crisis of regeneration in a very other way than mere *rapport* with the Regenerator, describes it as "a re-organization, a tangible luminous reality with every sense we have, but of a new essence. It is a whole constitutional change, not a change of state only"; and he adds, "If the deepest ground is to be broken up, the deepest and darkest and bitterest sufferings must be suffered. The very soul's constitution is to be rended,—how can we expect the work to be got over without the deepest feelings of anguish."[2] But such anguish is *not* known in anything like this degree to a great many sincere followers of the Lord Jesus Christ;—to many it is. Can it be that there has been in *another* prior existence what is equivalent to new birth? I cannot think it: the only alternative theory for my mind is that in these devout lives, unconscious of any of the pangs of rebirth, there is something that answers to impregnation of higher life, and that death to the flesh body may be literally the first bringing forth to embryonic perfection of the new creature so gradually and insensibly formed; possibly experiences that follow upon death.

As to the arch-natural body being transmitted to children when it exists in both parents, I doubt if Böhme would admit that such an inheritance is possible —favourable tendencies, but *not* the new creature. For "every angel and soul which will live in God's light and power *must* die to the selfhood of the fire's dominion in

---

[1] Incarnation, Part I., ch. xiv., pars. 51–53, 59.
[2] James Pierrepont Greaves, *Unpublished MS.*

the *desire*,"[1] and the selfhood of the fire's dominion is the origin of earthly life. Every child brings it to manifestation here; and as St Paul said, it is "first the natural, and after that the spiritual," because, though the one so little agrees with the other, in the natural body the soul has ability to form the heavenly—Böhme repeatedly asserts—as gold is formed in the matrix of its rough quartz. Mr T. L. Harris gives a similar report of the luminous body being formed within the opaque, in one of his unpublished pamphlets; and in another, with a realism all his own, tells his disciple to "take care of the cell-germs of the present form, because the new-natural grows from cell-germs evolved out of the present ones."[2]

As regards the arch-natural *in the flesh* enabling people to have "uncontrolled range of arch-natural senses," and to "see and handle spiritual forms," I should think it unlikely, but do not presume to have an opinion. Evidently, the inner senses—of the astral body as I suppose—have been very much quickened within the last century; and the inhabitants of an adjacent plane of being seem increasingly desirous to make us aware of their existence. Whether it is that the nerve body is better developed in our present generation, or whether the great judgment of spirits in 1757, reported by Swedenborg, did, as he averred, rid the regions contiguous to our earth of a dense crowd of spirits who obstructed higher astral influences, able to reach us ever since that great clearance, we cannot of course decide; but this is certain, that a new consciousness of unseen agents spreads amongst us more and more in spite of all denial, regret, and ridicule. It often leads me to think of Böhme's prediction that at the time of the end "*the gates of all three Principles shall stand open.*" Are

[1] Third Apology, Text I., par. 60.
[2] Wisdom in Council (the 2nd Part of *The Golden Child*), p. 27.

they not opening gradually now? So strange a mixture of the worst and the best spirit influences seems to be pressing upon us, like a mixed multitude trying to get into an enclosure at every least opening. Such eager seeking for access to the soul of man is quite intelligible so far as the rabble of astral spirits go, because from regenerate man they can learn more than the world-soul can teach (according to Böhme quite a degree lower in rank). But what for them can be the attraction of the mass of human beings? Is it not from eagerness to reveal some of their own peculiar knowledge? for "the stars," he says, "have in them the causes of every thing that is in this world: all that live and move are stirred up from their properties and brought to life."[1] And also "the outward instigation to manifest and reveal the mystery proceedeth from the stars, for they would fain be freed from vanity, and they drive mightily in the magical children to manifestation."[2] Well may he add, "Therefore we must prove and examine the instigation whether it proceed from God's light, from God's Spirit, or from the dominion of the stars."

It seems quite possible that as our astral senses quicken, astral bodies may become evident, and their indwelling spirits audible associates; the great danger is that from our non-acquaintance with the true paradisical body, we may mistake perishable astral glory for that in which the kingdom of Heaven may be seen—that *only*; and forming our soul's magical substance by this erroneous imagination find them at last divested *even of this*, and without eternal flesh and blood.

[1] Threefold Life, ch. vii., par. 73.
[2] Epistles (1649), Ep. 4, par. 115.

Here connection of ideas is wanted without knowledge of another doctrine of Böhme's, that until all the wonders the stars can pour out are opened by man, the illusions of time, the periods during which "the whole creation groans and travails," will not be brought to an end. Hence their interest in the "magical children"—query, mediumistic?

To Mr Lockerby's last question, "Can we follow Böhme in the spiritual law?" nothing short of his answer can honestly be given. "Searching is not the chief or most special means to know or apprehend the mystery, but to be born or regenerated in God."[1] If I have not already claimed too long patience with his doctrines from seekers of *Light*, I hope to be allowed another day to report his account of the seven-fold stratification of men in a man; about which he speaks, in one of his books, with almost as much exactness as an Eastern adept.

That such a paper as this can be allowed in an English periodical may do *something*, I hope, to remove an aspersion coming from Mr W. Q. Judge, in last month's number of the *Theosophist*. "How could European minds understand the statement that there may be an astral body and an astral shape also, each distinct from the other, when they have always known that *body* is a thing due to accretions from beef and beer?" We have got a little in advance of *that!*

[1] Forty Questions (1665), Ques. 1, par. 254.

BURIED TREASURES

PREAMBLE

"Now I know very well that I shall not only in part be, as it were, dumb or obscure to the desirous reader, but also tedious, and he will be somewhat troubled at me."—Böhme's *Three Principles*, ch. v., par. 12.

UNDOUBTEDLY I shall be tedious too, if from no other cause than that of frequently interpolating quoted words; but as my object in writing this is to put into intelligible shape the instructions I have gathered from teachers little read, it would be as foolish to apologize for quoting them so often as to express regret that pearls were threaded upon a string. The string is of no use or value, apart from drawing those pearls together into combined beauty. So of these attempts of my mind, which has been honoured with this use by the Giver of all good; and I am not going to neglect my own proper mission, however humble, in order to assume that which belongs to minds of higher calibre and more originality, therefore perhaps less free to seek out, and admire, and set in order treasure which has already been laid open to those who *could* seek and find, but do not. Because no one comes forward to remind contemporaries of all the wealth buried in the writings of Böhme and Swedenborg, offering proofs and samples, it is my misfortune, not my choice, to be driven again and again by my ardent desire that this should be done, to try and elucidate subjects quite too large for my grasp. If any one with adequate intellectual force would deal with them—presupposing equal familiarity with those writings—how it would rejoice me! For I am convinced that if Böhme and Swedenborg held that place in our Universities which they ought; if they were studied as Plato and Aristotle have been studied, Atheism and Materialism would be regarded by all intelligent people as the gross blunder of ill-informed minds. That must inevitably result from an unprejudiced study of the works of these two great seers; distinguished above all other teachers for having united intensity of love for God with knowledge inexhaustibly profound. Their writings are pervaded with a love equal to all the most ardent pietists can feel or desire to feel, and in those writings the most searching intellect (if but cognisant of its previous ignorance, and teachable) will find itself led on from one depth to another, till it rests from all the wearying uncertainties of modern thought, and begins to see that the permitted embodiment of the human race in its present fallible condition *is* compatible with Omniscient Love, and that all the woe and sin which now appear unconquerable will be made to evolve a yet larger purpose of Divine mercy in ages to come.

It is Böhme *alone* who can satisfactorily answer the taunt implied in a sentence such as this that happened to meet my eye in a recent number of the *World's Advance Thought*. Its drift is one of the commonest jibes against Christian faith, and is uttered on all sides as unanswerable; as indeed it *is* by theologians.

"Omnipotence applied to God must be a misnomer, or everything in which power is inherent is a part of God."

Briefly to intimate *how* Böhme solves this paradox, one may paraphrase that saying thus: "White is a misnomer for what we call whiteness, since it includes every colour."

Instead of accepting the help these wonderful mediums transmitted to us, by dint of labelling one with the title of *fanatic*, and on the strength of that title neglecting what he wrote; and adding an *ism* to the name of Swedenborg, and turning his vast science into the narrowness of a religious sect; we have disparaged both, and effected what the enemy of souls must strongly desire, the consecration and maintenance of darkness.

It is real grief to find thoughtful people poring, year after year, over a number of modern *views* of evolution, while Swedenborg's *Angelic Wisdom concerning Divine Love and Divine Wisdom*, and Böhme's *Sixth Epistle*, which meet every requirement for harmonizing difficulties on that subject, remain unstudied. When, after reading infusions of Darwin, in recent literature, I open either of those works, I find my despair at human perverseness taking expression in the outcry of Solomon, "Wherefore is there a price in the hand of a fool to get wisdom, seeing he hath no heart to it?"[1]

LOOKING-GLASSES

"Les plus éveillés voient encore le monde réel à travers l'illusion dominante de leur race ou de leur temps: et la raison c'est que la lumière illusionnante part de notre esprit même."—Amiel, *Journal Intime*, vol. ii. p. 75.

In the *Visions* of "M.A. (Oxon.)" this passage occurs:
"I want to ask whether those scenes are real—real, I mean, in the same sense as scenes in our world?

"In precisely the same sense. The scenes of the world

[1] Prov. xvii. 16.

If the question, "How can evil have arisen in a world called into existence by a God wholly wise, loving, and all powerful?" really disturbs the peace of any person rich enough to spend money on winning an adequate answer, it may be found, so far as a finite intellect can supply it, in a treatise by Dionysius Freher, on *Deity considered as manifesting Himself through Eternal Nature*. A very scarce work, but no doubt money could obtain it—in translation, and to reprint it would be a noble beneficence.

of spirit, and the surroundings of the spirit in any sphere of its existence, are just as real as are the scenes and surroundings of your earths. Each is impressed upon your own spirit; each is the result of your own state. They would not be real to you in your present state; they were real to you in spirit as you visited them, just as these scenes are not real to us."[1]

And again, referring to another, the seer asked, "Can you give me any message about that vision?" and the answer was, "*It was not a vision but experience.*"[2] These last words I have italicized as what most impressed me in that wonderful record. They set me thinking, very impertinently a metaphysician might have said, had he known my thoughts, for the first was that a direct assertion like this, coming from the source it did, was worth more than all the intricate theories of Kant regarding objective and subjective perceptions, which, according to the jesting old story, he complained, "no one was able to understand, except Fichte, and he misunderstood."

Do I then presume to understand the *rationale* of this simpler doctrine, that every spirit forms its own realities —not its *phenomenal* perceptions, its own delusive views of things only—but its surrounding facts, real as well as objective to itself? By no means; but putting together this statement of it, and several hitherto dark sayings of Böhme's—which for years have baffled my efforts to understand—I think I see a glint of a great law, valid in every world, which finds its best elucidation in the structure of looking-glasses; and by this word Böhme designates it. The requisite for every looking-glass is arrest of light at a certain distance from its source; and its office the giving back of objects which stand above or before it; on its smoothness and purity depends the accuracy of their outlines. Now as limitation is thus

[1] Page 11. [2] Page 20.

essential to consciousness, it is in that sense that he says, "The spirit is the life, the looking-glass is the manifestation or revelation of the life, else the spirit would not know itself."[1] And having in the next chapter to that in which these words occur given most profound insight as to the relations of the Wisdom, i.e., "the passive essence of divine operation" to Deific will, he continues: "The will in the looking-glass of the Wisdom discovereth itself, and so it imagineth out of the Abyss into itself, and maketh to itself in the Imagination a ground in itself, and impregnateth itself with the imagination out of the wisdom" . . . "for, the will becometh impregnated with the glimpse of the looking-glass."[2]

Parenthetically I must here observe that it is such passages as these, and many others susceptible of the same inference, which led Martensen and some English students to the hasty conclusion that Böhme's teaching involves a belief of the Supreme Creator first becoming self-conscious in His creations. If they would add *on that plane of self-manifestation*, I could entirely agree with them; but to suppose God to be only completed by and in the creaturely life seems to me quite foreign to Böhme's thought, so much so as to have prevented him from guarding his expressions from misprision in many passages—misprision virtually excluded from his doctrine by others—such as these: "God is in Himself the Abyss, viz., the first world, of which no creature knoweth anything at all, for it standeth solely and alone with spirit and body in the Byss or ground. Thus also God Himself in the Abyss would not be manifest in Himself, but His Wisdom is from eternity become his ground or Byss."[3] Now the Wisdom is antecedent to the creation of our universe. Even if careful study of all Böhme wrote had not led me to the same conclusion,

[1] Incarnation, Part II., ch. i., par. 43.   [2] Ibid., ch. ii., pars. 5, 7.
[3] Ibid., ch. iii., pars. 24, 25.

Freher's verdict on this point would be final with me; for he, who had read all his books ten times through, sums up the question thus: "If there is in the first world before and without Nature no perception, knowledge, etc., then there is also not only no Wisdom, but no God in no sense and manner"; and after examining arguments for accusing Böhme of "defining God as potentiality alone, which requires the aid of nature before it gain life, reality, and power of its own" (I use Martensen's words for the indictment) Freher says: "This explication, I grant, is plausible if looked upon from without, superficially, for Böhme's own words do plainly say all these things; and if there were but that one and true distinction observed between the eternal generation *without nature*, and the eternal manifestation *in and through nature*, nothing more could be desired."

It is because God does, in Böhme's phraseology, "only find Himself in man" on this earthly plane of Divine action, that until human nature is purified enough for His image to emerge from its troubled, turbid depths, the earth cannot be covered with the glory of the Lord. "The first Adam was contrived, or imagined, out of the light's essence, and substantiality,"[1] Böhme says, and the restoration of that image is only to be effected by the same process.

We now find our souls darkened, and to escape from that darkness which solar light cannot relieve for more than a hundred years at the longest, we must *will* to regain light. "A will is no substance, but the will's imagination maketh substance." That is the awful law of nature. "The mind is the wellspring where the one only will *can create* out of it evil and good, which is done through imagination or through representation of a thing that is evil or good. And so is the property of that thing capable of the same property in the life.

[1] Incarnation, Part I., ch. xii., par. 26.

The life's property catcheth or receiveth the property of the thing represented, and kindleth itself therewith in itself " . . . " all according to the *represented* substance : whatsoever the imagination caught, that it introduceth into the mind."[1]

Here we have, only at greater length and in fuller light, a reiteration of the fact that in man also " *the will becometh impregnated with the glimpse of the looking-glass,*" *i.e.*, with suggestive enticements to any subject on which the human mind can turn its attention. For as man was destined to be the "looking-glass of the Deity," so is all in this world a looking-glass for man, *relatively* speaking, a passive which can reflect upon his will every image which his desire—imagining—can impress upon it.

The enchantments we may work upon ourselves by this law of our nature, are often quite as gratuitous as the shapes and faces which a sick person's eye can trace out for pastime in every object before it, in wall-paper, folds of curtain, or hang of clothing thrown aside; in forming these we have no accomplice, and the slightest movement breaks the illusion. But the great sorcerer has legionary servants who can only see into our life through the mind of man, and well they know how to occupy that magic glass with a phantasmagoria to the tastes of each.

We each form our own looking-glass, it is true, and see everything there of inner or outer world, as it is seen by no other eye, for *every* object mirrored there reflects something which self has added or deducted from images of surrounding life. Nevertheless, it is constantly liable to cross lights, and to being tinted by other colours than our own "soulish fire." And with every change of these, and every new refraction of the light of truth, " the image in the spirit becometh altered, all according to what is contained in the will which the

[1] Great Six Points, Point III., ch. iv., pars. 7, 8.

soul hath framed or contrived"... "viz., according to the imagination."[1]

When Franz Baader says, "Jede Wille bringt seine Vision, mit dieser seine Lust und List damit," (*Every will brings its own seeing and with this its pleasure and its craft*), one's first thought is that the seeing is an arrangement of that will's cunning, made to secure its pleasure. Indirectly it is so, but not consciously. We often say with impatient surprise, "I cannot make him or her see so and so!"—glaringly evident to the speaker. In very many cases no human power could alter the mental perception of another; because the constant interaction of the reflex images in the mirror of the mind, and the spirit which has *immassed* them there, precludes the sight of actual facts as involuntarily as the breath of a person shut up in a small glass house would obscure the passage of light and obstruct the captive's vision. We are all prisoners within the magic circle of our own unconscious spells. The will has created images that suit its desire, and the images have corroborated the will.[2]

The momentary fury of irritation which will flare up in a narrow or despotic mind when its prejudices are controverted is solely due to this. No one likes to have his own special looking-glass shaken, or its plane confused by images foreign to those usually there. Hence the instinctive reserve of Englishmen: their fixity of opinion makes them impatient of every subversive thought. Nor can any imported ideas alter the proportions of our own. How often do we come from an audience with the inner thoughts of another—say, of a

[1] Forty Questions (1665), Ques. 7, par. 19. See also par. 18.

[2] This is no new truth, of course; long since well-worded by Fichte, "*Solltest du anders sehen so müssest du erst anders werden.*" (If you would see things differently you must first become different yourself.) But this is one of the facts so habitually disguised in self-conscious life, that it needs to be repeated to every rising generation afresh.

very conceited, very proud, or very melancholy friend—feeling as if we had been in contact with a mind partially deranged! Conceit has been in such comical disagreement with outside verdicts, pride so bewilderingly blind, and dejection so wholly out of keeping with the cause alleged, and yet so intense and immovable. We wonder; but if our secret chambers of imagery had been inspected probably there would be quite as much to startle on some other line; and I think we should all guard more carefully against foolish wishes and vain or angry thoughts, if we knew how surely, when habitually allowed, they "compact themselves into the substance of the phantasy."[1] Whoever *has* long entertained one of these befooling fixed ideas must know not only their tormenting force but their fascination: for as Swedenborg so profoundly observed, "The objects flowed from the representations and not the representations from the objects."[2] The slave of habit feels the truth of that, and still remains a slave.

It is in perceiving how very much we all make the world we see that deepest disquiet arises as to the reality of anything. Amiel felt this when writing in his *Journal Intime*:[3] "We produce our own spiritual world, our monsters, our chimeras, and our angels; that which ferments within us we make objective. All is a marvel for the poet, all divine for the saint; all is great for the hero; all mean, ugly, and bad for the base and sordid soul. The bad man creates a Pandemonium around him; the artist an Olympus; the elect a Paradise, which only each can see. We are all visionaries, and what we see in things is our own souls."

Undeniable; but it is the appropriation of what in the abstract really is, and not—chimeras excepted!—what does not exist. All those states of being are real in the soul,

---

[1] Election, ch. v., par. 25.   [2] Spiritual Diary, vol. iii., No. 3672.
[3] Vol. i. p. 66 ; English translation, vol. i. p. 62.

and with each we can so identify ourselves that we shall be cognisant of no others. This is the tremendous prerogative of man: his will, desire, and imagination bring into animate existence all that corresponds to their quest and, by intensifying their magic influence, blind him to any other. This has been neatly exemplified in a recent publication: " The other evening I looked up and saw over me a black sky. I supposed that the stars were hid. But I was standing under an electric light. When I had walked on and looked up again, the stars came out. There is a man who is living under the light of his one science and it is honest white light. But in it he loses sight of the whole heavens. He needs to go farther on in his life to widen the circle of his experience." . . . " He needs to step out from under his own blinding light in order that he may gain faith's larger vision."[1]

We do all step out from under one light to another as time goes on; yet each generally blinds us in some degree; and our visions change as from time to time our looking-glasses become clearer, or more dim and more warped by distorting modes of thought. Necessarily, too, imagination hungers for new delights: and phantasies—a more ephemeral brood by far—shift from year to year. We all prove in turn that "the universe is an infinite series of planes; each of which is a false bottom; and, when we think our feet are planted now at last on adamant, the slide is drawn out from under us."[2] How sharply and suddenly sometimes! and what a heart-sickening process it is!

Sooner or later every looking-glass, which reflects this world's images only, must break, and of the time inevit-

---

[1] Christian Facts and Forces, by Newman Smyth, 1887, pp. 102, 103; 1888, pp. 62, 63.
[2] Emerson, *The Preacher. Works*, Riverside edition, 1884, vol. x. p. 217.

able when this befalls Böhme has such words that he must be quoted again :—

"Outward Reason supposeth when the outward eyes seeth a thing, *that is all*, there is no other seeing more; indeed, it is bad enough when the poor soul borroweth the outward looking-glass, and must make shift to help itself only with that; but where will its seeing be when the outward looking-glass breaketh; wherewith will it then see? . . . It can see no other where. Therefore it often cometh to pass that when the poor captive soul descrieth itself in the inward root, and thinketh what will follow when the outward looking-glass breaketh, that it is horribly terrified and casteth the body into anguish and doubting. For it can nowhere discover where its eternal rest should be; but it findeth that it is in itself in mere unquietness, moreover in darkness; and hath the outward looking-glass only as it were borrowed."[1]

He calls it borrowed because it was not that for which man was born; he was imagined by God into existence in the world of Light, and brought himself by his own imaginations into a nature which—until eternal light is generated in its soulish fire—is wrath and darkness. Nor can the soul of man embody itself in any lasting substance till it brings its *desire* into light, and *wills* to be reborn.

"In which world now it uniteth itself and giveth up itself, from the same *it getteth substance in its imagination*,"[2] and "out of the light the *right* or true substantiality exists, for it is a fulfilling or satiating of the will."[3]

---

[1] Great Six Points, Point V., ch. vii., pars. 21, 23.
[2] Ibid., par. 29.
[3] Forty Questions (1665), Ques. 1, par. 278.

The *reason* of this may be better apprehended when the genealogy of water—principle of all corporeity—is remembered. From fire comes light, air from light, water from air; and from the quality of the fuel of the fire from which light proceeds depends the quality of resultant

I wish every reader of this paper could have access to the context of the words just quoted from Böhme's *Great Six Points*. It is too long to give here, but at pars. 38 and 39 a solution is offered to the all-concerning problem, How, with debased desires and a perverted will, is any soul to lift itself to higher imaginings? and that must not be omitted. It can

"*often not know itself;* it becometh oftentimes overwhelmed with the fierce wrath of evil and malignity; so that it is as if it were quite perished; and it were also perished if the *Looking-glass of the Deity* did not stand presented to it, wherein the spirit of the poor captive soul may draw breath and recover itself, and generate therein again. For, in the looking-glass of the light-world standeth the incarnation of Jesus Christ presented to the soul's spirit; and the Word that became man standeth in the *sound*, and is stirring;[1] the soul's spirit CAN *therein* draw breath or recover itself and anew generate itself, else it were often past help."

It is here that the wisdom of the Father of Spirits comes into very striking contrast with the unwisdom of His child—in the modern thinker who declares an historic Christ to be too limited a conception for operative influence on the whole race. For when our philosophers cease to deny the possibility of Divine incarnation (Eastern Theosophy having lamed *that* cavil), they still question the probability of such an event on these two counts; first, that under such narrow limits of time and

---

substance. There was profound spiritual *fact*, not only a figure of it, given to us by The Light of the World when He offers the waters of everlasting life to the soul of man. Till *that* Light is kindled *there* its thirst is never quenched.

[1] That sentence, "standeth in the *sound* and is stirring," is one of the insoluble little lumps of meaningless emphasis which seems to darken the whole context. It admits of very instructive explanation, which I hope to produce in a following attempt.

place a creaturely manifestation of God must be inefficacious, and, secondly, superfluous, because, teaching being the main thing for amendment of a fallen race, a higher standard of ethics was all that was needed for its uplift. It is their assumption; but no teaching and no abstract ideal of virtue has ever told on human imagination with any constraining force. The life of the Saviour did—His enemies themselves being witnesses. It does still, as everyone knows who has become a "new creature," who has won to a spiritual life which has joy, hope, and ambition quite independent of all that death ends. In the chaotic confusions of a self-pleasing heart, the shadows of happiness which flutter past, and the ever-broken and ever-renewed images of pleasure that occupy for a while and sooner or later mortify—all produce weariness, often ending in despair. In such states a soul truly does *not* know itself; at one time it feels somewhat good, at another hard as iron, almost diabolical; and to give it an imagination of what it ought to be and could be, and must be if it is to find rest, is a boon of unspeakable worth; because an ideal of this sort is as essential to re-birth as some little point is for fluids to crystallize around if they are to form themselves into right angles. From Jacob's days and onwards, an image which strongly seizes on the imagination always causes an attempt in some measure to reproduce it, as surely as an echo gives back sound and still water the outlines of a figure raised above it. Till Jesus came to mankind in the flesh there was no picture of Divine love and tenderness in the human imagination. He brought that, as well as the *undivided* tinctures of fire and light, into the soul of our race. Who will dare to say that these two saving gifts were, as regards Time, simultaneously bestowed? When we talk of tincturing material things we often refer to a very slow process, and I suppose that the human soul began to be thus tinctured when

Eve received the promise of victorious seed. When the Christ came ("*in His creature*," says Böhme, "*He is a man*") we must believe that the transmuting process had gone far enough for the *basis* of regenerative life to be evolved: the *substance* bought by the Holy One was then ready for the light of the risen sun of righteousness to quicken into organic existence. This light permeating one's life from within, as it ever does, intensified the prenatal throes of eternal life, and in that anguish man was born again. Suffering is inevitable, if supreme bliss is to be known, for there must be a solution of all an evil will has framed into the "substance of its phantasy" before the image of God, Christ *in us*, can begin to renew itself in the soul. With his usual accuracy of similitudes, Böhme represents this when saying that a soul which imagines according to the dark world's property

"loseth God's looking-glass: it becometh filled with dark, fierce wrath; as a man mixeth water with earth, and then the sun cannot shine in it, and that very water loseth the sun's looking-glass, and the water must again sink down from the earth, else it never becometh a looking-glass of the sun any more, but is captivated in the fierce, wrathful earth. Thus it goeth also with the human life; while it imagineth after or according to God's Spirit, so it conceiveth or receiveth God's power and light, and apprehendeth God; but when it imagineth after or according to earthliness and the dark world's property, then it receiveth the essence of the earthliness and dark world, and filleth itself with the same. And then is the life's looking-glass shut up in darkness, and loseth the looking-glass of the Deity, and must be born anew."[1]

Now when the crisis of true conversion comes—be it slow or sudden—a leaping-up of spiritual light seems to

[1] Great Six Points, Point IV., ch. vi., pars. 24-27.

shatter the compressed rubbish of our vain desires, and to purify the soul's vision from the foul dust of earthly-mindedness; but the *will* to convert must precede contrition, and the will to forsake sin is not always at our command: hence the mercy of a body, the soul's outward looking-glass; on this the weakest will can exercise some control; it can forbid itself both word and deed, and so doing, little by little it gathers strength, and the imagination is purified; and as its turbid products subside, the example of the Holy One of God can shine in it once more. Then we begin to be able to fix thought upon that example by "such a strong importunate imagination of faith"[1] that the soul "*bringeth its magnetic hunger into God's love,* and the soul then attracteth Divine substance, namely, the essential wisdom of God."[2]

That I may make more clear the difference in effect between this process and that of any amount of philosophical thought or ethical belief, I will cite the other greatest seer on record, who, never having read any of Böhme's works, exactly agrees with him in many vital points.

"The love which is of the will cannot be raised in the same manner as the wisdom which is of the understanding. The love which is of the will is raised only by shunning evils as sins, and then by the goods of charity, which are uses, which the man thenceforth accomplishes from the Lord. Therefore if the love which is of the will is not raised at the same time, the wisdom which is of the understanding, however it may have ascended, *still relapses to its love.*"[3]

This is precisely what happens to those deluded pietists

---

[1] Mysterium Magnum, ch. xxiii., par. 32.

[2] Four Tables of Divine Revelation (1654), Microcosmus. Table of the Three Principles (1661), Microcosmos, par. 6. (*Several Treatises,* 1662).

[3] Swedenborg's *Divine Love and Wisdom,* 1890, par. 258.

whose religion is notional and not a life; and I fear we must one and all know, that our devoutest feelings have wings, used often as swiftly and suddenly as those of birds quitting a branch, and our mundane feelings all the close persistency of earth-worms, which never leave *their* line of action. Human nature is now averted from God, cleaving to the dust. "In God's holiness it cannot take hold; for the will was rent off from that; therefore there must now be a *similitude* wherein the imagination of the human nature may take hold."[1] Now Jesus Christ is that similitude.

[1] Baptism, ch. ii., par. 33.

CREATION BY THE WORD[1]

"Of what the Word is in its power and sound, of that the *Mysterium Magnum* is a substance; it is the eternal substantial Word of God."—*Election*, ch. viii., par. 61.

"But now the human mind resteth not satisfied with this; it inquireth after *Nature*, out of that out of which this world is become generated and All created."—*Incarnation*, Part II., ch. ii., par. 30.

WHEN a learned friend of Böhme's asked him, "How and in what place the soul's seat in man is?" he answered that the soul "is a thing that is without ground, and yet seeketh and maketh ground in itself . . . it goeth forth out of itself and seeketh forward, where then it *maketh* one looking-glass after another till it findeth the first again, viz., the unsearchable limit."[2] He thus gave to the habitual illusions of life a far deeper origin than the senses; and possibly metaphysicians might have got a little beyond their intricate tangle of objective and subjective perception, had they accepted as revelation what Reason alone could never teach, that the soul creates its own objective world; and that thus, in the deeper sense, subject and object are one. This, of course, can only be said unreservedly of a collective soul,—of the soul of man as a whole, emerging fractionally during Time in a World, which the unknown entity, the World Soul, has projected by its imagination and which every soul of human kind shares, and *sees* into, as a consequence

[1] Light, 1888, vol. viii. pp. 268, 292.
[2] Forty Questions (1665), Ques. 11, par. 1.

CREATION BY THE WORD 355

of having at a former epoch imagined itself into the circle of its enchantments, and desired to submit to its spells (I give here what has been gathered from Böhme): for obviously we do not each form the world we are born into, we only form our perception of it, and so far it is true of everyone that "*the surroundings of the spirit are the result of its own state.*" Many years ago it used to perplex me when reading Swedenborg's *Heaven and Hell*[1] how it could be that the scene around every spirit alters as it alters; for one naturally thought—but what happened then to other spirits, if on a sudden proximate objects vanished? I suppose the key to that puzzle is his affirmation that in the world of spirits there is *place* but no *distance*; and failing to help thought into any clearness by such an abstraction, I persuade myself that from the unfailing law of likeness of mind drawing all spirits into societies in that world, there may be such a consensus of imaginations as would keep surroundings in accordance.

This, however, is a side issue, only touched upon because I wished to notice that one great underlying illusion must frame the life of every inhabitant of our world, where externals are *not* plastic to internal or spiritual change. Even in this world I have often been struck with the singular agreement of the vegetable products of different regions with their human natives. Take for one very good instance, the shape of blossom in the *Dielytra Spectabilis* (Fortune's Fumitory) found first in China by Mr Fortune, with its exact resemblance to the pagoda style of Chinese architecture; for another, the Japanese water-lily, which so startlingly recalls the

---

[1] "The things which are without the angels assume an appearance according to those which are within them" (par. 156).

"The exterior things which surround angels correspond to their interiors" (par. 173).

See also *Angelic Wisdom Concerning Divine Love and Wisdom*, Part IV., par. 322.

dragon-like outlines of common Japanese art. With this unauthorized theory in my mind it was pleasant to come across this saying of Mr W. Oxley's: "The surroundings in all worlds and states of existence are always the outbirths or representations of that which is within the organisms of the beings who inhabit them."

As the editor of *Light* has lately observed, delusions and illusions are not two names for the same thing. The first misleads, puts the mind on the wrong track where there is a right one; the second makes that objective which does not actually exist. The worth of these *illusions* must be considered in another paper; their origin and inevitability are the points aimed at in this.

In trying to offer some sort of answer to the question, *How* does the soul which is without ground, *i.e.*, an *abyss*, yet seek and make ground for itself? one must go some little way round to reach the mark, and patient, close attention must be supplied by the reader. For here the pathway of thought is necessarily obscure, and reader and writer must each take a share in the toils of exploration.[1] The Bible words, "He spake, and they were made; He commanded, and they were created," are read year after year without, I venture to say, any least guess of their full meaning. They are naturally taken as a simple assertion of God's omnipotence, as an equivalent to the human authority which secures the "go, and he goeth, do this, and he doeth it," style of obedience. No such meaning of arbitrary power as this remains in the thought of any one long taught by Böhme. He makes us understand that sound has a constructive effect; that it creates forms in what is virtually a plenum of potential spiritual life; and this from the highest supernal regions

---

[1] Those who are so fortunate as to have St Martin's *L'Homme Ministère* either in the original or in translation will find it worth while to read from p. 81 in the first, and 89 in the English copy onward, on this same theme.

of the infinite ether to our grosser air, derived from it by very long descent. We can help ourselves to imagine this by remembering that the musical notes of any stringed instrument can, at a certain distance, form shapes in sand spread on a quite smooth surface. Now the undifferentiated efflux of Deity—the Wisdom—was and is to the outgoing will of God, *i.e.*, the Word, what the sand is to the vibrations of air caused by musical sound. It is, "the one only substance out of which all things are": the atmosphere surrounding Swedenborg's great spiritual Sun, which, by graduated derivation, originates all inferior atmospheres, wherein the creaturely word continues to extend *existences* to the lowest ultimate of life. It is, I suppose, identical with what the instructors of the Baroness von Vay call "God's substantial expression—primeval light"; of which they further say: "Primeval light is just as omnipresent as God, but as God is everywhere present spiritually and unchangeable, so is primeval light in transformations; and as God is infinite, so is His light infinitely expanded. Thus He is not only ever present in relation to all that is in being, by His will and His love, but substantially also through all the transmutations and consolidations of primeval light."[1]

It is in this sense that Böhme speaks of "the substantial power of the great love of God, out of which all things have received their motion and possibility . . . an eternal habitation of the working love of God: a ray or beam of the omnipotent Spirit."[2] And "the spirit of the world, together with the configurations or stars of its science,

[1] Geist, Kraft, Stoff, ch. i., p. 4.
[2] Explanation of the Table of the Three Principles, par. 29.

The same connection between creative sound and vibration of light is beautifully touched upon by Mr Oxley's angel teachers: "The Father God works everything under the form of light; and the form of sound working under the form of light is one of the greater Divine activities."—*Angelic Revelations*, vol. i. p. 62.

and with the subtle body of the fire, the water, the air, and with its fixedness of the earth, and whatsoever is therein contained, all this now is the outspoken life and substance out of the inward eternal mystery, viz., *out of the inward substantial word of God*, which eternal word of God in the inward ground dwelleth and worketh in the holy power, and with the beginning of this world hath, through the inward mystery, outspoken itself into an outward mystery; and out of that is the whole creation of the outward world proceeded."[1] (*N.B.*—By the beginning of this world Böhme did *not* mean the beginning described in *Genesis*.)

Though modern expositions of Eastern Theosophy are all I know of it, even that smattering of knowledge convinces me that Böhme's "wisdom" is identical with the *Mulaprakriti* of Buddhistic lore and its *Prakriti* with what he calls "the outward mysterium of the formed word"[2] out of which "the whole creation of the outward world proceeded," in contradistinction to "the inward eternal mystery," a distinction most important to bear in mind, involving nothing less than the difference of individuality and personality (as I suppose), for when speaking of the influence of the spirit of the world, through the stars, on man, as to temperament and character, he is careful to tell of influences far earlier than these; thus "the inward property or disposition of the soul lieth now in the first created configuration of the stars, *in the eternal commencing ground*, that is not co-imaged or framed together in the outward bestial constellation or configuration of the stars."[3] In Mr P. Sreenevas

[1] Election, ch. viii., pars. 70-72. [2] Ibid., par. 73.
[3] Ibid., par. 121.

If any one would carefully read the Sixth of Böhme's *Epistles* (1649 ed.), the second and fourth chapters of his treatise on *Election*, and, if that rarest of his works can be got, his treatise on *Divine Vision*, I believe the process of creation, and all the series of involutions necessarily preceding the evolutions of nature, would become so far apprehensible that such a reader

Row's "Annotations" on *Light on the Path*[1] the same distinction is drawn as to the "unmanifested and undifferentiated condition technically called Mulaprakriti," "root matter or principle, and its particles in the latent germ ... have had no beginning and will have no end. ... Secondly, the manifested and differentiated condition which is not eternal, since its manifestation has had a beginning and will have an end. It is in this second condition that Prakriti forms the material cause of the universe and man."[2] It is in this lower plane of Divine efflux that the human will has its creative fiat; and not *only* the human will; for Böhme shews convincingly that the creation we see is all due to the *life* proceeding from the God of gods, manifested, perverted, or in some way or other deeply disguised by the will of *all* creatures themselves *naturing*, coming to be, while forming external existences, "re-outspeaking" their own self-life. Only thus is the marvel of good and evil combined made at all intelligible. "It is herein rightly understood, how the *inward* spiritual ground of *all* substances originally ariseth from the divine power, and how all *bodies* of the visible or palpable substance originally arise from the *desire* of nature."[3]

Accepting, unreservedly, the dogma of one of the keenest thinkers of recent times that "the material could never commit the gross blunder of crediting the High and Holy One with the creation of our world as we see it. As wisely might we complain of our sun's light making the clumsy shadows which so roughly correspond to objects around us. The sunlight does indeed make possible their projection, but the dense medium through which it shines and the impossibility of translucence where it is resisted—not the sun—causes all the dark shadows on our earth.

[1] By Mabel Collins.
[2] Theosophist, vol. vii. p. 53.
[3] Divine Vision, ch. i., par. 44.

(Will no one use twenty pounds, or less, in having a reprint made of this small but pricelessly valuable treatise? one of the most rare of all Böhme's writings.)

universe is a body of spirits,"[1] and Böhme's that "the magnetical attraction is the beginning of nature,"[2] we may begin to perceive *how* the fiat of the human soul—the desire "in the fiery essence of the soul figureth an image for the soul according to its imagination in the will."[3] Not unlike the method we must all have noticed among our embodied associates. A strong will attracts weaker wills to its own line of thought and action, as irresistibly as a strong current of air draws in its undetermined eddies. Let us admit that all spirits have something we can only describe as properties, and then "these properties constellate themselves now also into a figure, after their kind, wherewith the soul figureth itself either into an image or disposition of an angel or of a devil."[4]

"We affirm," said one of Mr Oxley's invisible teachers, "that no atom that hath commenced the outward journey to ultimate itself upon your earth, ever travels alone, but always meets with an innumerable number of atoms who attach themselves to the atoms thus coming forth, and by this action that atom becomes so condensed as to be able to enter upon the physical body. In the physical state you yourselves can bear testimony that even in that state there are always a certain number of atoms who attach themselves to a certain individual form of life, and this is only a symbol upon your earth of that which has transpired within; for when the angels speak of the numbers which form or compose the one, we speak of all the atoms it hath drawn to itself, for it could no more remove itself from the atoms that have been thus attracted to it than could an individual remove the material sun which shines in your outer universe."[5]

[1] James Hinton.   [2] Election, ch. ii., par. 41.
[3] Forty Questions (1665), Appen., par. 29.
[4] Election, ch. viii., par. 125.
[5] Angelic Revelations, vol. iii. p. 337.

Thus do these same authorities (whom I am persuaded the incoming generation will receive as such) explain the fact now increasingly recognized that "the human organism is a collection of spirits drawn together by the Divine Spirit."[1]

Now the outspoken ray of Divine light, sent forth by the will of the Supreme Unity, is—through however many mediates—that attractive, magnetic, divine spirit in man—the higher self, as I suppose, about which we read so much at present.

I please myself with an additional guess of my own, that the more or less of magnetic force in this central ray, this dominant constructive ego, is the cause of strong or weak constitutions, which have been a puzzle to me for tens of years, because the strongest are often found in connection with weakest health. Doctors might be able to tell us, if their attention could be drawn to such a theory, whether with good and strong constitutions, great firmness of purpose and persistency of will are not normally combined. Such wills have force both to attract and bind a host of weaker wills into glad subordination, and may yet be adverse to common physical well-being.

The idea of an expressed will, by its magnetic desire and consequent intensity of imagination, drawing together spiritual adherents, and thus forming its own organic body—for "the soul is the workman and framer of the body"—would not be at all foreign to our thought, if once this great truth, announced by Böhme in the following words, had been accepted, and applied to problems otherwise insoluble:— "Whatsoever can be thought to have a being anywhere in the creature, the same is likewise without the creature everywhere: for the creature is nothing else but an image and figure of

[1] Angelic Revelations, vol. iii. p. 325.

the separable and various power and virtue of the Universal Being."[1]

In his interesting work on *Primitive Mind Cure*, Mr Evans has given us something of the same teaching with great lucidity. "The cosmic matter, the primal stuff of which all things are made, and which is recognized in science as the universal Ether, and which is the same everywhere and in all things in the universe, is without form or quality. It is the original chaos. It only receives form and quality from ideas which are in mind only. Hence it is that mind shapes matter, and gives it all its properties."[2]

[1] Clavis, par. 96.
[2] Page 143.

I do not suppose that Böhme was the first to say this because to me he was the first; and when I call Mr Evans's *something* of the same teaching it is because I doubt whether Böhme would allow that anything in the Universe can be without form or quality. Swedenborg forbids the thought that one can be apart from the other, whereas Mr Evans seems to take for granted that what is unmanifest in dispersion is therefore homogeneous, and that forces which are negative in relation to one will and desire, are never positive with regard to others (an error which I suspect lies at the root of some of our modern theories about mind-cure of bodily ailments). Being as usual unable to justify this belief by any "well-reasoned" arguments, I call in Oken for its sponsor solely because one cannot refer to Böhme's doctrine of the seven forms of Eternal Nature in a footnote. "A chaos has never existed," Oken wrote with the unreserved dogmatism that charms a plastic mind. "The general never exists, but only the particular. Chaos was from eternity a multiplicity of ætherial globes" (*Elements of Physiophilosophy*, p. 40). And again : "There cannot be an atom that was not crystallized, not arranged according to central and polar forces" (*Ibid.*, p. 94) in the terrestrial world. So I venture to think there could not have been any "original chaos" ready to receive form and quality from ideas which are in mind only. There *was* a perfect harmony of qualities, but now human thought falls into an abyss of spiritual beings of what grade I know not—as eager to follow the magnetic line of man's will as the countless midges of summer evenings to crowd into a shaft of sunlight piercing shade. We are told that these hosts of subservients are elementals ; but I suspect that there is another host, also, disbanded at every dissolution of a human being's mortal life ; and such, having been polarized once, must have strong tendencies.

CREATION BY THE WORD

And as the "life principle," of which Madame von Vay's teachers say so much, pervades every sphere, it is certain that spirit *creates*, not only in earths, but in all regions of every plane. "Wherefore when affections and cupidities, which in themselves are spiritual, meet homogeneous or corresponding things in earths, a spiritual is present which gives a soul, and a material which gives a body. Moreover, in every spiritual thing there lies an effort to clothe itself with a body."[1]

Now a thought *is* a spiritual thing (as Mr Prentice Mulford has reiterated to his readers with sustained emphasis), and Mr F. Hartmann has very neatly described their creative magic. "Forms are isolated and materialized thoughts; if you can hold on to a thought and isolate it from others, you call into existence a form."[2] Precisely what desire does: it isolates and holds fast an imagination of want. "The own will is a ground of its selfhood, and shutteth itself in as a desirous will, whence the magnetic impression hath taken its original."[3] And so nature begins, and all its developing *comings to be*. "Each Ens of the forth-breathed word hath a free will again to breathe forth out of its own Ens a likeness according to itself."[4] For "our soul, before the beginning of the human soul's creature, was an *Ens* of the Word of God *in the Word*."[5] Therefore "man beareth the word, which created heaven and earth in his *Ens*,"[6] and every property in man "maketh unto itself a subject or object by its own effluence."[7] "Thus we understand herein the substance of all substances, that it is a magic substance, where

---

[1] Angelic Wisdom Concerning Divine Love and Divine Wisdom, Part IV., par. 343.
[2] Magic, White and Black, 1886, p. 66 ; 1888, p. 115.
[3] Divine Vision, ch. i., par. 38.
[4] Mysterium Magnum, ch. xxii., par. 24.   [5] Ibid., ch. lvi., par. 23.
[6] Ibid., ch. xxii., par. 36.   [7] Clavis, par. 123.

a will can create itself into an essential life, and so pass into a birth, and in the Great Mystery awaken a source which was not manifested before," . . . "and thus also apprehend whence all things, evil and good, exist, viz., from the *imagination* in the Great Mystery, where a wonderful essential life generateth itself. As we have a sufficient instance to apprehend it by, in the creatures of this world; viz., where the *divine* life hath once moved or awakened the *nature*-life; how the same hath generated such wonderful creatures out of the essential mystery, whereby then is understood how every essence is come to be a mystery, that is, to a life."[1]

Now, I hope that all the foregoing quotations from Böhme may bring some other minds to the rest I have found in consequent belief, that the effluence made by each property is the light proceeding from the soul's fire; that in the minutest area of soulish life that light is an exact equivalent to the Wisdom for Deific will (*i.e.*, "a passive substance of divine operation"), and that the light outflowing from our human will is the substance in which our desirous imagination has its own *fiats*, and creates. That such a sphere exists is proved. Asserted by Swedenborg, it is reported afresh by Mr F. Hartmann. "It has been often given me," said the first, "to perceive that there is such a sphere around an angel and a spirit." . . . "That the same thing obtains in the natural world is known from the experience of many of the learned; and that a wave of effluvia is continually flowing forth out of man, also out of every animal, and likewise out of tree, fruit, shrub, flower, and even out of metal and stone. The natural world gets this from the spiritual world, and the spiritual world from the Divine."[2] And Mr Hartmann says:

[1] Earthly and Heavenly Mystery, Text V., pars. 37-39.
[2] Angelic Wisdom Concerning the Divine Love and Divine Wisdom, Part IV., pars. 292, 293 (Dr J. J. Garth Wilkinson's edition).

"Visible man is, so to say, the kernel of the invisible man; the sphere of his mind surrounds him on all sides like an invisible pulp, blending with universal man and extending far into space, and he can become conscious of the objects existing within that sphere if he recognizes his relation to them. This invisible and ethereal 'pulp' is as essential to constitute a man as the pulp around a peach is essential to constitute a peach, but material science knows only the kernel, and nothing about the pulp."[1]

Our divinity (so called) is unfortunately as ignorant; it continues most wisely to exhort to control and purification of thought, as bearing upon our social life; had it been competent to reveal the awful outcome of even tacit thoughts and desires in a *creation* which *every* human soul brings into existence, surely its warnings had not been quite so ineffective!

It is the endless reproductiveness of the forces we produce so unconsciously that appals one on reflection. But this is when we think of our too common abuse of power. If our desires project into that magical circumference which is the realm of each human will, imaginations of self-advancement, self-indulgence and the like, we reproduce a worse and weaker caricature—even than ourselves—of what each was destined to be—the image and likeness of God. But if our imaginations seize on the characteristics of the perfect man, and our desire to secure them for our own maintains the force of its *fiat*; then do we literally enlarge the glory of God; acting, and speaking, and feeling so as to shew forth that glory. "Doing all to the glory of God" in a less vague and often less-deceiving sense than that which is ordinarily urged upon us, as if the Lord of Life could gain what we understand by glory from the conduct of any number of creatures! What is the glory of God but the reflected

[1] Magic, White and Black, 1886, p. 122; 1888, p. 184.

shadow of God? In calling the effulgence of any fire its glory, be it the glory of the sun of our world, or of the one Being from whom all that is proceeds, we unconsciously speak of that which not only shines and makes manifest, but which *substantiates* the products of fire—these again evolving *their* proportionate glory, their light, air, water, and *substance*—and thus, "as in every will of every essence, there is again a centre of a whole substance."[1] The creaturely will wholly given up to God's will, enlarges the substantial glory of the First Creator. I once believed that I had thought this out for myself, but of course Böhme had anticipated the idea: "God so highly glorified him as His own propriety, or, *as the soul is glorified in the body.*"[2] Fabre D'Olivet, in his *Cosmogonie de Moyse*, recognizes it; translating verse 20, *Genesis* ii., he renders it thus: "An auxiliary mate as a reflected light of him"[3]; (D'Olivet's translation being literal from what he called "La langue Hébraïque restituée"). On so obscure a theme every agreeing note has, I think, its value; this has encouraged me while weaving my network of quotations, from writings not easy of access to all students. With this web I have hoped to catch those films of suggestive thought, which in dispersion float away unheeded. An hypothesis, however crude, may serve to keep them together for further consideration; and, because there is a blessing upon all honest effort, I trust that clearer light may be thrown upon them by the unseen Helper who guides into all truth. Lest I should have confused complex ideas, by attempts to disentangle them, three more passages from Böhme are added as a summary. These are clear enough, and may perhaps remain in remembrance.

[1] Forty Questions (1665), Ques. 1, par. 115.
[2] Aurora, ch. xii., par. 125.
[3] *Glory* of the man is used in the same sense, 1 Cor. ii. 7.

"The desire is that by which God said *Let there be*. The desire is that fiat which hath made something where nothing was, but only a spirit. It hath made the Mysterium Magnum, which is spiritual, visible, and substantial." [1]

"Man is weak and ignorant, and can do little by his own power, yet he hath the imagination, and the choosing, or the free yielding to a thing, where then the maker is ready before hand, which maketh him to be according as his lust or desire is." [2]

How can that be, seeing that he has fallen in his own kingdom, and made himself subject to Spiritus Mundi? Thus:

"The mind is the god and creator of the will, *that* is free from the Eternal Nature, and, therefore, what it generateth to itself, that it hath." [3]

[This contribution to *Light* was finished before "Nizida's" very admirable paper on *Elementals* appeared in its issue for May 12th, and I had thus the satisfaction of finding some coincidence of her thought with mine; I value it much.]

[1] Clavis, par. 75. [2] Three Principles, ch. xx., par. 75.
[3] Ibid., ch. x., par. 49.

IMAGINATION AND PHANTASY [1]

I

"It matters not what our wills and imaginations are employed about; wherever they fall and love to dwell, there they kindle a fire, and that becomes the flame of life, to which everything else appears as dead. . . . That which concerns us therefore is only to see with what materials our prevailing fire of life is kindled."—W. Law's *Appeal to all that Doubt*, 1762, pp. 307–309; 1893, pp. 198, 199.

WHILE writing on these subjects I am aware that my treatment of them is as insufficient as the babble of a child, and that where I seem to myself to think clearly on the surface of depths unsearchable, that clearness is probably more due to ignorance than to knowledge. Minds scantily furnished with *received* ideas, and saturated with the less restrictive teaching of intuitional seers, are prone thus to presume. But what still emboldens me to do what I can with their dicta is the conviction that tentative outlines of thought, if but firmly and clearly presented, may serve as skeleton maps serve in the school-room. They do not pretend to suffice; they only make ready a frame for larger knowledge to fill up.

Böhme and Swedenborg agree in reprobating Phantasy. The first assigns to the arch rebel "the kingdom of phantasy," because, breaking the harmony of the seven spirits of God's Eternal *Nature* (I italicize the word as a reminder that they cause an eternal *coming to be* in ceaseless interaction), he "introduced the eternal will out of the temperature into division, viz., into the

[1] *Light*, 1889, vol. ix. pp. 56, 75.

disharmony of the phantasy; which phantasy instantly seized upon him, and therein brought him into an unquenchable cold and hot fire-source, into the opposition and contrariety of the forms and dispositions.[1] For the wrath of the Eternal Nature, which is called God's *anger*, manifested itself in them" [notice the plural pronoun; all those *forms* became creaturely] "and brought their will into the phantasy; and therein they still live, and can now do nothing but what the property of the phantasy is, viz., practise foolery, shows, tricks, metamorphose themselves, destroy and break things; also elevate themselves in the might of the cold and hot fire, frame and will in themselves to go forth above the hierarchies of God, viz., the holy angels."[2]

In another of his works Böhme credits these slaves of phantasy with originating the changeful fashions of dress that so often disfigure womankind, and indeed there has been much of late in the monstrous projections and elevations of its style to make one ready to believe it.

To sum up all, the self-will of the creature "set the phantasy in the place of God, and then the Holy Spirit departed from its nature, and now it is a spirit in its own self-will, and is *captivated* in the phantasy as we perceive in Adam. Now when the root of the soul, through the devil's inspiration or infection, elevated itself, then the Holy Spirit departed into his own

[1] "Consider, there are *two sorts of fire*, a hot and a cold" (*Threefold Life*, ch. viii., par. 41). "According to the dark impression a *cold fire* and a false light arising through the imagination of the harsh impression, which light hath no true ground. The *hot fire* hath a fundamental light arising from the original of the *divine will*, which doth also bring itself forth in nature through the fire into the light" (*Epistles* (1649), Ep. 6, pars. 29, 30).

This is Böhme's own account of the *two fires*, so unintelligible to me that sometimes I have thought, does he thus indicate what we call negative and positive electricity?

[2] Election, ch. iv., pars. 72-74.

principle, and so Adam became weak in the image of God, viz., in the temperature; and could not in the similitude, magically *bring forth* his like out of himself."[1]

(Swedenborg's definition of *image as the spiritual, and likeness as the celestial,* representative of God, is worth remembering here.)

In these two passages the most important doctrines of Böhme are comprised, and the essential difference of phantasy and true imagination implicit. Man was destined, in the kingdom of a great dethroned angel, to generate a race manifesting God, as His delegate and representative. The *phantasy* to which he became subject is but *a "theatric play of the geniture,"*[2] because it can never evolve light and heavenly substance without which God cannot be revealed to the creature. The "phantasy only imageth or formeth *itself*; and now that phantasy receiveth nothing into itself but only a similitude or thing like itself; and that likeness is the power of its life. If anything else did come into it, then the phantasy must cease and vanish, and then would that vanish with it, out of which it is generated, viz., nature; and if nature did cease and vanish away, then the *Word* of the Divine power would not be speaking or manifest, and God would remain hidden."[3]

There is given to reflective thought the cause of the *necessity* of the Redeemer of our race coming to it in a similitude—in the disguise of our phantastically monstered human nature. Had He come to our world even in its pristine glory, the consuming fire of His Divine love would have destroyed the object of salvation. But the Word was made flesh, and "re-out" spoke everlasting love, in the flesh, dwelling among us

---

[1] Election, ch. vi., pars. 93, 94.   [2] Ibid., ch. iv., par. 111.
[3] Ibid., pars. 121, 122.

amid the phantasies of earthly life, till the *imagination* of man was once more quickened in "the looking-glass" of Deity.

"The new fountain of Divine love and unity hath, with its outflowing in Christ, incorporated itself into the *true* life of the three principles of the human property, and is entered into the imaginary thoughts, into the natural, creaturely, apostated, image-like will of the life and assumed humanity; and broken the selfhood and own self-willing with the inflowing of the sole and only love of God, with the eternal one, and inclined or turned in the will of the life again into the *Temperature*: where then the devil's introduced will became destroyed, and the painfulness of the life became brought into the true rest."[1]

Throughout his *Spiritual Diary* Swedenborg tells of phantasy in various aspects—as a means of discipline carried on by divine wisdom through the permitted agency of "castigating spirits" often cruel in their mode of inflicting torture. And "the cruelty of the infernals can never be described; they act from phantasies in a most cruel manner against others, upon whom they practise such cruelties that if they were described they would cause horror." . . . "For such is the power of phantasies among souls that they can induce, as it were, a bodily sensation, and thus excruciating pains."[2] "It is wonderful that souls and spirits have sense (or sensation) altogether as in the body—thus they have the sense of touch, as when they touch their garments. In like manner as to cupidities and appetites, heat, cold, yea perspirations, which are as actual as in the body; when, nevertheless, they cannot be otherwise called than phantasies; but inasmuch as the sense is real, such as it is in the body, they are, as it were, real sensations. These and similar things are induced upon spirits by an

[1] Divine Vision, ch. ii., par. 14.   [2] Vol. i., No. 374.

imaginative direction."[1] "Unless the Lord should take away their phantasies, their corporeal things thus remaining in their minds, they would be tormented with much severer anguish than in their bodies; for evil spirits and the diabolic crew not only have such phantasies, but they inflict the like upon the minds of those whom they torment, which, unless the Lord took away and moderated, they would have a hell vastly more excruciating than would ever be possible from their *bodies* being held in the suffering of the most intense anguish."[2]

Our recently acquired knowledge of hypnotic experiments should enable us to believe this. By bending, or removing phantasies, Swedenborg tells us in the same book, gradual reformation in vicious spirits is effected, for with his usual sagacity he sees these phantasies to be so much a constituent of man's present nature on either side of death, that it would not be safe to remove them suddenly.

"At the present time," he wrote in 1747, "when there is no faith, and when scarcely any one can be prepared for Heaven in the earth-life" [*he* says, *other* life, referring to this from a transmundane position], "because they are in an inverted order of life, there is nothing but mere phantasies or hallucinations of the senses, which remain in souls, or in their natural mind, or animus, in which the life of the man living at the present time chiefly consists. This natural mind, full of so many phantasies, is not broken, that is, its phantasies cannot at once be shaken off and extinguished; for in this case the man himself would be broken down, and nothing as to his sensitive life would remain; for this life is composed of mere phantasies—a fact which from many things is so evident that no doubt can be entertained on

---

[1] Spiritual Diary, vol. i., No. 364. See also No. 376.
[2] Ibid., vol. ii., No. 1720.

the subject. There is an insanity in all things which compose and govern the life of man."[1]

Indirect confirmation of that saying, "phantasies cannot at once be shaken off, for in this case the man himself would be broken down," seems to me to have been given by the fact which Sir A. Helps noticed some thirty years ago in the *Spanish Conquests in America*, that "native tribes die out so soon as their ideas are conquered." Assuredly whenever habitual belief is sapped by misgivings the whole inner man is weakened and a state of nervous collapse results, which must injure bodily health.

II

"The deep sea of love is a leaven of fire, which shall break the adamantine nature in the man of sin, in both worlds; for it spreads itself over all worlds and reduces everything into the pure being and nature of God. Such is the true nature and property of Love."—JANE LEAD.

"Christ, the inbreathed Word, Who only can reach the soul's original ground, being the creating *Fiat*, can alone make all new again."—JANE LEAD.

Swedenborg seems to have noticed the surface similarity and intrinsic difference of phantasy and imagination, for in his *Spiritual Diary* we find, "I spoke with spirits concerning phantasies, yea, with those who supposed that they were wholly corporeal men, although they knew they were spirits" . . . "it was granted to tell him that hence may be known what is phantasy, and that man seems to live from himself, and yet it is such a phantasy, and that it is not wonderful that there exists phantasies of this sort concerning the body and corporeal things, so long as that phantasy of living in or from himself remains. Afterwards we spoke concerning angelic representations, that still they are not, although they appear. Concerning which it was granted to say, that such things are imaginations, or repre-

[1] *Spiritual Diary*, vol. i., No. 426.

sentative imaginations, signifying celestial and spiritual truths, and are thus exhibited to angels and angelic spirits. Wherefore, they are not phantasies, for they feel them and are intimately delighted by them. Such delight and felicity cannot come from any other source than from the truths of faith which are therein."[1]

And of *useful* phantasies he tells valuable truth in this other entry. "Spirits seem to themselves to dwell in houses and bed-chambers, and these indeed well furnished with utensils of every kind, and also with indefinite variety according to each one's inclinations; thus because initiated into the like, during the life of the body, they also retain after life, and desire similar things; thus the like are granted them with indefinite variety according to each one's genius, and thus they are bent to good, for they arrange those things according to use which the Lord disposes, and at the same time the use introduces quiet and innocence in their minds. Thus also peace and innocence are insinuated."[2] . . . "They do not stand in want of all these things in the other life; wherefore such a cupidity is false; but to receive such things as have been mentioned, from the Lord, and to arrange these according to use in tranquillity and innocence, this is the chiefest reality, because it conduces to their felicity. *Such imaginations so-called are real, because they have real things in themselves.*"[3]

(This is a lesson which many a discontented heart might profit by, before carrying its poison into the world of spirits.)

Here we have the vital distinction between phantasy and imagination vividly lit up. Contentment and consequent happiness *are* real, they proceed from facts;

---

[1] Spiritual Diary, vol. ii., Nos. 3172, 3173.
[2] Ibid., No. 2447. See also 2448.
[3] Ibid., No. 2449.
Italics are mine, where the point in question is specially impressed.

such and such pleasant phantasies are received from the Lord and tend to use. Compared with these, a phantasy proper is what the lovely vegetation seen in mirage is to the produce of fertile soil. The first must perish fruitless of all but deceiving and disappointment. It is but a seeming thrown upon barren ground by transient influences,—it is not *generated*. This is the difference emphatically marked in all Böhme says about imagination; so far from confounding it with any delusions he says, "the Magia is the greatest hidden secret, for it is above Nature, and maketh Nature according to the form of its will,"[1] and after a profound analysis of its efficacy in the antecedents of Nature, he gives the key to his frequently asserted problem that "all things arose from Divine imagination" in these few words, "*The Magia is the acting in the will-spirit, or the performance in the spirit of the will.*" . . . "This magic will which yet sticketh *in the desire*, may image itself in the looking-glass of the wisdom how it will, and as it imageth itself in the tincture, so it is comprehended in the Magia and brought into a substance."[2]

Tincture here means the light proceeding from the soul's fire, it is the most mysterious force in nature, and here only this much can be offered to explain it—Böhme's own definition in his *Explanation of the Table of the Three Principles*:—"Tincture is the *separable* word out of which the seven properties"—those of Eternal Nature —"flow forth."[3]

This *separable word*, man's will re-out speaking itself as "a child of the omnipotency," forms into a substance in a surrounding plenum of what St Martin calls "Matières Spiritueuses." "For every imagination desireth only substance in its *likeness* wherein it doth exist,"[4]

[1] Small Six Points, Point V., par. 80.
[2] Ibid., Point V., par. 88, Point VI., par. 89.
[3] Par. 41.   [4] Small Six Points, Point II., par. 21.

and it is by the strength of its desire the *performance*, not the mere project of the will. It is a forcible laying hold of impressions which, without a determinate vigour, would pass away like the shapes of fleeting clouds; and the will must be as steadily fixed, while imagining, as one point of the compass if the other is to trace the desired circle. It is to this central point that Böhme refers when he says, "in every will of every essence there is again a centre of a whole substance."[1]

Now the centre that generates substance must, according to his shewing, be a *fire*: the will, in the last analysis, is the soul's fire, and its light, and consequently the substance produced from light, depends on *what fuel of imagination* that fire is fed by. Let him explain himself here. "The fire of the soul must have the right fuel or wood, if it is to give a *clear*, bright, and powerful light; for from the soul's fire, God's Spirit in its power becometh separable, distinct, and manifest in the nature of the soul; as the light is *manifested* from the fire, and as the air is manifested from the fire and light, and as a subtle dew or vapour goeth forth from the air, which becometh substantial after its going forth, whence the light draweth the power and virtue again into itself for its food" ... "so in like manner can *Christ in Man* not be manifested, though indeed he be in man and draweth and calleth him, also presseth himself into the soul, unless it eat of the fiery Ens into its property ... and then out of the soul's fire, the right *divine* air spirit goeth forth out of the fire and light, and bringeth forth its spiritual water out of itself out of the light, *which becomes substantial*; whereof the power of the light eateth, and in the love desire introduceth itself into a holy substance therein—viz., into a *spiritual* corporeity, wherein the Holy Trinity dwelleth, which *substance* is the true temple

[1] Forty Questions (1665), Ques. 1, par. 115.

of the Holy Spirit."[1] It is difficult for me to stop short in such quotations—so helpful and enlightening is the context; and one sighs to remember how few can ever read it—even of those who fain would. It was in deference to this spiritual corporeity that J. G. Gichtel said when speaking of his contemporaries: "The inner body of virtue is dead; they are but skeletons of men." And it is because the rebel angel and his host fired their imagination with proud desires, and lost the only light that can produce enduring substance—for they have but flashes of unsteady light—that they long to be *creaturely*, to have something like substance for their unquiet souls to exist in. "Our selfhood hath no true *Ens* wherein its light may be *steadfast*; for it createth with its desire not out of the Eternal One, viz., out of God's meekness, but createth itself into substance, its light originateth only in the substance of the selfhood."[2] "Light in all forms is the master," Böhme says elsewhere, "*for it hath the meekness*,"[3] and "meekness maketh substantiality."

How *literally* true this is it is not here the place to shew; his writings will do that—especially in the *Treatise on the Incarnation*, Part I., ch. v., pars. 67 to 72. I can fancy how scientific readers may smile derisively at all this; but perhaps he knew something of science though not of our scientific formulæ. Sir Isaac Newton was glad to borrow from him one of his most valued theories. The general reader, too, would say, of course, what absurdity to suppose that all this goes on when we feel nothing of it. But while so many vital processes of our animal life go on unfelt, it is unreasonable to think that accretions of growth in the immortal body are likely to be perceived. Nevertheless there must be a

[1] Election, ch. viii., pars. 231, 234, 238–240.
[2] Knowledge of All Things, par. 35 (*Several Treatises*, 1662); also *Epistles* (1649), Ep. 6, par. 35.
[3] Incarnation, Part III., ch. v., par. 40.

conscious death of the apostate self-will before the Divine word can re-outspeak itself in the soul. That habitual self-suppression, that resolved dying to sin is now all the human will can do towards the rebirth of the image of God.

The practical issues of these doctrines are momentous. "Every will hath a seeking to do or to desire somewhat, and in that it beholdeth itself, and seeth in itself in the eternity, what itself is; it maketh to itself *the lookingglass* of its like, and then it beholdeth itself what itself is, and so finding nothing but itself, it desireth itself."[1]

If in every world we are liable to find nothing but ourselves, the unspeakable folly of setting our hearts upon *external* goods comes into clearest light. What we *have*, however delighting and desirable, is truly a matter of small importance compared to what we *are*, and if we could but see it, the habits of our mind, our thoughts, wishes, and aspiration are really bills of exchange upon our future lot, be it on this or the other side of bodily dissolution. A trick of being discontented with such things as we have is a flaw in our looking-glass which no change of existence can remove; it is a defect in our own hearts which will come before us wherever we may be till humility and love have been made magical by the "spirit of the will." If we knew all the ramifications of cause and effect in external circumstances, I believe we should discover that they are not only more of a response to secret desires, but a truer reflection of character than we generally suppose—antenatal character, some will say. But short of that length of causation, all might allow it if, besides seeing how character moulds events, we could estimate the impetus given to every turn of events favouring its peculiarities by accomplices unseen. For our wills attract others in the same cupidity. The immediate coalescence of chemical atoms

[1] Forty Questions (1665), Ques. 1, par. 22.

that have affinity one with another may give some notion of how instant and how strongly inviting and intensifying such attraction may be. Every human being is a mighty magnet, and, the will once determined, legionary subject spirits rush into coalition. We were lost if the Love which is the life of the world of light were not as eager to combine with the faintest beginnings of spiritual rebirth: and cruel, though so often an unconscious wrong, is the word or look from a human being which imperils *that* in the soul of another; for "the fiery essence of the soul figureth an image for the soul, according to its imagination in the will."[1] To throw upon the looking-glass of another an evil or dispiriting representation of the soul that there *seeks itself,* is to do much to poison the will, and deface its fair image, so fragile, so unsubstantiated still! Hence the inexpressible importance of fixing imagination on Divine love. "Whereinto a spirit introduces its longing imagination, the essence and property of that it receiveth in the great mystery of all beings."[2]

"Hold fast to love in your imaginations," says Gichtel, with the eagerness of a long-experienced victor over wrath. "Nothing can take it from you but your own imagination: as soon as our imagination goes out of the love, darkness enters the imagination." Merciful heaven, let this be believed! Let it not pass away from the thought as a mere opinion! For as "all things are generated out of imagination, so also the soul shall receive its property in the imagination: and *every imagination reapeth its own work which it hath wrought.*"[3]

[1] Forty Questions (1665), Appendix, par. 29.
[2] Signatura Rerum, ch. xvi., par. 25.   [3] Ibid., ch. xv., par. 41.

ALCHYMISTICAL PHILOSOPHERS [1]

In "K's" article on Mr A. E. Waite's book on *Alchymistical Philosophers* the question is raised whether "the genuine alchemists were in pursuit of worldly wealth or honours," or whether "their real object was the perfection or at least the improvement of man." Böhme's answer to this is very clear and emphatic, as any reader of his *Signatura Rerum* will know; and as he is known to have studied the writings of Paracelsus, and to have had friends of his own deeply versed in alchemical lore, I think his verdict will be worth offering. Had there been time for search I might have found briefer expressions of it; but throughout his many books he speaks on this point unvaryingly to the same effect. All Hermetists will, I believe, allow the writer of the *Suggestive Inquiry into the Hermetic Mystery* is a great authority on this subject; and but a few days ago I chanced to have from her pen this decisive sentence: "*Alchemy is a vital process psychically enacted and proven.*" Writing to a friend "concerning the philosophical work of the *Tincture*," Böhme says that it cannot be effected:—

"Unless a man first become that himself which he seeketh therein, no skill or art availeth; unless one give the tincture into the hands of another he cannot prepare it unless he be certainly in the new birth." [2] "The para-

---
[1] Light, 1889, vol. ix., p. 126.
[2] Epistles (1649), Ep. 23, par. 15. See context also.

disical image" (in man) "which is shut up, and captivated in the wrathful death, in which the Word of the Deity, viz., the Divine Mercury, ruled and wrought, did disappear as the gold is disappeared in Saturn, so that nothing is seen but a contemptible matter, until the right artist sets upon it, and again awakeneth the Mercury in the enclosed gold, and then the dead enclosed body of the gold doth again revive in Saturn, for Mercury is its life, who must be introduced into it again, and then the dead body of the gold appeareth, and overcometh the gross Saturn, wherein it lay shut up, and changeth its mean contemptible old body into a fair, glorious, golden body. Thus likewise it is with man; he lieth now shut up after his fall in a gross, deformed, bestial, dead image; he is not like an angel, much less like unto Paradise; he is as the gross ore in Saturn, wherein the gold is couched and shut up; his paradisical image is in him as if it were not, and it is also not manifest, the outward body is a stinking carcase, while it yet liveth in the poison." . . . "Till the artist who hath made him take him in hand, and bringeth the living Mercury into his gold or paradisical image disappeared and shut up in death" . . . "and a new man ariseth in holiness and righteousness—which liveth before God, appeareth and puts forth its lustre as the hidden gold out of the earthly property: and hereby it is clearly signified to the artist chosen of God how he shall seek; no otherwise than he hath sought and found himself in the property of pure gold; and so likewise is this process and not a whit otherwise, for man and the earth with its secrets lie shut up in the same curse and death, and need one and the same restitution. But we tell the seeker, and sincerely and faithfully warn him as he loveth his temporal and eternal welfare, that he do not first set upon this way to try the earth, and restore that which is shut up in death, unless he himself be before born again through the Divine Mercury out of the curse and death, and have the full knowledge of the Divine regeneration, else all that he doeth is to no purpose, no learning availeth; for that which he seeketh lieth shut in the curse in death. If he will make it alive, and bring it into its first life, then that life must be before manifest in him."[1]

[1] Signatura Rerum, ch. viii., pars. 46-49.

BÖHME AND THE "SECRET DOCTRINE"[1]

PRAY, for the sake of truth, allow room for a few remarks which can be of no interest to any but readers of Böhme and the *Secret Doctrine*. In vol. ii. p. 640,[2] Madame Blavatsky quotes as the Rev. G. Oliver's a passage taken almost *verbatim* from Böhme's *Signatura Rerum*, chap. iv., par. 34, of which, either by ignorance or oversight, the plagiarist has marred the sense wherever he alters the text. Thus, describing the seven constituent men in the individual man, Mr Oliver correctly gives No. 1, "the true, golden, divine man, which is the likeness of God"; and No. 2, "the inward holy body, generated from the fire and light in the tincture," but having, probably, no idea of what *tincture* means there, the adopter of a *seer's* words discreetly leaves the word out, and continues "like pure silver," *omitting* what Böhme added—"*if it were not corrupted.*" No. 3, by a similar omission, he misinterprets, calling it "*the elemental man.*" "The elemental man from the pure element resembling Jupiter" is the original sentence—a very other sort of man than what we should now mean by an elemental man. No. 4 Mr Oliver makes "the mercurial paradisical man," but Böhme said, "the mercurial, which is the growing, or paradisical man," words which I understand as little as Mr Oliver did, apparently; but I can see that

[1] Light, 1889, vol. ix., p. 386.
[2] Third and revised edition, 1893, p. 677.

by the word "*growing*" something was indicated which simply to omit is to leave the other adjective shorn of its full force. By turning No. 5, "the martial from the fire, viz., the soulick man according to the Father's property," into "the martial *soul-like* man," nonsense is substituted for quite intelligible sense. A soul-*like* man, when soul is the factor of *all* creaturely life, however various, is an absurd rendering of the old-fashioned soul*ick* for soul*ish*; one might as well say a psyche-like study when speaking of psychic study! The Father's property is what answers to the origination of the Trinity in man, *i.e.*, the *soul's fire*, from which light—son, and air—spirit, proceed.

If I understand anything in this summary of man's downward steps to material ultimation (much in it I do not), it is at this point that Böhme describes him as coming into touch with Nature on our present earthly plane; for the soul is *not* spirit, but instrumental for its manifestation. At No. 6, he continues, "The venerine man, according to the outward desire, and the water's property." Students of his writings should find no difficulty there, knowing that the desire and will of the *pre-existing* spirit strikes up the soulish fire, and that this by the media of light, air, and water produces "the water's property"—corporeity. But his rash interpreter, not seeing this, was like a puzzled schoolboy deluded by the word "venerine," and taking a leap at *probability*, renders the passage thus, "*the passionate man of desires.*" Again, Böhme's text is "seventhly, the solar man according to the sun's property, viz., according to the outward world, as a seer and knower of the wonders of God; and yet it is but the one only man; yet is both in the inward and outward world." His clerical quoter thought well to improve upon this, and gives it thus, "The solar man, a witness and inspector of the wonders of the Universe." It is quite foreign to the ecclesiastical mind to claim for man any knowledge of Deific life, *though* St Paul, speaking of what the spirit reveals to man, said that *the spirit searcheth all things, yea, the deep things of God.* Böhme did speak of *external* nature as part of the wonders and mysteries of God, but, had any one so mistaken his meaning as to suppose that bore on *outward* nature only, he would surely have replied, "Both suns shine unto us." His teaching as to the great spiritual sun, of which our cosmic sun is but an opened *point*—for manifestation of such light as we can now bear, and conveyance of "virtues" such as both our minds and bodies need—being in precise agreement with Swedenborg's.

Having completed this maimed extract from *Signatura Rerum*, Mr Oliver adds as a gratuity "Theosophers had also seven fountain spirits or powers of Nature." Also— one might as well say, after describing our earth's five continents, there was also a globe! Well may Madame Blavatsky call this a jumbled account, but it is not Böhme that *jumbled* it. The longer his writings are studied the more striking becomes his consistent accuracy even on points where at a first reading he seems to contradict himself. For example, though he has so often said that *body* is derived from *water*, and that the moon corporifies all that it receives from the sun and stars, yet here the *Venerine* man is said to have the water's property. The paradox is explained when, for one among many such passages, we find in his *Mysterium Magnum*[1] "this Venus, being she is mortified to the fire, is submissive and giveth the holy water, which is holy in the spirit, and yet in the substance it is captivated in the wrath" (i.e., *temporal nature*), "where it giveth the material water according to the deadly property." Let the student refer to *Threefold Life*, chap. v., par. 37, and to the first four lines of par. 10, chap. iii., for understanding *how* mortification to the fire maketh substance; and

[1] Ch. xiii., par. 18.

then to chap. ix., par. 103, in the same book, where we read that the moon "affordeth carcase, and all that belongeth thereto, it taketh all to it, and maketh the whole image as a beast; it is the corporeity; Venus congealeth in it."[1] "It is thus that her holy water is captivated in the wrath." Observe that Luna is not named in Böhme's summary of *Man in his Order* because this bestial corporeity, which elsewhere he calls his "Monstrum," is no part of true humanity. But nevertheless for one who is to be a seer and knower of the wonders of God in both the inward and outward worlds, the ancient saying quoted by Madame Blavatsky in the footnote of page 639[2] vol. ii. of *Secret Doctrine*, "*the moon is the mind, and the sun the understanding*" is confirmed by him who said "out of the substance the true intellective spirit primely proceedeth."[3] Without a body for reaction—on any plane of being—there can be no consciousness, the essential of intellect. And that the sun is the understanding he would quite agree who tells us that, "the sun is the king and heart of the deep, and the other six planets make the senses and understanding in the deep,"[4] that "all the stars are the sun's children,"[5] and "every one of them helpeth toward life, and to the revelation of the wonders of God."[6] Fabre D'Olivet, deeply versed in Hebrew, translating the first chapter of *Genesis*, says "it seems evident from the text

[1] In Mr Oxley's *Angelic Revelations*, Purity says (vol. iii. p. 251): "It was within the planet Venus that the pure virgin was clothed upon with an external form." See also as to this, vol. v. p. 20, *Ibid.* The holy corporeity from the meekness of love, is, no doubt, referred to here, but *much* more, which Madame Blavatsky would understand, and I cannot even guess at.
[2] Third and revised edition, 1893, p. 675.
[3] Mysterium Magnum, ch. iv., par. 9.
[4] Threefold Life, ch. vii., par. 77. "The whole deep between the earth and the stars."—*Ibid.*
[5] Ibid., ch. x., par. 17.
[6] Ibid., ch. xi., par. 35.

of Moses that this hieroglyphic writer regarded the celestial bodies as sensible luminaries destined to propagate intellectual light and to awaken it on our earth." Western theosophers are not all blind, nor I trust will astrology be much longer spoken of contemptuously by any but people of weak mind or imperfect culture.

ATMOSPHERES [1]

WHEN I had finished reading the charming article of "G. R. S." on "Atmospheres," I felt ready to say with old Quarles,

"Screw up the heighten'd pegs
Of thy sublime Theorbo four notes higher,"

to the pitch sounded by St Martin on the same key. It may interest readers who have not got his correspondence with Kirchberger to see what they say on this theme: the more so as for many people, either from lack of strength or of money, seeking recuperative atmospheres by change of place is impossible.

"The great question is," Kirchberger wrote, "how can we obtain this heavenly nourishment? And on this important point our friend Böhme is very luminous: he calls the sacred body [corporeity] *Sophia* (*Epistles*, 1649 ed., Ep. 1, par. 40). This Sophia, which is animated by the Holy Spirit, is substantial, without being corporeal like our bodies (*Threefold Life*, ch. v., par. 50). The substantiality comes from the pure element which serves for her envelope (*Ibid.*, par. 53). The pure element is nearest to our world (*Clavis*, par. 169). And I, I believe that the subtile ether is what approaches nearest to the pure element, because it is in the air that the Holy Spirit is hidden, as in His heaven, through the gradation I have just indicated; and this heaven is in our heart (see *Aurora*, ch. xxiii., par. 76)." Böhme's own words *must* be

[1] Light, 1889, vol. ix. p. 528.

inserted to light up the foregoing words, "And here we give the reader (that loveth God) to understand what the pure element is, wherein our body, before the fall of Adam, stood, and in the new regeneration now at present standeth also therein; it is the heavenly corporeity, which is not barely and merely a spirit, wherein the clear Deity dwelleth."[1] "Thus," Kirchberger continued, "every time we breathe with entire abandonment of self, and full trust in the loving kindness of our Divine Master, we receive the sacred body, which is everywhere, and we saturate our hearts with the pure element, in which, and by which alone, we can be born again to a new life. This is a great and important truth, and generally most hidden from man. It is founded, not only on the doctrine of Böhme, but also on experience."

To this St Martin replied: "You said everything, it seems to me, in placing the Holy Spirit in the pure element by means of Sophia. He cannot dwell elsewhere essentially, and what proceeds from Him, in the mixed elements and the ether, is only a ramification of His powers by which everything moves and exists in the universe. Unhappily they are corrupt influences of a very inferior order, that dwell in all these aërial elementary regions, as St Paul tells us. That does not prevent our souls from receiving it essentially from the Holy Spirit, because the soul also has the Sophia, and the element by which the Holy Spirit and we may unite, even without the breathing which belongs to the animal creature."[2]

[1] Three Principles, ch. xxii., par. 19.
[2] Correspondence between Louis Claude de St Martin and Kirchberger, translated and edited by Edward Burton Penny, 1863. Letters 35, 36, pp. 119, 121.

JESUS AND THE CHRIST[1]

THE "question of the Christ" is, as "S. K." says, both "a very delicate one" and "of much difficulty"; too much so to deal with briefly in restricted space; but as I know he cannot easily find the key which opened my mind into great light upon that question, I long for him and other inquirers to have what helped me; and hope you can find room for a few passages from one of Böhme's least accessible works, the *Apologies*. In them alone has he made the inestimable doctrine clear. Swedenborg, as to Jehovah *forming the Divine Humanity*, by taking the human soul (from a human *mother* only), gives precisely the same great truth, but at such length that no quotation from him could adequately give his meaning. This is Böhme's:—

"Jesu, the eternal Sun, shineth forth through the Christ; Jesus is Jehova, that is God; and Christ is the Mediator between God's love and anger. To Christ is *all power given* from Jehova, or Jesus: Jesus hath given the divine power to Christ, not that Christ should bear the power or authority for himself; but God, who is a spirit, He useth the Christ for an instrument, whereby He takes away the power or authority from the anger"—[understand the wrath of God *in man, i.e.*, the *discordant* spirits of Eternal Nature in man's soul].
"According to the humanity he hath a *given* power, and according to the Deity he is the *Giver* Himself. The

[1] Light, 1890, vol. x. p. 48.

man is our humanity; and the *Christ* is the anointed of God, which God hath manifested out of the name Jesus."[1]

"As the sun shineth in the whole outward world, *and impowereth* all and maketh it fruitful; and the world is not the sun, so also the Christ shineth as a revealed sun out of Jehova, or Jesus, in the creaturely humanity of Christ."[2]

In Text I. of the *Third Apology*, from par. 21 to 39, a very valuable summary of the distinction between Jesus the Anointer and Christ the Anointed will be found; and again in the *Third Apology*, Text IV., Point IV., the necessity of the Redeemer having *other* than a "*holy and perfect body*"—in a word, of being creaturely and not super-human in externals—is admirably stated from par. 5 to par. 11. With regard to creaturely limitations of Deific life in the Christ, it will repay any student of Böhme to turn to chapter viii. of Part I. of his treatise on *The Incarnation of Jesus Christ the Son of God*, and read from par. 45 to par. 51.

[1] Third Apology: Concerning Perfection, Text I., pars. 226, 227, and Text IV., Point III., par. 10 (*The Remainder of the Books written by Jacob Behme*. Sparrow, 1662.)
[2] Ibid., par. 13.

UNCONSCIOUS CREATION [1]

I

"We have received before now intimations from the unseen that the emanations of persons may, when of sufficient strength, give rise to separate existences, half spiritual, half material, like ourselves, yet finer, more subtle, less thoroughly manifested."—"G. R. S.," *Light*, November 30, 1889, vol. ix. p. 575.

"Every spirit in its degree must create . . . not another spirit do you thus create, but something which to your outerness may seem but an *idea*, for which you shall suffer, and which you shall enspiritize."—"Psychic Telegrams," No. III., *Light*, vol. ix. p. 572.

For some years past my mind has been warping round to this same belief, solely from deductions made from the significant hints of Böhme and other seers; and I would fain bring my guesses upon this subject into presentable coherence. So before machinery was perfected would the designer of a supposed new fabric long to weave a close, smooth pattern of the stuff he imagined. I have no adequate mental machinery, and only a little time left for throwing down samples of crudely tentative thought before contemporaries: therefore I crave pardon for venturing to offer it. If thus I can but set fast in other minds the various sayings which have served mine, like pegs from which to spin connecting, gossamer lines of hypothesis, they may help as outlines for more able thinkers to fill in and confirm. Of their suggestive worth I cannot doubt. But it will need some ductility of thought and imaginativeness to see where one is apposite to the other,

[1] *Light*, 1890, vol. x. pp. 236, 248.

UNCONSCIOUS CREATION

and unless the reader will kindly *try* to follow the writer's chain of ideas his impatience will be equal to his contempt. The first notion of our *inevitable* creativeness came to me from these words of Böhme: "Therefore there is also such great diversity in the spirits, as there is great diversity in the will of the essences; whereof we have an example and similitude in the will and purpose of our *mind*, out of which do spring so many various *thoughts*, where every thought hath again a centre to a will, that so out of an imagination a substance may be produced." "In such a manner are all spirits created out of the eternal mind."[1] In what manner? By the *ideas* of the Divine mind becoming substantiated in the wisdom—"the corporeity of the Holy Spirit." And at this point one may choose either Böhme's or Madame Blavatsky's teaching, for they are identical as to this, that the *idea*, the senseless unconscious image of man, extant millions of ages before it was *engrossed* in our coarse flesh and blood, was what subdeific powers *worked out* into creaturely existence; precisely as our brain holds an outline of the work the hands proceed to execute: let us have a saying from each of these great teachers to illustrate this. "A Divine imagination, in which the *ideas* of angels and souls have been seen from eternity, in a Divine type and resemblance; yet not then as creatures, but in resemblance, as when a man beholdeth his face in a glass; therefore the angelical and human idea did flow forth from the wisdom, and was formed into an image, as Moses saith."[2] "This true image it is which God from eternity hath beheld with His Holy Spirit in the wisdom, but without substance, which He created into substance, that is, brought substance into this image."[3]

---

[1] Threefold Life, ch. iv., pars. 30, 31.   [2] Clavis, par. 43.
[3] Third Apology, Text IV., Point IV., par. 18. See also *Incarnation*, Part I., ch. ii., par. 14, and *Threefold Life*, ch. x., par. 14.

After discussing at length occult doctrine concerning man's primeval evolution Madame Blavatsky says: "Finally, it is shewn in every ancient Scripture and cosmogony that man evolved primarily as a luminous incorporeal form, over which, like the molten brass round the clay model of the sculptor, the physical frame was built by, through, and from the lower forms and types of animal terrestrial life."[1] Now, an idea conceived in the human mind with any habitual intensity does not end as an imaged possibility; it prompts desire for carrying it out; we want, as we say, to realize it. So Böhme says: "Where there is a desire there is a mother, for no desire can make itself; it must arise out of a will,"[2] and, "In every will of every essence there is again a centre of a whole substance."[3] I beg for a stress of attention on that last sentence. How is that substance produced? Let him answer again. "We well know the similitude of the Deity in ourselves, if we know and consider ourselves, for the spirit giveth everything its name as it standeth in the birth in itself, and as it formed them in the beginning—in the creation—so it also formeth our mouth; and as they" [Heaven and earth, stars and elements just before named] "are generated out of the Eternal Being, and are come to a substance, so the *human* word goeth also forth out from the centre of the spirit, in shape, property, and form, and it is no other than that the spirit maketh such a substance, as the creation itself is when it expresseth the form of the creation . . . for God is Himself the being of all beings, and we are as gods in Him."[4] These words are of no dubious meaning. He has already taught us that creation in all worlds was and is effected by the seven

---

[1] Secret Doctrine, vol. ii. p. 112. Third and revised ed., 1893, p. 118.
[2] Threefold Life, ch. viii., par. 52.
[3] Forty Questions (1665), Ques. 1, par. 115.
[4] Threefold Life, ch. vi., pars. 1, 2, 4.

spirits of Eternal Nature; and that a desire for manifestation of spirit is invariably the hidden "lubet,"[1] which strongly concentrates diffused undifferentiated life, till contraction and motion generate fire, fire light, light air, air water, and water substance. That, in fewest words, is Böhme's account of the genesis of *manifested* life. My contention is that the desire of any human mind acts on its own plane, precisely as the Divine lubet in the wisdom—or Akâsa, if our Theosophic friends prefer the term; and as "the eternal centre, and the birth of life is everywhere, if you make a small circle, as small as a little grain or kernel of a seed, there is the whole birth of the Eternal Nature"; the intrinsic insignificance of the desire—given its sustained intensity —proves nothing against resulting substance; and, of course, by *substance*, I do not here mean matter or anything external senses can perceive, but, I fear, such substance as may often compact itself into materiality in other bodies, first as a model and then as a concretion formed upon it. For the wonderful and awful truth is by many great seers established that a spirit "*maketh out of itself a form of a spirit and the form maketh a substance according to the property of the spirit.*"[2] And Swedenborg warns us, that those who *suppose spirit to be* merely thought without substance are mistaken, and entirely ignorant of what spirit is, since a spirit is a substance and indeed a subtle organism.[3] Mr Sinnett will help us here, "Every thought of man upon being evolved

[1] "This pleasure, or lust, in the English translation" (of Böhme) "is very aptly and significantly expressed by the Latin word *lubet*. Such a sweet and meek lubet there is without or before all travailing nature in the eternal liberty" (Dionysius Freher.) The question, of course, occurs to one, What corresponds to *this* in the antecedents of the manifestations by *nature* of the human spirit? Must we attribute the previous lubet to the transcendental ego?
[2] Great Six Points, Point IV., ch. vi., par. 10.
[3] Spiritual Diary, vol. ii., No. 2366.

passes into the inner world and becomes an active entity, by associating itself, coalescing, we might term it, with an elemental, that is to say, with one of the semi-intelligent forces of the kingdoms. It survives as an active intelligence—a creature of the mind's begetting, for a longer or shorter period, proportionate with the original intensity of the cerebral action which generated it. Thus a good thought is perpetuated as an active, beneficent power, an evil one as a maleficent demon. And so man is continually peopling his current in space with a world of his own, crowded with the offsprings of his fancies, desires, impulses, and passions; a current which reacts upon any sensitive or nervous organization which comes in contact with it, in proportion to its dynamic intensity." [1]

To Mr Sinnett's lucid instruction, I wish to hang on what appears to me *additional* knowledge as to *how* our thoughts associate themselves or coalesce with those convenient *extras*, the elementals, this dictum of Swedenborg's. Writing of diseases he said, "With men who are in fevers, such spirits are present; for the sick man summons those who infuse heat. Such spirits rush where their sphere is." [2] A sad and angry thought has similar attraction; a loving or hopeful one no less. Chemical affinities in action should give us a lively idea of the instantaneous rush of spirits to the sphere *our* spirits betray. We can get a little further still on the lines of causation, as to *how this is done* by collating some of the dark—but gradually enlightening—sayings of great seers regarding *breath* and *sound*.[3]

[1] The Occult World, 1881, p. 131 ; 4th ed., 1884, p. 89.
[2] Spiritual Diary, No. 4571.
[3] The foregoing article was written some few months ago under the mistaken impression that its leading thought was—*constructively*—more my own than I find it could have been. For since then, turning over a four-year-old extract book, I chanced to see the following passage which I had copied from p. 139 of Dr. Franz Hartmann's *Magic*: "Man is a

II

"Every word, when it is expressed, is *outwardly* made and formed, for in the expressing or pronouncing thereof the outward spirit—viz., the *outward part* of the soul receives it to its own substance. . . . In what property every word doth form and manifest itself in *man's speech* when he speaks it forth, let it be either in God's love—viz., in the holy *ens* or in the *ens* of God's anger, of the same it is again received . . . everything entereth with its *ens* into that, whence it takes its original."—*Mysterium Magnum*, ch. xxii., pars. 16, 7.

Speaking of *ideas* in his *Spiritual Diary* (3499) Swedenborg says that they "*are moments and varieties of respiration,*" and at 3323 *Ibid.*, we read, "*The external of the idea belongs to such respiration, because the idea brings it forth.*" He has also said, "Every idea, or the least image of a man, entirely resembles a man in effigy; or there is the effigy of a man in every one of his ideas" (378 *Ibid.*) And a recent writer, Râma Prasâd, in the *Theosophist*, September, 1889, after explaining that every vibration of light in colour has its sound, goes on to say, "it is from this very easy to understand that the prototypes of all physical forms, with their inherent powers of appearance, duration, and disappearance, are all a set of sonorous phrases. It is sound that leaves on physical matter the various living organisms of the world. It is sound that creates, preserves, and destroys." Now he had elaborately taught in a foregoing paper, that from *every* human soul a coloured aura proceeds; hence, by his shewing, changes of mental or soulish state, *altering vibrations of light in that aura, emit some degree of sound*, quite in agreement with Böhme's, "mark centre from which thought is evolved, and crystallizes in forms in the world of souls. His thoughts are things that have life, and form, and tenacity; real entities, solid, and more enduring than the forms of the physical plane" (3rd ed., 1888, p. 208). A sentence which holds more than pages of mine could express with equal force and clearness; yet as *infusions* of herbs are serviceable to the body, so may an infusion of thoughts serve the mind, by carrying out and prolonging their effect.

this, every imagination maketh substantiality"[1] and "thoughts, which are also such an outgoing from the breathing of the mind, as the mind is an outgoing and object from the Divine mind."[2]

Again, in a most profoundly interesting book entitled *Swedenborg, the Buddhist*,[3] I find, p. 132: "The aura that exhales when a man thinks, speaks, acts, is not lifeless, and effectless; for it is an outflow of vital mites, intensely fiery and effective; a nervo-vital force that affects all things, animate and inanimate, with which it comes in contact. And note this strange fact, that it always re-acts, that it returns to the man from whom it issues." Nor must we forget how largely Van Helmont enters into this idea of "new spiritual bodies that go forth continually from man, which belong to him, and contribute to the whole man for to make out his full measure"; "and because these outgoing spiritual ideal beings are not mere spirits but spiritual bodies, and bodily spirits, as being born of the whole man, and that all these spirits have their original out of and form the central spirit of man, viz., out of the heart, and are sent abroad as his messengers, must not these messengers perform that which they were duly sent about, and go thither whither the central man designs them? and in like manner return by revolution to man again?" . . . "and forasmuch as the voice and word of man are his offspring and children, viz., his outflown spirits and angels which continually (from the beginning of his life until his death) go out from him," . . . "they are a spiritual and everlasting being as well as he himself is."[4] No; they must be what Böhme calls "choative" and

---

[1] Threefold Life, ch. x., par. 31.   [2] Divine Vision, ch. ii., par. 30.
[3] Swedenborg the Buddhist. By Philangi Dasa. (Well worth reading, though flawed by a prodigious falsity as to the great Swede's faith.)
[4] Van Helmont's *Paradoxal Discourses*, Part II., Concerning the Microcosme, pp. 8, 7, 63.

"temporary spirits," for they have no *eternal* origin; a discordant *quality* of Eternal Nature gives rise to them—and what thus *begins* in division must end. Van Helmont uses the above argument in support of the belief in Reincarnation; and I have often thought whether the embodiment of some of these derived *shadows* of a past existence—drawn by the magnet of some central spirit, naturing for the first time on our earth—may be the fact that the doctrine of *invariable* reinfleshment covers; but it is the influence of those creations in the present life, on which I want attention to be fixed. It would be waste of time and space thus to draw together authorities for believing that we are all involuntary creators of many a "vital mite"; but that unfortunately they escape from the "central man" with no *design* of his. If birth only extended existences; if bane and blessing only reached our fellow-creatures by conscious determination or bequest, life would not be the momentous force its every instant is. We need also to be aware of this *every* output of thought and will secretly, but as surely, enlarges and fortifies the spiritual state which prompts that emission. Anyone can prove it by closely observing what happens during an ill-tempered mood, when indulged. An angry or bitter word seems to relieve us, but for each that we utter, a dozen more spring to the doorway of the mouth, and want to find voice: so with an impatient gesture; snatch, or fling down, or stamp once or twice under extreme irritation, and the fretting impulse is now ripe for fury. Why, when we see how it shocks or pains another, and even alone disgraces ourselves with loss of dignity, if nothing worse, *why* does the wretched passion gather strength? Metaphysicians are, of course, content with the surface answer: all indulged habits are strengthened. But the question our seers have answered is *why they strengthen.* If we break a glass and cut our fingers, we do not do that again because it has been done. Now we often cause ourselves acute suffering, shame, and corresponding anger from companions by a jibe, a taunt, a reproach, and yet they best know how often the choleric friend repents and apologizes—and sins afresh. Because "the outward part of the soul has received the poison of wrath or scorn into its substance," and—spirits who can perceive what affects the *outward* part—congenial spirits "rush to their sphere" in that soul: hence, too often, seven spirits worse than the first, attracted like small boys in a street by any "row" hasten to make us justify a small outburst of temper, by one more angrily unjust. And over and above these *concurrent* spirits remember the awful truth revealed that the *will* of man "is a voice or sound, viz., a *word* of the spirit" . . . "in this *word*, there is *yet* a will, which there will go forth into a substance," . . . "from the mouth of the will forth into the life of the *magia*, that is into *nature*; and openeth the unintelligent life of the magia so that the same is a *mystery* in which an understanding lyeth essentially, and thus getteth an essential spirit. Whereas every essence is a secret arcanum of a whole substance, and is thus a comprehension, where many lives, *without number*, become generated, and yet is together as it were but one only substance."[1] These derivative lives form but *one substance*, presumably because they are not from eternity, they "arise out of time"; and are the emanations of no *whole* being. It is but a fanciful deduction of my own that as a consequence of being one substance with the generating soul which puts forth these anomalous lives, change of residence in mature age causes the uneasiness and depression it so often

[1] Earthly and Heavenly Mystery, Text IV., pars. 19, 20, 21.
Context is encumbered by expletives, and, to make the passage intelligible, I am obliged to detach sentences even in consecutive paragraphs. Italics in the texts not mine.

does, for really old people it is a recognized risk to health. Is there not something more than "use and wont" missed in a new home; in leaving rooms long occupied do we not cut ourselves off from an invisible *entourage* of spirits that corroborate the habits of the head of the tribe? Children who have not had time to people their home sphere thus are joyous in new places, but the *first* day in any such is more often depressing to their elders. This may be a fancy of my own: the influence of the *reliquæ* of the dead in their usual haunts before quitting the outermost body is a fact long proven. Readers of *Light* will not need to be reminded of the sentry-box that had to be destroyed, because three suicides had been committed in it. An exactly similar recurrence of these, in a lodging-house, and the last being that of a stranger who *could* not have heard of what had happened there before, has been reported to me, and only within the last few months, friends of mine, for whose veracity I can vouch, young, full of eager interests and activity, wholly ignorant of the theory their experience exemplifies, have suffered much from occupying the bedroom of a relation whose life, and last illness in that home, had been heavily weighted with temperamental melancholy, one of the kindest hearts, who could never willingly transfer suffering—but quite possibly for some little time, one of those whom St Martin calls the *non allants*. As I am not subjecting matters of private history to the analysis of the Psychical Research Society, I may quote a few sentences from the letters of my friends—both very unimaginative. One sister wrote saying she was about to leave the house for a year, having suffered so much from low spirits since she went to live in it. "We have felt," she said, "unaccountably depressed and more especially in the room where —— died. We neither of us sleep there now; not for fear of ghosts, or anything we may see, but we are so certain of waking up morning after morning miserable and dejected. We have tried it so often that now we leave it empty." And the other sister writes: "Whenever I slept in that room I felt hysterical, for no reason: a most unusual thing with me, for I am always bright early in the morning and fit for any amount of work. I am not afraid of her spirit, for I am not at all nervous, but I would not occupy that room again; there is no doubt as to the depression which troubled me, and I do not care for its recurrence." A very subtle thinker has lately told us that "biology resolves into a combination of living entities the living individual, who itself subsists, is nourished, and develops itself, by the help of a society more vast."[1]

My supposition is that death disbands these constituents of *seeming* individuality, and that in places where its *collective* life has been, the outbreathed ruling quality of that life remains in diffused incipient spirit life, and that these leaderless sparks of soulish fire combine afresh when living men and women afford a new magnetic centre; and *thus* the *débris* of a vanished life can affect us. Possibly these are what Madame Blavatsky has called "the residuum of the personality that *was*, dregs that could not follow the liberated soul and spirit, and are left for a second death in the terrestrial atmosphere."[2] A second life in another personality is what in some cases I apprehend: especially in *embryonic* life.

I have Mr Laurence Oliphant's full sanction for my belief as to involuntary creativeness. At p. 254 of his *Scientific Religion* he wrote:—

"The idea of procreation by respiration will, of course, seem fantastic to the natural mind, until it reflects upon

[1] Alfred Fouillée's "Les Transformations de l'Idée Morale."—*Revue des Deux Mondes*, September 15, 1889.
[2] Sinnett's *Incidents in the Life of Madame Blavatsky*, p. 179.

the fact that we actually do procreate by respiration every day of our lives. This is only brought forcibly to our notice in cases of infectious maladies, for nothing is more certain than that the exhalations of diseased persons are charged with microbes or bacilli, or minute living organisms which carry with them the germs of death, which are, so to speak, hatched in our bodies, and which we breathe out into nature, thus becoming their human parents. There would therefore be nothing strange in the phenomenon of similarly generated organisms being life-giving, instead of death-dealing. Such do, in fact, exist in the sentient atoms of healing magnetism, the quality of which largely depends on the respiratory processes of the operator." (See context to end of chapter.)

SPIRITUAL EVOLUTION [1]

I

"God giveth power to every life, be it good or bad, unto each thing, according to its desire, for He Himself is All; and yet He is not called God according to every being, but according to the light wherewith He dwelleth in Himself, and shineth with His power through all His beings. He giveth in His power to all His beings and works, and each thing receiveth His power according to its property; one taketh darkness, the other light; each hunger desireth its property, and yet the whole essence or being is all God's, be it evil or good, for from Him and through Him are all things; what is not of His love, that is of His anger."—Böhme's *Signatura Rerum*, ch. viii., par. 42.

THAT extremes meet is an axiom verified every day, but a more striking instance of its truth could hardly perhaps be found than in the similarity of mental attitude which so-called evangelical doctrines and those of Universalists [2] induce.

The net result of both is jubilant confidence in a blessedness not depending on the conduct of human beings.

Many years ago an old lady, nearing death, told me that she had no kind of anxiety about her readiness for it, because she had "rolled all her sins upon her Saviour." From what I knew of her antecedents I inwardly feared that they might roll back upon her conscience with

[1] Light, 1892, vol. xii. pp. 4, 15.
[2] Ill-fitting names which one has to use, in default of better, to indicate people who hold a recognized set of opinions, and often characterize these by such terms.

oppressive weight, when mundane spells were broken and introspective life began.

Those cheerful reasoners who call their mode of belief Universalism, roll all apprehensions arising from sin on a still wider breadth of repose—on the irresistible power of Divine order; shifting all responsibility from man to God; they seem to wonder that other people cannot make themselves as comfortable by a close application of logic to the designs of the Most High God. The express declaration that His thoughts are not our thoughts, neither our ways His ways,[1] seems to offer them no obstacle to this process: they will use the little measure of human reason for estimating infinitudes of Deific wisdom all the same. We have lately read in *Light* that this new Gospel of human irresponsibility is what "the pure theologian has missed; for he fails to see that salvation is no scheme, but an absolute, necessary, unhinderable evolution." It is no wonder surely that he fails to see what the whole tenor of the Bible contradicts, though here and there passages do occur which undeniably predict, the ultimate restitution of our race to lasting well-being; but at what a terrific distance from our own is the ultimation! Setting aside the consensus of inspired men, might not the records of geological science suggest a warning to people who expect release from evil by the irresistible force of evolution? Its methods are formidable enough when good is being evolved in a terrestrial orb. Think of the long periods of glacial lifelessness, the tremendous volcanic upheavals of successive layers of soil, the recurrent cataclysms from fire and water that took place before our earth was habitable, and imagine, when all this was necessary for securing material conditions, what convulsions of a spiritual nature may be the analogous preliminaries of evolution in undying souls.

The testimony of unhappy spirits still bound to earth

[1] Isaiah lv. 8.

by the anguish of a remorseful memory, must surely have too much weight with Spiritualists to allow *them* to accept this misleading *jeu d'esprit* of logic, which, because God will be all in all when our solar system has collapsed and Time is at an end, cruelly foreshortens the perspective between now and then, and urges that even for guiltiness, "good will be the final goal of ill,"—urges it upon us now while on all sides the conscience is made drowsy by the asphyxia of sin, while the struggle for spiritual life amid the chaotic confusions of thought is more and more relaxed, and the sorceries of this present life obliterate anxieties about the next. I doubt the bravest Universalist assenting to the term "unhinderable evolution" when enduring, for a seeming eternity the irrefusable wages of sin in his own nature, the will at enmity with God's order, and the heart alone, in the horrors of self-loathing, with no escape from self, for "the *will* cannot break, and the soul must continue in the will."[1] "All earthly food and lust passeth away at the end of days, but the will remaineth standing eternally and the *desire* in the will."[2]

At that stage of evolution we may be very sure the goal of evil will be undeniable torment. Nor can we suppose the despair of those who suffer it, if repentance begins to quicken, finding any solace in such a line of thought as this, "Ye must be born from above." "Such perfection of life is a debt which the All-Father owes, and which He will assuredly discharge to every one of His children in due time."[3] It is not what the Father owes the child, but what the child has owed, and not paid, of obedience and love that will occupy the conscience-stricken mind when once the veil lifts.

Now we must allow that the extreme Evangelical

---

[1] Forty Questions (1665), Ques. 18, par. 10.
[2] Threefold Life, ch. xv., par. 15.
[3] Things to Come (Elliot Stock, 1892, 1893), p. 6.

offers to "conscious sinners" a quietus fully as stupefying as those who teach the doctrine of irresponsibility; for example, in such lines as these taken from a popular hymn:

> It is finished, yes, indeed,
> Finished every jot;
> Sinner, this is all you need,
> Tell me, is it not?
>
> Weary, working, burdened one,
> Wherefore toil you so?
> Cease your doing; all was done
> Long, long ago!

But there is this difference between the two dealers in spiritual narcotics—absurdly erroneous as such expressions sound, I believe those who use them are nearer to helpful ideas than they who can think of sin as a phenomenal dream,[1] necessarily dispersed by death, for these seem to me both to deny the real essence of sin and to have no knowledge of what human will is. The acted or worded sin might be phenomenal if act and word were not consequent on the direction of the will— and even what is aimless at the time must always be an evidence of previous, if not habitual, motive; volition, however closely masked, being incessantly at work within; nor can any determination of the will be without reaction on itself, because the imagination of the heart which determines it is intensified by pursuit; and its truly magical stimulus strengthens attraction to any object of desire, be it good or evil. Nothing that the will is used to seek can be easily given up; the whole bulk of spirits' communications for centuries past assures us that it is not given up when means for its exercise are withdrawn.[2]

---

[1] Suicides evidently believe it to be so, and as the delusion gains ground suicide must become even more common than it is.

[2] "His substance is no more earthly, yet he carrieth along the earthly willing, and so plagueth and tormenteth himself therewith."—*Incarnation*, Part III., ch. iv., par. 16.

This makes sin "the sting of death," a famished will deprived of its prey.

The conversion of the will is therefore the one indispensable condition on which Evangelicals offer comfort before sinful habits are at all overcome, and any one who is intelligently Christian will see that there is better ground for such comfort than appears on the surface, for the will must be inclined to receive salvation through Jesus Christ before the seemingly precipitate offer, "Believe on the Lord Jesus and thou shalt be saved,"[1] can be accepted: and the will once converted from rebellion, all that desire to keep God's commandments and follow Christ's example can effect, is potentially won.[2] The truth of sudden and real conversion is often doubted because habits of sin are known to be almost ineradicable, and the assurance given to penitents that "all their sins shall be blotted out" naturally rouses contempt in minds hostile to Christianity; yet were such sayings interpreted by a deeper knowledge of human nature, what now appears foolishness might be justified even to rational people. From what are sins to be blotted out? Not, assuredly, from the imperishable records of all that has been, but from the imagination of the heart, which *must* be vain and evil, until the will has turned back from alluring images of good to its divine and central magnet. It is this magic faculty which must be cleansed by "the Blood of Christ" (the highest tincture of Divine love), not only from seductive images, but from the dismaying memories of sin, which can so dominate the unconverted mind as to make reformation seem impossible; and what people suppose themselves to be they generally are in conduct. And,

---

[1] Acts xvi. 31.

[2] "A new will is formed by the Lord, from which the will of the proprium is entirely separated."—Swedenborg's *Spiritual Diary*, vol. iv., No. 4711 *m*.

besides, the effect of all sinfulness is confusion: Selfhood unreconciled to God "loses itself in the dim anarchy of a sphere without a centre."[1] The thought of a loving Saviour strongly impressed on a mind in this state is like the first distinct indication of the sun's whereabouts on a hopelessly cloudy day.[2] "Thoughts open the spirit that it may come to the will"[3] and "the Divine fire of the soul was through sin shut up, which none could unshut and kindle, but only the love of God in this incorporated grace covenant."[4] "Now, if the soul doth but a little *imagine* into the love of God, the Divine life becometh stirring";[5] and if that spark of life is not quenched again by permitted sin, desire for grace and pardon will strengthen, and then all that man can do is secured; for "man hath the death in him whereby he may die unto the evil"[6] and "the desire standeth in our will, but the conversion standeth in God's mercy."[7] (I use Böhme's words because they give my meaning better and more briefly than any others could.)

[1] T. Lake Harris's Introduction to *Arcana of Christianity*, p. 18.
[2] Any one possessing Böhme's *Treatise on the Incarnation* will find in Part I., ch. v., pars. 124-126, what is well worth reading on this point.
[3] Threefold Life, ch. iv., par. 82.
[4] Baptism, ch. ii., par. 9. (Böhme's revised version.)
[5] First Apology, Part II., par. 553.
[6] Signatura Rerum, ch. xvi., par. 28.
[7] Second Apology, Part I., par. 109.

II

DIVINE AND HUMAN WILL

"Thou must create a will out of thy soul and with the same go forth out of evil, wickedness, and malice into God . . . the willing spirit that will kindle thy soul, and then reach after the life and spirit of Christ, and thou wilt receive it; which will new regenerate thee with a new willing, which will abide with thee."—*Incarnation*, Part II., ch. ix., pars. 26, 27.

"The idea of anything is its soul."—*Nature's Finer Forces*, p. 137.

It is while even the initiatory stages of conversion are precarious that one shudders to hear some modes of speech applied, such as "accepted in the beloved," to a person still a stranger to any kind of self-denial, though cultivating a holy imagination. It is true that in Christ's most gracious parable the father runs to meet the long-lost son while he was "yet a great way off," but the son *had arisen*; so must the will of every one rouse to lay hold on the righteousness of Christ, because that only can avail us which is substantiated by our own desire.[1]

It is the necessity of this initial action of the human will which both Universalists and Evangelicals seem to ignore. Both trust to the inevitable evolution of goodness; the one because omnipotent love wills it; the other because full assurance of salvation by faith in the completed work of the Redeemer cannot, they think be nullified by subsequent backslidings; with regard to this last persuasion, perhaps no better answer could be given to it than the words found in *Ezekiel* xviii. 26, and *Matthew* xxv. 11, 12. In one case iniquity, in the other a neglect of the conditions requisite for grace, hindered spiritual progress.

As to Universalists, I think some modifying ideas might be gained by them if the relations of a human father to his young children were attentively studied: he is

[1] "Justification is effected in the blood of Christ in man; in the soul itself."—*Election*, ch. x., par. 119.

comparatively omnipotent; he can alter their circumstances for weal or woe at pleasure, but he cannot—be they ever so weak—compel them to say or do what they have set their will against, for they brought in with life a force which the originator of their earthly existence cannot constrain to obedience. Tyranny can break down that force, and with it all the gladness and vigour of nature: a parent's love withholds him from any such risk, and thus limits power. This, on a very minute scale, is an exact picture of what Böhme teaches us as to the restraint of Deific Omnipotence in winning men or devils back to their allegiance—in preventing the arrest of orderly evolution caused by their own self-will. "God," he tells us, "cannot fight against God," and in every immortal spirit there is a "sparkle of Deity." If Divine love could put forth irresistible power and coerce the will of the creature, the deep sighs of its pity, which thrill here and there in both Old and New Testament, would be meaningless. Our own hearts feel them to be the utterance of sorrow and not figures of speech.

In such sentences as these the yearning expostulations of love cannot be mistaken:—

"Oh that they were wise, that they understood this, that they would consider their latter end!"[1]

"Oh that My people had hearkened unto Me, and Israel had walked in My ways."[2]

"Thus saith the Lord, What iniquity have your fathers found in Me, that they are gone far from Me, and have walked after vanity, and are become vain? . . . Have I been a wilderness unto Israel? a land of darkness?"[3]

"Oh My people, what have I done unto thee? and wherein have I wearied thee? testify against Me."[4]

"Oh, Jerusalem, Jerusalem . . . how often would I

[1] Deut. xxxii. 29.   [2] Psalms lxxxi. 13.
[3] Jer. ii. 5, 31.   [4] Micah vi. 3

have gathered thy children together, as a hen doth gather her brood under her wings, and ye would not."[1]

Having come to this point, "ye would not" yield to the will of Almighty God, there is no honest escape from reference to the unfathomable mystery of free-will; and perceiving, as I do, that no one, however wise or learned, tries to explore it without breaking thought against one or other of two opposing truths—that God is omnipotent, and that man has ability to choose or refuse what is presented to him for choice—I know that for me to pretend to throw any light on the subject would be absurd: not so to try and explain why its mystery never darkens my own intellectual light. Every docile student of Böhme's revelations could witness, I suppose, to having the same privilege.[2] For while philosophers reason about the will of man as an attribute, assigning to it in their theories more or less of intrinsic power, Böhme shews that in the last analysis it is the man himself;[3] that by his *will* he is a creature individualized in the ocean of life; proving that a will has separated itself from the whole will of the supreme God into divisional existence; and the method of this transition from an unrealized idea to creatureliness, is given in the following words as intelligibly, perhaps, as by any number of quotations.

"The eternal word breathes forth itself into an infinite-

[1] Luke xiii. 34.

[2] To such learners it is a grief and astonishment to see all that is spent year after year in publishing sermons, snippets of devotional reading, and torrents of tracts, while works of such inestimable value as Böhme's smaller treatises, which would cost little to reprint, cannot be obtained except in very rare copies. The answer to the third of his *177 Theosophic Questions* would appease doubts that shake the faith of thousands of people, but no one cares to reproduce what theologians discredit or despise.

[3] Swedenborg uses just those words in *Arcana Cœlestia, 10,777*: "No one can be compelled to good because nothing which is of compulsion inheres, for it is not his. That becomes his which is done from freedom, for what is from the will is done from freedom and the will is man himself."

ness of plurality, and brings the plurality of knowledge into imagination, and the imagination into desire, and the desire into nature and strife, till it comes to fire ... the fire giveth soul."[1] (By nature here understand the first forms of nature, the astringency and mobility which strive against each other till their conflict strikes out the involved fire of an antecedent will.) A yet deeper opening in the abyss was granted to Böhme, which I think Greek scholars may claim for Plato before him. He teaches that an idea or thought in the Deific mind[2] originated the separated creaturely will. "The image," he wrote, "was not a substance but a will to a substance." Nor does he allow us to think that the mode of man's creation was exceptional, though, as to this universe, it was the highest pitch of Divine imagination which brought into manifest life the image and likeness of God. "The centre of everything," he asserts, "is spirit from the original of the Word. The separation or distinction in the thing is own self-will, of its own self-impression, or compaction, where every spirit introduceth itself into substance according to its essential desire."[3]

[1] Epistles (1649), Ep. 6, pars. 21, 24.

Perhaps a few sentences of Râma Prasâd's most instructive book may afford some glint of light on this last sentence: "At every moment of time, *i.e.*, in every *truti*, are millions of *trutis*—perfect organisms in space. The units of time and space are the same ... every *truti* of space is a perfect organism."—*Nature's Finer Forces*, p. 80.

[2] Our minds "out of which do spring so many various thoughts, where every thought hath again a centre to a will, that so out of a conceived thought a substance may be produced. In such a manner are all spirits created out of the Eternal Mind."—*Threefold Life*, ch. iv., pars. 30, 31.

[3] Knowledge of All Things, par. 11 (*Several Treatises*, 1662); also *Epistles* (1649), Ep. 6, par. 11.

Anyone who has seen Mrs Watts Hughes' *Voice Figures* will better understand how "spirit is from the original of the Word" the breath that causes the vibration of sound determines the figure—the formative idea which is the first beginning of a "will to a substance," and the will spirit concentrating the action of the seven forms of nature in that focus (the idea) brings it to ultimation in a denser sphere of existence.

Everything includes, of course, crystals, plants, and animals: little as we can discern the action[1] of a will in plants, it is indisputable; a plant has its will and makes it valid, as many a weaker growth finds to its cost.

But are we to conclude that all creaturely wills originate from ideas in the Divine wisdom, *i.e.*, the efflux of Deity? What follows after the passage above quoted saves us from that supposition, "the formability of bodies existeth out of the experience of the willing, where everything's centre, as a portion of the outspoken Word, re-outspeaketh itself and frameth itself into separability, after the kind and manner of the Divine speaking."[2]

This justifies the belief that the idea, will, and desire of inferior beings in the supersensual world may originate creatures—not immortal, as on the highest plane the "spiration of the Word created man."[3] I find it helps my faith in the loving-kindness of God *not* to believe that all hideous animals and more loathsome reptiles were spoken forth by Him. Look at a rhinoceros or alligator, and even some kinds of fish, to feel this. The hypothesis that these embody the foul ideas of minds not holy will explain St Martin's curious saying about insects. "One need not," he says in a very striking chapter on *The Third Nature and Insects*, " worry oneself as naturalists do to classify insects in the regular order of animated nature. In relation to nature they are evidently apocryphal creatures; they are excluded or cut off, so to speak, from the true family line, and the name given to them, insect, from the Latin word *in-*

---

[1] See par. 66 of *Sixth Epistles* (*Epistles*, 1649).

[2] Knowledge of All Things, par. 12 (*Several Treatises*, 1662); also *Epistles* (1649), Ep. 6, par. 12.

[3] "Creation, which implieth chiefly a compaction and bringing down lower."—Dionysius Freher.

SPIRITUAL EVOLUTION

secare, alone implies what I have just shewn to be their origin."[1] Returning from this digression to the point chiefly in view—if the will is the factor of creaturely existence, all that exists having proceeded, by however many gradations, from the One Holy Will—two deductions appear to me to be inevitable. First, that no human creature can be a manifestation of the "sum of all beings."[2] For even in numbers no *one* can have for its product a unit of equal value.

Second, since every derivative fraction of the all-comprehending One, such as angel or man, is energized by the will of God (in nature), its will cannot be amenable to compulsion. To this may be objected the common fact of one human will being subdued by the force of another, and so in our own minds may one form of volition conquer another; but this is not equivalent to destroying a faculty which, if such things can be brought into comparison without profanity, would be similar to the Holy Will of God annihilating the will of a human creature. Besides, even between man and man or man and woman, where the will seems to be conquered, we may be sure that the semblance of self-interest led to the surrender: after which a kind of hypnotism prolongs defeat. Again, the hopeless slavery of habit, which seems to hold people fast to follies and vices they abhor, is often taken for proof that human will is not free. Might we not as well say that limbs have no power of movement because many are paralysed, and

[1] L. C. de St Martin's *L'Esprit des Choses*, vol. i. p. 164. Böhme seems to have entertained a similar thought. "Elementary qualities at *some* times generate living flesh therein, as grasshoppers, flies, worms or creeping things."—*Aurora*, ch. xvii., par. 14.

[2] "For myself I am no more assured of my own ultimate perfecting than I am of the perfecting of every Ego in which the sum of all beings is self-manifested."—G. W. Allen's "Address to the London Spiritualists' Alliance," Nov. 17, 1891, *Light*, Nov. 28, 1891, vol. xi. p. 571.

some can be made rigid and incapable of self-direction by mesmeric art?

I have no doubt that thousands of human beings are hypnotized by evil spirits to whose incitements they have yielded while yet free; in a very terrible degree proving the truth of the saying, "To whom ye yield yourselves servants to obey, his servants ye are to whom ye obey."[1]

To conclude, honesty obliges me to confess that since I firmly believe that after slow and tremendous discipline, at last the most discordant and violently fractional will is to be brought into divine harmony, it may fairly be said, Why, then, need you doubt God's ability to do now at once what by more slowly working influences is to be effected? and if that is possible must not the Holy One design and promote the discords of sin?[2]

If nothing already alleged prevents this inference I can only answer—by what may seem a weak evasion—that as all created beings in the strictest sense inhabit the life of the supreme source of life, it is necessarily impossible for us, minutest atoms of that life, to conceive aright of its modes of action: that, therefore, the attitude of thought prescribed by the Father of Spirits must be our nearest approach to wisdom. Now the tenor of Scripture from beginning to end is deceptive if man has not freedom of choice. Denying that freedom, we can hardly accept other Bible doctrines with any show of consistency. It is, I know, a very old-fashioned position to rest in when reason is non-plussed, but for me, the summary of wisdom recorded by Job remains most comfortably clear. "Unto man he said, Behold, the fear of the Lord, that is wisdom; and to depart from evil is understanding."[3]

---

[1] Rom. vi. 16.
[2] See on this point *Incarnation*, Part I., ch. v., pars. 132, 133.
[3] Job xxviii. 28.

ILLUSIONS IN LIFE'S TRANCE[1]

I THINK readers of Dr Wyld's very interesting and valuable notice of Dr Tuckey's work on *Psycho-Therapeutics* may like to see the following account of the fourth step of the soul's progress—surely not always *ascension*—to a state of Trance. Commenting upon the words of *Genesis* ii. 21, Böhme says: "Man fell into a deep sleep, viz., into the Magia; it was with him as if he were not in this world, for all his senses or thoughts ceased, the wheel of the essences passed into a rest. He was, as it were, essential, *not* substantial, he was altogether like the Magia; for he knew nothing of his body; he lay as dead, but was not dead; but the spirit of the body stood still. And then the essences have their *effect*, and the spirit of the soul only seeth or discerneth; and there is *portrayed* in the sidereal spirit all whatsoever the starry heaven bringeth forth. And stood magically in the mind as a looking-glass on which the spirit of this world gazeth and conveyeth whatsoever it seeth in the looking-glass into the essences; and the essences flow forth therein, *as if* they did perform the work in the spirit, and portray it in the spirit; which are *dreams*, and representations or figures."[2]

Now, if any one reading this should ask, What did Böhme mean by essences? my answer would be, I shall be very glad if any one can tell me. Though in the

[1] Light, 1892, vol. xii. p. 95.
[2] Incarnation, Part I., ch. vi., pars. 1–5.

original German text *Wesen* is both *essence* and *substance*, I understand by his use of the first word active psychical powers, and by the second their passive physical media. If his sense of "*the Magia*" were inquired for, I should humbly allow that its complicated depths of meaning baffle my understanding, as much as the mysteries of modern Mesmerism defy scientific analysis. Possibly two of his briefest definitions may help minds quick to seize an obscure inference. "The *Magia* is the greatest hidden secret, for it is above Nature, and maketh Nature according to the form of its will." . . . "The Magia is the acting in the will spirit, or the performance in the spirit of the will."[1] What most puzzles me in the passage describing Adam's trance, is that in which *the spirit of the world is said to have gazed into his quiescent mind, and to have set the essences at work according to the figures there reflected from the astral world.* This suggests a great deal. Taking for an established premise that *animus mundi* is inferior to the human *spirit*, though the parent of the elementary human *soul*, may we translate the process into modern mesmeric practice thus? The stronger will of the hypnotizer, having soporized the weaker will of his patient, injects imaginations into a passive mind, which elementary spirits—the world-soul's executive force—study as a determining model, and proceed to carry out in act, so far as they can: how far?—by moving the *plastic* machinery of the nervous system? Truly a rough translation.

This is, of course, a kind of sorcery, and a most dangerous kind; but to magic spells of some sort a very large proportion of human conduct is due. We call it influence, and think of what comes from fellow-man; Swedenborg called it influx, and taught that it proceeds also and *always* from a various host of unseen com-

[1] Small Six Points, Point V., pars. 70, 88.

panions, who at once share and intensify our illusions. Is there, then, no protection from the phantastic enchantments of universal *Magia*? None, so far as I can see. The fact admitted in our Bible that man was "made subject to vanity, not willingly," seems to forbid any idea of seeing things *as they are* in this life. Yet who can seriously doubt that this temporary enforcement of coloured glasses is the work of the wisest love? They admit light enough to work by honestly—guiding rays from the great Spiritual Sun: accepting, and working by their light, we shall at last reach "the way, *the truth*, and the life."

FORM [1]

I

"The beginning of every being is nothing else but an imagination of the outflown will of God, which hath brought itself into separability, formedness, and image likeness wherein lieth the whole creation."—*Treatise on Baptism*, ch. i., par. 4. (Böhme's revised text.)

WHEN I began to see the result of any fixed persuasion in our *entourage* of spirits, I never guessed where that seeing would lead me. But it happened to me as it does to a child playing on open ground when his ball rolls off into a pathless thicket close by; though he is pretty sure to miss the shortest way out, and now and then to lose his footing in rough and tangled obscurity, yet he saw the ball enter, and at all risks will follow to try and find where it went to. I saw that a fixed persuasion was a permanent attitude of mind, that every attitude was a form and amounted to the same thing as a figure on the visible plane; and then as remembrance of Böhme's saying, "The figure hath caused the spirit," [2] and Swedenborg's, that "Influx is according to form," [3] flashed upon me, I suddenly perceived that some unvarying law of creative action was to be discovered on this ground. Plato's Ideas came to my mind, of course, and many a dark saying of Böhme's in which the use of the words idea or figure had been so without context in my mind

---

[1] Light, 1892, vol. xii. pp. 123, 147. [2] Threefold Life, ch. x., par. 13.
[3] Conjugial Love, par. 86.

previously, that passages in which they occurred, had, for me, been a dead letter. If now I can suggest any interpretation of these worth having, or even any gleam of light upon them leading to fuller illumination, seeming presumption may be forgiven. The attempt is not made because I think myself equal to it, even in my best days, but because if I do not do what little I can *now*, I shall never be able to share with other seekers, finds—in my judgment—most precious; and it may be long before another student has had leisure and inclination for thirty years' quarrying in Böhme's works. This qualification is mine.

In par. 4 of his twelfth *Theosophic Question* he says: "The original of all things lieth in the idea."

In answer to his fifth *Theosophic Question*—all most instructive on this theme—par. 4, we read: "When God would have such an Idea in living creatures . . . then He moved and severed the central fire of the Eternal Nature whereby the Idea is become manifest in the fire, which is done through the breathing," and a few sentences before, "The central fire of the Eternal Nature, wherein the substance of the creature standeth." (How is substance to be accounted for therein? thus—all fire that is kindled enough to give forth shining light, produces first air from thence, and from air water distils; water is potential corporeity.)[1]

It should be remembered that in Böhme's language the "fire of God" and the "wrath of God" are equivalents for nature in our world, and the light that outshines from nature's fire is not wholly originated by nature, for "in the light are the powers of the not-natural life manifested,"[2] but out of light, he tells us, no creature

[1] "If anyone should demand of us what properly a body is, we say that a body is a tangible birth of the water, differing in shape and quality according to the power and activity of its former life."—Van Helmont.
[2] Election, ch. ix., par. 45.

could be formed; for *naturing* there must be fire, that which is always consuming and producing simultaneously. We see, therefore, *why* the central life of the Eternal Nature was moved in order that the ideas of the Divine mind should be manifested.

In many places in Böhme's writings we shall find him insisting on the same laws of nature ruling on highest and lowest planes, and this among others, that as in the mind of man a form or model of what it desires to effect must precede every acting out of the will, so in the "Wisdom" of God, and so in the world-soul it has ever been. It is interesting to see how exactly Madame Blavatsky's account of the creation of man tallies with Böhme's as to this: "The Dhyân Chohan creates man in his own form; it is a spiritual ideation ... that form is the ideal shadow of itself; and this is the man of the first race."[1]

"The first race was composed of astral shadows of the creative progenitors, having, of course, neither astral nor physical bodies of their own."[2] "The Father of Nature," Böhme wrote, "hath continually compacted the substantiality in the mystery" (by mystery understand a chaos of potentialities), "where it hath formed itself, as it were, into an image, and yet hath been no image, but as a shadow of an image."[3]

My object is to shew how that shadow of an image tends to creaturely existence, and in the attempt Böhme's track must be closely followed.

"The will is no substance, but the willing's imagination maketh substance."[4]

"The will maketh out of itself the form of a spirit, and

---

[1] Quoted from Commentary XIV., Stanzas of Dzyan, Stanza X., *Secret Doctrine*, vol. ii. (1888), p. 242; (1893), p. 253.
[2] Ibid. (1888), p. 121; (1893), p. 128.
[3] Incarnation, Part I., ch. i., par. 54.
[4] Ibid., Part II., ch. ii., par. 23.

the form maketh a substance according to the property of the spirit."[1]

"It figureth the willing into a form or shape, wherein we understand the centre of the spirit."[2] Without Böhme's key to the last sentence, what a totally unintelligible paradox that seems! One can hardly imagine words more senseless than "a shape wherein we understand the centre of the spirit," the centre of what we are used, in our ignorance, to think of as essentially independent of form! Yet with Böhme's key, we shall find in these words a most precise compendium of his revelations concerning the origin of all living creatures. To prove this a considerable digression is necessary. It is vain to try to give Böhme's meaning with any evasion of the fact, that as soon as one level of understanding is reached another yet deeper is perceived. But on the other hand, if once clear intelligence is gained of any obscure part of his teaching, light will break out from that part more and more, and shew such unforeseen agreement of assertions of his (previously seeming to lack point) with what little we know of the mysteries of nature, that conviction grows upon us of his having been used by a Divine teacher as a medium.

It is impossible, I think, to render his account of what the Wisdom is—*in* which, by the Word, all that was *first* created came into existence—with any words as clear as his own in the following passage: "The word is the speaking or breathing of the willing. . . . The Wisdom is the outflown word . . . the substantial power of the great Love of God . . . a passive substance of Divine operation."[3] Now, if content with this as *all* we can learn of the Divine Originator, Böhme's frequent refer-

[1] Great Six Points, Point IV., ch. vi., par. 10.
[2] First Apology, Part II., par. 493.
[3] Four Tables of Divine Revelation (1654), Second Table Expounded. Table of the Three Principles (1661), pars. 28, 29 (*Several Treatises*, 1662).

ence to the Mysterium Magnum will be a baffling patch of superfluous unintelligibility. Let us therefore heed his own definition of it in a small treatise, in which he seems to touch the most profound arcana accessible to man. In the fifth point of his book of *Small Six Points* he says that the Magia is "the original of nature . . . no other than a will, and that will is the Mysterium Magnum . . . the greatest hidden secret, for it is above nature and maketh nature according to the form of its will. It is the fountain of the Divine Wisdom, viz., a desire in the Number Three, whatsoever the will-spirit openeth in it, that it driveth into a substance through the harsh astringency which is the *fiat*,[1] all according to the model of the will. As the will doth model it in the wisdom, so the desiring Magia receiveth it in."[2] So we have to think of the Mysterium Magnum as the desirous activity of the Deific will to realize ideas in the passive efflux of Deity —the Wisdom.[3] Invited by Böhme to believe in a close analogy between the Divine and human mind, we can think of the ideas in the Wisdom as answering to such as we entertain in thoughts: so soon as we will to bring these to actuality, the concentration of desire is the magic that effects our creaturely word. We utter or outbring acts; the Word of God produced creatures. Now every definite purpose is, as such, a limitation of indefinite powers; as we say, it fastens the mind on a

[1] "The desire is the Fiat which hath made something where nothing was but only a spirit."—*Clavis*, par. 75.
[2] Pars. 65, 66, 70, 71, 73.
[3] Anyone seriously bent on understanding all that Böhme has revealed about that most mysterious Being the Divine Wisdom, should read, not once or twice, but repeatedly—some interval of time between each reading —the second and third chapters of the second part of his treatise on the *Incarnation*. Of course, pride and sloth would tempt with the thought that it is a subject unfathomably obscure. But so are logarithms, until they have been studied long enough. It is only adequate interest which is wanted for *standing* long enough *under* the weight of obscurity to be rewarded by growing intelligence.

point. "If there be a speaking, then the power must first contract itself that it may breathe forth itself; and then it begetteth that comprehensive magnetic impression, viz., the something [which is the beginning] wherein the *fiat* which attracteth the powers is understood."[1] Thus does the form or shape prove to be the centre of the spirit; the idea is the shape into which the will contracts itself with desire to bring that idea to ultimation; and with that contraction of the will the evolution of a self-conscious and embodied spirit begins; for "not substantial, but figured spirits without corporising have been from eternity."[2] Spirit must form some kind of embodiment before its self-consciousness can begin. "Out of the substance the true intellective spirit primely proceedeth, which before the substance is only a will, and not manifest to itself; for the will doth therefore introduce itself into substance and essence that it might be manifest to itself."[3] "Out of the spiritual form the corporeal form is generated,"[4] and as the spiritual form alters, so does its bodily exponent. "Being the first Adam had fixed his imagination in the earthliness, he is become earthly."[5]

The result for the race is a predominating sense of physical conditions. Böhme draws one of his most powerful arguments for securing regeneration before death from the certainty that sooner or later life-sustaining forces, both elementary and astral, must fail for mortal bodies, and when the last dies the spirit's outward "looking-glass" is shattered and no possibility of an altering consciousness remains, only what the magical

[1] Four Tables of Divine Revelation (1654), Explication of the First Table. Table of the Divine Manifestation (1655), 10, Tincture. [Usually bound at the end of the *Election of Grace*, 1655.]
[2] Forty Questions (1665), Ques. 19, par. 10.
[3] Mysterium Magnum, ch. iv., par. 9.
[4] Three Principles, ch. xi., par. 17.
[5] Incarnation, Part I., ch. x., par. 11.

will reproduces from the past with hungry, insatiable desires. Unless the new creature of heavenly flesh and blood is in some degree of life, there can be no consciousness of any other good than what the poor soul has groped after here. "The soul hath no image or body which remaineth eternally, unless it be through Christ regenerated out of its first substantiality. . . . In the time of the earthly life it may alter its will, and then the *fiat* altereth the figure, but after the dying of the body it hath nothing more wherein it can *alter its will*."[1] It is in this sense, as indispensable to conscious self-disposal, that Böhme calls the outward world of every inward life a looking-glass: "Every form maketh substance in its desire . . . and hath its seeing in its own looking-glass. Its seeing is a darkness to the looking-glass of the other."[2] There are, we know, many planes of consciousness besides that of the body, and each one makes what Böhme terms the "looking-glass of the imagination." "That is a looking-glass wherein the will beholdeth itself what it is, and in that beholding it becometh desirous of that substance which itself is, and the desiring is a drawing in." (Ah, yes.) "The will draweth itself in the desiring and modelleth itself in the desiring for what it is. That very model is the looking-glass wherein the will seeth what it is, for it is a similitude of or according to the willing."[3]

Now, if the human will were long bent on one form of desire, these looking-glasses would not be the brittle, disappointing things they are. We complain of the treachery of hope; but there is a worse traitor in the camp, the perverted will which seeks happiness in every other direction before it turns to the only source of any lasting joy.

[1] First Apology, Part II., pars. 265, 267.
[2] Small Six Points, Point II., par. 13.
[3] Incarnation, Part II., ch. i., pars. 36–40.

II

"Imagination occupies the mean between the existence endowed with, and existence deprived of, reason, between spirit and matter; it serves them as a medium and thus unites the two extremes: that is why its nature cannot be easily seized with exactness by the philosopher."—Synesius.

"All images do make something that is subsisting and substantial, but above all the images which Elohim conceiveth within Himself."—Van Helmont's *Notes on Genesis*, i. 26.

In *Lucifer* for October, 1891, there is an article on "Heat, Sound, and Consciousness," in which one sentence, "*a study of heat as will power*," might lead students of Böhme to recognize a mind on the right track in one of the most profound mines of hidden knowledge. By his own original line of thought, Mr T. Williams comes to conclusions which very nearly coincide with some that the old seer had asserted centuries before. This, for instance, "Will is an energy whose unique direction is always towards self-perception, so that its reflection on the material plane is that of work directed into its own centre. But this is the distinctive characteristic of the effect of gravity, which is therefore common to every atom composing our own globe, because it is the result of the impress of the nature of will (as an impulse to self-recognition) in all its agglomeration of partial activities."[1] Böhme with less brevity expresses the same truth thus: "Every will hath a seeking to do or to desire somewhat, and in that it beholdeth itself and seeth in itself, in the Eternity, what itself is: it maketh to itself the looking-glass of its like, and there it beholdeth itself what itself is, and so finding nothing else but itself, it desireth itself."[2] "It bringeth itself into a receivingness of itself, and compresseth itself to something, and that something is nothing but a

[1] Lucifer, vol. ix. p. 103.
[2] Forty Questions (1665), Ques. 1, par. 22.

magnetical hunger, a harshness like a hardness, whence even hardness, cold, and substance arise."[1] Of this self-exploring will Böhme says: "The Eternal Unity hath breathed forth itself out of itself that a plurality and distinct variety might arise, which variety hath induced itself into a peculiar *will* and properties; the properties into desires, and the desires into beings."[2] It is that "peculiar" will which makes creaturely existence. The "*magnetical impression is*" thus "*the beginning of nature*,"[3] for "by the desire substance is sought, and in the substance the desire kindleth the fire,"[4] and thus beings derive from desires, and desires from properties—and properties? "The original of all things lieth in the Idea, in an eternal imaging."[5] In Böhme's revelations this is an ever-recurring statement, though variously worded: "All spirits are created out of the eternal mind."[6] "Whatsoever the eternal mind figureth in the eternal wisdom of God and bringeth into an idea, that nature frameth into a property."[7] And we may well ask what did he mean here by nature? So far as I have been able to follow him, he attributes to what Fabre D'Olivet describes as "the fathomless contingent potentiality of being,"[8] a latent imagination stimulated to activity by the ideas thrown upon its depths; as outlines just seen may lead an artist to elaborate a perfect picture.

"Thus we understand the substance of all substances, that it is a magic substance, where a will can create itself into an essential life, and so pass into a birth, and in the great mystery awaken a source" . . . "and

[1] Clavis, par. 70. [2] Epistles (1649), Ep. 6, pars. 8, 9.
[3] Election, ch. ii., par. 41. [4] Small Six Points, Point III., par. 45.
[5] 177 Theosophic Questions, Ques. 12, par. 4.
[6] Threefold Life, ch. iv., par. 31.
[7] Clavis, par. 58.
[8] Fabre D'Olivet's translation of *Genesis* i. 2, in his *Cosmogonie de Moyse*.

thus also apprehend whence all things, evil and good, exist, viz., from the imagination in the great mystery, where a wonderful essential life generateth itself.[1]

It may well be asked why, when deeply learned Theosophists, such as Messrs Subba Row, Mohini Chatterji, Râma Prasâd, and Madame Blavatsky, have given our Western world copious and precise teaching about cosmic formation and mighty primordial beings who effected it, with such masterly lucidity of style as to make it impossible to say that *they* wrote what cannot be understood, I should presume to approach those themes with obscure fragments of arcane knowledge, selected from Böhme's books and loaded with the uncouth verbiage of his day?

If knowledge was all I drew from them it would indeed be folly to do so. As to that, no one can feel more than I the greatness of our obligation to those modern instructors, for enlightenment and information not to be gained from any other source. But hard as it often is to understand Böhme, the teaching he gives to heart and conscience is never doubtful, and helps me far more than theirs, precious as it is to the intellect, because it always bears upon the spiritual fate of man, whether in the past, present, or future; on the originating causes of his position *now*, and the tremendous alternatives which hang upon his choice *here*. However far he may seem to wander from these main lines, they underlie all he wrote. His many reiterations of the same occult truth, urged by intense desire to give to others what he knew to be of inestimable value, secure for patient readers impressions that can hardly fail to affect conduct: in these there is no obscurity—however clumsy the vehicle which conveys them—to the inner man. Theosophists adopt what was called of old the

[1] Earthly and Heavenly Mystery, Text V., pars. 37, 38.

Wisdom Religion. No doubt it was a well-deserved title before "grace and truth came by Jesus Christ," but when compared with His later revelations one great defect stamps them with insufficiency. Humility is not inculcated, and without that neither wisdom nor peace is possible for human beings. Recommendations of this virtue may be implicit in the literature of Eastern Theosophists, though of these no trace appears in English versions of it; nor does it seem possible that a religion excluding any idea of a Personal God (*i.e.*, one who responds to human conceptions of such a God) should admit humility to its list of duties. Of love to all, Buddhistic teaching is eloquently full, but, as Gichtel said, "Humility is the throne of love"; unless that throne is firmly established, love is quickly deposed by every spasm of self-will. That the Divine Man Himself is meek and lowly was a discovery no human wisdom could have made; it was first declared by Him Who came in the fulness of time to be the Saviour of all men, even of Theosophists, who believe that they need no redeemer, and scout the offer of pardon as childish and irrational.

Apart from intellectual gain, I think Theosophy must become popular, when every bond is resisted; requiring neither submission nor obedience, it exactly suits the insubordinate temper of our day.

If it were honest to evade difficulties when professing to try to lessen them, I would not notice a sentence quoted just before this long digression, "The imagination in the great mystery," because it is only one sample of a most inexplicable part of Böhme's doctrine. Again and again he refers to imagination as that by which everything in the universe has been caused to exist. I help myself dimly to interpret this by what little is yet understood of hypnotic methods, of the injection of forms of thought by one mind strongly imaging what it wills should effect the imagination, into that of another. To this process he attributes the fall of Adam into material conditions: after saying that the earth was corrupted by its former ruler, and that Adam was sent to restore it, Böhme goes on: "God forbade him the false lust, which the devil stirred up through the *limus* of the earth in Adam's outward body with his false imagination.¹

"The devil opposed man in his enkindled envy, and insinuated his venomous imaginations into the human property." . . . "Whence Adam's imagination and earnest hunger did arise that he would eat of the evil and good, and live in his own will."²

The expression, "insinuated his venomous imaginations," might have puzzled any philosophical reader some years ago before the famous hypnotic experiments in France gave a degree of notoriety and credit to their results never attained by the similar discoveries of Dr Darling and Mr Braid³ some forty years sooner, though under the name of Electrobiology, they had both fully proved the power of inducing states of sensation by the control of the operator's will. But now even scientific men are obliged to own that this is done, and strain their intelligence to find out *how*. They would scorn to learn of Böhme; yet he told centuries ago precisely what Oriental Theosophy had announced ages before, that all which *seems to be* is the work of imagination, the effect of *Maya*, "the veil that is spread over all nations."⁴ He assures us that "all things are arisen through the Divine imagination and do yet stand in such a birth."⁵ And he

¹ Mysterium Magnum, ch. xviii., par. 18.
² Ibid., ch. xvii., pars. 36, 37.
³ The late Mr James Braid, of Manchester, first applied suggestion to the treatment of disease, the patient being previously put into a state resembling deep reverie, artificially produced, and which he called hypnotism.
⁴ Isaiah xxv. 7.
⁵ Epistles (1649), Ep. 6, par. 78.

copiously declares the momentous fact that human spirits determine their fate by what they imagine (observe that this is but an enlargement of the thesis, "the figure hath caused the spirit"). It need scarcely be added that the direction of such a magical power by a right will, is the only safeguard against being infested by a stronger one.

Nothing ever gave me such a lasting fear of leaving this life unpurified as Swedenborg's account of the cruelties practised by evil spirits on others, amenable to their diabolical arts from having been servants to sin while in the flesh. In his *Spiritual Diary* he records the process of torturing by hypnotism exactly as it has been done and observed on this side of death. Those among us who are wont to speak of hell and its despots as the dream of old-world superstition, would do well, I think, to reconsider their verdict by the light of modern science. What has perplexed me with regard to Adam and his dethroned enemy, is the doubt whether in that case the paralysis of true vision was effected by one great being subduing and then binding the mind of another, as one World-soul is supposed to influence another, or whether, as usual, the single name indicates a race, which yields in detail to the seductions of adverse hosts. This, however, is of no practical interest: we know well enough that for every human being unseen promoters of sin abound. But it is far less commonly known that our own imaginations affect all that concerns us so strongly, that giving, or having given, to us a different idea of what we are, will often cause radical change of character. Probably the belief that he or she is a reprobate, hopelessly subject to bad habits, as firmly rivets their chain, as the remark (or annoyed consciousness) that one seems to be in a bad temper makes it difficult to feel otherwise for the next hour or more. This makes *snubbing* almost criminal, and to encourage people about themselves, as much as sincerity allows, a duty we owe to the public.

Christian scientists seem to have a juster sense of the immeasurable force of imagination than most of us entertain, only, as it appears to me, they antedate the time of its release from penal fetters. In the world of spirits, *will*, we are clearly taught, makes all the surroundings of the spirit, and as its state alters, so will every object in view: just as it now is in our minds; *their* eyes

> "See all around in gloom or glow,
> Hues of their own, fresh borrowed from the heart."

But in the mind and in the spirit-world all is homogeneous. Not so in the world we now occupy, for our bodies are here in their own element, our spirits are but "strangers and sojourners." The spider can weave its delicate web wherever it will in the light atmosphere in which it was born; falling into a basin of gum it would be as impossible for it thus to energize, as it is for a Christian scientist who denies the reality of pain, because it is unspiritual, to ignore the torment of toothache or sciatica—when felt.

THE ADVANTAGES OF CHRISTIANITY [1]

I AM much obliged to Mr Williams for explaining the omission of humility among the requirements of Theosophy. What he says about this brings into a strong relief the happiness of Christians, whose faith frees them from the cares of self-disposal, and from an attempt so vague and difficult as that of trying in a world where "*without singulars the universal is nothing,*"[2] "to merge self in the universal." I say trying, because I am incredulous of the sneers of an effort that contravenes the originating law of all creaturely life. The ideal of a Christian is not to abrogate this law, but to restore its first beneficent use. It is our happiness to know that our trance of selfishness *must* end, because we are being organized by the only life in a universal body, "fitly joined together and compacted by that which every joint supplieth";[3] and so far from wishing to merge ourselves in the universal we rejoice to think that not one recipient of life in that organization is without a special use—that our Lord "*hath need*" of each one of us in it, as in the flesh and blood body there is need of each constituent muscle or nerve, or blood vessel, that regulates the proportion of its growth. We look for gains of infinite love and infinite wisdom, not from loving "the limited interest of personal aims," but from con-

[1] Light, 1892, vol. xii. p. 214.
[2] Swedenborg's *Arcana Cœlestia*, par. 6482.
[3] Ephesians iv. 16.

sciously devoting them, as means, to the end for which a merciful Father has given to every one his work, his faculty, and opportunities of service. What barrier can arise from separateness like that of the fingers—restricting power to *parts* for the help and perfection of the *whole?* Apart from the mystical body of Christ (the grand man of Swedenborg) we are worse than nothing— refuse of disease and disintegration. In that body self-seeking is a monstrous excrescence of misgrowth which self can never reduce to health. We therefore submit to the Head and Saviour of that Body as to the only one who can heal us: and of His methods we know enough to be sure that controversy will only inflame spiritual disorder. Any approach to it, therefore, I earnestly avoid, though wishing to show the attitude of Christian faith which necessitates humility. If in practice this attitude had been maintained as well as it is in theory, I doubt if the excellent highly aspiring Theosophists of our time could desire to merge self in anything so comfortlessly indefinite as the universal. For if Christendom was worthy of its name it would have been evident that in "the love of Christ, that passeth knowledge," there are depths which can swallow up the wretched limitations of self-endedness; and, freed from those hereditary bonds, what equivalent has Theosophy to offer for the joy of grateful adoration?

Mr Williams will forgive me, I hope, for submitting to him here a *précis* of the remedial process by which Christians hope to be divinized. To give coherency to brief selections from writing not lucid, I shall run them together, omitting superfluous words and context likely to divert thought by opening side issues.

To his own question, "Seeing the mind together with the senses and thoughts is an inceptive natural life, which standeth in a Time and corruptibility, how may it then in this time be brought to the supersensual Divine life? or how is the Divine inhabitancy in this life?" Böhme, the great Theosopher, answers: "The life of man is a form of the Divine will, and is come from the Divine inbreathing into the created image of man; it is the imaged word of the Divine skill and knowledge. . ." But "the life's will imaged itself with the outward earthly object of the mortal nature . . . and did introduce itself into an own self-image . . . into the desire to own selfhood, and comprised itself into selfhood . . . and the inward Divine ground of the goodwill and substance extinguished; that is, as to the creature became *workless*. . . . For the will of the life broke itself off therefrom, and went out of the Unity into the multiplicity: and strove against the Unity, viz., the one only eternal rest, the eternal good. . . . In this earthly imaging and own self reception it cannot know its ground and original wherein its eternal rest stood; for it hath brought itself out of the *Divine Ens* into an *earthly*, and set it into a corruptible substance, and will rule in that which yet breaketh it, and suddenly as a smoke or vapour passeth away. . . . This captivated life the great love of God is come to help again. . . . As a new fountain of unity, love and rest, out of which it may now frame the life, and quench its painfulness and disquietness in the centres of the own selfhood. . . . This new fountain of Divine love and unity hath with its outflowing, in Christ, incorporated itself into the true life of all the three principles of the human property, and is entered into the natural *apostated* will of the life and assumed humanity, and broken the selfhood and own self willing with the inflowing of the sole and only love of God. . . . And thus hath powerfully demonstrated how the Eternal One can mightily rule over the multiplicity, and own selfhood, that the might of the imagibility may not be a god; but that the might of the *non* and *super*-imagibility may rule all: for the imagibility is only an object or representation of the un-imagible will of God *wherethrough the will of God worketh.*"[1] I beg for stress of attention on those last six words.

If the life of man with all its illusions of personality, its unavoidable solicitude for self, its varying flux of hopes and fears, is the instrument of God, wherewith He works, why should its folly, in the abstract, offend us? No weapon is cognisant of the use to which it is to be put—not even man. Mankind is not the only race of beings in this world for whom the Father cares, and we in our short existence here are doubtless subserving ends of which the cause lies in Eternity before Time, and the consequences in Eternity beyond it. While we try habitually to merge blind self-will in the holy Will of God, *consciousness* that it *is* "a form of the Divine willing" gives to life a calmness and dignity which no other effort can secure.

[1] Divine Vision, ch. ii., pars. 1–17.

BÖHME AND RÂMA PRASÂD[1]

"As there is a nature and substance in the outward world; so also in the inward spiritual world there is a nature and substance which is spiritual, from which the outward world is breathed forth and produced out of light and darkness, and created to have a beginning and time."—*Regeneration*, ch. ii., par. 31.

"There is only one life, and this is not capable of being created, but is eminently capable of flowing into forms organically adapted to its reception—all things in the created Universe, in general and in particular, are such forms."—Swedenborg's *Intercourse between the Soul and the Body*, par. 11.

No habitual student of Böhme's works could study Râma Prasâd's work on *Nature's Finer Forces* without noticing the agreement of account given by both these writers of many recondite facts. With point of view quite different, and diction most unlike, each confirms the evidence of the other: but they give two sides of the same phenomena, Böhme the spiritual, Râma Prasâd the supersensuous material. Take, for example, the often recurring mention of "the powers, virtues, and colours of the wisdom" (efflux of Deity), by the old seer, and what we find about the varying colours of vibrations of ether (*tatwic* phases) on pp. 42[2] and 57[3] of the modern book. Calling to mind Böhme's frequent assurance that everything in temporal nature has its analogue in Eternal Nature, close attention to such an admirable teacher as Râma Prasâd should help to a clearer conception of the mysteries Teutonicus laboured so

[1] Light, 1892, vol. xii. p. 219.   [2] Revised edition, 1897, p. 44.
[3] Ibid., p. 58.

earnestly to expound. I think "desirous seekers" after truth must always be pleased when one mystic or seer endorses the report of another. For instance, Böhme teaches that a figure—a passive model—has invariably preceded the origination of creaturely life, whether emanating directly from divine or from spiritual beings, and these are the words of Râma Prasâd: "It might, however, be said that all formation in progress on the face of our planet is the assuming by everything under the influence of solar ideas, of the shape of these ideas. The process is quite similar to the process of wet earth taking the impressions of anything that is pressed upon it."[1] To those who have not seen this valuable book—almost given away at its very low price—this much of its tenor must be offered to make further comparison intelligible. The great Breath of Life acting upon undifferentiated cosmic matter, "throws itself into five states, having distinctive vibratory motions, and performing different functions."[2] Of the five sensations of men each of these ethers (tatwas) gives birth to one, "the evolution of these tatwas" [five modifications of the "Great Breath"] "is always a part of the evolution of a certain definite form."[3] "Thus form can be perceived through every sense: the eyes can see form, the tongue can taste it, the skin can touch it, and so on. This may appear to be a novel assertion,[4] but it must be remembered that virtue is not act. The ear would hear form, if the more general use of the eye and skin for this purpose had not almost stifled it into inaction."[5]

The identity of Böhme's doctrine about the Breath of

[1] Page 137.   [2] Page 1.   [3] Page 19.

[4] In his essay on the *Sublime and Beautiful* Burke broached the theory that the perfect roundness of every granule of sugar caused the sensation of sweetness. It is quite thirty years since I have seen the book, to which I have not now access, and I forget whether it was salt or acid to which he attributed sharpness of taste from acute angles in their atoms.

[5] Page 94.

God and those of Eastern Theosophists is too striking to need indication, but the following coincidence might be easily overlooked. One of his most frequent sayings is that the effect of the first form of Eternal Nature is to darken previous light by a concentrated desire to *manifest the imagination of a spirit*. Thus in one passage, "we ought to know from whence darkness originateth: for in the Eternity, without or besides nature, no darkness can be, for there is nothing that can afford it.[1] We must only look into the will and into the desiring, for a desiring is an attracting, and whereas in the Eternity it hath nothing but only itself, it attracts itself in the will, and maketh the will full, and that is its darkness."[2]

Râma Prasâd having already said that the colour of the Akasic Tatwa is black, and that that is the first vibration in evolving Prâna, *i.e.*, soul—be it the cosmic or the human soul—says also, "Certain measured portions of the solar *âkâsa* naturally separate themselves from others, according to the differing creation which is to appear in those portions."[3]

Again, the initial vibration is called by him the "*sonoriferous ether*," and Böhme, after mention of the seven forms of nature, says of the first, "That which proceeds forth in essence according to the properties of the will, is dark and causeth a strong pulsation, which is a cause of the tone or sound."[4]

With regard to the colours, his account differs from Prasâd's in that he admits green and excludes black. As to this I must give his own words: "Here meeteth us the great secrecy which hath from Eternity lain in

---

[1] "The Sidereal Spirit is the soul of the Great world which depends on the *Punctum Solis*, and receiveth its light and life from it."—*Mysterium Magnum*, ch. xi., par. 20.
[2] Forty Questions (1665), Ques. 1, par. 8.   [3] Page 23.
[4] Signatura Rerum, ch. xiv., par. 17.

the mystery, viz., the mystery with its colours, which are four, and the fifth is not peculiarly belonging to the mystery of Nature, but it is the mystery of the Deity which shineth in the mystery of Nature, as a life of the light. And these are the colours wherein all lieth, viz., blue, red, green, yellow; and the fifth, the white, is God's own, yet also hath its glance and lustre in nature. The black belongeth not to the mystery, but it is the veil, the darkness wherein all lieth." [1]

(Mystery, it will be remembered, is used by Böhme in the sense of a chaos.)

He repeatedly warns us that nothing happens in our present life without leaving ineffaceable impressions—that they will outlast both it and time. "The multiplicity of things come into one again, but the figure of everything remaineth standing in the one only element." [2]

"The figure and shadow continue eternally, as also do words, both the evil and the good, which were here spoken by a human tongue; they continue standing in the shadow and figured similitude." [3]

What we read in *Nature's Finer Forces* [4] of the "Cosmic Picture Gallery" exactly agrees with these statements. The old seer affirms that it *is* so—the modern, *how* it is so.

On one very interesting point, the agreement of these two, seems to me inferential, though not fully proved. When Râma Prasâd begins to tell us about the origination of mind—*Manas*, his term for it—he writes: "*Virat* is the centre and *Manu* the atmosphere. These centres are beyond the ken of ordinary humanity, but they work under similar laws to those ruling the rest of the Cosmos. The suns move round the *Virats* in the same

---

[1] Earthly and Heavenly Mystery, Text VII., pars. 65, 66.
[2] Threefold Life, ch. v., par. 122.
[3] Three Principles, ch. ix., pars. 21, 22. [4] Page 122.

way as the planets round the suns."[1] "The composition of the *Manu* is similar to that of the *Prâna*. It is composed of a still finer grade of the five tatwas; and this increased fineness endows the tatwas with different functions."[2]

If we turn to p. 69, to see what the laws regarding Prâna, which rule the Cosmos, are, we read: "The planets each of them establish their own currents in the organism . . . the real tatwic condition of any moment is determined by all the seven planets, just like the sun and the moon." This the disciples of Böhme will readily believe; but unless I greatly mistake, I think they would say that he often, directly or indirectly, refers to constellations higher than any our solar system includes, as influential over the human spirit. Does not the following sentence imply this? "The inward property or disposition of the soul lieth now in the first created configuration of the stars or constellation, in the Eternal commencing ground, that is not co-imaged or framed together in the bestial configuration of the stars."[3]

And here again: "For as man hath the outward constellation or astrum in him, which is his wheel of the outward world's essences and cause of the mind; so also he hath the inward constellation of the fire-essences, as also in the second principle he hath the light-flaming Divine essences."[4]

I must refer the reader to chap. ix. of *Threefold Life*, pars. 71 to 77, for a passage so imperfectly understood by me that I cannot feel at all sure whether its true sense would confirm my theory; these words seem, however, to look that way. "The image in the Revelation hath twelve stars upon the crown; for the image representeth God, it is the similitude of God in which

[1] Page 91.   [2] Ibid.
[3] Election, ch. viii., par. 121.   [4] Incarnation, Part I., ch. v., par. 11.

He revealeth Himself, and wherein He dwelleth. . . . The number twelve containeth two kingdoms in the doubled number of six, viz., an angelical and a human, which together make twelve."[1] But surely it is very probable that the stars to which Böhme referred so mysteriously in pars. 17 and 22 of the next chapter as beyond ken, because of prevailing evil, are those which produce spiritual substance (or form) in the already evolved human soul. Jane Lead, who learned much from him, is very clear upon this point, saying in her *Revelation of Revelations*, par. 33: "The outgoing power of the Holy Ghost sets the soul free in the Eternal liberty, from all conflicts which the dragon, or the starry region, hath introduced; for the soul is now influenced by those superior planets, to which these outward planets are subject"; and again at p. 42, "The suns and stars which were seen about the head of the woman in the Revelation signify those superior planets, which cannot be adulterated with the defilements of this inferior orb, as possessing far higher and more exalted powers, carrying dominion over all that is beneath them. For as the lower planets hold down in subjection to the curse, so these deliver and set free from it." Böhme appears to justify her assertion, and my inference, in the following passage: "The whole outward visible world, with all its being, is a figure of the inward spiritual world; whatsoever is internally, and howsoever its operation is, so likewise it hath its character externally."[2]

Now he abundantly shews that the operation of lifegiving in all three principles has been by breathing in of life; as here: "All whatsoever hath life liveth in the speaking Word, the angels in the eternal speaking and the temporal spirits in the re-expression or the echoing forth of the formings of Time, out of the sound or

[1] Pars. 75, 77.   [2] Signatura Rerum, ch. ix., par. 1.

breath of Time; and the angels out of the sound of Eternity, viz., out of the voice of the manifested word of God."[1]

The *formings of Time* I take to be the substance produced by the ethereal vibrations of our sun and planets; for he says: "By this partition, comprehension, and framing of the power of the stars, and of the four elements, we understand Time and the creaturely beginning of this world."[2]

By the *manifested word* of God, I understand "the angels which are mere imaged powers of the word of God," of whom he says: "Now as man with his senses and thoughts governeth the world and all things and substances, so God, the Eternal Unity, ruleth all things through the management and doings of angels, only the power and work is God's."[3]

Speaking of "their princely dominion" in another of his books, he says "that they rule in the properties of nature above the four elements, yea, also above the operation of the stars in the soul of the Great World; which also bear the Names of God."[4]

And again: "Each angelical prince is a property out of the voice of God and beareth the great name of God; as we have a type and figure of it in the stars of the firmament . . . which are altogether one only dominion, and have their princely dominion in power under them."[5]

These are the mighty beings who seem to answer to Jane Lead's "superior planets," and if Böhme's dictum holds good, "This is the right or law of the Deity, that every life in the body of God should generate itself in one

---

[1] Mysterium Magnum, ch. viii., par. 32.
[2] Election, ch. v., par. 43.
[3] 177 Theosophic Questions, Ques. 6, pars. 2, 7.
[4] Mysterium Magnum, ch. xxxv., par. 10.
[5] Signatura Rerum, ch. xvi., par. 5.

uniform way;[1] though it be done through many various imagings, yet the life hath one uniform way and original in all,"[2] must we not consequently infer that from "the imaged powers of the word of God" creative breath has proceeded? given forth, as Böhme anxiously insists, not *out* of, but *in* the voice of God; from mighty beings, in the highest regions to their subordinate officers in our visible solar system, who in their turn out-breathe those slower vibrations which form soul-life on a lower plane, and continue to elaborate its substance till it is able to receive and retain the finer and swifter action of supersolar breath?[3] How consonant is such an hypothesis with Swedenborg's report (he who assures us that our sun is but a small representative of the great spiritual sun from which all life derives).

"The quality of intelligence from the Divine," he wrote, "was shewn, and this also by a light which was brighter and more luminous than the noonday light of the sun, extending to all distance and terminating like the light of the sun in the universe" . . . "for intelligence is nothing else than an eminent modification of the heavenly light which is from the Lord."[4]

Does he not also help us to understand *why* the slower vibrations of ether have to evolve the grosser forms of soul-life before other finer and swifter begin to be perceptible? "That forms or substances are arranged in

---

[1] "Heaven and earth and all whatsoever there is therein, and all that is above the Heavens, is together the body or corporeity of God."—*Aurora*, ch. ii., par. 28.

[2] Aurora, ch. lii., par. 5.

[3] "The outward flesh received the outward air, and its constellations for a rational and vegetative life, to the manifestation of the wonders of God; and the light body, or heavenly substance, received the breath of the light of the great Divine powers and virtues, which breath is called the Holy Ghost."—*Regeneration*, ch. ii., par. 39. "First the natural body and after that the spiritual," St Paul had said long ago. We are enabled now to understand a little how such bodies are formed.

[4] Arcana Cœlestia, 4419, 4414.

a manner most suitable for the influx of life, may be manifest from every single thing that appears in our living bodies. Unless life were received in substances which are forms, there would be no living thing in the natural or spiritual world" . . . "for substances or forms are the determining subjects."—*Animal Kingdom*.[1]

If the bearings of this truth on spiritual life were perceived, these essays on form would not seem, as I fear they must, a fruitless waste of time as well as a too ambitious direction of thought. If in another attempt I can make good my purpose, neither the reader's nor the writer's patience will be thrown away.

[1] Copied from an old notebook where neither page nor number was given.

[It is very doubtful whether the above quotation will be found in Swedenborg's *Animal Kingdom*. The following passage is from the *Arcana Cœlestia*, No. 7408. "That forms or substances are recipient of life, may be seen from every single thing that appears in living creatures; and also that recipient forms or substances are arranged in the way most suitable for the influx of life. Without the reception of life in substances, which are forms, there would be no living thing in the natural world, nor in the spiritual world. Series of the purest filaments, like bundles, constitute these forms. It is the same with those things therein that are highly modified; for modifications receive their form from the forms, which are substances, in which they are, and from which they flow, because the substances or forms are the determining subjects."—ED.]

PLANETARY INFLUENCE [1]

"All material forms exist by virtue of correspondence with some spiritual form. All material forms exist directly, from the correspondential spiritual forms in the degree next to them, and these spiritual forms are the mediums through which the activities flowing from the Creator enter the lower forms. . . . Every change, therefore, however minute—yea, all of those changes for ever beyond the ken of the most powerful microscope, which occur in organized material forms, are so many ultimations on the material plane of changes occurring in the correspondential forms on the spiritual plane.

"These changes, let us ever keep in mind, are the results of activities and relationships between the different planes of existence, which extend into the infinite particulars of each plane."—J. L. WILLIAMS, *Was Swedenborg a Theosophist?* 1889, p. 42.

THAT the position of planets in our solar system affects the character and fate of all human beings, either from birth or from the first kindling of the soul's fire, is not yet among generally received opinions; none the less is it firmly believed by a large number of educated people, as well as by the multitude who trust to *Moore's Almanack* for reliable readings of the stars. Though wholly ignorant of astrology, I am among those firm believers. The concurrent testimony of wise men, in ancient and modern times, is enough for me when I find such a seer as Böhme entirely agreeing with them as to this. Here, for one example of his frequent reference to the stars: "Every seed of the body, according to the outward world, standeth in the power and under the authority of the Spirit of the world in the configuration

[1] *Light*, 1892, vol. xii. p. 285.

of the stars; for as the great clockwork or machine standeth in the figure at that time, such a figure also the *Spiritus Mundi* giveth it in the condition of the outward life; and such a beast it modelleth in the property of the outward life: for the spirit of the outward world out of the four elements can give nothing else but a beast. And so now it distributeth itself always in the *beginning* of every *child's life*, in the figure: as the stars' constellation or configuration standeth in its wheel, such an image it maketh in the property or constitution, out of the *limus* of the earth, viz., in the four elements. From whence many a man from his mother's womb, according to the outward man, is of the condition of a malignant evil serpent, or of a wolf, a dog, toad, or of a sly fox, of a proud lion, or of a filthy swine, a haughty peacock; also of a self-willed, stubborn, unruly horse; or else of the condition of some good, gentle, tame beast, all as the figure is in *Spiritus Mundi*."[1]

And "the starry spirit worketh in the flesh and blood, and maketh the soul to long and lust that it also may do as the starry spirit doth,"[2] so that "man is many times in the outward world so very evil natured from the stars that he becometh loathsome to himself."[3] Thus "the soul is always according to its constellation which stood in its birth, as also hath stood in its conception; as that it is at all times aspected with the conjunction of the constellation, with the imagination of the constellation; so is also the outward will-spirit, unless it be that the soul do attain the divine light again in the new birth, and then the soul constraineth the outward spirit with the power of the divine light and leadeth it captive."[4] Belief in this subjection of man to astral

---

[1] Election, ch. viii., pars. 106, 108, 109.
[2] Threefold Life, ch. xviii., par. 21.
[3] Three Principles, ch. xx., par. 71.
[4] First Apology, Part II., par. 547.

influences has long made me intensely curious about its mode of action; and from Râma Prasâd I hoped to learn something that might in some degree explain it. My own slowness in understanding what he writes may be the cause of disappointment; and on the chance of other people gaining more, I will give a brief epitome of what I did definitely gather from his pages on this subject. It leaves me seeking still. "A *truti*," he tells us, "is the astral germ of every living organism."[1] "They might be spoken of as solar atoms. These solar atoms are of various classes according to the prevalence of one or more of the constituent *tatwas* [ethereal vibrations]. The different classes of these solar atoms appear on the terrestrial plane as the various elements of chemistry."[2] "The units of time and space are the same —a *truti*." "At every moment of time, *i.e.*, a truti, there are millions of trutis—perfect organisms—in space."[3] "Individual man or woman is the most perfect ixpression [sic] of a truti" . . . "it is a phase of solar existence having in it every power of life that is manifested on earth. It is the most complete original of individual human life."[4] If I rightly understand *Nature's Finer Forces*, p. 139, every truti is said to be composed of the tatwic rays proceeding from the other trutis on the same plane, whether of psychic, or mental, or externalized life; for here we read: "Each truti on the plane of Prâna is a life-coil; the rays which give existence to each of these trutis come from each and all of the other trutis, which are situated in the space allotted to each of the five tatwas and their innumerable admixtures, which represent, therefore, all the possible tatwic manifestations of life." Similarly, "on the plane of *manas*,

[1] Nature's Finer Forces (1890), p. 256; 1897, p. 249.
[2] Ibid., p. 22.   [3] Ibid., p. 80.
[4] "Thoughts on the Prasnopnisat," *Theosophist*, vol. x. p. 469, May, 1889.

each mental truti represents an individual *mind*. Each individual mind is given birth to by mental tatwic rays [coming] from the other quarter, which represent all the possible tatwic phases of mental life. On the psychic plane each truti represents an individual soul brought into existence by the psychic tatwas flying from every point to every other point."[1] In the saying that follows, "The latter class of trutis on the various planes of existence are the so-called gods and goddesses," I get the nearest approach to my desideratum. The two next pages are profoundly suggestive, but nothing in them explains *how* stars instigate to such and such conduct, when in certain positions relative to each other. With moral character such a statement as the following seems to have absolutely no connection: "As the earth moves in her annual course, *i.e.*, as the truti of time changes, these permanent trutis of space change the phases of their life, but their permanency never is impaired. They retain their individuality all the same; all the planetary influences reach these trutis always, wherever the planets may be in their journey: the changing distance and inclination is of course always causing a change of life-phase."[2] This leaves me no whit nearer any idea of what those planetary influences are, thus constantly affecting these "astral germs" of individual human life. And I doubt whether reading the whole of the interesting work I quote from would supply it.

At the risk of earning ridicule, I confess to believing those we call heavenly bodies to be as much self-conscious individual beings as we are ourselves,—that in their bodies, as much as in our own, a multiplicity constitutes a seeming unity,—that from organizations, in some unimaginable way corresponding to our own, they effect a divine purpose, by the vibration of their breath,

[1] Nature's Finer Forces (1890), pp. 139, 140; 1897, pp. 140, 141.
[2] Ibid., 1890, p. 81; 1897, p. 80.

—that they are responsible agents of the Most High God, not always guiltless in the use of power,—and that their influence is as much due to character as that of human beings. Only on such theoretic grounds can I reconcile Böhme's words about the prompting and imagination of the stars, and his emphatic assertion that they are powerful but not compulsive in regard to the human soul; and as to the *new creature* in man *powerless*. For he is precise in his report of their spiritual *status* relatively to man; and even of the sun, "the nature God" as he terms it, he is careful to make us know that it is "without divine understanding,"[1] and that "though God's fire is at its root, yet it belongeth not to God's kingdom."[2] Râma Prasâd agrees with him here pretty well, saying that the gods and goddesses in Prâna, which inhabit the sun and superintend human souls, are "self-conscious. But they are in comparison to men absolutely elementary beings. They live in absolute conformity with time and space. They have but one idea, one work, and they are always full of it. They are always true to their nature. Transgression is impossible to them."[3] But no conception of the nature of these astral beings helps me to guess how that tells upon character in our planet, *unless we admit the possibility of spirits coming from other orbs to this*, attracted by the figures which ethereal vibration deposits on its surface, and associating with human spirits born when such and such vibrations prevail. To attribute spiritual tendencies to a material cause is only possible to materialists, who are here out of court; but Swedenborg has taught us that by the great law of correspondence spirits can find in material conditions a language to us unknown, to them so forcible as to be sometimes compelling. With wonderful pre-

---

[1] Mysterium Magnum, ch. xii., par. 4.
[2] Great Six Points, Point IV., ch. v., par. 29.
[3] Theosophist, vol. x. p. 472, May 1889.

science of knowledge only lately acquired by Europeans in our time, he wrote in 1741, "The substance of the soul is produced by the aura of the Universe,"[1] and elsewhere he speaks of "the form of the ideas that constitute the nature of the soul."[2] May not these ideas, originating in the sun or planets, and impressed on the astral germ of a human organism, become disturbed by other vibrations in certain positions of the planets? and consequent irregularities of its form invite disorderly spirits?

Here words of L. Oken come to mind which will serve to give better expression to my thought. "The vibration of air is a progressive motion of sonorous figures: if the sonorous figures are not incommensurable, several may be at one and the same time in a single portion of air without interfering with each other. They harmonize because they have originated according to concordant laws; but if they are products of different laws they are then confused, and an indeterminate and offensive vibration originates; just as savours become loathsome if they depart from their law." Now, if, as I cannot doubt, the figure causes the spirit in a sense secondary to that already enlarged upon, *i.e.*, when the idea of an *eternal* being separates itself, by desire to realize that idea, into a peculiar self-will; if the figure causes elementary spirits by attracting atoms of life to cohesive solidarity, "for things naturally indefinite are subservient to such as are definite, and definite natures give an orderly arrangement to such as are borne along indefinitely according to an all various transmutation,"[3] then it is easy to conceive of offensively irregular figures from discordant vibrations, drawing evil influx to a soul. One can push such an hypothesis no further; but the malign effect of some vocal figures is well understood by those

---

[1] Economy of the Animal Kingdom, Part II., No. 311.
[2] Animal Kingdom, Part I., p. 341, footnote (*i*).
[3] Proclus, *On Providence*, p. 17.

who are versed in black magic. Speaking of these, Mohini Chatterji writes: "It is not unusual for sorcerers to adopt some of the formulæ of true religious rites, and with change of accent turn them to their own purposes. It is generally believed that when a spell is muttered backwards its effect is reversed. The truth being, however, that the effect is not so much due to the arrangement of words as to the sound produced and its accompanying psychic disturbance."[1] Practices which our ignorance of spirit-life has classed among mere superstitions, testify that geometrical forms have a force inexplicable to reason. Not to speak of what is known to initiates in occult science, any one who has read Benvenuto Cellini's *Autobiography*, with its graphic account of his attempt to summon spirits; or studied the Ritual prescribed by Eliphaz Lévi for their evocation, will not forget the importance attributed to pentagrams and other cabbalistic figures. I used to think they were designed to affect the mind of the operator, predisposing it by artificial tension to imagine supernatural sights, but when I had learnt from St Martin that music opened different spiritual spheres, according to its quality,[2] I dismissed the shallow thought; for music produces sonorous figures by vibration just as does the human voice on a smaller scale. May not these figures attract spirits to whom such shapes are a language? Is not this implied when in answer to the question, "How are statues said to have enthusiastic energy?" Proclus replies, "Telestic art, through certain symbols, and arcane signatures, assimilates statues to the gods and makes them adapted to the reception of divine illumination."[3] Madame Blavatsky noticed lately a curious fact, relative to forms and spirits, "the remark made in *Theosophist*,

---

[1] Man: Fragments of forgotten History, p. 102.
[2] See his *L'Esprit des Choses*, vol. i. p. 185, and *L'homme de Désir*, sec. 112.
[3] Proclus, *Ten Doubts Concerning Providence*, 1833, p. 35.

September, 1886, page 793, that if the rules (on mathematical proportions or measurements) are not accurately followed in every detail, an idol is liable to be taken possession of by some powerful evil spirit, *is quite true*,"[1] an assertion which common experience may help us to believe. Let violence of anger be feigned by gesture or play of countenance, and anger will soon be felt. Even in our faces attribution of character appears to give it something of reality. As I try to leave this subject, my thoughts are coasting round an abyss of mysteries connected with language, written or spoken, that Böhme has indicated rather than revealed. He speaks of "*the spirits of the letters*" in several of his books with unmistakable fulness of conviction. In his *Fifteenth Epistle*, we find: "It is opened to me in some measure to sound out the spirits of the letters from their very original."[2] And in chapter xxxv. par. 49, of *Mysterium Magnum*, "the spirits of the letters in the alphabet are the form of the only spirit in the language of nature." There is no temptation to try and elucidate sayings that baffle one's own understanding utterly. This, however, may well be glanced at here, the notorious congruity of language and the character of those who speak it in many parts of the world. Take for example the crowding consonants of German, the vehicle for thought *par éminence* in Europe; and that of the simple-hearted, sensuous natives of islands in the Pacific, where the language is said to be almost made up of vowels, and as soft in sound as the other is stringent and guttural. If the connection between the form of letters and the psychological characteristics they express should ever be discovered, no doubt the frequently recurring x in the Mexican tongue will be found to represent some marked peculiarity of nature. Anyone who wishes to examine

---

[1] Lucifer, vol. ix. p. 186, Nov. 1891.
[2] Epistles (1649), Ep. 15, par. 27.

what Böhme has said about the hidden life of letters will find in his *Explanation of the Table of the Three Principles*, an unfolding of the letter sense of the word "Adonai," pars. 13-20; of "Jehovah," pars. 30 and 31; and "Tincture," from pars. 41-50. Chapter xxxv. of *Mysterium Magnum* should also be read; and pars. 18 and 19 of *The Fifth Theosophic Question*.

RESURRECTION BODIES [1]

IN reply to "E. S. W.," as to what sources of information I possess regarding these, my answer is, that from the Bible I gain the knowledge of faith, and that I have been saved from this being reasoned away by such knowledge of understanding as I am able to gather from Böhme. For other minds this might have no weight; to me it has been a revelation which brought rest to many perplexing thoughts. Some day I hope to deal with the subject at greater length, but that will necessitate many quotations from the *Philosophus Centralis*: too many, I doubt, for the patience of readers of *Light*. This in briefest summary is what I understand from his intimations. That at the time of the general resurrection, all earthly fixities of state will be dissolved and every force set free. That the laws of spiritual affinity will then be irresistible and every magnet will draw its own natural adherents. Of all creaturely formations Böhme said: *"The magnetical attraction is the beginning of nature,"* [2] the same creative law will rule when to the spiritual body a body in ultimates is restored. Not, of course, by the revivification of corrupt corporeity, but by the return of undying powers previously involved in its perishable matter. These, according to his report, are from the quintessential part of the earth from which the bodies of our race were evolved. At this point I must drop the clue of his teaching from inability to

[1] Light, 1892, vol. xii. p. 569.   [2] Election, ch. ii., par. 41.

justify my own deductions from it, without copious reference to the original text. What I suppose it to contain is this, that in our bodies, by their nutriment both before and after birth, we unconsciously assume, and supply, naturing conditions to the comatosed spirits of a past Æon fallen into a darkness even more profound than our own (as to spiritual light and life), and that these form in every human body a constituency which is disbanded at death. Some of these as *temporal* spirits beginning in time may end when the body is returned to earth, but those which had an earlier origin, having taken influence for good or for bad from the central spirit of man, *have a future before them*; escape from the baser ingredients of mortal flesh and blood certainly; but between the time of dissolution and the time of magnetic attraction to their old leader, even Böhme gives not the faintest hint of what that future is. Only on one certainty he insists: "All things enter again into that whence they proceeded."[1]

"Everything entereth with its Ens into that whence it takes its original."[2]

It is interesting to know that "the ancient Egyptians believed that the life atoms of the mummy did, notwithstanding the embalmment, keep on for three thousand years to throw off invisible mites, which at the end of this time would again come together for a one-ment into a new body, for the man in whose service they had formerly been."[3]

St Martin has a mysterious saying to which my thought reverts when musing upon those discharged servants of the human will. "It is," he says, "in the earth that the

[1] Signatura Rerum, ch. xv., par. 42.
[2] Mysterium Magnum, ch. xxii., par. 7.
[3] Philangi Dàsa's *Swedenborg the Buddhist*, p. 61.
Having seen the same statement elsewhere, I venture to quote it; *though* from a writer who could persuade himself that Swedenborg was a Buddhist.

substance is prepared which serves for a basis and a first step to the reintegration, or to the new birth of all beings in the universe." (I cannot find chapter and page reference for this, but the words are his.) Further, our thought cannot follow, any more than it can on some other lines of occult history which we believe in none the less. These outgone spirits, which build the perishable body they afterwards forsake, are not the only constituents of that which is reformed at the general Resurrection; Böhme shews that man has in his measure a creative work: himself the re-outspeaker of *the* Word, by whose breath all things come into existence, by the breath of *his* mouth, the unconscious fiat of *his* will, man also produces spiritual entities which are not ephemeral. Dr Franz Hartmann puts this fact before his readers very clearly: "Man is a centre from which continually thought is evolved and crystallizes into forms in the world of souls. His thoughts are things that have life, form, and tenacity; real entities, solid and more enduring than the forms of the physical plane.[1]

They differentiate and organize powers previously *indefinite* by the magic of an attractive focus; so at least have I read the riddle of "the figure causeth the spirit." For these, as the outbirths of our own spiritual nature, we are responsible, and whether we believe this or not it is these that will return to their source, when all disguises and all artificial separating restraints fail in the terrible light of that day which will make the whole past of every human being a vividly present *now*. Analogy is not valid as argument, yet to my mind the received belief among Christians that redeemed souls will form the mystical body of Christ, not to speak of Swedenborg's Grand Man, formed of myriads of generations of human beings, goes far towards justifying the belief that each of these, when perfected, will be

[1] Magic, White and Black, 1886, p. 139; 1888, p. 208.

in like manner an organized host of spirits trained and made subject to the central spirit from which they took their direction. Though Van Helmont does not connect his ideas on this point with bodies re-forming at the Resurrection, they so well express what Böhme's dark sayings have led me to believe, that I shall give here two quotations from his *Paradoxal Discourses* as an interesting enlargement of thoughts suggested already:—

"And because these out-going spiritual ideal beings are not mere spirits, but spiritual bodies and bodily spirits, as being born of the whole man, who consists of the soulish body and spirit, and that all these spirits have their original, out of and from the central spirit of man, viz., out of the heart, and are sent abroad as his messengers; must not, therefore, these messengers perform that which they were duly sent about, and go thither, whither the central spirit or will of man designs and aims them; and in like manner return by revolution to man again? And must not therefore the works of man follow him which he hath done in this lifetime, whether they be good or evil? Especially seeing (as was mentioned before) that new spiritual bodies go forth continually from man, which belong to him and contribute to the whole man, for to make out his full measure until that member which he supplies in Adam or Christ do attain to that perfection which suits with such a head, that so a perfect member may be joined to a perfect body, and a perfect body united to a perfect head?"

"Must not also finally those spirits (as a great and well-ordered army under their captain general or Adonai Zebaoth), and every least atom, after they have wrought out their revolution, return to man again and unite themselves with his central spirit, and so all these spirits being united with the central spirit, make up the whole man?"[1] "And forasmuch as the voice and word of man are his offspring and children, viz., his outflown spirits and angels which continually, from the beginning of his life until his death, go out from him and make up the whole man ... and all his out-births are a spiritual, endless, everlasting being, as well as he himself is; how is it then possible that ever they should be separated from man, or that they should lose themselves or perish in the great world, which is man's mother, any more than a man is able to lose himself?"[2]

What one would like to know is how they are employed in the great world during their *temporary* separation from man. Upon that mystery neither Böhme nor Van Helmont offers any gleam of light.

[1] Concerning the Microcosme, p. 7. [2] Ibid., p. 63.

THE IMAGE

I

"The right true human essence . . . lieth not in the outward man, it lieth within, for it was given to Adam in an image. But it is shut up and lieth in death, and cannot qualify or operate; and hath also no moving in itself, unless it becometh stirring in the power of the Deity."—*Great Six Points*, Point V., ch. viii., pars. 1-3.

IF it may be assumed that ideas generate spiritual existence in higher spheres than this now occupied by mankind, and that, in this, congeries of spirits are attracted by mental figures which serve as a rallying point for their specific modes of operation, we are supplied with a theory that may well explain the deterioration so often observed in people whose leading ideas have undergone a radical change, and the worst change of all, total discredit after having been long held sacred: this has, I believe, been noticed in all countries where Christian doctrines have dislodged the hereditary belief of Mussulmans and Hindoos before their morals had been revolutionized: a process that *must* require more lengths of time than fervent missionaries like to believe. Too often a baptized convert is a more unmendable rogue than he was before the little light of conscience he had was disturbed and the claims to his obedience undoubted. When trying to extricate the essentials of religious faith from tangles of gross superstition, it is hardly possible

[1] Light, 1892, vol. xii. pp. 629, 638.

to leave the first uninjured in average human beings; but the ill effect of subverting old forms of belief, old habits of imagination and tricks of thought, is not at all confined to religious life. Sir A. Helps says, in one of his books, that "when the ideas of a people are overcome, the nation is virtually conquered and will soon die out" (his remarks bore upon the effect of Spanish conquest in America, among the many tribes who first resisted, and gradually became extinct, by no other modes of extermination). In later times the dying out of uncivilized peoples wherever Europeans and European ideas have established themselves, may be due to this in great measure; and not only to newly-imported vices.

It may seem a fancy, but I deem it to be a fact, that among ourselves declining health begins in not a few cases with the removal of old mental landmarks: for loss of confidence wherever it fails is a loss of vitalizing energy. But why? Because "a city divided against itself cannot stand." If caprice invalidates lasting affection, how much more must concentration of will be lost when frequent misgivings disturb the ground of former assurance? But how should this affect bodily health? Surely by scattering spiritual associates from whom confirmation of faith and combined forces of will are unconsciously gained, as long as certain forms of thought are fixed and dominant. Swedenborg affirms that if the spirits who make up man's life were suddenly withdrawn, he would drop down dead: that they often gradually withdraw we may well believe, as by his shewing, they are changed according to the changes of man's ruling affections. These statements helped me to see a use, not perceived before I met with them, in the fixed ideas of weak and narrow minds; for they may serve their turn well enough: should we try to enlarge them, how often the fate of the fabled dog and the shadow might befall! an inadequate notion foregone, only a blank is made; what the mind had a firm grasp of, on Time's frail bridge is dropped; what shone fair in a larger reflection of Truth is beyond its feeble apprehension. Again, puerile details of religious observance may have higher use than we could suppose, while leaving out of thought their efficacy on the unseen side of worship: until we have learned—the last thing modern thinkers care to learn,—that the human mind has no solitary action, that it is in every attitude a leader for subordinate spirits, we shall never duly estimate the importance of all our habits in both inner and outer life.

It is now time to report what has been my best reward for searching in Böhme's depths for the causative relation of form to spirit. Only those who have tried to make a clear pathway of thought to his meaning when he wrote of *the image* can appreciate the worth of my find. While trying to trace out the bearing of his axiom, "the figure hath caused the spirit," the dense obscurity surrounding his use of the word *image* began a little to disperse. It remains to be seen if I can lessen it in other minds. I appeal to any docile reader of his books for assent as to the impossibility of understanding what he meant when referring to the image; in nine passages out of ten they seem to me even more baffling than those which bear upon "The Wisdom." But at last I have been enabled to see that for us they are more practically important. As *no* one will read this essay who is not a very determined student in Böhme's school I feel at liberty to treat the subject with some thoroughness. I think everyone must recognize the curious inadvertence with which, when reading books hard to understand, the mind passes over sayings which answer to nothing already within its scope of vision; it is natural; flippancy in passing judgment after such imperfect study is often natural, too; I fell into both these errors a few years ago, when saying in print (*Light and Life*, September, 1886, p. 23) "Why

Martensen judged it suitable to speak of the Virgin Sophia as *The Idea* when *all* ideas of the Abyssal God, prior to nature and creature, are said by Böhme to have been reflected in her, as in a passive mirror of the divine mind, I cannot understand."[1] Though this mode of speech is exceptional in all he wrote, to confess here my mistake rids me of a little burden of shame. Nothing can be clearer than these words of his "which spirit the Idea, Jesus, an efflux from the Divine Unity came to relieve,"[2] and of course the inseparableness of the Word from *the Wisdom* is here implied, when Jesus is called an efflux from the Deity—the invariable definition of Virgin Sophia; but I had not noticed the sentence when criticizing a writer who had. Remembering this, it is with diffidence that I offer the little I apprehend of the relation of the Idea to the image.

A passage in *Nature's Finer Forces* will best explain my conjecture. When describing the origin of the sun, moon, and planets, Râma Prasâd says, first that *Prâna*, the lifecoil, is the shade of *Manu*, the atmosphere enlightened by the Logos. As the body in sunlight casts a shadow, "the suns are given birth to in this shade by the impression of macrocosmic ideas into this shade; these suns, the centres of Prâna, become in their turn the positive starting points of further developments. The *Manus*, throwing their shades by the intervention of the planets, give birth to the moons,"[3] so that according to him, the shadow of some object that intercepts light,

[1] See page 274 of the present vol.
[2] 177 Theosophic Questions, Ques. 12, par. 24.
[3] Page 79.
["The suns owe their birth in this shade to the impression upon it of the macrocosmic mental ideas. These suns—the centres of Prâna, become in their turn the positive starting-point of further development. The Manus, throwing their shade by the intervention of the suns, give birth *in* those shades to planets, etc. The suns throwing their shades by the intervention of planets, give birth to moons."—Third and revised edition, 1897, page 79.]

becomes the first original of the transmitted light which proceeds *instrumentally* from itself.

Rather a new idea, is it not, to most of us, that the shadow of one orb lays the foundation of another? Yet it had been implied as to other foundations by other teachers long before. After saying that "the soul was not substantial but essential, and was apprehended where the fire originated," Böhme adds, "but the shadow of itself hath fashioned itself into a figured image in the desirous will of God."[1] In his literal translation of the first chapter of *Genesis*, Fabre D'Olivet gives this reading of verses 26 and 27: "And he said, the Gods, declaring his will, we will make Adam in the shadow of us." ... "And He did frame out, He, the God, the self-sameness of Adam [universal man] in the shadow of His own. In the shadow of Him, the Being of Beings, He created him."

By the help of Râma Prasâd's words, quoted above, I can better conceive of the image to which Böhme attributes so much efficacy in the regeneration of the soul. Dwelling in the light from which all light derives, may not the Sun of Righteousness, "the first-born of every creature," have cast a shadow, which was the formative figure of the first Adam? Is the image the shadow, the Idea? To most readers this will seem too fanciful to be worth writing down, but what Böhme repeatedly asserts equally offends both reason and common-sense; this, that in every human soul an image is propagated, which, when substantiated by regenerate life, becomes "the true temple of the Holy Spirit, yea, even God in His manifestation and revelation of Himself."[2] When trying a few years ago to find a place for this incoherent thought, a passage, quoted from De Mirvelle's *Pneumatologie*, v. 516, in Madame Blavatsky's

---

[1] Forty Questions (1665), Appendix, par. 4.
[2] Election, ch. viii., par. 240.

Secret Doctrine struck me as possibly referring to the same unintelligible fact; it is curiously in agreement with Böhme's report, though given in such different terms. "Here we have the Word of the *second* Jehovah and His *face* ['presence,' as the Protestants translate it] forming both but one, and yet being two; a mystery which seemed to us unsolvable before we had studied the doctrine of the Mazdean *ferouers*, and learnt that the *ferouer* was the spiritual potency, at once image, *face*, and *guardian* of the soul, which finally assimilates the ferouer."[1] On the next page we read, "The ferouer is the spiritual counterpart." Now when the image in the soul comes to life, the soul is represented by Böhme as regaining the "wife of his youth," spoken of in *Mal.* ii. 14, the divine womanhood of Adam's androgynous perfection, until his treachery to her disqualified him for the heavenly consort and left him only fitted for an Eve.

It is indispensable here to give Böhme's own words and with this much of preface; he frequently speaks of heavenly substantiality as if he only meant that in the abstract, though no one used to his writings can fail to see that by those words an organized corporeal vehicle for the indwelling spirit of God is often signified, "Seeing that the soul in the beginning of its creation was clothed and adorned with this heavenly substantiality, and it was the soul's right inward body, and that the soul in Adam is gone forth with its imagination from this substantiality, whence that substantiality is become again shut up in death, viz., in the still *nothing*, and the soul is entered with its imagination into the earthly kingdom, and nevertheless that very first image which became shut up without the life, yet hangeth to the soul, but without its apprehension or understanding; therefore now when the light of the soul becometh kindled again, and the heavenly substantiality, out of God's majesty,

[1] Secret Doctrine, 1888, vol. ii. p. 479; 1893, vol. ii. p. 502.

receiveth the life, viz., the *light in the soul*, then the dead substantiality becometh living in the light's power, and becometh with the now new introduced substantiality, one spiritual body, for it is of one only essence; and here death riseth up in Christ, here God and the inward man becometh one person. Understand it aright, this new light-life is Christ."[1] And thus is Christ formed in us. This image "hanging to the soul" is the effaced, too generally the inoperative image of God; our birthright ever since the treader down of the serpent—the hydra-headed serpent of self-love—was promised; the image which can give to our soul's magically creative fire, the fuel that produces Heaven's light, and from the meekness of that light comes the water of eternal life which alone can make immortal bodies.

. . . .

This article was half written seven months ago, but having then found out, or fancied, that the supporters of *Light* began to feel my measures of Böhme's lore insupportable, I resolved to refrain long enough to give their fatigue a rest. To leave unfinished what I had begun was not for a moment in my thoughts, as I find I was trying to share with others [what] seemed to me of value. It was this, that the heavenly image in the soul, about which he says so much and so unintelligibly, until one can seize the clue, is pre-eminently "the figure that causeth the spirit," the indwelling spirit of God. With one more article I shall finish what, perhaps, was a mistake, in *Light*, to begin.

[1] First Apology, Part II., pars. 373-376.

II

" Because it was a departure from the regular academic rules, I am afraid they will want to make learned Reason its judge."—Gichtel's *Letters*.

" Take pity of your life, and of your fair, heavenly image. Ye are God's children; be not the devil's."—Forty Questions (1665), Ques. 17, pars. 28, 29.

Commenting on *Genesis* iii. 15, Böhme says: "In that inspoken voice the poor soul obtained breath and life again; and that inspoken voice was in the human life as a figure of the true reflex image."[1]

All that has been discovered about voice figures gives a significance to these words, which will not, I hope, be overlooked.

It is impossible, I think, to escape the conclusion that our souls have perceptions of which the mind can take no cognisance. Plotinus wrote: "The whole of our soul also does not enter into body, but something belonging to it always abides in the intelligible, and something different from this in the sensible world." . . . "We do not know everything which takes place about any particular part of the soul till it arrives at the whole of the soul."[2]

Assuredly any quickening of desire for man's long-lost glory, from seeing its faded image, does not come within range of present consciousness. But how many physical processes persist within us unperceived: is it likely when so many vital transactions in a flesh and blood body are inscrutable that those of our spiritual life should be less secret?[3]

---

[1] Election, ch. vii., pars. 45, 46.

[2] Five Books of Plotinus, translated by Thomas Taylor, 1794, pp. 282, 283 : " On the Descent of the Soul."

[3] " Those purer or interior forms which are inscrutable, are what form and fix the internal senses, and also produce the internal affections."—*Arcana Cœlestia*, 4224.

Blinded as we are by the specious powers of reason, we are slow to imagine that anything of importance can happen in our inner world unknown to what we call ourselves; as little can we believe that a number of subordinate spirits act in that hidden sphere, building up the existence which we suppose is all our own. Such ideas are scouted as unreasonable: they are so, but that does not prove them to be untrue; our rational senses being as limited on their own plane as those of the body are on another. Even science accepts as momentously certain, what its most learned professors ridiculed as absurdly unreasonable twenty years ago.

Böhme teaches that on every level of creation, nature, as a derivative of Eternal Nature, has similar laws of action, however diverse the factors by which those laws are carried out. Now, as we know that in surface life a plan or outline serves in the construction of every material work, it seems possible that the formation of the spiritual body goes on according to a pre-existent design; and that for the recovery of true *human creatures* this image of it is engendered in every child of man as naturally as other instincts of the race. Inherited aptitudes, as we know, may long remain dormant or overborne by stronger impulses, yet without becoming extinct, so with the Heavenly image while animal passions and worldly cupidities predominate, it *must* remain lifeless, as Böhme admits, "in truth with most it is so," for "Man now lieth shut up after his fall, in a gross, deformed, dead, bestial image; he is not like an angel. . . . His paradisical image is in him as if it were not, and it is also not manifest."[1]

Any tolerably advanced student in Böhme's neglected school will not need to be told how this image is first brought to life and then to its full evolution in heavenly

[1] Signatura Rerum, ch. viii., par. 47.

substance; but a brief recapitulation of his account of this process may be welcome to others, the more so as it is identical with what he teaches about the organization of man—as a creature.

The idea of the deific mind in that beginning was seen in the Wisdom;[1] it was impressed on the human mind after the severance of the divine and human nature in man; and henceforward born in all mankind. If that image rouses the will to desire its fulfilment, the will involves its concentration of desire in that image. Hence what Böhme calls the astringent form of nature, *contracting*; next resistance to that restraint—*mobility*; the conflict of those antagonistic forces causing ceaseless unrest till the fire of life breaks out (the involved spark of soulish life, *i.e.*, will), and this gives life to the meek munificence of light with its resulting vibrations of sound, which doubtless aid in forming the substance of that perfect creature that, when fully evolved, manifests the purpose of God in the previously revealed image. This summary is what one might call Böhme's account of creation by the seven forms of Eternal Nature in the abstract: by a very other line of instruction, not excluding, but involving with practical counsels this bare outline, does he teach *how* "the first Adamical image of God may again appear; and become seeing, hearing, feeling, tasting, and smelling."[2]

Instruction not to be epitomized in an ephemeral page for the hasty glance of an unconcerned reader. His *Epistles* are accessible in reprint for but a few shillings, and in the first of these, all that may not be cast before a careless public is impressively opened to an attentive mind. The dangerous and ignorant doctrine of salvation

---

[1] "Where the word is, there is also the Virgin or the Wisdom of God; for the word is in the Wisdom; and the one is not without the other, or else the Eternity would be divided."—*Threefold Life*, ch. vi., par. 78.

[2] Epistles (1649), Ep. 1, par. 16.

by imputed merits, by any efficacy of the blood of Christ *external* to the soul, is powerfully impugned in this epistle; and without any obscurity comparatively speaking, it proves that "out of man's willing must God's spirit become generated; it must itself become God in the willing spirit, or else it attaineth not divine substantiality."[1]

Applying this to the inanimate image in the human soul, we can understand that unless the will of man desires its restoration to life it cannot become a living, breathing creature, and how truly it was said by J. Pierrepont Greaves, that "the creative process is neutralized by contradictory emotions."

For the animal soul and its astral associates creaturely evolution is secured by nature—an organism good for a term of years, usually; or as our friends, the modern Theosophists say, for many recurrent periods of time. But time has beginning and end; the human soul neither; and being a fire-spark out of God's might, no effect of man's will can be *only* negative; it is inalienably at his own disposal, to surrender to good or evil; and by yielding habitually to evil, he forges his own fetters. Even when not earnestly aiming at goodness he is incurring future results which no wise thinker could leave unconsidered. For by the habitual bent of his will and desires now, he forms his future external appearance. Let him look to it. "The image in the spirit becometh altered all according to what is contained in the will which the soul hath framed or contrived."[2]

Who would willingly enter the world of spirits, where disguise is impossible, disfigured, monstered by diseased imaginations and loathsome grovelling tastes? Such souls "will have lost the right and true image; what

[1] Incarnation, Part II., ch. x., par. 56.
[2] Forty Questions (1665), Ques. 7, par. 19.

the daily lust and delight hath been, such will their image be."[1]

Shameful, *not* human, appearance will not be the heaviest part of the penalty. Bodily form, as we all know, conditionates consciousness. In vain should we bring a dog, or cat, or ape, into a fine library or lovely garden, hoping to rejoice *them*; with their bodies they cannot even perceive what would delight a creature more perfectly organized. God is Love, but his omnipotence could not make degraded animalized human beings sensible of angelic joys. It is not God, but man who, when leading an animal life, shuts himself out of Heaven, for "Thy holy body must be regenerated if man's spirit would see God; otherwise he cannot see him except he be born again in the water of the holy element in the spirit of God (who hath manifested himself in Christ with this same water source) that his disappeared body may be made alive; else he hath no sense or sight in the holy life of God."[2]

This is what is gained by assimilative union with the "noble image," heavenly consciousness. This the "*figure that causeth the spirit*" that can be one with the Christ. One more quotation from Böhme will explain the relation of the image to the soul more decisively, perhaps, than any other that could be selected. "The *soul* hath the seven properties of the inward spiritual world according to nature; but the *soul's spirit* is without properties, for it standeth without or beyond nature, in the unity of God, and yet becometh manifest through the soulish fiery nature, in the stillness, for it is the true real express or reflex image of God, viz., an idea, in which God Himself worketh and dwelleth; so far as the soul bringeth its desire into God, and giveth itself up to the will of God. But if not, then is this

---

[1] Forty Questions (1665), Ques. 30, par. 61.
[2] Mysterium Magnum, ch. ii., par. 21.

THE IMAGE

idea, viz., the soul's spirit, dumb and workless; and standeth only as an image in a looking-glass, which disappears and hath no substance, as befel Adam in the fall."[1]

It should be noticed here that Böhme's use of the words "the soul's spirit" in this passage implies what he has elsewhere fully demonstrated—that of the three souls which co-exist in man's nature only the first "out of the Eternity" outlasts Time. Both the animal soul and the astral soul have necessarily their spirit and their proceeding breath, or they could have no bodily organs; but the original soul, "the child of Omnipotency," is the only one in which the image of God can be revealed by *that* soul's spirit. Students of Böhme will find this a very needful difference to keep clearly in view, as without it his various use of the terms soul and spirit leads to much confusion of thought.

[1] Four Tables of Divine Revelation (1654), Microcosmus. Table of the Three Principles (1661), Microcosmos, par. 5 (*Several Treatises*, 1662).

APPENDIX

ADDITIONAL ESSAYS AND LETTERS BY MRS PENNY IN *LIGHT*

VOL. PAGE
- II. 181. Miracles—and Free Will.
  - 201. Free Will.
  - 355. Esoteric Views of Church Doctrine.
  - 407. "The Perfect Way." [Also p. 478.]
  - 480. Vision at the Moment of Death.
  - 497. The Divining Rod.
  - 577. Materialization, and the Human Body.
- III. 38. A Personal or Impersonal God?
  - 141. God and Nature.
  - 273. Death : *Romans* vii. 24.
  - 309. Esoteric Buddhism.
  - 323. Buddhism and Christianity.
  - 381. Agreement of Spiritual Instructors.
  - 403. Ideas of Supreme Deity.
  - 453. Bell-ringing by Spirits.
  - 470. Involution and Evolution.
- IV. 47. A Statue Weeping.
  - 367. Conditional Immortality.
- VII. 44. Teachings from Swedenborg.
  - 128. Have Animals Souls?
  - 208. "An Astounding Ghost Story."
  - 256. Insects. [Also p. 267.]
  - 261. Spiritual Old Age.
  - 302. Spirit and Body.
  - 518. Dissolving Views.
- VIII. 8. A Midnight Dialogue.
  - 10. The Astral Body.
  - 23. *Re* "Nizida's" article on "Progression in Spiritualism."
  - 38. Astronomical Theories. [Also p. 71.]
  - 57. Transmission of Light.
  - 94. Chirognomy.

VOL. PAGE
VIII. 100. Ignorant Credulity. [Also p. 111.]
335. The Point. [Also p. 379.]
391. Suppressed Memory.
495. "Kokowaars."
514. Keats a Medium.
523. The Divining Rod.
552. Were-wolves.
567. Testimony of the Unseen.
604. Judgment to Come.
IX. 57. Doubles.
95. The "Spectator" and Laurence Oliphant.
101. Biblical Criticism.
123. Suicide.
140. Blood Sacrifices. [Also p. 168.]
183. Christian Science Healing.
235. Madame Blavatsky's "Secret Doctrine."
279. On making the best of both Worlds.
290. Suggestive Remarks on Animal Sacrifice. [Also p. 324.]
368. F. A. Tindal's Music Master.
386. Memory after Death.
500. James Hinton's "The Law Breakers" and "Coming of the Law."
600. An Inquiry. [Also p. 612.]
X. 11. The Fading Grasp of Spirit on Body.
63. An Indictment.
83. Associated Spirits.
151. Old Age.
159. "Exploration of Lives."
256. Capital Punishment.
380. Animals Mediumistic.
400. Poem : A Haunted House.
XI. 9. Swedenborg. [Also p. 65.]
340. Man not only a Spiritual Being.
497. Unseen Confederates.
509. Poem : Left Alone in the House.
520. Results of Assurance.
XII. 322. Genius Mediumistic.
369. Hair.
434. An Assortment of Masks. [Also pp. 453, 465, 472.]
483. Ignorance of Contempt. [Also p. 501.]
528. "Religio-Philosophical Journal" misquotes Swedenborg.
545. Personal Reminiscence of William Stainton Moses.
XIII. 39. Arrest of Thought.
201. Music. [Also p. 208.]

www.ingramcontent.com/pod-product-compliance
Lightning Source LLC
Chambersburg PA
CBHW071135300426
44113CB00009B/976